WILD BILLY EARP
(AND WHERE TO FIND HIM...)

MIKE MARTIN

Text © Mike Martin, 2024
Illustrations © Ross Lee, 2024
All rights reserved.
Without limiting the rights under copyright reserved above, no part of this publication may be reproduced, stored, or introduced into a retrieval system, or transmitted, in any form or by any means (electronic, mechanical, photocopying, recording or otherwise) without the prior written permission of both the copyright owners and the publisher of this book.
First Edition
Paperback ISBN: 978-0-9571967-1-1
Hardback ISBN: 978-0-9571967-2-8
www.softwoodbooks.com

ABOUT THE AUTHOR

Mike Martin studied and qualified in film and television production at West Surrey College of Art and Design in 1974.

He was born and raised in the English home counties just to the south west of London, the youngest son of a well known variety comedian who went on to become a prolific television scriptwriter.

In a long career, he has appeared in numerous areas of the entertainment business as a concert and cabaret performer/musician/actor in the U.K. and across the continent. He has also worked as a freelance London tour guide, specializing in such topics as the Jack the Ripper murders of 1888. His informative public talks cover diverse subjects within history and show business. Venues for these talks have included Leeds City Armouries, Wilton's Music Hall, the Water Rat's Theatre and educational facilities in Denmark and Germany.

He has also been regularly commissioned as an article writer and reviewer for various publications, notably The Stage newspaper.

Previously published books:
NODDIES; THE FILM EXTRA'S GUIDE (Arlon-1997) ISBN 0-946273-22-7
FROM CROCKETT TO CUSTER (Trafford-2004) ISBN 1-4120-1878-1
BE LUCKY; THE STORY OF GEORGE MARTIN "THE CASUAL COMEDIAN" (MGM9-2012) ISBN 978-0-9571967-0-4

Mike Martin is a long standing member and officer of the show business charity brotherhood The Grand Order of Water Rats, also serving as freelance secretary to the Order's Trustees. www.gowr.co.uk

WILD BILLY EARP (AND WHERE TO FIND HIM...)

INTRODUCTION

PART ONE: WILD BILL HICKOK

1. Showdown
2. Young Jim
3. Jayhawking and Freighting
4. Rumble at Rock Creek
5. Wild Bill goes to War
6. Onto the Plains...
7. A Law Unto Himself
8. Abilene
9. Hickok's Theatrics
10. The Road to Deadwood
11. The Final Hand
12. Legacy

PART TWO: BILLY THE KID

13. First Blood
14. Apprentice Outlaw
15. Lincoln County
16. Roots of War
17. Regulators
18. Vengeance
19. Buckshot
20. Siege
21. Regulators Adios
22. Amnesty
23. Moving On
24. Granted
25. On the Outlaw Trail
26. The Noose Tightens
27. Cornered
28. In Chains
29. Escape
30. Freedom
31. The Reckoning
32. Requiem

PART THREE: WYATT EARP

33. Blood for Brothers
34. Wandering the West
35. Lawman
36. Dodge
37. Tombstone
38. The Cowboys
39. Trouble Brewing
40. Lines Drawn
41. The Summer of Ill Intent
42. Near the O.K. Corral…
43. The Smoke Clears…
44. Resentment and Revenge
45. Riding for Vendetta
46. Arizona Farewell
47. A New Life
48. Boxing and Prospecting
49. A Tale Worth Telling
50. *"The Good Lord owes me an explanation…"*

With huge thanks and appreciation for the artistic talent of Ross Lee whose caricatures and portraits illustrate this book.

INTRODUCTION

Another book about cowboys, gunfighters, outlaws and sheriffs?

"Not that lot again!" some may wail, raising their eyebrows as they mutter amused complaints about hackneyed, even childlike, characters who belong to a past which does not deserve to be taken seriously.

Wild Bill… the Kid… Earp… for Pete's sake, have they not had their day? Surely any interest in their overblown, exaggerated sagas has been done to death … every possible shred of wonder squeezed out during a bygone time when the Old West became a fad in the mid twentieth century. Roy Rogers, John Wayne and their ilk on the big screen, then all those interminable and repetitive 1950s and 60s television series … *Bronco, Maverick, Cheyenne, Gunsmoke, Wagon Train, Rawhide, Have Gun Will Travel, The Rifleman*… blah, blah, blah…

And I remember it vividly… I grew up in a time when kids still regularly played at Cowboys and Indians. I loved it… and all those shows and films too.

Then, later on, a Western reboot, to breathe life back into a predictable format where the good guys beat the bad guys, where all those native people were savages, fit only as cannon fodder for the hero's gun, where white settlers were the saintly souls who opened up the United States to civilization.

How much mileage could be wrung from a limited period of history, the classic time zone of which could only really be stretched from the end of the American Civil War through to, just about, the turn of the twentieth century? Barely three decades… how many stories could there be? How many variations of the same theme which basically boiled down to taming a wild frontier?

A European film director, an Italian, found the solution, for a while at least, when he came up with the concept of the "Spaghetti Western". With the arid landscape of Spain substituting the real Wild West for locations, Sergio Leone cleverly turned the genre on its head, creating a harsher, grittier West, populated by ugly, nasty characters, where even the so called heroes crossed the line of morality… anti-heroes, in fact. And this made a star of Clint Eastwood who, of course, went on to popularise that kind of character globally.

The masses loved this new take on the old style and Hollywood caught on, giving the Western film a few more years of popularity as a whole glut of revisionist movies dominated cinema. Some may argue that this new vision went way too far in the opposite direction, many of the films becoming totally unrealistic for another reason. One extreme to the other.

Iconic Western star John Wayne openly hated this new look at the culture he had helped to create. He had been there since almost the very beginning of Westerns, starring in Raoul Walsh's *The Big Trail* way back in 1930, the year after Wyatt Earp passed away. Following an apprenticeship in a string of B features, he went on to become an enormous star in classics like *Stagecoach, Red River, The Searchers, Rio Bravo* and *True Grit*… great films but, many would argue, of their day. Wayne was still making movies way beyond the time when everything changed and his popularity remained intact with his millions of diehard fans, despite criticism from the younger generation. He fought hard to maintain his standards, yet even his final film, *The Shootist*, in 1976, contained elements of the more modern impression. It is an intelligent and very moving story, about an aging gunfighter facing his mortality, brought on by terminal cancer. Wayne's performance is superb; he was never better, and the uncharacteristic vulnerability he brought to the role was very human. It was a perfect farewell from the old cowboy.

Anyway, my intention is not to write a condensed history of Westerns. This was just to emphasize how a popular form of entertainment reached a stage where it was seen as stereotyped and corny, no longer valid. Although Western films have yet again found an audience with a new generation, it is largely because they have, as a rule, become far more authentic in look and feel to most of those which were made back in the day. The stories and characters have become complex, rich in texture which relates to issues of today. Writers, directors and stars understand the importance of addressing the deeper issues which helped to open up the mid nineteenth century frontier and, arguably, a better informed and, perhaps, more sophisticated audience responds to this. It is fair to balance plots with the portrayal of viewpoints not often seen in previous productions. To see the western expansion through the eyes of the Indians (or Native Americans as they are now insistently referred to) is one example, with respect for their customs and beliefs.

Indeed, fair enough, but there are two sides to every story. So, for every awful tale of brutal savagery by the whites against the Indians; the scalp hunters, the attacks on peaceful Indian villages, the slaughter of women and children, the theft of their land, let us balance these true horror stories with the other side of the coin…

How about Apache and Comanche raids on homesteads and travellers when women would be raped to death or taken with their children into slavery? Of the gratuitous torture of captives, skinned alive or roasted over slow fires? Horses ridden to death, domestic dogs eaten, The Lakota Sioux's delightful habit of excessive mutilation of their dead enemies? And if we are talking about seizure of land, tribes all over the continent had been doing it to each other since long before the settlers began their encroachment.

None of this justifies acts of evil intent, but I mention it because nothing in life is simply a shade of black or white. The human element comes into everything and colours it all, good, bad and indifferent, regardless of race.

Personally, and I am not alone, I got somewhat tired of the moral high ground which began to paint a false picture of "Native Americans" as noble guardians of nature, courageously defending their families and land, at one with the Great Spirit and cast by impossibly good looking actors.

Don't get me wrong… the Indian peoples were, and are, indeed very spiritual, and sincere about it. There is much to be gained by looking into these beliefs, but it all got so out of hand. Cheyenne Dog Soldiers and Comanche and Apache raiding parties had no feelings of benevolence towards their fellow man. They were out for themselves, believe me. And they didn't all look like Rock Hudson either. The menfolk were dedicated to war and hunting. A woman's role was to deal with all other aspects of work.

Looking back at these times with just a surface knowledge of the real history can be most deceiving. And seeing 19th. century figures dealt lines and attitudes which are way out of kilter with the period they lived in. Making them "politically correct" to tick the boxes of virtue signalling is totally out of place in an historical setting. For many of us, that is extremely galling.

"Reimagining history" it is often called… well, history is history and should only be imagined as it most likely was, surely.

Anyway, I digress. This book does not deal with the conflict between this clash of cultures. I have addressed that in other writings.

Here I wish to detail that other main topic which dominates most folks view of the Old West… the gunfighter.

There are many familiar names I could have chosen, and it was tempting to extend this work to include far more than I have. As it stands, after much thought, I have chosen just three… Wild Bill Hickok, Billy "The Kid" Bonney and Wyatt Earp.

Why them, in particular? How about Jesse James and Butch Cassidy? Bass Reeves and Wes Hardin? The Daltons and the Doolins? The list could go on and on…

Well, in this study, I have decided to concentrate on the three who I personally feel are most representative of the entire topic. Even today, that trio will ring some kind of bell with many people, especially those of a certain age... and that does not mean having to be *too* ancient!

Two of them died by the gun, one under forty, the other hardly out of his teens. The third lived on, incongruously, into an old age where he seemed out of place. All three lived in a violent age where law was cloudy and life was cheap. As we shall see, death by gun or other savage methods was common, but not quite in the way we have been led to believe by the traditions of Hollywood. Life in the Old West, for most, was harsh and largely dreary, save for those all too common bursts of sordid action.

But surely, I hear some cry, everything we historically know about these characters has been written about over and over again. Why do we need more? What else is left to be said?

This can be construed to be true, BUT when it comes to history, the facts can always be subject to interpretation. What is history anyway? We are dealing with a time which none of us experienced physically first hand. All we are left with are accounts from those (long dead) who were there (and they often contradict each other... just like differing reports of incidents seen today), some handed down artifacts, newspaper reports, some faded photographs, archaeology ... the sum of all this adds up to a wealth of material and serious researchers are left to analyse and present their own conclusions.

This is what I have done, my starting point being the great heartfelt passion I have had for history since I was a small child. All history fascinates me, it always has, but my dedication to the Old West burns particularly bright. Why is this so? I simply do not know... it just is. At the end of this book I try to offer some kind of explanation and, if you get that far, dear reader, you may be in a position to understand me a little more than here at the beginning.

As an Englishman it may seem odd that my most absorbing interest is for events which took place in a different age, thousands of miles away across a wide ocean. In fact, I have been criticised by American friends who question my "right" to delve into their past and "dare" to pass comment on their national icons. One, who I actually have great respect for as a researcher, even asked me how I would like it if he wrote about the British Royal Family!!!

My response is *"Go ahead... write away... do what you want... it is **your** right!"* I would like to think that he would treat the subject with respect and do his research, but that is how I feel about anyone who writes about any subject, regardless of nationality.

I have done the work, treated everything I have perused with that respect, spent years gathering information from every source available, joined historical societies, spent much time in discussion with fellow enthusiasts sharing viewpoints, always keeping an open mind to new information and forever giving it all deep thought.

In addition. I have devoted much of my life to travel, exploring and experiencing in person the historical sites which intrigue me. From the home based battlefields of Great Britain, most of which are built over now, I have walked the bleak moor of Culloden where Bonnie Prince Charlie's dreams were shattered forever in 1746, traipsed across the fields of Stirling Bridge (William Wallace victory – 1297) and Bannockburn (Robert the Bruce's golden moment – 1314), tried to find what remains of the battlefields of the Wars of the Roses (1400s) and the English Civil War (1600s). Of the latter, I am fortunate to live below the slopes of the Battle of Roundway (1643), a great Royalist victory, when the Parliamentarians were routed away from their siege of Devizes. It is one of the only battlefields in the U.K. which is still pretty much as it was, and I have spent many hours walking across those undulating, grassy slopes, imagining the conflict, almost feeling it at times.

Likewise, the World War Two Normandy landing beaches of Utah, Omaha, Gold, Juno and Sword (1944) are deeply emotive, bringing a chill when one realises the enormity of the enterprise and immense human cost. I felt a similar chill, but with extra darkness, when I walked the grounds of the Nazi concentration camps at Belsen and Buchenwald. And across the car park in central Berlin which now covers the bunker where Adolf Hitler committed suicide in 1945.

The Norwegian fjords and Danish flatlands furnished me with an appreciation of Viking battles… and that was another book which spilled out of me, as yet unpublished.

I made a solo pilgrimage to Kwa Zulu Natal in South Africa, criss crossing the country to remote areas so that I could appreciate the battles of the Boer and Zulu Wars. I stayed at Rorkes Drift and drank in the incredible story of the defence of that tiny mission station, also nearby Isandwlana where an entire British army column was wiped out by the Impis of King Cetshwayo in 1879. I even spent a day trekking along Fugitive's Drift, the same route taken by those who tried to escape the slaughter. And I gladly faced the challenge of swimming the Buffalo River at the spot where Lieutenants Melvill and Coghill did the same in their futile attempt to save the Queen's Colour. That was particularly exhausting and emotive for me, but at least I didn't have swarms of assegai wielding Zulus on my tail!

Blood River too (1838) where the Boers decimated a series of Zulu attacks, plus a long trek out to the bleak spot where Louis Napoleon the Prince Imperial and heir to the throne of France fell victim to a chance Zulu assault, an incident which proved highly embarrassing for Queen Victoria.

I also stayed much further north at Spion Kop where the British suffered another terrible defeat during the Boer War (1899 – 1902). With a terrific guide, just the two of us, I was taken on a brilliant day's appreciation of the Battle of Colenso and the lonely spot where Winston Churchill, as a young army officer and correspondent, was captured by the Boers.

Sorry to digress again, but I just wanted to make the point about how serious I am when it comes to history.

Getting back to the U.S.A, I spent several years touring areas of the continent which took me to sites of interest like Valley Forge near Philadelphia where George Washington collated his revolutionary army in the winter of 1777-78. Civil War Battlefields too… Vicksburg (1862-63) and others. Americans really do a first class job of preserving their battlefields…

I loved spending time researching at the Alamo in San Antonio, even though it is in the middle of the modern city … and San Jacinto and Goliad … all significant to the Mexican/Texan War of 1836.

As for the Plains Indian Wars, research for another project took me to the site of the Fetterman and Wagon Box fights (1866 and '67), then on to the Little Big Horn (1876) and many other places. (See my book *From Crockett to Custer*.)

And then, as you will see in the forthcoming pages, I scoured the country from east to west coasts, from New York to California, in my search for information to include in this book.

So, do I have anything new to offer?

I must confess that the basic information here will not educate any existing aficionados of those I write about. We who care and have done the work will already be more than aware of this material. It is presented in my own style and I would like to think that it is clear and concise yet laid out in a form which will intrigue those who are new to the subject, hopefully inspiring them to learn more. I have simplified much of it so that readers will not get bogged down in too much extra fact, frills which will not be needed for the essential tales.

That can be found elsewhere. I have made a point of not including a bibliography of my sources as that can be easily found, if interested beyond the essentials.

What I have written is my own deeply considered interpretation of what I believe happened, having absorbed all the information that is available. Some of it may differ, albeit slightly, to other conclusions, but I feel confident that I have never deviated far from the generally accepted historical facts.

And, because I am a writer, I have made a point of doing my best to make the text flow in a readable and entertaining form. If that does occasionally, and very minimally, stray into the realms of artistic licence, then I make no apology for that. This has been done to bring life and humanity to the characters and incidents I present here.

Finally, I would be immensely happy if American readers accept my version of their history, but, to be honest, it was not written with them in mind. Essentially, I am bringing the fascinating stories of these shootists to those who may be considering them for the first time; an introduction. If those who already know the facts can find something else, and respect, for my efforts, then I really will be delighted.

So, let's saddle up and take those big beeves by the proverbial horns...

In England we might be doing this by settling down over a jolly nice cup of tea (unashamed cliché!) but a finger of red eye will do just as nicely...

PART ONE
WILD BILL HICKOK

CHAPTER 1
SHOWDOWN

Friday, July 21st. 1865… Springfield town square, Missouri.

"He shouldn't come across that square, wearing my watch, unless dead men can walk."

Those were the sombre words of Wild Bill and the warning was crystal clear.

Davis Tutt had been pushing his luck. He should have known better than to goad a man with Wild Bill Hickok's reputation, but Tutt was no tenderfoot himself. Arkansas born, Tutt grew up in an atmosphere of violence, surrounded by a fierce family feud which had robbed him of his father. During the recently ended Civil War, he had served in a Confederate Infantry Regiment but it seems he probably deserted, drifting north to Missouri along with other members of his family.

He disliked the name Davis and preferred to be called Dave. By 1864 he was settled in the town of Springfield, an important commercial hub which had received the placing of the furthest western telegraph lines just a few years before. In 1861, at the start of the War, the population was expanding from 2,000 and was a hive of activity, its loyalty split between settlers from both North and South, as well as a large influx of German immigrants.

Both Union and Confederate armies embraced the importance of Springfield's strategic location and they swiftly sought to seize it, resulting in the Battle of Wilson's Creek close to the town, where General Nathaniel Lyon became the first high ranking Union officer to be killed in the conflict.

Control of the town zig zagged back and forth between Northern and Southern forces but, by the time Tutt arrived, it was in Union hands and would remain so for the remainder of the war, used as a supply base and nucleus of operations for all military activities in the region.

Tutt had little interest in the war by now, concentrating on his gambling career, and probably being low key about his military past. He had enough skill in this risky trade to eke out a living, as were many characters who inhabited the saloons and murky dens where card games were continuously in play.

It was during this period that Davis Tutt and James Hickok (who was becoming better known as Wild Bill) became acquainted. Most accounts tend to suggest that they were friendly rivals across the poker tables, regardless of the fact that their loyalties in the recent hostilities had been on opposite sides. Hickok had fought for the Union and had a colourful history of adventures as a scout and spy behind enemy lines, although how much of this was true is open to debate. Wild Bill was a flamboyant character, softly spoken but self assured and certainly not averse to holding court about himself. He basked in the attention of an audience, it seems, and enjoyed the presence of an enthralled crowd.

There is no doubt that Hickok drew attention wherever he went. He was over six feet tall with broad shoulders and a lithe, athletic physique. Confident in the calm, graceful way he carried himself, he cut a striking figure, enhanced by his penchant for fancy clothes... frock coats, flowery bow ties and scarves, shirts with lacey cuffs and bibs, striped or checkered pants, broad brimmed/flat crowned hats... this is an image which Hickok would embroider as the years went on.

In leather holsters, he favoured the securing of a pair of Colt Navy pistols folded within a red sash around his waist, their handles pointing outwards.

His reddish brown hair fell luxuriantly to his shoulders and a broad, drooping moustache reached to the level of his chin. Piercing blue/grey eyes never missed a trick.

Hickok and Tutt were well known figures on the gambling circuit and enjoyed an affable relationship. Tutt had even loaned Hickok money on several occasions.

The post war atmosphere in Springfield was confused, the streets thronging with travellers passing through on the Old Wire Road, settlers, freighters and a whole army of ex soldiers, Union and Confederate, who were now left idle and aimless. The War had ended in April 1865, throwing many prior enemies into a melting pot of resentment.

Gambling was a common pastime. Many were broken by it, but experienced hands like Hickok and Tutt appeared to get by, their fortunes rising and falling. Wild Bill appears to have been killing time after his wartime experiences with no particular plans to move on. At this stage of his career, many stories surrounded him, tales of *derring do*, and he had been around, for sure, with a verifiable history of action under his belt, as we shall see. But, right now, he was enjoying his gaming pursuits and flirtations with local women and this might have been part of the reason he and Tutt fell out.

Was it to do with rivalry and/or jealousy? Maybe, but the rumours are largely unsubstantiated. Hickok fathering the illegitimate child of Tutt's sister? Tutt carrying on with Wild Bill's woman? There is no real evidence of these accusations, but problems did arise between the men when gambling disputes and other debts surfaced. Simmering tension reached the point where Hickok refused to gamble at the same table as Tutt.

Hickok was staying at the Lyon House Hotel where he was ensconced in a game in his room with several other players. Tutt was not playing but stood by, encouraging Hickok's opponents, loaning them money and giving advice on how to win. This must have irritated Wild Bill but he put up with it, especially as he began to win, rather handsomely, to the tune of about $200; a lot of cash in 1865.

Seizing the moment, Tutt reminded Hickok, in front of all present, that a recent horse sale meant that $40 of that money was his. Unfazed, and not willing to take the bait, Hickok handed Tutt the sum without argument, but it seems that the aggrieved man was spoiling for trouble.

"What about the other thirty five you owe me from that poker game?" demanded Tutt confrontationally.

Hickok looked at him and coolly replied, *"I think you're wrong, Dave. It's only twenty five, and I have a memorandum to prove it."*

Tutt had a lot of friends present and it must have boosted his confidence. His eyes fell upon Wild Bill's Waltham gold pocket watch which was lying on the table beside his winnings. It was a prized possession with sentimental value for Hickok but Tutt reached down and snatched it away.

"Then I'll keep this until you pay me the thirty five..." snapped Tutt.

Wild Bill's jaw tightened but he fought to keep a grip on his anger. This was pure humiliation but it would have been madness to resort to any kind of force against these overwhelming odds.

"Put it back on the table, Dave..." he requested, quietly but firmly, but, it was noted, Tutt just responded with a sarcastic grin before stalking out of the room.

The following morning, in the cold light of day, and after a long night mulling over the issue, Hickok was considering what best to do. Not out of fear but through common sense he had no desire to be drawn into an actual fight with his former friend. Word had already spread throughout town that there was trouble brewing between the two men and it created an edgy atmosphere. Pro Hickok and pro Tutt factions were murmuring to each other and bets began to be taken.

It was a hot and humid day, but the streets of Springfield were busy with the normal hubbub of a bustling frontier town as the crowds mingled with the billowing dust and clatter of horses and wagons.

Both protagonists stubbornly held on to their determination in the matter to not give way, although several attempts were made, by mutual friends, to find a compromise which might help each of them save face. To make matters worse, Tutt was insisting that the amount he was owed had now grown to $45.

Following a long afternoon of negotiation and passed messages, Hickok, Tutt and a couple of associates could be found seated on the porch of the Lyon House Hotel in one last attempt to find a solution to the problem. Tutt produced the watch from his pocket and dangled it in front of its owner with the simple statement that for $45, Hickok could have it back.

"I simply do not owe you that much, Dave…" muttered Wild Bill.

Even at this stage the pair were insisting that they did not want any *"fuss"*, taking a drink together but getting closer to an inevitable stand off. Eventually, with no headway being made, Tutt walked away, heading towards a nearby livery stable and leaving everyone present no wiser as to the possible outcome.

At this point, one of Tutt's brothers approached Hickok, apologising for the difficulties and suggesting that if Wild Bill were to *"come down"* and pay up, then all would be settled.

Out of the question. Hickok got to his feet, shook his head and straightened his wide brimmed hat. A fresh determination and resolution now crossed his features as he adjusted the pistols at his sides. It was pointless to debate the problem any further. The time had come to act.

As he strode unhurriedly, but purposefully, up South Street towards the central public square, Wild Bill cut a striking figure as the townsfolk parted to clear a path for him. On the corner of the square, where Crenshaw's Store was located, the tall, long haired shootist paused and looked north across the dirt surfaced clearing towards the Courthouse. It was a big, imposing building, fronted by stone arches and Tutt could be seen entering the north western corner of the square about thirty paces from it.

How evenly matched were these opponents?

At this stage it seemed one could not predict a clear winner. They were both in their approximate mid twenties and had each seen action in and out of the war. As the more flamboyant of the two, and with garish tales attached to his name, Hickok probably had the popular edge, but Tutt had a reputation too.

The main thing was that neither man was backing down as they faced each other, diagonally, across that wide square.

Davis Tutt's young face had been hardened by a typically rough life on the frontier. A chin beard and thin moustache decorated his triangular features and a pair of pale, staring eyes. Although he was fairly small and slight in build, he looked tough and could act it.

On this day, he was wearing a long, light coloured duster coat and his holstered pistol was visible beneath it.

It was just before 6.00pm.. Just moments before, the square had been bustling with a busy crowd of folks going about their business, but the appearance of these two gunmen had brought about a rapid exodus as the throng scattered and took shelter in every nook of the clearing. Even so, everyone wanted a clear view of what might happen next.

The field of fire was without obstacles and the range between the opponents was approximately 75 yards; quite a distance. Each shooter was presented with a target equivalent to viewing a toy soldier.

Witnesses spoke later of how Hickok and Tutt stood rooted to their positions and called out to one another. Wild Bill was heard to warn Tutt not to walk into the square with that watch.

Tutt reached beneath his coat and drew his pistol. As he raised it, Hickok swiftly produced his Colt Navy ball and cap revolver, 1851 model, raising his left forearm to eye level to steady his gun barrel on it.

Both men turned sideways on to each other, a classic duelling stance to minimise the target, and fired simultaneously; the retorts so close together that all present swore that it sounded like just one shot. Tutt's bullet missed, but Wild Bill's found its mark, tearing into Tutt's body between the fifth and seventh rib and exiting on the adjacent side.

It was an amazing piece of marksmanship and, in that moment, Wild Bill Hickok commenced his legendary journey into the history of the Old West.

Some said that Hickok's next act was to spin around and cover the crowd behind and on each side of him, daring anyone to attempt to avenge his victim.

Tutt rocked on his feet, staggering towards the Courthouse almost at a run. As he reached the porch, he circled one of the stone columns before falling face down by the boards gasping, *"Boys, I'm killed…"*

Such a face to face gunfight, man to man, was a rare occurrence although television and films would have you believe that it happened all the time. True, gunplay was common in the Old West but not like this, and the famous duel between Hickok and Tutt was probably the incident that started the notion of the noble gunfighter.

Wild Bill, visually and in many ways factually, was to tick the boxes of what a Wild West hero was meant to be… and there were those, including him, who took great strides to make sure that the world believed it.

CHAPTER 2
YOUNG JIM

The Hickocks family (often confusingly spelled in historical records as *Hitchcocks*) can be traced back to origins in England in the 16th. and 17th. centuries; Stratford-upon-Avon, Warwickshire, of all places, the birthplace of playwright William Shakespeare. As such, the ancestors of one of the Old West's most notorious figures were contemporaries of the great Bard; an amusing thought. There is nothing more traditionally English than this delightful little town... a whole world away from the Great Plains, prairies, mountains and vast wilderness of the 1800's American frontier.

However, it was a Hickocks, also a William, who took a ship across the Atlantic to Boston on the eastern seaboard and planted roots which soon expanded all over New England. By the late 1700s, his descendants were well and truly American, fighting against their erstwhile British countrymen and King in the War of Independence, and later, yet again, in the War of 1812.

Wild Bill himself was not yet a glimmer in his father's eye, he who was born in Vermont in 1801and dubbed... William! The Hickcocks were indeed fond of that name. This William was to marry local girl Polly Butler in 1827, settling for a short time in New York State where they commenced raising a large family, before moving west to Illinois, finally finding contentment in the small hamlet of Homer in La Salle County.

It was 1833 and the state was enjoying a newly won era of peace following the recent victory of the Blackhawk Indian War when all hostile natives had been expelled from the region. Settlers were soon flooding into this rich, fertile country and farms began to spring up everywhere.

By 1850, following a few lean years for the Hickocks, William and Polly managed to establish a modest farm of their own. When first arriving in the area, William had opened a store, the first in town, but when this venture failed, had spent a few years hiring himself and his young sons out to the local populace, grabbing any kind of work they could to scrape a living.

In all, William and Polly had seven children, although one son, named Lorenzo, had died when still a baby. Four sons grew to manhood... Oliver, another Lorenzo, Horace and James... plus two younger sisters, Celinda and Lydia.

The youngest son, James Butler Hickocks, the subject of this book, was born on May 27th. 1837. At some point the second C and end S appear to have been dropped from the family name and it became Hickok.

The name of their town changed too, from Homer to Troy Grove, to save confusion with a larger settlement named Homer, further north. All members of the family pitched in to help on the farm although William and Polly did make sure that, between the essential chores, their offspring received a reasonable level of schooling. The work was hard and seemingly endless, but all the Hickoks appeared to accept their lot in life. Only James seemed to expand his interests at this stage. He certainly did his part but it was noticed, early on, that, more than his siblings, he possessed an intense affinity with the outdoors. Indicating the path he would pursue in adulthood, James also embraced an early passion for firearms which became quite handy for the family as he would take off into the woods and hills to hunt game for supper. No one minded his absence from plough pushing because he would return with plenty of game. Indeed, young James Hickok certainly had a talent for marksmanship.

Slavery was at this time still practised widely across the country but the abolitionist movement was growing rapidly. The elder Hickok, William, was soon involved with the local factions and expressed deep sympathy for the plight of the enslaved black population. Quite a few of them passed through the Troy Grove area as they tried to escape to the north with bounty hunters on their tail. William Hickok, and others, did all they could to help them with food, shelter and advice… part of what was known as the illegal Underground Railroad. William's sons were recruited to do their part in this dangerous activity and it was claimed that James would have heard his first shots fired in anger as they dodged the bullets of those hunting down the fleeing slaves *en route* to the sanctuary of Canada.

This early indoctrination with an emphasis on freedom and justice had a deep effect upon the Hickok boys. Their father was passionate on this matter and was willing to risk his life, and that of his family, for these principles. James, in particular, took it on board it seems, as could be seen by the path he trod in later life, a very different one to that of his brothers.

Maybe that would not have happened had William not died in 1852 when James was just fifteen years old. The sudden loss of their father threw the family into confusion and desperation. Without a guiding force at their head, the boys and girls all had to do their bit to support each other and their grieving mother, Polly, working harder than ever to survive.

The youngest Hickok boy had been restless and wanting to expand his options for years. When his eldest brother Oliver had left home for the California Gold Rush, young Jim was anxious to follow but his father had forbidden it, telling him that his time would come. Now he was more anxious than ever, though he probably felt strong ties of responsibility to the family. That said, it does appear that he experienced a conflict of personality with his overbearing mother who did possess certain traits of possessiveness. It could have been that which drove him away with his brother Lorenzo when they both left home in 1856. Then again, further evidence suggests that James' life took another course...

He took all kinds of employment, including hunting wolves for the price that could be gleaned from their pelts. Local businesses engaged him to drive their wagons and further work could be found on the huge project which involved the extension of the Illinois/Michigan Canal. James was employed driving a mule team back and forwards for these canal builders, tough crews who laboured over such back breaking toil. They worked hard and played hard, their idea of fun being to get roaring drunk, gamble and rough each other up.

Young James Hickok, now aged eighteen, was to get very familiar with such characters in future years but in his youth he was a quiet figure, something of a loner which was probably the product of all the time he spent in solitude hunting.

Hickok's siblings, in years to come, all spoke of James' nature at this time, describing him as far from gregarious, although he was, apparently, fond of practical jokes within the family. His manner was pleasant, even gentle, they said, polite and a good listener. All the Hickoks had been brought up to be respectful of religion and were quite well educated. James may have read such adventures as *The Life of Kit Carson*, the renowned scout and Indian fighter, and saw himself in such a role one day.

Although he was tall and physically well built, James, at this point in his life was a little green around the edges. He found himself in the midst of these gangs of roughnecks without really playing an active part, just getting on with his work and keeping mainly to himself.

A story was to grow from this situation, something else to add to the Hickok legend. It was said that young James' low key demeanour was mistaken by some as weakness and led to a character named Charlie Hudson picking on him. Hickok finally cracked and went for his tormentor, resulting in a savage fight which sent them both tumbling into the canal. Hickok struggled ashore with the belief that his opponent had drowned, although he had, in fact, been rescued by others. Not wishing to face the music, the teenaged teamster fled blindly in panic and just kept going.

Or so it was claimed by certain early biographers.

Actually, the lack of provenance for this dramatic flight seems to point to the simple truth that James and his brother Lorenzo just decided the time had finally come for them to vacate the family nest.

What does seem likely, however, is evidence that Hickok did show some backbone in standing up to a foreman who was ill treating a team of horses. It got a bit physical between them and, as a result, Jim was dismissed from his teamster's job.

The Hickok brothers were young and yearning to expand their horizons, and that is what they did, full of optimism and not under any cloud of threat.

Young Jim had been dealt a hand to go West and he never really looked back.

He was on his way to becoming Wild Bill.

CHAPTER 3
JAYHAWKING AND FREIGHTING

Records are scarce regarding the initial path of young Jim Hickok and his brother but it seems probable that they did not look back over the next few days until they reached the banks of the wide Mississippi. Sternwheel steamboat traffic was pretty lively up and down this massive waterway so, finding a landing stage, maybe they would have found work on one of these vessels to work their passages further west.

Reaching St. Louis, Missouri, perhaps Jim and Lorenzo made themselves busy around the levees district, securing jobs on another paddle wheeler to head upriver into Kansas.

Thus they wound up in the newly founded township of Leavenworth, a rough and ready settlement which was seething with the tension of rival loyalties. Kansas was still a territory, not yet an American state, and Leavenworth was a central hub where trouble was forever at boiling point.

It was an important trading centre for traffic between all points of the compass, therefore all manner of folk were thrown together, regardless of their sympathies. The country was split between proslavery and abolitionist viewpoints and this caused a great deal of stressful conflict between factions which were growing more passionate, and violent, by the day.

Tension in the overcrowded town was so bad by the time Hickok's boat arrived that the local authorities forbade anyone to disembark and thus add to the already out of control trouble. However, as arguments raged between vessel and shore, the Hickoks might have slipped over the side and managed to make their way to the landing stage, mingling with the chaotic activities of the roughnecks unloading freight on the dock before quickly vanishing in the teeming crowds.

What they did next is uncertain, but it seems they parted company for some reason. It was probably easier to cope as single units and Lorenzo slipped away to seek his own fortune. Jim may have spent a while just working as a farm labourer before finding himself gradually drawn into the gathering confrontations which were increasingly dominating the territory, especially along the Missouri border.

With his lifelong held abolitionist sympathies, it was inevitable that he would throw in his lot with the Free State Militia, also known as *Jayhawkers* and later on as Kansas *Redlegs* (owing to their trade mark coloured leggings).

Clashes between rival factions were heartless, unforgiving and brutal, giving rise to a period referred to in history as *Bleeding Kansas* and the *Blood Dimmed Tide* as the savagery grew in intensity. Pro slavery Missouri *Border Ruffians* staged regular raids across the boundaries, burning, looting and murdering in an orgy of pure hatred. The *Jayhawkers* responded with equal ruthlessness and fought an undeclared, but filthy, form of war, a blood spattered precursor to the looming conflict between North and South which was to tear the country apart and change history. No pitched battles as such, but plenty of ambushing, burning of homesteads, mini massacres and lynching. Guerrilla fighting of the worst kind.

In essence, each side was as bad as the other, financed respectively by the motives of the rich Southern slave holders and the Northern industrialists, all of whom were stoking up the troubles.

The Free-Staters liked to style themselves as the *Army of the North* but there was nothing noble or official about them, any more than their opponents from Missouri. Both sides whooped and hollered, waved their weapons, galloping around and causing mayhem to each other, the result being that the general populace suffered greatly.

Samuel Colt's development of the revolver in the 1840s had dramatically changed the face of combat, replacing the limitation of single shot sidearms. Both sides in the *Bleeding Kansas* conflict embraced the deadly new technology with wild enthusiasm, arming themselves to the teeth. It was not unusual for men to carry as many as eight revolvers stashed in holsters, belts, saddlebags and deep pockets, along with spare loaded chambers for maximum firepower. Hickok's prowess with such handguns was undoubtedly refined during this period.

The *Jayhawkers* (Free-Staters) may have been named after a bird which acts ruthlessly, but more likely from an early abolitionist named John Jay. Their leader was a colourful character named James Henry Lane, an ex-lawyer and congressman who had commanded an infantry regiment in the Mexican/American War of 1846-48. He was very energetic and charismatic and did a lot to unite the numerous anti-slavery groups with his fiery speeches.

Hickok was impressed by James Lane and enlisted in the *Jayhawkers* along with his friend John Owen, a farmer. Lane soon became aware of the youthful Jim Hickok because he was always around, hanging on every word and expressing a degree of hero worship for his commander. Aware of Hickok's impressive skill with guns, and of his loyalty, Lane accepted him as his unofficial bodyguard. It was reported that on at least one occasion, Hickok acted to prevent Lane's assassination. Lane responded by calling him one of the most effective men in his command.

It was 1856 and the Border War was at its height, fed by sordid skirmishes but never reaching fully fledged confrontation, although it did come close.

The key anti-slavery township of Lawrence, Kansas, was attacked by a large force of Missourians, who raked the hotel with cannonfire and set fire to it. Looting and burning was rife as the town was sacked, the printing presses of the Free-State newspapers were thrown into the river and a couple of people were shot dead by the drunken *Border Ruffians*. By the time an opposing force of *Jayhawkers* had been rallied the Missourians had dispersed and fallen back across the border.

This stirred up a fierce desire for vengeance, not least in the heart of fanatical John Brown, a loud and active abolitionist who swore that far more needed to be done to release the slaves. His dream, he declared, was to *"drown the South in its own blood"*.

Frustrated at having missed his chance to do battle with the Lawrence assailants, Brown decided to act himself in retribution. Within a few days of the attack on the town, he led a gang of followers, including his four sons, to a pro-slavery hamlet along Pottawatomie Creek and by night randomly hacked five men to death with swords.

This caused a frenzy of threats and cries for revenge. Pitched battles were predicted and one nearly came to fruition in the late summer near Osawatomie, but it was not to be. The two armies cautiously approached each other on opposite sides of Bull Creek. There was plenty of shouting and waving of weapons, with a few half hearted shots exchanged, but no one seemed willing to commit to the expected bloodbath. The tension was finally eased, probably to the general relief of most, by the intervention of a squadron of United States Cavalry from Fort Leavenworth who persuaded both sides to withdraw.

But the Missouri/Kansas War continued in its underhand manner with bushwhackings, raids and general mayhem. By now, Hickok was well involved and doubtless played his part enthusiastically in much of this although there is a lack of surviving detail. It was a confusing time but we can be sure that it was young Jim's true baptism of fire as he grew accustomed to the excitement and tension of flying lead.

It is also worth noting that during this period it is said that Hickok made his first acquaintance with a young boy, aged about eleven, who was to grow up to become the legendary Buffalo Bill Cody. Cody was apparently working as a messenger for Lane's followers when he was set upon by a bully. Hickok stepped in and saved him. This cemented the bond which later grew into a strong friendship between the two, as we shall see.

After a while, things began to grow somewhat quieter along the border, although there was still the odd flashpoint of violence. This was deceiving, however, because it was just the calm before the coming storm of the Civil War.

Resentment, blame and hatred still simmered, bursting for an outlet whilst men like John Brown just pushed harder. Brown eventually, in 1859, attempted to incite a full blown slave rebellion by attacking the Federal armoury at Harper's Ferry, Virginia, but he was captured, tried for treason and murder and hanged.

Hickok, his thirst for action and adventure satisfied for now, drifted back to a more settled and peaceful existence. He occupied himself for a while with mundane pursuits like cutting hay and farm labouring again and even attained a few acres of prairie land where he established a dugout style home. Unfortunately, he was to lose this land owing to some complicated claim via a land treaty with the Indians. Sad, because around this time he had written home optimistically speaking of inviting his other brothers out to join him in the *"beautiful prairie that can't be beat…"*

He had also joined the expedition of an English adventurer named Williams who was looking for land to settle and this, in 1857, resulted in the foundation of the village of Monticello in Johnson County, northwest Kansas.

Hickok spent a lot of time in the tavern of this fast growing little township, and he was a popular figure, locally respected and described as a *"cheerful worker and a nice fellow"*. He took on the job of managing the stables and tending the horses of passing stagecoaches. Monticello was becoming an important, though small, staging post for fur trading and passages to the West.

In March 1858, aged nearly 21, Hickok's popularity was such that he had no problem being elected as a constable, along with three others, to serve the local magistrates of Monticello. For the first time, young James felt responsibility as a representative of the law, but being such a quiet town, it was a mild apprenticeship compared to what he would face as a frontline lawman in later life.

Right now, however, he was to be distracted by romance.

John Owen, the farmer who Hickok had enlisted with in the Free State Militia, had become a close friend. Considerably older than young Jim, Owen had married a Shawnee woman, consequently earning respect and warm relations with her tribe. They had a daughter named Mary and Hickok fell in love with her.

Mary was said to be beautiful and intelligent, as well as an excellent housekeeper and cook.

Writing his rare letters home, Hickok mentioned her and seemed proud to have made her acquaintance. He wrote of her blackberry picking and unbeatable biscuit baking, and of cutting off a lock of his hair to send to his mother. All seemed well... he was content and settling down, it seemed, and he even reported that he was no longer drinking or gambling, although whether this was true is a matter of conjecture.

It was a serious relationship, apparently, but something led to Hickok reaching out again for further adventure. This was a trait deeply ingrained in his nature, so maybe it was just that an uneventful life in a small Kansas town did not appeal to him. Loving sweet Mary was not enough and he began to question his priorities... at least that is my guess... for once again, for whatever reason, Jim Hickok took the open road, in search of something new.

***

The old Santa Fe Trail was the scene of the next chapter of Hickok's eventful life.

Though still youthful, Jim already had quite a parcel of frontier experience under his belt, and so he had no trouble getting work as a driver of freight wagons between Independence, Missouri, and Santa Fe itself. For about $20 a month, including his board, Hickok took on these regular hazardous journeys which included straightforward trails across the prairie before negotiating rivers like the Arkansas and Purgatoire. From there it was a winding, treacherous route into the Mountains of Raton... narrow paths, gorges and the constant danger of losing everything over the edge of a precipice.

Wagon drivers needed nerves of steel as well as exceptional skill in handling their freight. Hickok was a master of this trade, good with animals and supremely confident with a whip and reins in his strong hands.

It was not long before he is said to have progressed to driving stagecoaches carrying mail and passengers. As his confidence grew, the strapping young character gained a reputation too as he turned these journeys into events for all on board. He cut quite a dashing figure high up on the coach seat, already cultivating an image which he was to perfect in just a few years hence. Tall and broad shouldered, dressed the part and cracking his whip, Hickok delighted in putting on a show, giving his team of horses their head as he drove them full pelt, but expertly, into that ancient Mexican town of Santa Fe. The passengers would be shaken but exhilarated by their wild ride, as Hickok grinned over his therapy of what he called *"jolting out the cricks"*.

Jim was quickly accepted by the tough fraternity which filled his line of work. He was respected and popular, because he was more than capable of handling things, plus, although he could be quiet and solitary, he exuded an aura of affability and generosity of spirit. And it was during this period that he came to be addressed as Bill, although the "Wild" bit would come later.

Why this should be is not fully clear, although the Hickok family did confirm that Bill was his nickname when a child, probably in deference to the fact that William was such a popular moniker for their generations. His brother Lorenzo, who, by now, had become a well known wagon master, had also adopted the name of Billy amongst his contemporaries, so perhaps it was just a natural progression for the youngest brother. However, the newly named Bill Hickok would always be known to his close family back in Troy Grove as James.

So, Santa Fe became a regular haunt of Bill Hickok's and he was soon enchanted by the wild nightlife which revolved around the saloons, gambling houses and other dens of questionable virtue. It was loud, raucous, exciting and often violent. Hunters, freighters, mountain men, traders, outlaws and travellers passing through on endlessly mysterious business of their own, of all nationalities and of all manner of temperament. Beer and whisky were a staple diet and Bill quickly acquired a taste for it, accompanied by a constant cacophony of shouts, quarrels, songs, ripe language (in many tongues) and ribald humour. Music laced the air to the tune of piano, banjos, guitars, fiddles and anything anyone could thump out a rhythm on. But, life was cheap and gunplay and knife fights were common occurrences.

Bill observed all this and absorbed it with interest, a world where he knew he belonged. Above anything else, it gave him his lifelong love of gambling and he took to the card tables enthusiastically.

Legend has it, and maybe there is truth in it, that it was in this rowdy environment that Hickok met his hero Kit Carson.

Carson was truly a legend in his own lifetime although he was confused and unhappy about his fame. None the less, here was a man whose exploits, both real and wildly exaggerated in dime novels, was unequalled across the Continent. He had a proven record of hair raising adventures as a trapper, scout, trail blazer and Indian fighter going back decades, yet to meet him in the flesh was a little surprising. Yes, he looked weather worn, leathery and tough, but he was not big in stature. His demeanour appeared low key, modest and calm, yet everyone knew that he was not to be tangled with. He was almost thirty years older than Bill, but did they actually meet? Sadly, there is no tangible evidence to confirm it.

Hickok would have learned a lot from any association with Carson, not least how to carry himself in the challenging environment which surrounded them. Tolerant dignity was the key to respect, along with a confident ability to strike back only when necessary.

Of course, such a philosophy was effective in general dealings with his fellow man, but Hickok was shortly to discover that it cut no ice in the animal world. Or so the long held story says...

In the latter part of 1860 young Bill was doing regular work as a wagon master for a freighting company. Russell, Majors & Waddell ran a massive operation which dominated the transport trade in this part of the country as well as recently establishing the short lived, yet famous, Pony Express. Although it only ran for eighteen months, before being overtaken by the new technology of the telegraph, this enterprise dramatically etched its place alongside the legendary symbols of the Old West. At the time, the idea of swift ponies galloping across the wilds at top speed was exciting and groundbreaking, changing mounts and pushing on to deliver the mail between Missouri and California in record time... ten days, which was pretty impressive until that first telegraph made it all redundant.

By necessity, the Pony Express riders needed to be slightly built and jockey like, so that kept the well built, tall physique of Bill Hickok out of the saddle.

Instead, he carried on as a much valued guide and driver who could be relied upon to get the lumbering trains safely through the treacherous, rock strewn gullies and paths of the Raton Pass. Until fairly recent research unearthed contrary evidence, it was long believed that Hickok was actually quite a long term employee of R., M. & W.. Instead, it is more likely that he was working for the rival company of Jones & Cartwright.

All those who carried out this demanding work were of a particular breed so it is amusing to reflect on the sanctimonious rules of the R., M. & W's contract which all had to sign. Before God, they were required to swear that whilst in the employ of this company, they would refrain from drinking alcohol and using profane language, not fight or quarrel and behave honestly for the good name of their employer! What a joke... one wonders if *any* of these hard-bitten workers kept even slightly to those terms!

Anyway, it came to pass that Hickok allegedly had an early encounter which was a major step in the solidification of his growing legend...

The story goes that he was making his way back on his own from a delivery to collect another wagon when, in a batch of pine trees, he came across a large bear blocking the narrow trail. This creature was female and of the rusty brown furred cinnamon variety and she was not happy. It seems she had a couple of her cubs concealed in the nearby foliage and there is nothing more dangerous than a protective, disturbed mother bear.

The bears sudden appearance on the trail had startled Hickok's horse which reared up and threw him to the ground before galloping back the way it had come. Bill was swiftly on his feet, his eyes locked with the grumpy creature which was moving towards him threateningly.

It was not exactly a situation wherein he could use his human behavioural skills. No point in trying to run from a bear or to try and climb a tree to escape. They excel in both these acts. There was no reasoning with this angry beast as she closed in for the kill, so Hickok pulled out his pistol and opened fire on the big, hairy head and body.

The bullets appeared to have no more effect than angering her further and Bill just about had time to reach for his hunting knife before he suffered the first slashes of her lethal, sharp claws.

In the next few moments Hickok must have felt his time had come as he wrestled and fought back as best he could. His scalp was torn and hanging loose, his arms legs and torso ripped and gushing blood in torrents. As the bear enveloped him in a bone crushing hug he grew faint and made one last effort to survive by driving the long blade of his knife deep into the bear's midriff, cutting upwards and across.

The enraged, stricken bear roared and squeezed harder but Bill was determined as he worked the blade inside her until, at last, she released her grip and they both collapsed to the ground.

It was quite a while before the next wagon up the trail came upon the horrific sight of Hickok lying unconscious beneath the huge bulk of the dead bear, the pair of them tangled in a gruesome mass of her entrails and lashings of both human and animal blood.

He was rushed back to Santa Fe as quickly as possible where it was doubted that he could survive his terrible injuries. But he did, although it was a long, slow, painful process.

Well, that is what the long believed legend claimed as gospel but, yet again, recent research sadly seems to confirm that the bear incident simply did not happen. It was all part of stories which grew and were retold via many separate accounts.

So why do I include it here?

I do so as an example of how Hickok's legend often blends imperceptibly with the verifiable truth.

It was also long thought that within a few months, the company decided he might have recovered sufficiently to take on some lighter work. They found him a job assisting at their Rock Creek station out on the Oregon Trail.

But, Hickok's tenure with Jones & Cartwright had terminated in April of 1861 so why did he find himself at Rock Creek that summer?

It has been suggested that perhaps he was working temporarily for Russell, Majors & Waddell or that he just happened to be passing through and got hired directly by the station manager.

Whatever, a peaceful period of his life it was not destined to be.

***

In mid September 2004 I drove from Denver Colorado down the Interstate 70, turning south onto the 25, crossing the border into New Mexico where the ascent began up the famed Raton Pass.

The scenery is stunning, almost too much for an unaccustomed Englishman's eyes. Back in the days of the Old Santa Fe Trail it was remote in the extreme, save for the stream of wagon bound traffic lumbering up the rocky road. I could not resist pulling over regularly to get out and explore a little way from the highway, but I was cautious not to venture too far. Whether or not Hickok actually fought that bear, there is always the danger of one of its fierce descendants still roaming around with a taste for human blood!

When out of sight of the road, (but making sure you do not lose awareness of your bearings!) an impression is swiftly given of how it was for Hickok in his freighting days; the sheer stark, rawness of the land... so beautiful yet frighteningly threatening in its vast solitude.

Also took a quick look at the little town of Raton (which means MOUSE in Spanish) established by the scout Uncle Dick Wootton. He would eventually establish a toll road through the Pass which was rather enterprising of him. At its summit, this glorious landmark is 7,834 feet above sea level and, if clear, it feels like you can see to the ends of the Earth.

I mentioned the name of the town in a store en route and was immediately pulled up on my pronunciation by a bewildered local clerk behind the counter.

Only having ever seen the word on the written page, I said Rat-on, as in "on a rat" but the correction which came back to me in a frontier drawl was, "Yuh min Rat-TONE?"... as in rhyming with "bone".

This reminded me of my days working as a London tour guide when American tourists would ask about Leicester Square which, for the benefit of any non-English readers, is pronounced LESTER. Visitors invariably, yet understandably, would say LAYCESTER.

It was George Bernard Shaw who famously stated, "England and America are two countries separated by a common language".

I spent time in Santa Fe too, but I will go into further detail about that later on in these pages.

CHAPTER 4
RUMBLE AT ROCK CREEK

The grassy plains of southeast Nebraska are relentlessly bleak, especially back in the mid 1800s. There was precious little settlement then and once travellers set out west across that harsh, unforgiving wilderness, at the mercy of the elements, thirst, hunger, bandits and hostile Indians, they would need a whole lot more than luck to emerge unscathed, or even alive.

One last oasis before pointing hopefully towards the tempting Pacific Northwest was the thriving station at Rock Creek. All traffic on the Oregon Trail passed through here; gigantic ox drawn wagons, freight vehicles, overland stage coaches, traders, mysterious strangers and, for a while, those wiry little Pony Express riders who never dallied for long; just a swift exchange of ponies.

The station was the last chance for provisions, water, fresh mounts, advice and any repairs that may have been needed to wagons and coaches before plunging into the unknown. Here could be found twin ranch houses on either side of the creek itself which wound away to join the Little Blue River in the distance. There was also a barn, stables and a corral. A toll bridge across the creek was a further healthy source of income.

This outpost was managed by Horace Wellman, an agent for the R. M. & W. company. Accompanied by his wife, Wellman had taken the position in the spring of 1861, the station itself having only been recently acquired from its previous owner, Dave McCanles, who had settled here and built up the place on his way west from Carolina a couple of years before.

His station and control of traffic established, McCanles had become something of a dominant figure in the area who even had quite an influence over the nearby township of Palmetto. He was a big, brash, loud man who towered over most. Overbearing and demanding, he usually got his way, his various interests bringing him in a small fortune every month.

It was said that he had abandoned his wife and children to head west, taking with him his lover, Sarah Shull. Once having settled himself at Rock Creek with a thriving business, he sent for his family and they hurried out to join him in his success. As for Sarah, she was sidelined and apparently tolerated by McCanles' wife, for Dave himself was not averse to rekindling regular trysts with her. A convenient arrangement for the burly bully as Sarah was ensconced in one of the ranch houses just across the creek from the family home.

For some reason, maybe the awkward proximity of his lover, McCanles decided to sell the station, including the toll bridge and all the buildings, to Russell, Majors & Waddell, moving his family to a ranch a few miles away.

Horace Wellman and his common law wife, Jane, now ran things with a small team of workers. His stable hand was a man named Doc Brink and newly arrived Bill Hickok was engaged to tend stock.

Hickok welcomed the genteel pace of his new position. When not actually working he enjoyed his own company and most likely made the most of the therapeutic benefits gained from his solitary dugout just beyond the stables.

It is also possible, although not certain, that he found additional comfort in the arms of Sarah, McCanles part time lover, and that may have been one of the reasons why the big Carolinian took such a dislike to him.

Hickok was not looking for trouble but McCanles seemed determined to stir it up. The entire region, in fact the whole country, was in a state of restless turmoil owing to the recent declaration of war between the North and South. Men were dropping everything and enthusiastically rushing off to join the Confederate or Union armies. At this time they were all filled with a joyous, patriotic fervour, ignorant of what would become the horror of the next four years which would tear the nation in two.

McCanles too would be picking a side, but, in the short term, he was keen to settle matters locally. The R. M. & W Company were being somewhat lax in keeping up the agreed payments on the sale of the station, also on settling their supply bills with the previous owner. In fact the company was in serious financial trouble and facing bankruptcy. Understandably, McCanles was not happy about this and he began to take his frustration out on those who now occupied his old property.

Although he had a point, McCanles chose to take an unreasonable approach, making increasingly regular and belligerent visits to Rock Creek to demand a solution. Wellman tried reasoning with him, explaining that he was doing his best to extract what was owed from his employers but this just made McCanles angrier and more impatient.

Bill Hickok tried to keep out of it but McCanles honed in on him, finding excuses to make accusations and to try and humiliate the young stock tender at every opportunity.

Now, Hickok was no coward. Despite his youth he had already lived a pretty eventful life of action and was no stranger to violence and danger. However, by nature he was not one to seek trouble and always preferred to stay out of it unless it was totally unavoidable. Keeping to himself, he did his best to avoid involvement in the politics of the situation but McCanles was pushing hard and began goading him personally.

Hickok's good looks were slightly marred by a protruding upper lip and a rather pointed nose. Eventually he would cover these features with long, sweeping mustachios which became such a trademark of his yet to be famous image. But in the summer of 1861 McCanles apparently took advantage of this and, it is said, began taunting Hickok by openly, and laughingly, referring to him as "Duck" Bill. This, however, may also not be true, being a possible misunderstanding of the fact that Hickok was known as "Dutch" Bill. Why? No one, so far, has come up with a certain explanation

Hickok tolerated this, but there were occasions when McCanles took things further by finding excuses to physically accost him. Even then, young Bill refused to take the bait, not out of fear but by making the sensible decision not to escalate matters for his employers. Also, could he be bothered with the repercussions resulting from a full on frontier brawl? He was biding his time.

McCanles mistakenly took Hickok's reluctance to defend himself as weakness and it encouraged him to take further liberties. The station agent Wellman was under enormous pressure to find the money owed to his tormentor and so he travelled to the company's office at Brownsville to plead that the debt be settled without further delay. With bankruptcy looming, the representatives of Russell, Majors & Waddell still seemed reluctant, or unable, to pay up quickly and Wellman returned to Rock Creek empty handed and with nothing more than further empty promises.

With Wellman away, Hickok had been left in charge of Rock Creek and, consequently, had suffered almost daily increasing abuse from McCanles. Now that Wellman had returned with disappointing news, matters were about to overflow to the next level.

McCanles exploded with rage and made it known to everyone in the area that he was going to *"clean up on the people at the station"*. (As quoted years later by Sarah Shull herself.)

Wellman was close to panic, but he knew that the time had come to stand up to such a threat or face the likelihood of a humiliating, violent eviction from his home and job. McCanles was capable of carrying out such extreme measures and obviously meant to see it through.

On the morning of July 12th. 1861, Wellman discussed the crisis with Hickok and the stable hand Doc Brink. They knew they could expect another visit from McCanles and this time he would take things to the extreme. He had already shown up early in the front yard demanding that the station be handed over to him. Wellman had not complied, of course, claiming that he had no such authority to surrender, and McCanles responded with further threats, riding away with the promise that he would return with help to take the place by force.

There was no time to send for assistance so the defensive trio resigned themselves to resist as best they could. They had no idea what kind of support McCanles would return with… maybe a small army… but, in fact, when he did appear, late that afternoon, he was only accompanied by his cousin, James Woods, a ranch employee, James Gordon, and his twelve year old son, Monroe.

Wellman, Hickok, Brink, Wellman's wife and a girl who helped out in the house watched from the windows as McCanles and his party reined in by the barn. They dismounted and their leader told them to wait while he made his final demand.

McCanles, with young Monroe at his side, marched boldly up to the west door of the house, clearly not expecting any serious resistance. Wellman did not want to face such hostility again and sent Jane out in answer to the roars of the man but McCanles just insisted on seeing the agent in person. Jane hated McCanles because her father had recently taken a beating from him. She tried standing up to the big man but he shouted her down.

Wellman could not be persuaded to leave the house. What would be the point? Eventually, with no chance of McCanles' furious demands subsiding, Hickok stepped onto the porch to see what he could achieve.

Unsurprisingly, *"Duck or Dutch"* Bill's appearance made matters worse. McCanles yelled insults at him, demanding to know what business it was of his.

Hickok stayed calm but McCanles was having none of it. More threats forced Hickok back into the shelter of the house and McCanles and son moved around to the south door, peering into the building and trying to make out what was on the other side of the calico curtain which divided the inner sanctum of the front room.

The women had been sent down into the shelter of the cellar by now and Hickok and Wellman had armed themselves with revolvers and a rifle. Both of them stood behind the curtain waiting to see if McCanles would dare to enter the room.

He did. Stepping across the threshold, McCanles had crossed the line, along with his shouts to come out and fight. Was he armed? Almost certainly.

That was the cue to pull the trigger. Whether it was Wellman or Hickok is still debated by historians, but it was probably the latter, especially as the well aimed shot through the curtain took McCanles directly in the heart, knocking him backwards where he fell dying in the doorway.

That moment changed the odds dramatically. Emboldened by this sudden shift in advantage, Wellman stepped over McCanles' body as Doc Brink appeared beside him holding a shotgun. Hickok came forward too, facing Woods and Gordon as they rushed over from the barn at the sound of the shot.

The sight of McCanles' bleeding corpse pulled them up abruptly just as Hickok opened fire on them. Woods was hit twice, wounding him badly but he turned and did his best to flee. Gordon ran to the other side of the house but another blast from Hickok grazed him as he blundered in terror into the surrounding brushwood, his faithful bloodhound bounding after him.

Hickok left it at that, turning back to the front door and the poignant sight of the boy Monroe cradling the head of his dead father. The women had emerged from the cellar now and the vindictive Jane was screaming after the fleeing men. It was said she told Hickok to kill the boy too but he shook his head. Monroe fled into the woods before the furious woman could do him any harm.

James Woods, bleeding heavily, did not get far. Pursued by Mrs. Wellman, her blood lust up, the wounded man stumbled into a patch of weeds and collapsed where Jane set about him with a long handled gardening hoe, chopping out any last signs of life.

Gordon might have escaped, but his dog's barks and whines gave him away. Doc Brink, Wellman and Hickok followed the sounds and caught up with him along the creek bottom. The stricken man backed up against a tree where someone, most probably Brink, blasted him to death with both barrels of the shotgun.

The bodies were hurriedly buried but the killers were open about what they had done, allowing themselves to be arrested by the Sheriff of Gage County within three days of the incident. The McCanles family were swift to swear out warrants against Hickok, Wellman and

Brink and they were taken to the town of Beatrice, Nebraska, to stand before the Justice of the Peace.

It was an odd hearing because it appeared to be rather one sided with only the accused being permitted to speak. Wellman's biased partner, Jane, represented the territory, and McCanles' twelve year old son, Monroe, although an obvious witness, was not called to give evidence. The hearing had all the hallmarks of a set up, maybe because McCanles had not been popular with most people in the area.

Self defence and protection of government property was the plea from the accused and the matter never even went to trial. The Justice of the Peace decided that the charge of murder could not be sustained and the case was dismissed.

Those with blood on their hands went free.

It was not the most distinguished event in Hickok's colourful career but it was the one which was to kick off his reputation.

But that was a few years in the future when a certain writer saw the value of embellishing Bill Hickok's exploits into something fictitiously spectacular.

First, however, he had a war to fight.

CHAPTER 5
WILD BILL GOES TO WAR

The increasingly savage conflicts of the Civil War were gaining momentum as the armies of the Union and Confederacy fought it out on the battlefields of the States further to the East. This part of the country saw the most intense action and here it would continue for the next four years.

The South West also saw its share of bloodshed and mayhem but, on the grand scale of panoramic spectacle, in most ways, it was a lesser sideshow.

Many States and territories had seceded from the Union, forming their own southern based government under Jefferson Davis. The Union in the north remained sound under the steady hand of President Abraham Lincoln.

Once again the bitter rivalries of the 1850s flared up all along the Missouri/Kansas border lands, this time heavily stoked and spreading wide under the official banner of outright war. But it was still a messy affair, dominated by guerrilla activity… raids and chaos.

There was no question as to which side Bill Hickok would take. As the dust settled on the Rock Creek affair, he grew restless again. His strength regained, he felt the pull towards involvement in doing his part to restore the unity of the country under the principle of his abolitionist heritage.

But he was an individualist… a frontier warrior who needed to fight in his own way. As such, there would be no formal army enlistment for him. He offered his services to the blue clad Army of the Union at Fort Leavenworth, but it would be on his chosen terms, in a manner that would prove far more effective and useful than if he had donned a uniform and shouldered a musket as one of the rank and file.

Acquitted from any charges relating to the Rock Creek killings, Hickok wasted no time in vacating the area, but inflated stories about what had happened were already spreading far and wide. Retold over and over again, the actual facts were swiftly receding into myth and the low key, sordid truth was morphing into something else altogether. People from far away were learning of an imaginary version of events in which the vicious and much feared McCanles' Gang, numbering a dozen or so desperadoes, had been single handedly wiped out by an heroic superman named Bill Hickok.

By the time Hickok was volunteering himself for wartime service, this reputation had preceded him and wherever he went people regarded him with awe. These were early days, but it was the precursor to what would dog his every move for the rest of his life.

Major General John C. Fremont, commander of the Army of the South West, may have known of this reputation and, presumably, saw the benefit of taking advantage of a man with such qualities.

Fremont had already made quite a name for himself as an heroic military commander, politician and explorer, having led a series of expeditions which helped to open up the West, paving the way for the Oregon Trail and the Transcontinental Railroad. He was drawn to men like Hickok and therefore had no hesitation in appointing him brigade wagon master, but with an eye on using his skills in various other capacities.

One of Hickok's first assignments was to lead a supply train from Leavenworth to Sedalia in Missouri, but the wagons were attacked and captured by an enemy band. Hickok managed to get away, claiming to have killed several of his pursuers as he fought his way free. Making it to the town of Independence, where he was to rest up for a while, this is where, according to legend, young Bill acquired the attachment of "Wild" to his name.

It is not verifiable, as such, but the story goes that Hickok was taking things easy in town before considering his next wartime mission when a friend of his, a bartender, shot a troublemaker in his saloon. The man's friends took exception to this and about a score of them formed a "neck-tie party" to administer some crude frontier justice to the shooter. Cornering their terrified victim, the bartender would have been strung up for sure had not Hickok intervened.

Facing down the vengeful mob, many witnesses later spoke of the imposing figure of Bill who strode out to block their path, hands on the butts of his pistols.

The armed potential lynchers were fazed by this... what could one man do against twenty? They could overwhelm him, surely, but how many of them would he take with him?

Hickok's steely gaze and rigid demeanour spoke volumes as all those he faced weighed up the odds. His reputation was familiar to all of them.

Steadily, calmly but determinedly, Bill ordered the mob to disperse immediately or *"there will be more dead men here than can be buried"*.

Heads down, muttering, the formerly angry crowd chose self preservation over vengeance as they began to drift away from each other.

Hickok watched until they were all gone, at which point, it is said, an excited, and much impressed, female admirer amongst the surrounding spectators cried out either, *"Good for you, Wild Bill!"* or maybe, *"My, but ain't he Wild?"*

Whatever the truth of this, the fact remains that from around this time, the name of Wild Bill Hickok is how he would be known for the rest of his days and beyond.

***

There were only really two, maybe three, of what could be considered major battles in the South Western theatre of the Civil War, everything else taking the form of skirmishes, ambushes, raids and personalized conflicts, but it was a blood soaked and dangerous time for all.

Wild Bill's experience and talents were utilized beyond his wagon driving skills and he was soon engaged by the Union forces as a real asset in civilian clothes. Ordered to scout way ahead of General Lyons' army a few miles outside of Springfield, Hickok was tasked with locating Confederate batteries of cannon which put him under the fearsome reign of artillery fire for the first time. This led to the Battle of Wilson's Creek in August 1861 in which it seems Hickok played quite an active part, especially when the Northern troops were routed from the town by Shelby & Co.'s grey clad rebels. Although Lyons himself was killed in the retreat, Wild Bill and other scouts helped others escape by offering covering fire.

An interesting little side-note here is that the victorious Confederate forces may have included Frank James (brother of Jesse) and their cousin Cole Younger as members of the Missouri State Guard. Jesse himself was, at this time, too young to participate although he did join his brother, along with the rest of the Younger boys, later in the war when they rode with the notorious guerrilla leader Bloody Bill Anderson, and, consequently, with the even more notorious William Quantrill. In 1863, Quantrill's raiders sacked the town of Lawrence in a murderous attack which took the lives and destroyed the property of over 200 civilians.

The James and Younger brothers never really stopped fighting the Civil War and carried on their own version of hostilities as outlaws for years afterwards.

Lyons had been Fremont's replacement as commander of the Army of the South West, so now that the former was no more, the post was given to Major General Sam Curtis. President Lincoln was determined that the complications of a war front in this area be eradicated as soon as possible, there being already enough to contend with in the east, so the pressure was on.

Curtis also made use of Wild Bill and eventually promoted him to the position of Chief of Scouts. In the meantime, Hickok was given pretty much free reign with independent scouting assignments largely behind enemy lines, gathering information on troop movements and, along with others in his position, making things generally difficult for the Rebel forces, harassing them and planting false information. He also carried dispatches between various commanders, travelling the back trails of the Ozarks, largely by night to avoid detection by the vigilant Confederate patrols.

Hickok and his fellow scouts worked mainly in disguise, masquerading as hillbillies and even donning Confederate uniforms to obtain maximum potential for infiltration. In this way, Wild Bill was even accepted into the ranks of the Rebel Army for quite some time.

Many years later, an old war veteran recalled seeing Wild Bill, just once, in passing. Hickok was passing through a busy troop movement, going about his mysterious business when he was respectfully acknowledged by seasoned soldiers who had heard of his adventures fighting for the Union. Wild Bill's appearance on this occasion was surprisingly bedraggled and weather worn, drooped over the saddle of a weary mule. No doubt he had recently been involved in some dangerous scrape, but a green young trooper, unaware of who he was, made the mistake of making fun of him. Hickok merely responded by glaring blankly at the recruit whilst plodding on. When the soldier was told by his comrades who he had just insulted, he was terror stricken and spent a while lawing low in case Wild Bill returned to take revenge!

Wild Bill undoubtedly lived a colourful and adventurous life in this role throughout the War but, sadly, very few official records of his exploits have actually survived for perusal. Such written evidence probably never even existed owing to the clandestine nature of his work.

However, we are left, inbetween the outlandish tales, with a reasonably accurate picture of what he achieved and it emerges as pretty impressive.

For instance, he is said to have been overjoyed at the opportunity to take part in a glorious cavalry charge which temporarily drove the enemy out of Springfield, although they did swiftly retake the town.

In addition he apparently paved the way for the destruction of the Rebel arsenal at Yellville, Arkansas.

And he also probably played a significant role in the battle of Pea

Ridge in March 1863, a ragged and confused affair which was fought out messily in ravines, creek bottoms, copses and meadows.

A more doubtful yarn concerns his flight from capture by the enemy in which he killed the rider of a magnificent black mare, taking the animal for himself and naming her Black Nell. This horse became part of the Hickok legend and was credited with almost as many unbelievable adventures and talents as Wild Bill himself, but I think we can take all this with a large pinch of salt.

Even so, although officially unverified, enough anecdotes have drifted down through the ages for a generally convincing picture of Hickok's war, involving, pursuits, fire fights, swimming rivers to escape, close calls, etc.. Like in any war, the many participants experienced all manner of things, much of it heroic, outstanding and incredible, yet the bulk is lost to history. Whatever, Wild Bill was most certainly in the thick of it all and emerged, more or less unscathed, with a name which placed him at the forefront of those who made their mark.

After Pea Ridge, the South West grew quieter for the remainder of the war, although it was still punctuated by guerrilla activity, keeping Hickok and his ilk busy. In 1864, Hickok worked briefly for Springfield's provost marshal, plus he was hired by General John Sanborn which led to involvement in the second Battle of Newtonia that year.

Wild Bill remained under Sanborn and Curtis' command and was still regularly found things to occupy him, even beyond the Confederate surrender at Appomattox in April 1865.

In January of that year, with the hostilities grinding towards an end, signs were recognised of a possible diversion against a very different enemy.

Various Indian tribes in Kansas, notably the Choctaw, were reportedly plotting to wipe out white settlers in the region, encouraged by the distraction of the Civil War. This was taken seriously as a similar crisis had occurred three years before when the Santee Sioux in Minnesota had risen up and killed hundreds of settlers before being subdued in a brief and bloody reprisal by the Army. As a result, over 300 warriors were sentenced to hang, but President Lincoln reprieved most of them and just 38 actually went to the gallows… but it was still the biggest mass execution in US history.

Now, this is a tale which was told by Hickok himself to his biographers, so, as we shall see later, these accounts of Wild Bill's life, largely encouraged by his own amused impishness, cannot exactly be fully trusted, to say the least.

Never-the-less, it does fit the bill and I would like it to be true…

A Sioux chief named Conquering Bear had proved himself loyal to the Union by serving alongside Hickok's old commander, Jim Lane and his Kansas Free Staters Brigade. Conquering Bear swore his allegiance and friendship with white folks and he approached General Curtis with a warning that a large band of Choctaws were camped dangerously close to Lawrence, a town which had suffered more than its fair share of destruction and tragedy.

Curtis asked Hickok his opinion and Wild Bill replied that he was suspicious about any Indian who expressed such love for white men.

But it was enough of a potential danger for Hickok to volunteer to investigate further and he was sent off, with Conquering Bear, to sound out the Choctaw settlement on the Kaw River outside Lawrence.

It was an uneasy alliance, with the scout and the chief riding together in a state of intense distrust. Conquering Bear tried to assure Hickok that the Sioux had their own problems with the Choctaw and would welcome any excuse to rub them out.

According to Wild Bill, Conquering Bear led him into a trap where he was attacked by a Choctaw war party, but Hickok managed to shoot his way out of trouble and ride to safety.

Incensed by such treachery, Wild Bill plotted his revenge.

By gaining the confidence of another Sioux tribesman, Hickok managed to arrange a meeting with Conquering Bear without giving away who the meeting would actually be with.

The Sioux chief turned up at the rendezvous in a clearing some miles outside of Lawrence and was shocked to find the scout waiting for him.

To satisfy their honour, both men drew their Bowie knives and agreed upon a fight to the death. In a ten foot circle they battled it out in classic Wild West style, blood flowing as they cut and slashed at each other.

Finally, following a lengthy duel, Wild Bill triumphed as his blade tore open the throat of his opponent. Conquering Bear fell heavily, choking on dust and blood as he died.

Well, it really is a classic Wild Bill story and ticks all the boxes but can we be sure it happened? We only have Hickok's word for it and it sounds like his kind of antic. He certainly had plenty to do with hostile Indians as the years went on…

As I said, I would sure like it to be true, so I will concede to chalk it up to something he was capable of, and even if false, then I do not doubt that there are plenty of unverifiable, even unreported, adventures in Wild Bill's life which would equal this at least.

CHAPTER 6
ONTO THE PLAINS...

Emerging from his wartime experiences, Hickok was seemingly in no hurry to get back into action.

He hung around Springfield where he was already well known, devoting much of his time to the card tables which resulted in several demands for him to attend court charged with illegal gambling. It seems he ignored these orders and carried on with no one bothering to enforce such legality. Several years before, he had failed to respond to similar demands when serving as a constable in Monticello, accused of not fulfilling jury duties. Wild Bill apparently considered himself above the law in this way.

Surrounded by many friends and admirers, who outnumbered his potential enemies, Wild Bill enjoyed a leisurely summer in his favourite atmosphere. Rising late from his lodgings, he would saunter down to one of the many establishments he frequented, seated with his back to the wall at all night poker sessions where his skill and luck enabled him to make a variable but acceptable living. In those smoke fogged rooms, crammed with the colourful populace of that ribald frontier town, Hickok was quite a celebrity.

By this time, and able to concentrate on his social life, he paid much attention to the importance of image and appearance. Tall, well built, upright and classically handsome, Wild Bill liked the fact that he could make quite an impression just by entering a room. He was already striking to behold, but he quickly learned to enhance this by investing in an expensive and eye-catching wardrobe of clothes. As mentioned earlier, fine quality embroidered waist coats, tailored frock jackets, flowing silk neck ties, crisp white shirts, top quality boots, wide brimmed headwear, capes even, became his daily attire around town. At times he would don a mid-thigh length buckskin overshirt, fringed and brightly beaded at the hem and chest. His neatly brushed shoulder length locks, parted in the middle, and long, sweeping mustachios were a recognisable trademark already.

And, naturally, he was never without the open display of those long barrelled .36 calibre Navy Colt pistols, usually tucked butt forwards in leather holsters or a colourful sash around his waist. Eventually he would extend this armoury with a pair of concealed Derringers in his pockets and a Bowie knife across his midriff.

Unlike most men of his kind, that is to say typical frontier types, he was fastidious when it came to hygiene, bathing regularly. As a consequence, regardless of such dandyish behaviour, he was all man and took advantage of rather intense female attention.

Wild Bill was comfortable with his already glowing reputation and enjoyed the attention and admiration, but he was wary of danger from those who might bear a grudge, especially ex Confederates. However, his demeanour was not that of a loud braggart. Once again, not typical of his contemporaries, he remained softly spoken, calm, pleasant and courteous with all but those who challenged him.

The exaggerations of the McCanles fight, stories of his war exploits and numerous other tales grew in the telling, so, generally speaking, few viable threats came his way. A respectful fear seemed to protectively surround his presence until the unfortunate incident involving Dave Tutt in July 1865.

The highly dramatic and indisputably impressive marksmanship which resulted in Tutt's demise sent Hickok's reputation soaring through the roof. It swiftly became the talking point for miles around and Wild Bill's name grew synonymous with heroic gunplay of the highest order. There may well have been many characters whose ability and actions equalled and/or surpassed that of Hickok but when it came to image, he shone, and it most certainly accelerated his fame.

The power of charisma and showmanship.

Immediately following Tutt's death, Hickok willingly surrendered his guns to the local sheriff and allowed himself to be arrested on an initial charge of murder, but this was swiftly reduced to manslaughter.

Tutt did have a large circle of friends and there were murmurs of a lynch mob forming before his killer could take advantage of authorities who were biased in his favour.

Hickok faced a trial a couple of weeks or so after the duel but he was acquitted; a not unexpected result. It had been a very public gunfight with countless witnesses and there could be no dispute that the defendant had beaten his opponent in a fair stand off. Both armed and evenly matched; the better man had emerged triumphant.

Of course, it did help that Wild Bill had much sympathy and support from the town's hierarchy, some of whom had even covered his bail. Two of the jury members were even said to be officers who had served with him in the war.

In any case, the overall verdict was that Hickok had acted in self defence against Tutt's insistent and unreasonable aggression.

Case closed, although this result was somewhat controversial and did not satisfy everyone, by any means.

Hickok just resumed the life he had been leading previously, back to all night poker and a string of lady friends. By September he was a serious candidate to run as town marshal, receiving a lot of support but losing out to his rival Charlie Moss. Perhaps the townsfolk felt that Wild Bill was just a tad too "wild" for peacekeeping duties.

That same month someone came to town who was to play a huge role in the development of Hickok's destiny. This was Colonel George Ward Nichols who had served on the staff of the Union's top brass during the Civil War. Nichols had returned to his pre-war career in journalism and would become a music and art critic of some renown. He had already penned a well received book about General William Tecumseh Sherman's famous "March to the Sea".

This journalist was now in his thirties and hungry for a scoop. As soon as he was made aware of the presence of Wild Bill, his eyes lit up as he knew he had found one.

Hickok impressed the Colonel at first sight. When introduced, they hit it off immediately and Wild Bill was probably amused and intrigued by the attention. Not that Hickok was a stranger to such, but here was a distinguished gentleman of renown, a well known, published author who was keen to note down everything he had to say. It would have been enough to massage the most modest of egos.

And so Wild Bill Hickok sat with Nichols for a leisurely interview, conducted in comfort, his eagerly welcomed words eased out with the probable flow of good whisky.

The Colonel was enthralled by Hickok's recollections, wisdom and his adventurous life on the plains and clandestine wartime activities. The Rock Creek incident seemed to particularly intrigue the interviewer.

Wild Bill was open and seemingly square shouldered and honest. He was not gushing but spoke with an easy, self assured manner. Nichols scribbled it all down with every answer leading to twice the number of questions.

Flattery and maybe alcohol encouraged Hickok to tell all, even if it was not always *all* exactly the way it had *actually* happened. In the Colonel, Wild Bill had a captive, awestruck, sycophantic audience and consequently, largely for his own amusement and devilment, he let his tongue run loose. After all, as they say, why let the truth get in the way of a good yarn?

Eventually Nichols ended up with an overflowing notebook which pleased him no end. He could barely wait to collate it all into readable form.

The two men parted affably and went their separate ways; the

Colonel to his desk and Hickok to his next real life adventure.

Wild Bill probably scarcely gave any further thought to that enjoyable little interlude, spilling out his heart to a fan who questioned nothing, but in sixteen months time the result would be life changing.

***

Weeks rolled into months and Hickok began to tire of the comfortable yet ultimately hum-drum familiarity of life in Springfield. It was a lively enough place with plenty of comings and goings. He gambled and partied, held court, passed many a ribald evening with friends old and new, but Wild Bill began to hanker for something fresh.

Records of what else he actually did during that time are scarce, although he probably did venture out and about. Sadly, whatever he might have got himself involved in has been lost to history. He certainly was the type to attract attention…

Whatever, the next notably verifiable part of Hickok's adventurous life came when his old military and state connections contacted him officially again in early 1866. He was summoned to the new U.S. Army post of Fort Riley in Kansas where he was offered the role of a government detective at the handsome salary of over $100 per month. This was a position Hickok gladly accepted and he soon proved to be exceptionally good at it.

Life for a post Civil War trooper on the frontier was pretty grim, hence the rate of desertion from the ranks was unacceptably high, especially as these runaways more often than not took to the hills riding government mounts. Wild Bill tracked them down with ease and soon racked up quite a record of bringing them back to face military discipline. Very few offered serious resistance when faced with a man of his fierce reputation and threatening countenance.

With his knowledge and experience of the country, coupled with his proven courage and multiple skills, Hickok was in demand for various detached assignments. In the spring he was engaged to guide a pair of top ranking Generals, Sherman and Pope, to Fort Kearny, Nebraska. On the way, the column camped near Rock Creek, the scene of the famed conflict with McCanles five years before, but Hickok kept his distance.

When they reached Kearny, the column divided and the scout led Pope on to Santa Fe where Wild Bill most likely reaffirmed a few old friendships.

Of course, Hickok was only one of many scouts and guides who operated all over the west during this colourful period of America's history, but most of them are largely forgotten now.

Earlier characters such as Jim Bridger and the formerly mentioned Kit Carson made their mark, and rightly so, yet there are so many others who perhaps deserve equal fame.

Their names alone can conjure up exciting images of bearded, buckskin clad giants of folklore; trusted scalp taking warriors in whose hands you just knew would be safe when taken cross country, protected from all dangers... California Joe Milner, Old Bill Williams, Uncle Dick Wootton, Buffalo Bill Cody and Medicine Bill Comstock, for instance.

Buffalo Bill became the most famous of them all, naturally, but there was a flamboyant reason for that as we shall see later.

These scouts were a unique bunch and Wild Bill was prominent and well respected amongst them. However, regardless of stories which spread to the contrary, he was no linguist and could not speak the languages of the Plains tribes fluently. He understood Indians and knew the land but his communication with them was limited. Scouts who actually could converse were particularly valued, for obvious reasons; men like Ed Guirrier who was the son of a French Trader and a full blooded Cheyenne mother. Guirrier had been present at the horrific massacre at Sand Creek in 1864 when Chief Black Kettle's camp had been sacked by the Colorado Volunteers under the command of Colonel Chivington, a psychotic preacher. The 1970 film *Soldier Blue* was based on this terrible stain on U.S. history and it paints a graphic and fairly accurate impression of what happened. Guirrier was in the camp and saw women and children he knew raped, murdered and mutilated. Although he went on to work for white soldiers, it left him with an intense distrust of them.

Scouts, interpreters and couriers were well paid too, reflecting how much their skill was valued by the Army which relied upon them. Some received as much as $125 per month which was quite a contrast to a private trooper who got $13.

The romanticised image of these frontiersmen galloping majestically across the plains on handsome stallions is flawed too. Most preferred to be mounted on long eared, plodding mules; animals which were much hardier for the kind of work required of them.

Scouts worked alone under their own rules or sometimes with a partner. Hickok was often solo but he did also partner up with a character named Wentworth and another named Jack Harvey. Wild Bill and Harvey as a team were pretty adept at capturing mule thieves and returning stock but Harvey died of consumption before the decade was out.

During the Christmas and New Year period of 1866–67, Hickok

was working out of Junction City, Kansas, lodging with a family named Dunstan. By now he was also engaged as a deputy U.S. Marshal alongside his commitment to the Army, so he must have been very busy.

And then, in February of 1867, the latest edition of the highly popular and nationally circulated *Harper's New Monthly Magazine* hit the public. The main featured piece in it was a long illustrated article entitled *"WILD BILL"*; the result of Col. Nichols' creative and highly embellished version of his interview with Hickok himself back in the fall of '65.

In flowery prose, the Colonel portrayed Wild Bill as some kind of superman; a noble knight of the plains whose courage and skill were without equal and whose adventures and daring exploits could put fictitious works in the shadows. Based upon what Hickok had told him, tongue firmly in cheek, Nichols added his own interpretation of events, inflating them to the realm of pure fantasy.

Strange then that the Colonel mistakenly named his hero *"Hitchcock"*!

Hickok's Civil War activities morphed into a virtual single handed destruction of the Confederacy, his personal body count of Rebs dwarfing battle casualties. As for the Rock Creek affair in which three men had died under sordid circumstances, this was described as a battle royal between Wild Bill and the *"M'Kandlas gang of murderous cut throats"* in which he dispatched about a dozen villains in hand to hand combat with gun and knife, emerging peppered with buckshot and cut in thirteen places!

The fable of the fabulous horse Black Nell began in these pages too, alongside a wealth of other tales which were either total fabrication or exaggerated beyond recognition.

Newspapers picked up on this too and were soon printing their own versions of Nichols' hero worship. Nationwide, especially back east in the big cities, the North American populace swallowed it all with innocent gullibility. They could not get enough about the wild western frontier and yearned for blood and thunder heroes who they knew were carving out a new nation for them, making it safe for settlement. Civilization could be expanded across the corpses of those savage redmen and evil outlaws who had fallen at the hands of the brave and virtuous.

Wild Bill was a perfect symbol for all this and he became America's darling almost overnight. Of course, fame back then was dependant upon the written word or rare personal appearances, so everyone seemed hungry and desperately keen to believe all that they were reading, the more outlandish the better.

As Hickok's glowing reputation spread outside of the West he knew as home, those who dwelt there with him were somewhat bemused. Yes, he was Wild Bill and was respected for the life he led and things he had done. As previously stated, he was one of the larger characters of life and known for it, but certainly nothing like to the degree to which he had been portrayed in the Harper's article.

Those who knew him, or were at least familiar with him in Kansas, Missouri, Arkansas, and surrounding areas were stunned by what they read. Some were amused as well as perplexed, whilst others were irritated, even angered by this false picture of a man who was largely regarded as just one of their own.

Some of the more local newspapers began printing pieces to address the balance, questioning the outlandish stories, even subtly mocking them, but the die was cast and Hickok's reputation took a quantum leap.

Wild Bill himself seemed to just absorb it all in his stride and his true ability was still enough to instil wariness and even fear in those who met him face to face. Any criticism or mockery was conducted behind his back and he carried on as he always had. Passing visitors to the West who made his acquaintance were inevitably impressed by him and he happily played up to it. His appearance always matched his reputation and his calm, courteous manners surprised all those who were expecting the persona of a roughneck born of the wild.

Hickok cannot have been deterred by the result of the Nicholson interview because he was happy to be grilled again by a noted journalist; none other than Henry Morton Stanley at Fort Zarah just two months after the publication of the Harper's piece.

Stanley was quite an adventurous character himself. Born in Wales, he emigrated to the U.S.A. aged eighteen just before the Civil War broke out. He served on both sides of the conflict, including an active part fighting in the Battle of Shiloh where he was taken prisoner. From there he somehow ended up in the Union Navy where he fought further battles at sea.

After the war he became a freelance journalist and explorer who wandered widely across the globe to pursue his writing ambitions, taking part in expeditions which took him all across Europe, the Crimea, Persia, India, Egypt and beyond. In 1871, in a deep, dark corner of Africa he discovered the long missing famous missionary Dr. Stanley Livingstone, greeting him, it is said, with the legendary words, *"Dr. Livingstone, I presume?"*

But now, on April 4th. 1867, Stanley (who was eventually knighted thirty two years later) was in the presence of Wild Bill Hickok, intrigued by what he had read and heard about the great scout and spy.

One of Stanley's first questions was to challenge Hickok about all the men he had allegedly killed and why.

Unruffled, Wild Bill considered the enquiry carefully before claiming that he thought he had slain more than a hundred, but adding, *"I never killed a man without good cause"*.

Their conversation was a relatively short one, but it still resulted in Stanley's write-up soon afterwards in the *Weekly Missouri Democrat* which further enhanced Hickok's blossoming reputation.

All this news about their kinsman reached the Hickok family who were still domiciled in faraway Troy Grove. They were pleased to hear about him but ever since his flight from home some ten or so years previously, they had known little contact. A very occasional letter would arrive from him and since the end of the war they had barely heard a thing, save what they were now seeing in public print. Hickok's brother Lorenzo, who was a frontier character himself, would sometimes encounter him but that was rare. Lorenzo wrote to his other brothers, sisters and mother telling them not to expect much from James (now Bill) owing to his busy, adventurous life. Hickok's mother Polly, whose relationship with her youngest son was strained, could only accept it.

Amidst all this praise and attention, Wild Bill was chosen to guide a major expedition against the Southern Cheyenne and other plains tribes (such as the Kiowa and Comanche) who had been making mischief murdering settlers, burning homesteads and harassing workers on the Kansas-Pacific railroad.

Major General Winfield Scott Hancock was to head a punitive force against them, subjugating their aggression before any large scale uprising could take place. That was the intention anyway, but Hancock was to find that he had bitten off more than he could chew.

Not that he did not possess the manpower. His 1,500 strong force included several companies of the newly formed 7th. Cavalry, likewise the 37th. Infantry, a battery of artillery, supply wagons and scouts, both white and Indian, even a couple of journalists.

The problem lay in the sheer lumbering, slow progress of such an expedition which was totally unsuited to face a highly mobile and elusive enemy. There would be no chance of any kind of pitched battle against these fast moving Indian braves whose favoured method of combat was in the swift hit and run variety before melting away into the wilderness.

General Hancock sought a parley with the chiefs but they did not want to know. The efforts of Hickok and his fellow scouts were frustrated by the troops inability to act swiftly on any intelligence they were able to gather about the tribes movements.

Hancock was a proven, battle hardened soldier, but he was experienced in the tactics of the Civil War where troops faced an obvious, similarly equipped enemy, not the whooping, devious methods of who were rapidly being recognised as the finest light cavalry in the world.

The General's second in command was in a similar situation. Lt.Col. George Armstrong Custer, who had field command of the 7th. Cavalry, was a Civil War hero, much admired for his bravery and dashing behaviour in battle, which included leading reckless cavalry charges. He had even had several horses shot from under him. He knew how to fight, but he needed to be able to engage his foe before he could do so.

It was Custer's first experience of facing Indians and he was learning fast. He recognised the value and need for experienced plainsmen like Wild Bill and was influenced by him and his kind. Custer was soon adopting frontier dress in the form of a fringed buckskin jacket over his uniform and wide brimmed light coloured headwear replacing standard army issue. He retained his trademark though, a bright red neck-scarf which he had worn since leading his Wolverines regiment during the war.

Custer found a kindred spirit in Hickok. They both wore their hair long, flowing to their shoulders, complemented by their heavy moustaches.

Wild Bill was much admired by the 7th.'s commander who even put his praise in writing. Custer wrote a series of articles about his Indian fighting experiences for various magazines which eventually were compiled into book form; *My Life on the Plains*.

Custer described Hickok as the *"most prominent and famous of the scouts"* and *"a plainsman in every sense of the word"*. He also noted how Hickok possessed the *"ability to sort out trouble between others just by his presence"*.

Custer's wife, Libbie, also expressed a liking for the dashing scout and the way she wrote about him in her own books says a lot...

"Physically, he was a delight to look upon... fantastically clad... his word was law..." Hmmm... calm down, Libbie! (Actually, her words went

on and on in the extreme, even comparing Hickok to a kind of Greek godlike figure!)

The nimble Cheyenne and their allies were always a step or two ahead of Hancock's lumbering columns and Custer's men were sent on a series of wild goose chases. When it was finally, with difficulty, arranged for Hancock to meet with some chiefs, his attitude and threats merely succeeded in offending them and they left hurriedly with nothing gained. Hancock responded by torching their deserted encampments. Shortly after this, a ten man squad of the 2nd. Cavalry taking dispatches to Custer were ambushed and wiped out fuelling the fires of frustration and anger to boiling point, but all to no avail.

The hostiles simply could not be pinned down.

Eventually it had to be accepted that nothing was being achieved and Hancock was forced to withdraw, humiliated, to be replaced by another Civil War General, "Little Phil" Sheridan who became Commander of the Department of the Missouri. Custer, who by now had learned all the initial lessons of Indian fighting was left in overall charge of the situation. However, by the end of the year, he was to disgrace himself by *"absenting himself from his command without proper authority"*. This had come about when he heard of flooding and a possible outbreak of cholera at Fort Hays where Libbie was staying. Deeply concerned for her safety, he left his troops and rode with a small escort to be with her.

To his great relief she was actually safe at Fort Riley but his behaviour led to his arrest and court martial along with an additional charge of executing deserters without trial. Within a few months, his experience needed, he was back on active duty and *en route* to his eventual date with destiny at the Little Big Horn.

***

Wild Bill carried on with his duties, regularly ferrying dispatches between Forts Hays, Wallace and Harker. This was highly dangerous work, operating alone in hostile country, much more perilous than guiding and scouting when at least one was never that far from strong supporting forces.

Hickok's skilful intelligence kept him safe, as a rule, but there were occasions when misfortune would place him in peril. Such as when he and his partner reportedly ran into a war party and had to shoot their way out of trouble.

He is also said to have successfully ridden for help to bring relief to a besieged group bogged down at Gomerville, Colorado.

Others were not so lucky. The famed Medicine Bill Comstock, who Custer also openly praised, seemed indestructible. *"No Indian knew the country more than did Comstock..."* wrote the 7th.'s commander, *"... he spoke the language of many tribes and was perfectly familiar with every divide, watercourse and strip of timber for hundreds of miles in every direction."*

Whilst wanted for the shooting of a man who owed him money, Medicine Bill was killed by the Cheyenne, leaving a camp having played his part in a supposed peace mission.

Through the latter part of 1867 into '68, Wild Bill was also employed by Captain George Armes of the 10th. Cavalry, a regiment, along with the 9th., which was made up entirely of black troopers, except for the officers. They were known as Buffalo Soldiers because the Indians said that the colour of their skin resembled the hue of a buffalo cow's teat. The captain was impressed by Hickok's knowledge, also by his natural ability to get along well with the men. This was a real bonus as racial conflict was a troublesome issue for many during this period on the frontier, causing a lot of friction between the scouts and their charges.

Hickok rose above most of this in his collected, calm way; that is until he was confronted.

Although his reputation and affability assured his popularity, or, at least, respect from most in his circle, there were a few with whom he was not so popular.

One was General Eugene Carr of the 5th. Cavalry who apparently took an instant dislike to the flamboyant scout. Maybe it was a form of jealousy and resentment regarding Hickok's standing within the fraternity, but Carr also took exception to his passion for gambling which was something of an obsession for Wild Bill. Then there was an issue when Hickok uncharacteristically lost some important dispatches in the chaos of a heavy snowstorm.

Carr used this as one of the excuses to demand Hickok's dismissal but Wild Bill had friends in high places, not least of all Little Phil Sheridan himself who was familiar with Hickok's impressive Civil War career. Sheridan was keen for the scout to stay in place to keep the negro troops happy and quell any possible problems between them and less affable types.

In addition, during the campaign, tension had arisen between the white and Mexican scouts who were led by Charles Autobees, supported by his sons.

Buffalo Bill Cody was riding with Wild Bill at this time, along with others, and it does seem that the problem erupted into violence. Cody himself said years later that threats from the fifteen Mexicans under the Army's command led to a brawl with the white contingent which resulted in the Mexicans being severely beaten.

A newspaper report from the time described how Hickok had *"come to blows"* with Autobees' son, Mariano, and that Wild Bill was the victor.

Whatever the details of this *contretemps*, it was presumably resolved amicably because the Autobees personally addressed General Carr on the matter of Hickok's dismissal and requested that he be allowed to stay.

And stay he did, at least for a while.

Other incidents took place which confirm Hickok's willingness and ability to deal with problems without needing to resort to using his guns.

Wild Bill was sharing overnight lodgings at Monument Station with Medicine Bill when the troopers guarding the place were reassigned elsewhere. A man named Wiggins was employed there, accompanied by his wife, and when replacements for the troopers arrived, trouble came too.

These replacements, about ten of them, were not soldiers but volunteers who had recently been in jail. They were a rough bunch, led by the roughest of them, Dolan by name.

Wiggins was sent away on some mission and the roughs took advantage of the situation by giving his wife a hard time. Dolan insulted her at which point Hickok stepped in to teach him some manners. The fight was savage but Dolan ended up sprawled on the ground. Wild Bill then terminated the contest by jumping on the beaten man's face with both boots! He then turned on the others with a warning to make themselves scarce which they unhesitatingly did.

This showed just what Hickok was capable of when pushed. It took a lot to rile him, but when provoked, he would go the limit and leave no doubt as to who had won.

The old time scout Luther North, for instance, would eventually tell of witnessing Wild Bill dish out a severe beating to a hard bitten mule skinner; just another of many similar tales which added to the legend.

It is actually pretty significant to take on board this aspect of Wild Bill's character.

Contrary to what we have seen in so many Western movies over the decades, "fist fights", as such, were not common in the West.

Fights certainly were, but not played out in the semi comical fashion we see on screen; clean blows to the jaw, acrobatic hurling through saloon windows, shattering of balsa wood chairs over seemingly unaffected heads and shoulders, etc.. A shaking of the head and those fighters are on their feet again, maybe with a little tear in their shirt and a dribble of stage blood showing at the corner of their mouth...

Oh no... the reality was dramatically and savagely different.

Frontier brawls were vicious in the extreme and often resulted in permanent maiming of the participants. Imagine the actual real effects of a sturdy chair being broken over a human skull or body or a broken jagged glass or bottle rammed into an unprotected face.

When those tough characters of the real Old West were forced into a weapon-less fight, they battled to win and gave it everything they had. No rules, just pure animal savagery. If nothing else was to hand, they used whatever weapons they possessed naturally. That's why many of them cultivated the long length of their thumbnails, hardening them in brine for the very purpose of eye gouging. Indeed, a lacerated eyeball hanging by its stretched stalk on a well bruised cheek was usually a sure way of terminating a brawl. And then as the half blinded loser rolled in agony in the dirt, you could always make sure he stayed there by stomping on his face a few times!

Another favourite tactic was to get an opponent's ear, nose or cheek in one's teeth and clamp down with all one's might, chewing away until the sinews gave way. Grizzled characters with sections of their faces gnawed off was a fairly common sight.

Following the initial flailing of arms and attempted shin or knee shattering kicks, the combatants would close in and embrace each other in rib crushing bear hugs while their gnashing teeth sought something to clamp down upon. They would then roll around in a kind of bizarre, desperate dance, crashing into the furniture of wherever they happened to be, or maybe the muddy or dusty street or some prairie campsite. Sooner or later, unless an observer lent a hand, one of them would find an opening to turn the odds in his favour, perhaps by grasping the opportunity to grab his opponent's genitals and twist them with all his might.

So, this was the vicious world in which the often outwardly genteel and refined James Butler Hickok could survive and even thrive in. He proved he was as tough as they came and possessed the necessary "killer instinct" with or without guns.

Having just described the savagery of frontier brawling and the evidence we have of Wild Bill's involvement, the photographs we have of him (and there are quite a few… he seemed to love having his picture taken) show that he appears to have emerged from all these combats unscathed. His handsome face is unmarked, right to the end of his life, ears, nose and eyes intact, which I guess is proof enough that he was the toughest when it came down to it.

Throughout 1868, Hickok continued to lead an active life scouting, guiding and delivering dispatches for the Army, interspersing it with his duties as a deputy marshal.

Many stories have emerged from this period, exciting tales of gunplay, hair raising adventures and heroism but, alas, most of it is unverifiable and has been subject to a great deal of exaggeration or plain fiction.

Isolating the probable facts has been a mind bending task for historians ever since, which is a great shame because Wild Bill undeniably did live a pretty wild life, the details of which have largely been lost. We are certainly left with plenty of what are undoubtedly tall tales, but I strongly suspect that there are strong elements of truth in many of them. The gullible public of the time swallowed them whole and that is where it all got foggy.

What we do know is that by the summer of 1869, Hickok's life was about to move into its next phase. Up until this point his fame centred almost exclusively on his supposed Civil War heroics, the duel with Tutt, the fictional version of the McCanles fight and his scouting for the Army against hostile Indians.

There is some evidence that Government Senator Henry Wilson, who later became Vice President, engaged his services as a guide to lead an expedition into the wilds of the West. This was purely for leisure purposes so that Wilson and his high brow eastern friends could experience a taste of the frontier. If it actually took place, Hickok made sure to keep them out of danger, carefully selecting areas which he knew to be safe as they quaffed champagne and left a trail of bottles and debris across the prairie.

Prior to this, Hickok was wounded in a hand to hand skirmish with some Cheyenne braves leaving him with a broad bladed lance sticking out of his hip. The wound became infected and caused complications so he made the decision to return home, for the first time in many years, to his family in Troy Grove to recuperate. It was probably the last time he was ever to see them.

His skill with firearms was renowned too and his much witnessed shootout with Dave Tutt was a legend spread throughout the land; a feat which did not require exaggeration. Wild Bill's marksmanship, dexterity and speed with his pistols was well known, skills which he was happy to demonstrate in public displays and shooting matches which he invariably won. His trick shooting always attracted an admiring crowd as he put multiple slugs into airborne cans, fired over his shoulder or split playing cards.

This ability came to him naturally, an inborn talent, but it required regular nurturing. Hickok therefore made a virtual daily routine of dismantling and cleaning his weapons to ensure that they were always in tip top condition and ready for use at a moment's notice. He invested in a lot of ammunition too so that he could indulge in constant target practice.

His favoured choice of weaponry never really altered throughout his life. The cap and ball Colt Navy revolver, .36 calibre, with its seven and a half inch octagonal shaped barrel. A well balanced, quite hefty weapon, it was renowned for its reliability and accuracy over 200 yards. Originally produced way back in 1851, its design never faltered over the next couple of decades as it grew in common use on the frontier and throughout the Civil War.

Why was it called the Navy? It was originally named the Ranger but was soon known more widely as the Navy, although company records do not appear to record the reason. Maybe it was inspired by engraving on the cylinder which depicted Texan warships in action during the war against Mexico, or the fact that .36 calibre was popular in a sailor's armoury.

Whatever, Hickok possessed a pair of them which he could handle with great dexterity and speed, almost as if they were an extension of his arms and hands.

In the early part of his career he carried his Navies with standard walnut stocks but by 1867 he had replaced them with the fancier white ivory handled version.

Wild Bill spoke quite a lot about his attitude to gunplay. To him it was a serious matter; an art and a science, both in ability and psychology. It was one thing to be capable of pulling a pistol swiftly and hitting a target accurately, but a wholly different matter when in a life or death situation where your intended target may well be shooting back at you.

Speed was not really the deciding factor. Many men drew weapons and fired almost blindly in gunfights, events which usually occurred on the spur of the moment in smoky saloons or gambling dens between angry, drunken novices.

Hickok, and serious shootists of his ilk, always maintained that remaining cool and calm was the answer. Act swiftly and decisively but always retain those dignified nerves of steel. A well placed bullet would inevitably take precedence over a flurry of blasts.

And he may have been a master of the cross draw which involved pulling the butt forward facing pistols from their holsters by crossing the hands across the body, grasping those butts and cocking the weapons before they were levelled for firing. It is known, however, that his preference was for the reverse or plains draw. This required drawing those Colts with palms twisted outwards, without reaching across the body, and yet again cocking them in motion. These manoeuvres were swiftly, smoothly and slickly achieved in Wild Bill's skilled hands.

Hickok operated in some of the most remote regions of the frontier where the law was largely unenforceable. Consequently, these areas attracted the lawless of every description. Outlaws, thieves, cattle rustlers, crooked gamblers, blatant exploiters in all fields, and it seems they felt themselves untouchable.

Any chance of bringing order and civilisation to these out of control places would require the services of a special kind of "civilizer", someone who could instil instant respect and fear.

None seemed to fit the bill more than Wild Bill himself.

CHAPTER 7
A LAW UNTO HIMSELF

Hays City as a settlement had expanded considerably since its rough hewn foundation in 1867. From a ragged shanty town of tents, false fronts and makeshift saloons, two years had seen it grow into a mini, yet lively, frontier metropolis. It was an attraction for the trade brought in by the extension west of the Kansas Pacific Railroad, wagon trains and as the major supply hub for the South West. That and the business generated by the hundreds of entertainment starved soldiers stationed at nearby Fort Hays.

By the summer of 1869, Hays was as wild as they come. Heaving with life, it housed teeming crowds of visitors and residents who forged a living largely dependant upon exploitation in all its forms. Soldiers, railway workers, drovers, freighters, gamblers, hunters, criminals of every description, "soiled doves"... they were all thrown together in a melting pot of human chaos, overseen by a desperate little band of city fathers who did their best to maintain some kind of order as the dollars rolled in. Violence and drunkenness were rife; the air, especially when darkness fell, being almost endlessly split by random bursts of gunfire, discharged either in boisterous fun or with lethal intent. All this tempered with a few lynchings for good measure.

In a lawless land, Hays City had swiftly gained its reputation as the most lawless of all, and that was really saying something. Matters were getting out of control and it became essential that a force needed to be installed to calm the waters. A series of peace keeping officials had proven themselves not up to the job and, by the spring, the latest sheriff simply disappeared leaving the town without any law enforcement.

In August a specially arranged election resulted in Hickok being offered the post of acting sheriff of Ellis County (wherein Hays was situated) until the official elections could be called in November. Wild Bill rose to the challenge without delay and immediately took to the streets, his imposing figure on patrol bristling with sidearms and a sawn off shotgun cradled across his chest.

The sight of him, and his reputation, was enough to achieve the desired effect. Within a very short time word had spread that Wild Bill was on the streets and would take no sass from anyone. Most of the loudmouths were instantly silenced and the atmosphere in Hays was noticeably transformed as a kind of hushed respect descended over the populace. Not that it resembled a church picnic overnight, of course. It was still Hays City, but a city with someone in authority to answer to now, and that someone could back it up with action when required.

Naturally, there were still characters who felt that they could carry on as before. No long haired, fancy dude was going to spoil their fun, they declared. That is until they found themselves facing the cool, hard stare of the new sheriff, and this was usually enough to take the wind out of their sails.

Those who made the mistake of trying to resist were swiftly dealt with. Wild Bill was always ready with his guns but pulling the triggers was not usually necessary. One of those Navy Colts would appear in an instant when reason had failed, followed by the barrel connecting sharply across a skull… pistol whipping. That inevitably led to a prone body on the sidewalk and if that did not do the trick, a boot heel in the face always did.

However, there were still occasions when Hickok was called upon to use his most deadly skill and he did not hesitate to do so.

Having made an instant impression in the job, Wild Bill had been wearing his star for less than a month when a boisterous hoodlum named Bill Mulvey drew attention to himself by riding up and down the streets of Hays taking potshots at passersby and, it is said, shouting loudly that he was gunning for the new sheriff.

Mulvey had the excuse of being roaring drunk so his aim was fortunately bad as the citizens ran for cover. Hickok appeared on the scene before too much damage could be done and swiftly dealt with the problem.

Conflicting versions of the duel were recalled by witnesses but the result was the same. Mulvey received at least one of the sheriff's bullets through his body and died within hours.

As if to consolidate the fate which awaited any potential challengers, Hickok shot and killed another man within a few weeks. The victim this time was a teamster named Sam Strawhun who, with a crowd of work companions, all drunk, were causing havoc in John Bitters' saloon, turning over furniture, removing glasses from the premises and threatening to wreck the place. It was after midnight but Hickok was summoned and soon turned up.

The sobering sight of Wild Bill as he strode into the smoky room instantly took the edge off the ruckus. The hollering ceased, the inebriated teamsters silenced as the sheriff faced an unsteady but unfazed Strawhun as he leaned against the bar. It was said that Sam and Wild Bill had some history and that there was bad blood between them but this is doubtful. Whatever, they were certainly now in a tense stand off as Hickok determined to terminate the cause of this trouble by whatever means necessary.

One version of what happened next claimed that Strawhun went for Hickok with the jagged shards of a broken glass, another that he pulled his pistol. Whichever is true, the drunk teamster was not quick enough as Wild Bill's Colt roared again sending a bullet through Sam's head.

These two killings are verified by the official records of the time but in years to come several other old timers who were around during Hickok's tenure as sheriff swore that there were others. By the end of the year it could have been as many as eight, some claimed, but the details are so mired in hearsay and lack of evidence that they are not worth recording here.

Not that it really matters. What we do know for sure is that Wild Bill could shoot to kill when he had to. How often and how many is a matter of conjecture.

As it happened, he was not to stay in the acting sheriff's job for very long. The official elections did actually take place in November and, although Hickok stood for the post, he was beaten by his deputy, Pete Lanahan. Wild Bill had certainly been effective in bringing order to Hays City, but his appointment had never been an overly popular one. Some felt he was heavy handed and too fond of drinking and gambling. Also, politically he made no secret of his Republican sympathies, although he did try to cover this by standing as an "independent". In a region which was dominated by Democrats it was no surprise then that Lanahan, as a Democrat, won by a fair majority.

Hickok did not seem bothered by this and by January 1870 had hit the trail again, wandering across the West rekindling old connections and still serving as a deputy U.S. marshal. Kansas City, Topeka, Ellsworth; he drifted from one to the other and beyond, spending quite a bit of time at the marital home of his friend Buffalo Bill Cody. Louisa, Cody's wife, was, at first, full of doubt at the prospect of meeting "that man killer" but, introduced to him at a dance, she, like so many other ladies, was instantly won over by his genteel manners, dashing looks and charm. Indeed, Wild Bill always maintained that side of his character when in the company that warranted it.

For some reason, whether business or personal, he was back in Hays City in mid July and not everyone was pleased to see him.

One evening in Paddy Welche's saloon, he was drinking at the bar when a row broke out with a pair of 7th. Cavalry troopers. Hickok had quite deep connections with Custer's boys going back to when he spent much time with them as a scout and guide during the Hancock expedition. Of course, once he became sheriff he had regular reasons to tangle with many of them, cracking heads and dragging them off to jail when they got out of line.

Consequently, troopers from that period, especially newer recruits who had not served with him on the plains, bore a grudge and harboured thoughts of vengeance for their humiliation. What followed is related here using the most reliable of accounts, although as the years went on, hugely inflated versions found their way into the legend of Wild Bill.

On this particular night, two of them, Kyle and Lonergan by name, bolstered by drink, decided that the time had come to get some payback.

Hickok, it was said, was at the bar with his back to the room when they jumped him. Seized in a crushing bear hug, Wild Bill was dragged to the floor as a desperate tussle ensued, the troopers doing their best to immobilise the struggling ex-sheriff as one of them held a pistol against his head.

As Lonergan fought to maintain his hold on Hickok, Kyle cocked his Remington and pulled the trigger, but good fortune smiled on Bill. Just a sharp click… misfire! Hickok knew he had just a second or two before Kyle re-cocked his weapon and the chances were that this time it would send a bullet through his skull. In that brief moment, Wild Bill managed to wriggle one hand to one of the pistols at his waist, drawing it just enough to discharge a shot into Lonergan's leg.

This was enough to make the soldier release his grip, enabling Hickok to turn his attention to Kyle and put two slugs into him.

With his attackers disabled and the onlookers stunned, Wild Bill leapt to his feet amidst the haze of drifting gunsmoke and made a hasty exit through the saloon window. Picking up his belongings from his hotel room he set off into the night, laying low just outside of town until the heat died down a little.

Corporal John Kyle passed away the following day, an ignominious end for a trooper who, just about a year before, had won the Congressional Medal of Honour for his bravery in a skirmish against Cheyenne Dog Soldiers at the Republican River.

Private Jeremiah Lonergan spent weeks recovering from his leg wound and was eventually killed in a further brawl.

Custer, the 7th.'s field commander, and an ally of Hickok's, was away at the time so the latter could not expect any sympathy or support from the regiment in general. In fact there was a lot of resentment and murmurings of vengeance from the rank and file. Although the citizenry of Hays City more or less agreed that the shootings were an act of self defence, Wild Bill realised that it was probably in his, and everybody else's best interests, if he were to leave the area pronto.

And so he did, leaving the legend to expand yet again.

***

The latest news on the rumour telegraph spread like wildfire and it was soon common "knowledge" on the frontier, and beyond, that Wild Bill had taken on the entire 7th. Cavalry and had sent as many as a dozen of them to their graves already!

Hickok was far from happy about this addition to his volatile reputation. His fame had become a fickle thing. Some of it glorified him to the extreme whilst other exaggerated tales of his supposed incredible deeds demonized him as a murderous back shooter, wanton evil killer and coward. Understandably, he was becoming more and more wary of potential glory seekers who sought to be the one who "beat Wild Bill". Wherever he went, people increasingly regarded him with fear or even a growing, cautious contempt based upon hearsay.

Plus he had a new worry to concern him.

For quite some time he had slowly become aware of problems with his eyesight. A life spent in the glare of the prairie sun, the white outs of mountain snow and the shadowy, smoky atmosphere of scores of barrooms had probably contributed to his condition. He largely kept these concerns to himself for as long as possible but, from about 1871, the symptoms were gradually worsening... itching, swelling, sensitivity to light, a yellowy discharge from his eyelids, pain and loss of vision.

Eventually, and reluctantly, he was to seek medical advice from a city doctor and the diagnosis would not be good. Opthalmia, glaucoma, trachoma... any one of these conditions could lead to blindness and, in the mid 1800s the hope of treatment was minimal. It would inevitably get worse but all he could do was accept it.

He took to wearing darkened, smoked glasses on occasion, especially when out in the sun, but he hated this, feeling that it demeaned his well cultivated appearance. And, as a renowned shootist, the last thing he needed was for news to get around that he was going blind. That would bring the opportunists flocking like buzzards to a carcass.

However, life was not entirely full of despair for it was around this period that he was to meet someone who was to play a positive role in his future.

Her name was Agnes Lake Thatcher.

Agnes had been born in France but was brought to North America when a little girl. Her father coached her to become a skilled horse rider. By the age of 21 she had joined a circus troupe, developing her own equestrian act and high wire routine. All this was helped by having married a professional clown, one William Lake Thatcher, and together they partnered up with veteran impresario John Robinson to found the Robinson Lake Circus which toured successfully for several years. Agnes and William created their own company on the back of this, the Lake Circus, which they took all around the States; a big production which required 35 wagons to transport it. Agnes even took her own Equestrian show to Europe.

Agnes and William also produced a daughter; Emma.

Their show was quite an attraction and they took it as far west as Abilene, Kansas. Crowds flocked to see it and, in rough and ready Abilene, a large proportion of the audience lacked civility, one might say. More about this wild town later…

At a show in Granby, Missouri, in August 1869, Agnes's husband William caught a man who had managed to sneak into the circus tent without paying the full ticket price. Thrown out, the man reacted by pulling out a gun and shooting William dead.

Deeply shocked, naturally, Agnes put the show on hold for a respectful period as she weighed up her options but soon decided to resume the tour. As well as a talented performer, she also proved herself to be a shrewd and successful businesswoman and the circus carried on from strength to strength.

Somewhere along the line out west, she met Hickok. Maybe he saw the show. Whatever, they made a connection which carried on long after the circus moved on and they corresponded quite regularly.

Agnes was about a dozen years older than Wild Bill but there was certainly something between them which was to carry on for the rest of his life, as we shall see.

No doubt this was a pleasant distraction to Hickok's growing problems but his fortunes were soon to go in yet another direction.

CHAPTER 8
ABILENE

One of many small stagecoach stops on the vast expanse of the Kansas prairie was dismissively known as Mud Creek but, in 1860, a decision was made to give it a Biblical reference, renaming the place Abilene which means "grassy plains".

By 1867 the Kansas Pacific Railway had pushed westwards through this expanding hamlet giving it a new lease of life. Then along came entrepreneur Joseph McCoy whose vision really put the place on the map. He purchased land to the north and east of town and, with his eye on the potential fortune to be made, built his Drover's Hotel, also investing in the construction of vast cattle pens and stockyards.

His ambition was to transform Abilene into the first "Cowtown of the West" by encouraging the ranchers and cattlemen in Texas to drive their vast herds north, 600 miles up the Chisholm Trail to the largest stockyards west of Kansas City. A spur line was added that ran into town and there the beeves could be loaded onto rail cars and transported to the lucrative meat markets of Chicago and other big eastern cities.

The livestock would be the beefy Texas Longhorn breed whose hard hooves and tough long legs were ideal for making the arduous and lengthy journey up that trail which was rife with hazards.

Guiding them on their way would be an army of Texan cowboys who faced many weeks in the saddle battling the elements, crossing rivers and dealing with tough challenges, discomfort and dangers in the extreme. Many of these drovers were ex-confederate soldiers, familiar with the hardship of the recently ended war, dealing with the policy of reconstruction and glad to be working.

It became a huge, booming enterprise and, very quickly, other cowtowns sprung up to rival Abilene; places like Wichita, Ellsworth and later on, Dodge City.

Between 1867 to 1871 something approaching half a million head of cattle were shipped out from Abilene alone, tended by those energetic cowboys who were desperate to cut loose once the job was done.

The town was ready for them with its rows of saloons, gambling dens, dance halls and brothels, anxious to relieve those lively souls of all that hard earned cash which they had just received from their trail boss after months of eating dust and little else.

When they first hit the red light district of town, south of the tracks, those buoyant Texans generally followed a routine. Their pockets bulging with dollars, they would first queue at the barbers and bath house for a thorough grooming, shedding their chapaderos and weather worn work clothes. Emerging with clipped locks, smooth chins and soaked in what passed for cologne, the next stop would be the fancy goods store and clothing suppliers for a whole new set of fine duds. Three piece suits would be purchased and maybe a derby or top hat in place of their working headgear of a felt, wide brimmed, flat crowned item or Mexican sombrero. Not that many wore the newly introduced Stetson because it was expensive.

As they headed for their first of many drinks, to line the bars and fill up with copious amounts of beer and raw whisky, there was an essential tool from the trail which they were reluctant to shed... their firearms... and beneath their fine new frock coats one could still usually spot a brace of pistols holstered to cartridge belts firmly strapped around their waists.

Before long, just about the whole teeming bunch of them, in their hundreds, were transformed into a whooping gaggle of inebriated humanity, out of control and out for fun.

At first, the city fathers tolerated it, happy to receive the vast profits which came their way to the benefit of the town. However, the sheer bedlam which resulted from such drunken behaviour, carried out by what had become nothing better than a crazed mob, had become intolerable.

It could be argued that much of the chaos was shed in the spirit of pure fun; well oiled young men cutting loose after months of deprived hardship. Had they not earned the right to enjoy themselves? They were loud, boisterous and reckless as they galloped through the streets or rolled wildly between the houses of ill repute, exploited by wily gamblers, plied with rotgut liquor and fleeced by women who had, to turn a phrase, been around the block several times.

The cowboy's guns were discharged regularly, shooting out lanterns and windows and fired into ceilings, pockmarking virtually all establishments. Reckless action indeed, but not usually with harmful intent... this was just letting off steam. But there was also malicious violence. Arguments over card games or women, or just plain being "ornery" when the whisky took hold. Inevitably fights broke out and it was deeply ingrained in the Texan psyche to solve things with gunplay as the first resort.

Trail bosses took no responsibility. These men had done their job, were paid off and that was that. The town would just have to bear the brunt of the situation.

Order would have to be restored. Abilene was being wrecked. It would need an effective team of peacekeepers to enforce law against the mob.

A pair of experienced police officers were brought in from St. Louis but, faced with the enormity of the task, they simply could not handle it and resigned on the day they arrived.

Technically, the wearing of firearms was not permitted within the city limits but how could such a rule be enforced? Any signs put up making any such declaration were soon shot full of holes.

This was going to require a special solution, overseen by someone who could deal with the problem head on.

Hickok?

Not yet…

***

Tom Smith bore a name which hardly stirred excitement; one might even say his given handle could hardly have been more bland, and that may be one of the reasons why he did not achieve the same level of lasting fame as most of his more memorably named contemporaries.

Yet when you look at what he did, and how he did it, it hardly seems fair that historic recognition and admiration eluded him.

Originally from New York, Smith headed west to try his chances at prospecting but little detail has survived of his activities. It does seem probable that at one time he was making his living as a professional middleweight boxer and that would explain how he gained his later reputation as a man who solved problems with his fists.

He was tall and muscular and carried himself with a self assured presence. Handsome too. Piercing eyes, a thick mop of dark hair and a large but well groomed moustache topped off his fearless nature.

At some point he was drawn into the profession of law enforcement, serving as a deputy in various small frontier settlements, notably assisting the renowned lawman Pat Desmond in Wyoming and soon proving that he could do the job well. He even earned himself the moniker Bear River Tom following the prominent part he played in quelling a riot in Bear River City.

The 1870 cattle season was getting into gear and the pressure was on to find a suitable marshal to balance the coming storm.

Tom Smith's name was mentioned, highly recommended by various men in the know. Meeting with Abilene's city fathers, Bear River Tom impressed them with his courageous and confident bearing. He did not seem at all fazed by the prospect of taking on the responsibility of taming all those drunken cow punchers. What's more, he claimed that he would be able to achieve peace and order without the use of weapons.

It was not an idle boast. Smith took to riding slowly up and down the raucous avenue of Texas Street, the very centre of action, his steady eye on the lookout for any hint of trouble. He replanted the "no guns" signs and wasted no time in enforcing the order.

The cowboys quickly recognised that he meant business as he methodically approached all those who resisted. Time after time he marched up to swaying loudmouths waving pistols, always giving them the chance to surrender their weapons before laying them flat with a swift and well aimed one two from his hammer-like fists. Then it would be an over the shoulder carry to sleep it off in jail.

Bear River Tom only had to demonstrate his unique method a few times before the cowboys got the message, and they admired and respected him for it.

As a result, things quickly got more peaceful in Abilene. Not that the place turned into Toytown overnight, but Smith's effective style certainly made a difference. The city fathers were highly pleased. They had no desire to alienate the big spending Texan visitors but Bear River Tom seemed to be balancing matters to just the right degree. No wonder they were happily paying him a record salary of $250 per month.

All seemed fine until early November when Smith and his deputy, Jim McDonald, were called upon to serve a warrant on farmers Andrew McConnell and Moses Miles who were wanted for the murder of a neighbour.

These farmers went to ground in a dugout about ten miles outside of town having already chased off County Sheriff Joe Cramer who now turned to Smith for help.

Bear River Tom probably took it in his stride and approached the dug out with his usual confidence. McConnell was inside and Miles was in the open air. Smith left his deputy to watch Miles, taking on the task to enter the dugout to confront the other farmer. But McConnell was nervous and trigger happy. As soon as Smith entered his space he shot him in the chest. Reeling from the blast, the plucky and determined marshal soon gathered himself, grappling with McConnell and dragging him outside.

By this time, Miles had turned the tables on Deputy McDonald and was holding him at gunpoint. Though sorely wounded, Bear River Tom was managing to subdue the struggling farmer and their fight drew the attention of Miles. McDonald took advantage of this distraction and as soon as Miles turned away from him, he took to his heels, running for his life and leaving Smith to face the music alone,

Miles raised his gun butt, rushing to help his partner. Busy with holding McConnell, Smith probably did not see the other farmer closing on him until the stock of the gun connected with his skull, knocking him down.

McConnell wriggled free and Miles tossed his rifle aside, reaching instead for a nearby wood axe. Smith may have been unconscious or at least stunned and would not have stood a chance to defend himself as Miles swung the axe in a vicious blow which almost decapitated the marshal.

And so died the stalwart and courageous Bear River Tom, at the age of forty, a far from fitting end for such an upright and effective lawman.

The sordid horror of his demise probably contributed to the lack of enthusiasm for Smith's story, alongside the fact that he did not rely on guns in the traditional style of the Old West. But he deserves recognition at a much higher degree than he has received. The citizens did, however, grant him an elaborate funeral and, later on, a memorial was erected in his honour.

Dwight "Ike" Eisenhower, World War 2 icon and American president, spent much of his childhood in Abilene and he, at least, sung the praises of this worthy lawman.

The two farmers were eventually tracked down, tried and jailed for murder, but the loss of Tom Smith had a profound effect on Abilene and its inhabitants.

At least it came at a time when the cattle season was winding down, but the 1871 season was looming and promising to be the biggest one yet of an already booming trade.

Who could step into Bear River Tom's boots? He was one hell of an act to follow…

The new mayor, Joseph McCoy himself, considered several applicants but one name kept coming up… Wild Bill Hickok.

***

Hickok was offered the job as Abilene's marshal in the spring of 1871 and he willingly accepted. The salary was good, but not as good as had been granted to Tom Smith.

The town was just beginning to get busy again, in anticipation of the cattle season. Newcomers were arriving by the trainload, many of them desperadoes, pimps, whores, crooked gamblers and con artists, all anxious for the rich pickings which could be gleaned from those gullible, drunken cowboys who would soon be hitting Texas Street and its offshoots.

Wild Bill took on a trio of deputies to assist him, one of them being Jim McDonald who had let Bear River Tom down just when he needed him. Hickok, understandably, did not trust McDonald and he was dismissed after a few weeks.

Hickok's methods were somewhat different to those of Tom Smith but were similarly effective. Comparisons were inevitably made and there was much criticism of what was regarded as Wild Bill's heavy handedness. Smith had a quiet, almost gentlemanly approach to law enforcement, up until the point where his fists were needed, but Hickok was more blunt, steaming into a problem with less subtlety. Wild Bill was more inclined to use his pistols to resolve things, but not usually having to fire them. He was still fond of pistol whipping if the need arose, following it up with that savage boot heel in the face.

Smith had been a generally well liked figure, in tandem with respect and fear of his fighting skill. Hickok was certainly feared by most but many folks were wary of him. He seemed aloof, something of a loner with few real friends, standing apart from the crowd yet drawing attention with his dandified dress sense.

Unlike Smith, who was regularly seen patrolling the streets on horseback, Hickok was not quite so commonly visible. He left such mundane duties largely to his deputies, although when he was seen around, it was noticed that he moved about cautiously, favouring the proximity of a wall to his back. It was said he would "slide into a room" and stand for long moments surveying the scene before making a proper entrance. One old timer who knew him described the way Hickok regarded his surroundings as being like that of a "mad old bull".

By this time in his life, much of Wild Bill's apparent eccentric behaviour could perhaps be excused as the result of his eye concerns. Although it was still not common knowledge, the condition was slowly getting worse and it must have affected him in many ways. He covered it well, however, and was obviously still able to convince most people that he was as dangerous as he had ever been. In fact, he probably was.

While his deputies did the legwork, Hickok made his headquarters at the card tables of the Alamo Saloon, one of the higher class establishments amongst the many dens of iniquity in the Texas Town area.

He was always swift to react whenever trouble reared its head and was on the spot within moments of being informed. Yet again, as ever, stories abounded of the deeds he supposedly did during his first few weeks overseeing the law in Abilene. Without doubt he would have been busy, establishing his authority with proof of action whenever necessary.

The Texan cowboys did respond to his tough treatment of their "hurrahing"; fearing, respecting yet also hating him.

They despised his appearance along with his contemptuous attitude towards them. But also, more than anything, they objected to the most basic fact that he represented "Yankees" whilst most of them were "Rebs". They knew of his war career, his spying and his abolitionist stance. He was the antithesis of all they stood for.

It was reported that Hickok broke up a mass brawl in a saloon, which was not a rare thing, and had cracked a few heads amongst the instigators who went back to camp bearing a grudge. Seething and vowing revenge, they gathered a group of friends, about twenty to thirty strong, and rode brazenly into town, loudly voicing their intention of stringing up the marshal.

Wild Bill was warned of their approach and, as they cantered along the street, they were met by him, standing alone, blocking their path with a Winchester rifle aimed at their leaders.

The riders were not expecting this. They reined in, pulling to a halt in a tight bunch before their intended victim.

Hickok cocked the rifle and raised the barrel. His expression was hard and stern, his voice firm.

"Hide out, you sons of bitches!" he snarled.

And they did. The street cleared in moments as the vendetta mob took off back the way they had come.

A favourite haunt of the cowboys was the Bull's Head Saloon which stood right in the heart of Abilene's ribald action. Gambling, drinking, women; it was all on tap at the Bull's Head and the place was always packed and very lively. The back room was well known for its impressive faro set-up which was probably more crooked than a bend in the Colorado River.

Overseeing this gold mine of an establishment were a pair of Texan legends by the names of Ben Thompson and Phil Coe who had entered into a business partnership.

Both of them were renowned gamblers and Thompson, in particular, had a firm reputation as a deadly gunfighter.

Although regarded by the cowboys as one of their own, Thompson was an Englishman by birth, raised initially in the county of Yorkshire, although his family brought him over to Austin, Texas, as a child. Therefore, he also considered himself Texan through and through.

He had lived a colourful life on the frontier, involved in various adventures. During the Civil War he saw lots of action as a soldier in the Confederacy. After the war, in 1866, he fought as a mercenary in Mexico during the Juarista rebellion against the Emperor Maximilian.

He was tough and cool headed, but there is a photograph of him looking very dapper in a smart frock coat, brushed top hat and holding a cane like an eastern city gentleman. Ben had a younger brother, Billy, who had a swift and violent temper, known for flying off the handle in a much more volatile way than his elder sibling. Consequently, he was often in trouble which Ben usually found himself covering for. Both brothers were killers, but Billy was the more openly wild of the pair. That said, Ben became the famous one.

Phil Coe was raised in Gonzales, so he was a thoroughbred Texan. Like Thompson, he fought under the rebel stars and bars during the war and maybe also in Mexico. Coe then made his living as a gambler, building a reputation in a series of frontier townships before winding up in Abilene where he partnered up with Ben Thompson to open the Bulls Head.

A photograph of Coe also portrays him in a smart suit, looking reserved and quite pompous with his neat tie and long chin beard. In contrast to Thompson who, in appearance, was a fairly dumpy fellow, Coe was a big strapping character.

The saloon was soon doing great business and was regarded as the Texas cowpuncher's home from home. Out of sheer devilment, and in the supposed interests of promotional advertising, Thompson and Coe decided to commission a huge painting for prominent display on the side of the building. To the whooping delight of the high spirited clientele, it was a caricature of a lusty Texas Longhorn bull, complete with an oversized erect penis! By all accounts, this appendage was of such attention grabbing proportion that it gave the impression, when passing by, of virtually taking one's eye out!

All most hilarious to your average cowboy on a drunken spree, but not quite so amusing for some of the less boisterous Abilene citizens who tutted and complained to the authorities at such an outrage to moral decency.

Hickok himself was most likely not that bothered by it personally, but when the city fathers approached him, insisting that he do something about it, he agreed to act.

Wild Bill had no motive to unnecessarily provoke the town's life source, so he initially made a request that the picture be altered. When this was ignored, he addressed the problem personally and took a painter down to the building where he stood guard with a shotgun under his arm as the necessary alterations were made. The bull's modesty restored with a coat or two of slosh, Hickok went on his way while the saloon's proprietors stood by, wryly accepting it.

Thompson took it in his stride. He and Hickok possessed a kind of mutual respect for one another, but Coe added it to his list of the grievances he felt about the marshal. Coe was often heard to make threats against Hickok, boasting in the barroom about his own deadly prowess with a pistol.

When Wild Bill heard that Coe had said he could *"shoot a crow on the wing"*, the marshal is said to have responded with a smirk, *"But will that crow be shooting back? I will..."*

That summer another notorious character arrived in town as an employee of one of the cattle drives... none other than Texan John Wesley Hardin, known as Wes.

Hardin was still in his teens but had already earned a name as a much feared killer, his list of victims having been steadily growing since the age of fifteen.

Thompson and Coe became familiar with him at the bar of the Bull's Head and were soon putting it to him that he might like to try his deadly skills on the town marshal who, they said, had it in for Texans.

Hardin was not afraid but he was cautious and youthfully amused. *"If Hickok needs killing so bad,"* he reportedly said, *"why don't you do it yourselves?"*

The Texan gamblers waffled their way around this question and Hardin sashayed around town, still wearing his guns. That is what Hardin claimed anyway... Thompson was actually more than tough enough to fight his own battles.

Wild Bill was well aware of Wes Hardin's reputation and did not want to immediately indulge in gunplay with him. His initial approach was to affably engage the young killer socially, drawing him in and gaining his confidence.

It worked and they became unlikely friends for a few weeks. Hickok even allowed the young Texan the virtually unknown privilege of permitting him to wear his guns in town, as long as he promised to behave himself.

Anyone who questioned this was no doubt dealt with.

However, it is said that there was one occasion when young Wes stepped out of line and Wild Bill was forced to insist that he hand over his weapons. According to the autobiography which Hardin wrote in his prison cell many years later, he said he complied with the demand, offering his pistols in each hand, butts pointing forward. As Hickok reached out to take them, Wes said he neatly performed the classic "Border Roll", or "Road Agent's Spin" which involved rotating the pistols so that the butts dropped back into the palms, fingers on the triggers and barrels aimed forward.

Frankly, this anecdote is very unlikely to be true. For a start, the only source is from Hardin himself who, by that time, was probably quite desperate to enhance his long faded reputation and could not resist planting the idea that he had got the drop on Wild Bill. Also, Hickok was certainly too long in the tooth to fall for such an old trick.

Soon after all this, Hardin did actually shoot and kill a man in town and consequently left in a hurry before having to face the marshal again.

The main focus of enmity in Abilene grew around the tension between Hickok and Coe. Apart from the simple fact that they seemed to take a natural dislike of one another, there was also a heavy element of competition between them. Wild Bill's flamboyant image found a rival in Coe who was similarly striking in appearance. Tall, handsome and richly garbed, he strutted around enjoying the attention of Abilene's womenfolk, on both sides of the tracks.

A recurring theme in Hickok's life were the complications thrown up by his dalliances with various females and, yet again, it seems that a lady added to the problems. A girlfriend of whom he was fond had begun sharing her charms with Phil Coe who openly flaunted the relationship. This was somewhat humiliating for Hickok and he made his annoyance known.

Coe grinned and, as the summer drew on, he announced that he intended to put Abilene's marshal in his grave *"before the frost"*.

Things were beginning to change for the town's fortunes, even more rapidly than they had begun. Following a bumper season, the cattle trade was showing signs of slowing down in Abilene. The ever expanding railroad was pushing further on to other areas and the first of the cowtowns was being left behind.

The many and varied opportunists saw what was happening and recognised that their market was drying up. They began to pack their belongings and leave in droves to set up elsewhere.

The signs were also apparent at the Bull's Head and the proprietors decided that it was time to move on. Thompson left things to Coe and was away when he broke his leg in a carriage accident. Coe stayed around Abilene but sold his saloon interests. By September he was just killing time carousing around town, drinking with his Texan buddies and idling away at the gaming tables.

A period of relative peace descended upon the streets, to the extent that the authorities dispensed with the services of Hickok's deputies as it was felt that it had reached the stage where the marshal could handle matters on his own.

The red light district's dance halls were forced to close, much to the frustration of the cowboys and other mixed goodtime seekers who were still hanging around town. A general feeling arose that, before the winter set in and the mass exodus of visitors began, there should be some form of last chance blowout, a celebration of what had been.

On October 5th., with the first fierce stormy winds beginning to ravage the surrounding plains, the County Fair was a pleasant distraction for the gloomy times ahead. Farmers and their families were in town celebrating and Hickok was determined to keep them away from the cattlemen who had an intense dislike of "sodbusters". Wild Bill made it clear that he was intending to enforce the "no firearms in city limits" ordinance strictly and warned the cowboys that they must stay on their side of the tracks or they would have to answer to him.

Confident that he would be able to deal with anything that might arise, Wild Bill stopped into the Novelty Theatre for a word with his friend Mike Williams who was employed there as a bouncer. Williams could be counted upon for support but Hickok told him that all would be fine and, whatever happened, not to get involved.

The boisterous behaviour would inevitably get out of hand. Drinking in the Bull's Head had begun early and Phil Coe was holding court at his table where he still spent much time employed as a high rolling gambler. Drunken cowboys flocked around him and at about 9.00pm. a big crowd spilled out onto Texas Street with Coe at their centre. He was openly, and defiantly, wearing a holstered revolver.

It was a quite a mob which began careening up the street, noisily disturbing the peace, such as it was, and seemingly with no particular intention. They rolled from side to side, whooping and hollering, with Coe at their head, laughing and encouraging it all. Just high spirits or was something more sinister being planned?

Some said that a stray dog appeared and, whether provoked or not, it apparently growled and bit at Coe's heels. The gambler responded by drawing his gun and snapping off a shot at the animal which scurried away.

Over in the nearby Alamo Saloon, Hickok, seated with his back to the wall and trying to enjoy a card game, heard the shot and was on his feet in an instant.

Adjusting those Navy Colts at his sides, he strode purposefully out of the building and towards the source of the commotion.

This was to be a standoff which had been a long time coming.

Coe was motionless in the middle of the street waiting for Hickok who he knew would appear at any moment. With his smoking pistol still in hand, the gambler stood his ground as the marshal approached, drawing to a halt just a few feet away.

The formerly noisy crowd of cowboys drew back, silenced by the tension of the situation as Wild Bill, somewhat pointlessly, demanded to know who had fired the shot.

Coe's defiance and cocky attitude was unruffled as he said, *"I did. I shot at a mad dog."*

The next few seconds were unbearably tense as the old rivals glared at each other. Coe moved first, raising his pistol and firing twice. Hickok was lucky. One shot tore through the tail of his frock coat and the other kicked up dirt between his boots.

The gambler had spent his only chance. Wild Bill's pistols were drawn and discharged in an instant, both heavy slugs ripping into Coe's stomach. The gambler hit the ground groaning.

The stunned silence of the crowd was interrupted almost immediately by more movement. A figure was pushing through them and Hickok became aware of it over his shoulder and through a haze of gunsmoke.

What happened next was the result of instinct and gut reaction. Wild Bill span around to face this new challenge. In a split second he registered the gun in the rushing man's hand and reacted by discharging both his pistols again, stopping the figure in its tracks and hurling him lifeless into the dust.

Hickok lowered his pistols, stepping towards the man he had just dropped and it was then that he realised the terrible error which would haunt him for the rest of his life. This was no Texan drunkard rushing to help Coe. Wild Bill had killed his friend Mike Williams.

Putting his guns away, Hickok knelt beside the body, overwhelmed by the enormity of what he had done. The mob of cowboys and other onlookers stood and stared in a state of shock as the marshal lifted the corpse of Williams into his arms and carried him over to the Alamo.

Coe was moaning and writhing in agony, clutching his double punctured gut just paces away, but Hickok was oblivious to his suffering. Inside the Alamo, Wild Bill gently laid the body of his friend on the green baize of the billiard table and within moments he began to weep, a sight unfamiliar to all those who knew him.

Wild Bill Hickok was in a state of shock; his cool, collected demeanour rocked with grief and disbelief. No one wanted to speak to him… he was in a world of his own, shattered, although he could hardly be blamed for what had happened.

In the drama and highly charged adrenalin inducing moment of action, surely any man would be forgiven for instinctively reacting to a perceived attack. Hickok had just gunned down an enemy in a fair fight, surrounded as he was by scores of potential back-shooters. Hearing rushed footsteps behind him and glimpsing an armed man, the marshal had made a snap decision to defend himself. Williams had been told to keep away and his disobedient good intentions had cost him his life.

But none of this comforted Hickok. The result was that he had killed an innocent man who had been trying to help him… and a friend to boot…

As the minutes ticked by, the suffering figure of Coe was carried to a nearby house to be examined by a doctor. The verdict was grim. Gut-shot… twice… no way could he survive but it would be a lingering, painful passing… it took three days.

At last, Wild Bill emerged from the Alamo to face the crowds which were still standing around on the street, murmuring and passing judgement about what they had witnessed.

Hickok, his face set in stern resolve, went for them without hesitation. He roared at the gawping faces in fury, demanding that they clear the streets, before pacing the length and breadth of Texas Street, bursting into every brightly lit building, clearing rooms with his physical and verbal demands that everyone *"get out of town and do it quick!"*

The celebrations were well and truly over and Wild Bill was determined that everyone, without exception, would comply. As streets and rooms emptied, riders lit out to spread the word in the surrounding camps that Marshal Hickok was on the rampage and no one had ever seen him so Wild.

Hickok was desperate to make amends, but what could he do? Working in Kansas City as a bartender, Mike Williams was only visiting Abilene to make some extra money and now he was gone. Still grief stricken, Hickok made a trip to see Williams' young widow to try and explain what had occurred and to express his deep regret and sorrow.

The least he could do was cover all the funeral expenses, which he did.

Everyone who knew him always said that Wild Bill was never quite the same following this harrowing incident. It rocked him to the core and it was believed that his whole attitude to the essence of his very being was affected, as if he was re-evaluating his existence.

That said, he still maintained his essential bearing, caution and courage which was demonstrated within a few weeks when on a train journey between Abilene and Topeka. A quintet of vengeful Texans thought they might be able to take advantage of the marshal's lone trip. Their clumsy attempt at assassination was quickly foiled by Wild Bill who easily got the drop on them. He was way out of their class and, holding them at gunpoint, he forced them to remain on board and light out as he departed.

Back in Abilene it was all very different following the violent deaths of Coe and Williams. The salad days were over for the town and it was announced by the city fathers that the cattle drives would no longer be welcome. This was arguably a little late in the day as the beef business had already moved on to establish itself in towns further along the far reaching train tracks. A residue of life had remained for a while but the vast majority of inhabitants had got the message.

The weather was rapidly turning too. Rain and icy storms culminated in a lengthy blizzard which decimated the territory, the worst which had been seen for years. Thousands of unsold cattle perished. Quickly made fortunes were just as quickly lost and bankruptcies abounded.

The game was up.

As for Hickok, his position as marshal became redundant and in mid December he was informed that his services were no longer required. His high salary could no longer be justified.

It was a muted dismissal and when Hickok handed in his badge to the City Council there was barely a mumble of thanks. Wild Bill left town that same night after eight months of overseeing law and order. He was no Bear River Tom but his methods had certainly got the job done, albeit somewhat more crudely. It seemed that the town resented him and could not forgive the tragic events of October 5th..

Hickok boarded the train to Kansas City with hardly a backwards glance.

He had no regrets save the mistaken killing of Mike Williams.

But Wild Bill was older and wiser now, unexpected lessons learned and a deep resolve never to wear a lawman's badge again.

CHAPTER 9
HICKOK'S THEATRICS

What now for Wild Bill?

The Wild West he had always known was shrinking rapidly, swallowed up fast by the encroaching advances of civilization from the east. Disillusioned by the way he had been treated in his last stint as a lawman, what were his options? Scouting and guiding for the army again? This was no longer appealing for him as he had to accept the reality of health issues. He was still only in his mid thirties but it had been a hard, tough life on the plains enduring savage conditions. On the face of it, he was still hardy and strong but he knew in himself that he was slower than he had been... and his eyesight was definitely an issue now, aggravated by the searing relentlessness of the weather and burning sun.

There was always gambling... a risky business, but his fortunes and skill had seen him through before. And it was a past time he shamelessly enjoyed, basking in that smoky environment of late nights, whisky and loose women who were always happy to cling to his arm, especially when he was winning.

His reputation was still largely intact and most folks he encountered still regarded him with awe, having totally swallowed the outlandish tales which had been dogging him for years, especially since Nichols' stirring yarns in *Harper's Monthly* magazine back in '67.

Ever since then, Hickok had been featuring in the highly popular *Dime Novels* or *De Witt's Ten Cent Romances* which were distributed nation and even, eventually, world wide. Graphically illustrated tales of *Wild Bill the Indian Slayer* and *Wild Bill's First Trail* were convincing many thousands of gullible people that Hickok was a super man and glowing, infallible hero of the frontier. *First Trail* claimed to be Hickok's life as *"told by Wild Bill himself"*... really?

The writer and notorious legend spreader Ned Buntline also increasingly played his part in building up the glorious image of Wild Bill, although his main subject was Buffalo Bill Cody who Buntline seemed determined to make into the real star of the West. Hickok played more of a supporting role in the Buffalo Bill novels but it all helped to add to his fame.

Cody, inbetween his trips back to the frontier where he played his part as a scout and Indian fighter in reality, was beginning to be lured by the temptations of a show business career back in the big cities of the eastern states. The concept of restaging his colourful and exciting adventures (albeit highly dramatized) on stage for greenhorn audiences, at a handsome price, was becoming very appealing.

Of course, Buffalo Bill was destined to become the legendary creator of his glamorized version of the theatrical Wild West which eventually enthralled many millions over decades on stage and screen.

However, Cody was pre-empted in this venture, just slightly, by his friend Wild Bill.

***

By early 1872, Hickok was drifting on a fairly aimless course again. He settled himself in Kansas City once more where he knew he could survive at the gaming tables. Reluctantly, he even returned to do some scouting for the army but his heart was not really in it anymore. His experience pulled him through but he was not quite the vibrant, young, trail blazing character he had once been. And his eyes were troubling him, quite severely at times.

He already had an impressive history behind him; albeit that much of it was embellished fiction. How many men had he *actually* sent to the happy hunting grounds? Rumour claimed it was dozens, scores even, but the official records verify far less. There is much in Wild Bill's story which lacks authentication, but that does not necessarily mean that lots of it does not have a basis in truth.

Hickok himself did not contribute much to verifying this truth. He was aware of the stories and much of it appeared to irritate him, but he did not seem bothered about putting the record straight. Sometimes, for the sake of pure mischief, and, presumably, fun, he entertained himself, and an enthralled saloon or front porch audience, by relating tales from his past. He must have cut quite a figure, sitting back in his chair, long legs stretched out before him, hat tipped back, as he yarned away.

It is recorded that his legendary sense of humour often cut through the drama of his exciting stories, of how he had battled armies of rebs and whooping savages, or gunned down gangs of bad men. When he paused at the apex of a hair raising dilemma he had endured, when the odds seemed impossible, an awestruck listener might exclaim, *"But Bill... how did you escape?"*

Hickok would squint at them, his blue/grey eyes sparkling impishly. *"I didn't..."* he would drily say, *"I was killed!"*

Then everyone would collapse into laughter and urge him to tell more.

Well, I believe we can be pretty sure that many (if not most) of Wild Bill's adventures were simply not witnessed or recorded and are sadly lost to history.

And so he was probably more than ready to consider an offer which came his way in the summer of '72.

An entrepreneur and promoter named Sidney Barnett approached him, well aware of the pulling power Wild Bill might have to front an extravaganza he had in mind. He wanted to bring the Wild West, in all its exciting splendour, lock, stock and barrel, to the eastern states to present the spectacle live to the awe struck crowds who would surely flock to see it all in the flesh. It was certainly an ambitious idea which, if staged correctly, had the potential to make a fortune.

Easterners loved the West, but, so far, had only been able to enjoy it through the limited pages of those dime novels with their lurid illustrations. Most of them would never venture anywhere near the frontier so, to see it for real, brought to their doorstep, would be a dream come true.

Logistically, to transport all that was required from west to east would be a chaotic nightmare, but Barnett was convinced it was do-able.

A headlining name to sell the show would be a huge asset and there was none bigger than Wild Bill Hickok.

This was something totally new to a man who had lived the real thing all his life. An alien idea and he must have had pretty enormous initial doubts. He probably found the thought absurd, to be prancing around play acting like some prissy dude, making an act out of his life for a bunch of greenhorns.

But the convincing factor was the money, and, in his current situation, he could not discard that lightly. Offered a fee he could not bring himself to refuse, Hickok signed on, committing himself to a couple of performances in the summer as Master of Ceremonies.

It was to be called *The Grand Buffalo Hunt* and staged in a specially selected park area on the Canadian side of the border at Niagra Falls on August 28th. and 30th. 1872. A small herd of buffaloes had been captured (and this was no easy task) at the foot of the Rocky Mountains, plus quite a few head of genuine Texas cattle. Feather bonneted and colourfully costumed Indians would be in the cast, alongside a Mexican Vaquero Troupe whose *"wonderful dextrous feats with the lariat, throwing and capturing"* must be seen. *"A colossal undertaking"*... *"No expense has been spared..."* ... *"accompanied by a full regimental band"* and all this for just 50 cents at 3.00pm. each day.

It all seemed impressive and promising but, unfortunately, the general public were not as convinced as had been hoped. Over the two days, the expected crowds of 50,000 were closer to 6,000 which turned the entire enterprise into a financial disaster. To cap it all, the buffalo were virtually uncontrollable.

Hickok did what was required of him, galloping skilfully around, looking magnificent, but his heart was not in it. It probably put him off theatrics for life and he was glad to distance himself from the whole venture... that is until something similar came along later the same year.

***

Bill Cody had been making himself busy out west for all his adult life.

Since before his teens he fulfilled many roles on the periphery of frontier activity, perfecting his riding and shooting skills as he worked as a runner and go-fer for seasoned frontiersmen. As mentioned previously, it was during this period that he first met Hickok who apparently rescued him from rough treatment.

Cody was to make many claims in his grandiose autobiography which was written on the back of his eventual fame, so he can probably be forgiven for his words reflecting the showman within him. He no doubt embellished his deeds but the fact remains that he most certainly served a genuine apprenticeship in the Wild West and would have experienced the real McCoy.

He might have ridden for the Pony Express... he did work for the company, at least, and in 1863, during the height of the Civil War, he enlisted in the Union, serving as a teamster in a cavalry regiment. By 1866 he was engaged as a scout, often with Hickok, during the Plains Indian wars and saw a fair slice of action.

There is no doubt that he was a very good marksman and this led to his first bout of fame when, between 1866 to '68, he excelled in employment as a buffalo hunter for the Kansas Pacific Railway, supplying a bountiful supply of meat for their hordes of track layers. During this period it was recorded that he killed nearly 4,300 bison. He also won a shooting match against Medicine Bill Comstock when, over an eight hour active hunt, Cody dropped 68 of the beasts beating Comstock's 48. Thus he was aptly named Buffalo Bill.

General Sheridan appointed him Chief of Scouts for the 5th Cavalry and in 1872 he oversaw that prestigious expedition when the Grand Duke Alexis Romanov of Russia took a tour of the West with Sheridan and Custer. That same year he was to win the Congressional Medal of Honour for gallantry during his Indian fights and scouting forays.

So, regardless of some modern day cynical debunking of Buffalo Bill, it is irrefutable that he did his part. That he was to gain his worldwide fame in showbusiness is secondary to his real life pedigree.

He first met Ned Buntline in 1869 and the ambitious writer and promoter immediately saw Buffalo Bill's potential as a money spinner.

Cody had the looks as well as the experience, his many surviving photographs proving his striking appearance. His natural image was that of a comic book hero and that is what Buntline set out to exploit. At first it was a glowing story in the *New York Weekly*, but that quickly grew into a novel, *Buffalo Bill; King of the Bordermen*.

But Cody was partnered with another similar character… one Texas Jack Omohundro, an ex Confederate and Chisholm Trail cowboy who had also earned a reputation as a scout and guide for American and foreign tour groups. He could also perform some impressive tricks with ropes.

Buntline decided to team Buffalo Bill and Texas Jack together and persuaded them to try and present their dual charisma on stage, to bring the West to the East where he was sure they could all make a fortune.

In December 1872, they debuted their show *The Scouts of the Prairie* in Chicago and it was an immediate hit, a sellout. The critics were not overly impressed, but the public loved it. And Cody and Omohundro had found their vocation… they loved it too, garish costumes, painfully dramatic script and all. City folk who had never experienced the wonders of the Plains were enthralled by the spectacle of the real men who were protecting their borders and carving out civilization. Or so it seemed…

Meanwhile, Hickok had returned from his own brief toe dipping into the world of entertainment and was killing time again in his old haunts around Springfield. He was staying out of trouble and probably doing his best to keep as low a profile as someone like himself could, but it was inevitable that he would attract attention.

In September, the gate at the Kansas City Fair was robbed by the James/Younger Gang, netting around $1,000 dollars in spoils and wounding a young girl in the crossfire as they made their escape. Hickok was not there that day but he was in attendance the following day when tempers were still on the boil from what had occurred.

It must have been like a replay from his Abilene days when he came across a bunch of drunken Texans who had surrounded the musicians on the bandstand, browbeating the terrified bandmaster as they loudly insisted on a rendition of that old Rebel favourite *Dixie*.

In his unique way, Wild Bill soon put a stop to this bullying and order was restored, but this was a rare return to what had once been a routine for Hickok.

His life was now an endless round of gambling; a risky business as such pursuits were against city ordinance but what else did he have to do? Therefore, when approached by his old friend Cody with a tempting offer, albeit not ideal, he was swiftly persuaded.

Buffalo Bill and Texas Jack had been successfully touring for several months with Buntline's show and they had really embraced a taste for the stage. However, when the season ended in New York in June 1873, their relationship with Buntline had soured somewhat, mainly over money and what they felt they were due.

They parted company and, at first, Cody felt that he had fulfilled his theatrical ambitions. He was pining for the real West again but Texas Jack talked him into reconsidering. They did not need Buntline. Why not carry on by themselves? They were experienced now and understood the theatre world.

Cody thought it over as he went back to buffalo hunting for a while but Omohundro's reasoning made sense. There was a great deal of money to be made, especially if they were running their own show.

Some ambitious ideas were bandied around... a play based upon Cody's expedition with the Grand Duke Alexis... a tour of Europe... Although these particular plans were not to happen... yet... the two stagestruck scouts put all their energies into creating a show of their own, but this time they had their eyes set on another name to help draw in the crowds.

Listening to the convincing words of his old friend Cody, Hickok was eventually persuaded to tread the boards again. His initial doubts were overturned by the motive of going on the road with kindred spirits who understood the frontier, but it was the handsome fees which finally got him to sign on.

Buffalo Bill and Texas Jack had already been touring their new show, *Scouts of the Plains*, for several weeks when Wild Bill agreed to travel east to join them. It was late August 1873 and Hickok's much anticipated arrival in New York City was highlighted by a characteristic dramatic incident. The driver of a horse drawn cab, who picked up Hickok after he had stepped off a train at the central station, made the mistake of underestimating a man he presumably felt he could take advantage of. He tried to overcharge Wild Bill for a short journey across town and received a sound thrashing in return.

Having thus swiftly made his mark on city life, Hickok joined what was now known as *Buffalo Bill's Combination*, a theatre show which starred the trio of legendary scouts (much being made of Wild Bill's *Harper's* and dime novel fame). The supporting cast included Texas Jack's new wife, dancer/actress Giuseppina, and several genuine Indians to serve as cannon fodder to the onstage heroics.

Hickok was uncomfortable in his new role from the very start. They rehearsed him in quickly, the feeling being that his very presence would be enough to satisfy the packed houses of sycophants. The staging was very much of its day and the plot wafer thin, punctuated with excruciating dialogue. The heroic scouts all looked the part, regardless of what they were actually required to do.

Wild Bill soon proved that he was no actor, and had no desire to be. Cody and Omohundro revelled in their roles, pure naturals who played to the crowd, but Hickok despised the falseness of it all. He had problems delivering his lines, missing cues and even favouring a tendency to almost hide behind the scenery. The shooting and gun handling displays were easier for him but he quickly grew annoyed and bored with the nightly repetition of such hokum. To pacify these feelings he began to entertain himself by discharging his guns alongside the legs of the Indians to make them howl and leap around.

At one performance, when a spotlight shone directly into his troublesome eyes, he apparently responded by hurling his pistol at the lens and smashing it.

It was a relentless, busy tour, rolling along from state to state. From New York it trundled across a wide variety of venues in New Jersey, Ohio, Kentucky, Indiana, Pennsylvania, Rhode Island, Maine, Maryland, Connecticut, Massachusetts and New Hampshire.

To alleviate the boredom and frustration he felt, Hickok did his best to take advantage of his new environment. This was a part of the country which had previously been outside of his experience... the civilized states... and, inbetween shows, he enjoyed exploring whatever town they found themselves in.

In Buffalo Bill's ghost written autobiography, penned in 1879, it was claimed that Wild Bill lived up to his reputation yet again on November 6th. 1873 at the Parshall Opera House in Titusville, Pennsylvania. Hickok wandered into a nearby billiard hall where some local toughs tried to make fun of his appearance. Arming himself with a chair or maybe a billiard cue, Wild Bill took them all on and soon cleared the place out.

The tour continued and Hickok stuck it out for just over six months before deciding that he had really had enough. Cody and Omohundro understood his reluctance to continue and released him from his commitment in Rochester, New York, following his final performances in early March 1874. Buffalo Bill and Texas Jack were to carry on as a headlining duo for the remainder of the run, but they thanked their scouting friend with a golden handshake of $500 each plus a gift of a fine pair of Smith & Wesson No.3 "American" revolvers.

***

One of many highlights for me when exploring the sites of the Old West was the time I spent in the wonderful town of Cody, Wyoming.

During the height of Buffalo Bill's runaway success and fame, he founded this unique place as a symbol of all he held dear and it retains its old world frontier charm. The atmospheric Main Street may be festooned with gift shops, because tourists are attracted here, naturally, but the vibe of history is strong.

I was lucky to be able to book into the Irma Hotel which Cody built and dedicated to his daughter. The entire structure emanates a lived in 19th. century feel which I found to be a sheer joy, especially when settled in my Caroline Lockhart Room (Caroline being a renowned journalist, author and rancher who actively promoted all things Western). One may miss the presence of air conditioning, but this is more than made up for by the vibe of authenticity... brass bedstead, jug and washbasin on a crocheted cover, battered old dresser, hat stand and chaise lounge.

Buffalo Bill used to glory in holding court on the veranda here and the long redwood bar was presented to him by Queen Victoria.

The Buffalo Bill Heritage Centre is simply brilliant, the ultimate delight for Western enthusiasts. It is massive with a huge section devoted to the Plains Indians. Countless items which had belonged to Cody, costumes and genuine frontier working outfits, plus a vast collection of vintage firearms. This includes what is claimed to be one of Hickok's ivory handled Navy Colts which, they say, was auctioned off in Deadwood following his death. There is even an original Cheyenne to Black Hills stagecoach which operated in the 1870s... oh, the tales that could tell... and many items pertaining to Custer's 7th. Cavalry.

The Whitney Gallery of Western Art is full of paintings by the likes of Remington and Russell and I was taken aback by the gargantuan depiction of Custer's last Stand which Edgar Paxson painstakingly laboured over for years. Paxson contacted many of the battle's participants in his desire to make his work as authentic as possible. I handled a letter penned by Lt. Godfrey, commander of K company, which he sent in response to Paxson's request for details, and it is rich with gory and precise information. (Paxson, understandably, omitted these hair raising and frankly sickening descriptions from his work.)

This visit gave me a much deeper appreciation of Buffalo Bill and his huge significance and contribution to the creation of the genre.

As Annie Oakley said of him, "Essentially he was a simple and good man; as comfortable with cowboys as he was with kings"

CHAPTER 10
THE ROAD TO DEADWOOD

So, yet again, the living legend known as Wild Bill was at a loose end.

He wasted no time in wending his way back west to the familiar territories where he knew he belonged. Before long he had settled himself in Cheyenne, Wyoming, where the dollars he had earned in show business were soon diminished as his fortunes rose and fell at the card tables. Renting a room, long term, above a saloon, or, possibly, in a house on West 27th. Street, Hickok fell back into an aimless routine.

But it suited him.

Following the turmoil of the last few years, Hickok was most likely ready to take things more easily, at least for a while. And there is little doubt that the anguish and guilt he felt over the accidental killing of his friend Mike Williams had a lasting effect which haunted him constantly. It seems that he willingly began to embrace a lower profile and those who knew him personally respected that.

He largely kept to himself, enjoying his gambling which was his overwhelmingly main occupation. His popularity grew as he became a more familiar figure in the city, avoiding trouble and living up to a new reputation as a quiet and gentlemanly figure.

Despite this, Cheyenne's authoritative leaders seemed to take exception to his very presence in their midst, even though he was laying low and paying his own way. Perhaps his past reputation as a mankiller made the city fathers uncomfortable. And the notion of anyone making a living from the turn of a card was not only undesirable but also illegal.

The town's marshal apparently put the pressure on and ordered him out of Cheyenne on more than one occasion, although the marshal himself later denied this. Why Hickok still remained in an environment where he was unwelcome can only be guessed at. The thing is, he still had many friends in town and perhaps felt protected in a way whilst not taking the threats of removal seriously. He just carried on in quiet contentment, acting very differently to the way the Wild Bill of old would have reacted.

Even so, by mid summer of '75, he was officially branded with an accusation of vagrancy which led to his arrest and a bail order for a court appearance in November. Quite a demeaning comedown for a man whose celebrity and real life exploits had made him one of the most famous figures in the United States.

Looking at this from a distance, the whole dilemma faced by Wild Bill at this point in his life does smack of a kind of sad injustice. The quick shooting lawman, Indian fighter and icon of the West reduced to arrest for vagrancy? Did he really deserve this? The answer is almost certainly a resounding "no" and the answer probably can be found in an objective appraisal of the city father's nervousness in having a man of Hickok's calibre in town on a seemingly permanent basis.

He may have been a model of good behaviour (even as a professional gambler) but it was just having him around that bothered the more fastidious members of society. It was like living on a powder keg. Who knew what little matter it might take to set off such a volatile and potentially dangerous character?

Hickok dealt with all this suspicion with benign tolerance but, for whatever reason, he did leave Cheyenne by the fall, although he would intermittently return until well into the following year. His movements became something of a mystery again but it is very possible that he sought the help of a specialist doctor in Kansas City for many weeks in the hope of alleviating his worsening eye problems. His treatment included the use of strong mineral drugs and, as before, he would presumably not have wanted any of this to become common knowledge. Judged today, it would seem that his condition was probably trachoma; a serious infection which, in those days, would almost certainly have led to blindness.

During these long, fact shrouded months, some further evidence has filtered through that Hickok may have been part of an expedition to the Black Hills of South Dakota. During the previous year's major military expedition into the area, led by Lt. Col. George Armstrong Custer, gold had been discovered, resulting in a wild rush of prospectors into the sacred lands of the Lakota Sioux. The government had made a treaty with the Sioux promising that the Hills would be reserved for them alone, but the lure of gold put paid to that. It was to lead to the long, tragic and bloody death knell of the Plains tribes.

Whatever, Hickok was spotted again in early 1876, this time in St. Louis, before making his way back to Cheyenne where he continued to ignore his bail conditions. It is likely that he was already making plans to return to the Black Hills, maybe to try his luck at making his fortune in mining, but, on the face of it, this seems out of character. Wild Bill with a pickaxe, toiling away in the dark? This would be a direction he had never ventured into before, but maybe he was ready for it. He certainly needed something new in his life…

As it turned out, fate was to deliver something positive for him, something so synchronistic that one cannot help but wonder if it did happen purely by chance.

Hickok had continued to correspond, by letter, with the widow Agnes Lake, whenever possible. They were obviously fond of one another and possessed a connection which survived such long periods apart. She was forever on tour with the circus but they had managed to meet up briefly in New York towards the end of Hickok's partnership with Buffalo Bill's Combination. She was in town with her own show and they were able to spend some quality time together before circumstances pulled them apart again.

And now, in Cheyenne, as luck would have it, as Hickok reappeared, Agnes was there too, visiting resident Minnie Moyer, an old friend from the circus.

It must have been a delightful reunion. It seems that Agnes brought out the best in Wild Bill and the timing was perfect. Hickok had mellowed, a condition brought on by wisdom, age and unavoidable health considerations. Apart from his eyesight, there are indications that he was suffering from rheumatism which probably would have been brought on by his previous harsh life on the plains and in the mountains. By the time Agnes met him in Cheyenne, at the age of 39 (she was over 50), the famous lawman/scout/gunfighter was using a cane which he had fashioned out of a billiard cue. Some said it was to ease the persistent problem which had never left him since receiving that Cheyenne lance in his hip.

So, he was slower and more tolerant than the human coiled spring he once had been, although still a force to be reckoned with if pushed hard enough. He was done with trouble and was ready for peace. Agnes appeared like a gift, just what he needed.

Many observers of Hickok's story have expressed surprise by how quickly things moved in his relationship with this woman who he had barely seen over the years, but, on reflection, it made sense. They had reached a point in their lives where they needed each other. Comfort, security, companionship, peace. Their long term continuous relationship by letter had kept the spark aglow and now destiny had brought them together once more.

They were not kids... far from it. Their love was mature and, in that way, contained a depth which was lasting. Little wonder then that they quickly decided that the time was right to marry... and so they did, in Cheyenne, on March 5th. 1876.

It was a well attended occasion and the happy couple set off for their honeymoon, first to St. Louis and then on to Cincinatti, Ohio, Agnes' hometown.

Whilst away and taking it easy, they must have indulged in a lot of talking about their future because, after just a fortnight, Hickok took leave of his new wife and headed back west.

***

At the end of March it was reported that Hickok was bunking at Cheyenne's "Miner's Home" which was a kind of headquarters and rendezvous point for optimistic treasure seekers with their eyes on the fortune to be found within the Black Hills.

A correspondent who interviewed him for the *Republican* newspaper described him as *"looking pale now, because of a recent illness..."* but that he *"spoke favourably of the prospects in the new El Dorado as soon as the weather permits"*.

Hickok seemed serious about this venture and must have agreed it all with his wife, the plan being, presumably, to make a fortune so that they could set up home together and live happily ever after. His affectionate letters to her during this time did intimate this but also that he had postponed his own expedition until June owing to complications with competitors and the intended route.

Having drifted around again for a while, Hickok returned to Cheyenne where he teamed up with Colorado Charlie Utter, a colourful character who, with his brother Steve, was taking a large wagon train into the Black Hills with the intention of establishing a transportation line. Wild Bill and Charlie had long been friends and left together near the end of June, at the head of about thirty wagons, bound for the ramshackle newly established shanty town of Deadwood.

The journey took about two weeks and, on the way, via Fort Laramie, they picked up another lively soul who was already establishing herself as one of the gigantic names to emerge from the Wild West... none other than Martha Jane Canary (or Cannary)... famously known as Calamity Jane. More about her later...

The train also lumbered its way through rough country and a ranch belonging to one John Hunton. They halted here for a brief spell and Hickok, presumably by mistake, left behind his billiard cue walking cane which eventually found its way into a Wyoming museum where, many years later, it was put on display.

Deadwood itself was situated in a narrow gulch, flanked by steep rock walls and slopes which were festooned with tall pine trees. There had been no plan when the prospectors began arriving in undisciplined droves throughout 1875, unofficially naming the makeshift settlement after the plethora of dead trees and rotting stumps which littered the canyon floor.

At first the newcomers established themselves in tents and dugouts along the length of the single main thoroughfare, panning for precious sparkling dust in the streams which gushed down from the hills. Then, in the fall of '75, a thick, rich vein of gold was discovered deep in the rocks of the northern Black Hills and the rush was on. By the spring of '76, thousands of would be gold seekers were pouring into Deadwood Gulch and the town grew accordingly as claims were staked in every section of the surrounding area.

All of this was, of course, in direct contravention of the Fort Laramie Treaty of 1868 when the Lakota tribes had been granted their sacred Black Hills as a haven from white expansion. Dakota was still a territory and would not become an American state until 1889 so it was largely a lawless land where *"anything goes"*.

Naturally, this caused great resentment and hostility from the Sioux whose warriors watched this invasion of their spiritual homeland with dismay. They hit back when they could, massacring isolated mining parties, but the influx was simply too great to make much difference. The digging went on and the government authorities could do precious little to stem the uncontrollable flow.

By the time Hickok arrived in Utter's wagon train, in the early part of July, Deadwood Gulch was a thriving raw boned metropolis, buzzing with activity as newcomers appeared sporting picks, shovels and shedloads of wide eyed hope.

As with any newly opened market in the West, it was inevitable that the thousands of naïve hopefuls would be followed by an equal number of those who would always be on hand to exploit them… the card sharps, the whores and their pimps, thugs, thieves and con artists of every description, quack medicine men, the bent gold dealers and their dodgy scales… it was a thief's paradise.

That long, narrow Main Street was by now lined with hastily erected log or clapboard structures, most of which appeared to be saloons, all of which were forever crowded. Horses, mules, oxen and an endless train of groaning wagons jammed the muddy, dung infested thoroughfare, and the stench must have been truly overpowering.

As for any semblance of law, a man would make his own and police it with his personal ability to defend himself. After all, the land officially belonged to the Lakota so the U.S. government kept its distance. Therefore violence was rife and most of the many disputes were settled in blood by gun, knife or whatever weapon came to hand.

Newly arrived men of vision, like Colorado Charlie, did their best to establish some form of order in their own small corner of this chaotic world. Stores opened and other forms of business flourished to furnish the necessity of supplies and services to this melting pot of humanity.

Utter's wagons brought yet another injection of life to the town, not just Wild Bill and Calamity Jane, but also memorable women of brazen charisma such as Madame Mustache and Dirty Em whose newly opened bordellos, hosted by fresh *"soiled doves"*, were soon doing a roaring trade.

Hickok's arrival in town was met with some level of excitement from those who were aware, and/or cared about his fame. Wild Bill had, for over a decade now, been a widely recognised figure, feared, admired, even hated, and he was used to creating an impression wherever he went. Deadwood was not quite the same as most places he had frequented before, because gold was the star here and everything else took second place.

He could still pull a crowd and his appearance in Main Street's saloons were something of a novelty for a while as he leaned on the plank/barrel bars before taking his place, back to the wall (so that he could keep his eye on the whole room) at the poker tables.

An old friend of Hickok's, Carl Mann, part owned Nuttal & Mann's No. 10 Saloon, plus the bartender was Harry "Sam" Young who he knew from his Hays City days. They made Wild Bill very welcome and he and Colorado Charlie (with Calamity Jane in tow) agreed to make the No.10 their headquarters in town.

Hickok and Utter pitched tents as canvas covered homes but, by all accounts, it seems that most of Wild Bill's time was spent gambling in the No.10. Whether he spent any of his waking moments out at the diggings is doubtful. Although his incentive for being in Deadwood was supposed to be prospecting for gold, it is apparent that old habits were not going to diminish and once he was seated at the card table, that is where he was going to stay.

His optimistic letters to Agnes, who was still living at her daughter's home in Cincinatti, gave the impression that he was beavering away at raising that fortune for them, but he had other ideas. What his long term intentions were, I guess we will never know.

Colorado Charlie was more industrious and set about creating some business interests in town, As for Calamity Jane, who was only in her mid twenties whilst giving the impression of someone who had spent decades living it hard on the frontier, she lived up to her reputation by kicking up a storm wherever she went, hurrahing, drinking and carousing with the roughest element in town.

It is hard to pin down any accurate information about this lady because her entire life, mainly encouraged by her own tall tales, was surrounded by nothing more than rumour and unverified facts. She claimed to have been a scout for the army, fighting the Sioux and Cheyenne and taking part in numerous heroic scrapes, but what evidence there is suggests that she was more like a camp follower, and occasional prostitute, on the periphery of any action. Mule skinner? Bull whacker? Well, she certainly mixed easily enough with the roughest and toughest of them, drinking many under the table. Her personality was coarse and loud, her language fruitily profane but she was regarded as entertaining company when in the kind of circle which suited her style. That is until her short fuse was lit and her fierce temper exploded to the extent that she could clear a bar.

She almost always dressed in male attire, buckskins and leather britches, slouch hats and riding boots and was usually armed to the teeth. Physically, she was thick set, her features heavy and a touch brutish. No wonder she often passed herself off as a man. One story tells of how when employed by the army on an expedition into Indian country, no one was aware of her gender until she stripped off to bathe with the other men in a river. The outraged commanding officer immediately sent her packing.

I feel it is not ungentlemanly of me to observe that, in the spirit of accuracy, for Doris Day to have played her in that wonderful 1950's film musical was a milestone in mis-casting! Having said that, Howard Keel as Wild Bill was also in the same league... (I love that film, though!)

So, regardless of what she claimed in later life (and even at the time he was alive), Calamity Jane's relationship with Hickok was nothing like as close as she would like to boast. She had only just met him in the summer of '76 and it seems to me that she was drawn to him in the way that many were. I think she amused him and he tolerated her, in small doses, and she was, no doubt, around a lot in the saloons as just one of his many acquaintances. In the years to come, she loved to exploit and exaggerate this tenuous connection.

Many of the darker, unsavoury elements in Deadwood were unhappy with Hickok's presence, even though he was keeping to himself and proving to be a popular attraction. Some thought he might have been invited to town by certain ambitious people who would like to see the famous ex lawman tame the place.

It is possible that Hickok was approached and offered the equivalent of a marshal's role but he simply was not interested. Those days were behind him, his confidence rocked by what had happened in Abilene. In addition, he was very aware of the limitations which he was now facing. Eyesight, reflexes... he knew he was not the man he had once been and wanted to be left in peace to enjoy more gentle pursuits.

CHAPTER 11

THE FINAL HAND

There was nothing very notable about the slouching, sandy haired man who leaned on the bar of the No.10 Saloon. He was drunk and unsteady on his feet, but his eyes were locked on the small group of men at a nearby table as they sat engrossed in their game of poker.

His name was Jack McCall and he was particularly interested in one of the players; that tall, long haired dude who everyone seemed to admire so much... the notorious Wild Bill Hickok.

It was the evening of Tuesday August 1st. 1876.

McCall was cross eyed with a nose that had been broken and naturally set at a crooked angle. His scrubby, small mustache topped lips which drooped in a malicious frown. He was fascinated by the game taking place and wanted to be in on the action... but there was no room for him.

He had not been in Deadwood for long. Originally from way over in Kentucky, McCall had spent most of his 26 years or so on the move across the mid western states, maybe working a spell as a buffalo hunter before winding up in the Black Hills. What brought him there is not recorded but, by this time, he was calling himself Bill Sutherland, for some reason.

Suddenly, one of the card players threw in his hand and left the table. McCall quickly stepped up and invited himself to take the departed man's place. No one objected and he was dealt into the next round. He had money and placed his stake but he was no match for such experienced gambling company. His inebriation probably did not help matters.

He played several hands throughout the night, but lost continuously until he was totally cleaned out beyond his last dime. Humiliated but reluctant to leave the table, McCall just sat there until Hickok apparently took a little pity on him. Offering some calm and well intentioned advice to the drunken loser, Wild Bill also offered him cash to buy breakfast, adding the suggestion that he had best not join another game unless he was sure he could cover his losses.

McCall left the table seething with resentment it seems. Drunk though he was, his pride did not stretch to accepting Hickok's breakfast offer. Witnesses said that the loser staggered out of the bar feeling insulted.

But maybe that was not all he had against Wild Bill.

***

The following morning, Wednesday August 2nd., erupted with Deadwood Gulch's usual pandemonium as the town burst back into the turmoil of an average day. A lot of rain had fallen during recent nights but the morning sun burned bright, evaporating the warm dampness and dissipating any early mist.

Lamplight from the endlessly busy saloons gave way to the natural bright rays of that golden orb as it began to peak above the valley's eastern rim, sending streaks of heavenly glitter through the trees. Likewise, the loud and raucous chatter, whoops, music and occasional gunshots of the night morphed seamlessly into the buzzing commerce of a town getting back to work. Horses, mules, oxen and wagons filled Main Street again, grizzled miners packed their pokes for yet another session of backbreaking toil, the stores opened, the brothels took a breather for a brief lull…

Wild Bill Hickok, following his usual early hours retirement, had most probably slept in late again, as was his usual routine. Midday was a normal wakeup call for him when he would rise from his tent and often take breakfast with Colorado Charlie. The sun was high in the sky by now and it was proving to be another broiling hot afternoon, humid yet fierce out of the shade, the temperature hovering in the nineties.

Not a day for hard, physical labour up at the mines, although many were doing just that. Not Wild Bill though. His chin clean shaven, long locks and mustachios brushed, he took his time to dress fastidiously as he always did, paying careful attention to that dashing image he had cultivated since the end of the Civil War over ten years ago. Despite everything, he had a reputation to maintain, standards to uphold.

It was early afternoon before Hickok began his casual saunter along the wooden boardwalks, trying to avoid the swirling dust clouds which billowed from the constant traffic of hooves, wheels and boots. A few idle souls sat with their legs stretched out across the planking of the walkways, puffing on pipes and taking in the sites, but mainly the crowds were a jumble of jostling men going about their business.

Tall, graceful and as immaculate as the atmosphere would allow him to be, Wild Bill still drew attention and he played up to it naturally. Most folks would willingly, and instinctively, make room for him as he strode along, tipping his hat to those few ladies who were around and greeting the many mutually recognisable faces.

Sometime around 1.00pm., he reached the doorway of the No.10

and swung into the welcome shade of the darkened room. The heat was still oppressive, however, and just about everyone was in shirtsleeve order. Apart from sunlight piercing the doorway and a window or two, kerosene lamps provided the only lighting.

Custom was not heaving... just a few drinkers and the inevitable card game going on as if it had never ended from the previous evening. Maybe it hadn't...

Hickok acknowledged the clientele... regulars... he knew just about everyone. At the bar, Harry Young greeted him and served his drink. Four players were ensconced in their game at an adjacent table, nodding to the newcomer who they knew would be joining them soon...

Hickok, witnesses would later say, had seemed melancholy of late. Only having been in Deadwood for about three weeks, he had put himself about, but, in years to come, several of those who knew him well, or made his acquaintance during that time, spoke of a philosophical mood which seemed to have affected him.

Some spoke of his spirituality, aligned with an ominous forboding which, it was said, began to obsess him. When arriving in Deadwood, he had apparently remarked to Colorado Charlie, and others, that he felt this would be his last camp and that his time was up. Harry Young claimed that Hickok said that he sensed something was about to happen to him, and that on the evening of August 1st. he was seen leaning against the door jam of the No.10 looking morose before wandering away in a kind of dreamlike state.

Back in his tent, this is when Hickok penned his last ever letter to his wife; words which were prophetic as well as bringing out the poet in the ailing shootist.

"Agnes Darling: If such should be we never meet again, while firing my last shot, I will gently breathe the name of my wife – Agnes – and with wishes even for my enemies I will make the plunge and try to swim to the other shore..."

When one of the four players rose and left the game, Hickok was invited to join his friends at the table, and he willingly did so. They were all well known to him... Carl Mann (the saloon proprietor), gambler Charlie Rich and 46 year old Missouri river boat pilot Captain Bill Massie.

They were all seated on stools around the table, no chairs. Hickok hesitated because the vacant seat would mean he had his back to the door. Still on his feet he asked if he could swap positions with anyone but his companions laughed good naturedly and assured him he would be quite safe. Reluctant but not wanting to push it, Wild Bill sat down with a probable sense of discomfort. He was unfamiliar with making himself vulnerable but did his best to shrug it off as they dealt him in.

Enjoying their poker, probably none of them noticed a skulking figure enter the room. It was Jack McCall, making a re-entrance from his previous night's losing streak. He was probably drunk already but he slunk up to the bar and ordered a drink from Harry Young.

Shortly before that, Captain Massie's luck paid off and he raked in a sizeable pot of winnings. This cleaned out Hickok who remarked, *"The old duffer broke me on the last hand..."* and asked Young to lend him some dollars in chips so that he could stay in the game. The bartender complied.

It was approaching 4.15pm. and Charlie Rich had dealt the next hand of Five Card Stud. The four players were concentrating on their cards as McCall crept awkwardly towards the table and positioned himself behind Hickok. Massie sat across from Wild Bill with Mann and Rich on either side, the latter with his back to the wall.

McCall stood rigid, less than a yard from an oblivious Hickok, his intended victim's back a perfect, unmissable target. It was now or never...

Staring intently at his cards, Wild Bill may have been slightly hunched over, face tilted down as he weighed up his next move. It is probably accurate to surmise that this poker hand had his full attention in this moment. A brain filled with the memories of a full and wild life, the only source of the real truth behind the legend. He alone possessed the knowledge of all he had actually done... secrets that he would take to the grave...

Nobody recalled seeing McCall suddenly produce an old Colt .45 revolver which he aimed point blank at Hickok's back before crying out, *"Damn you... take that!"* and pulling the trigger.

The ball took its victim almost squarely in the rear of his skull, slightly to the right, just below the ear and into the base of that richly enhanced brain. At such short range that ball was unstoppable, ripping through the oral cavity between the jawbones and bursting through his right cheek.

It was an instantly fatal wound.

Hickok sat stock still for just a moment before slowly tilting sideways off his stool to crash heavily to the wooden floor.

Wreathed in gunsmoke, McCall stared incredulously at the result of his action. Everyone in the room was frozen to the spot with abrupt shock, save for Captain Massie who was the second victim of the ball which had just killed Wild Bill. That .45 slug had carried on from Hickok's face across the table to bury itself in the Captain's left wrist and his first thought was that the old shootist had plugged him in a fit of pique.

McCall could scarcely believe what he had done. With the evidence of Hickok's prone and bleeding body curled up in front of him, the assassin quickly processed the situation and realised he had best move fast. One version of the events which immediately followed the shooting described how McCall turned on the others in the room, forcing them all out into the street at gunpoint before fleeing out of the rear door.

Other reports say that those in the room were already making a move towards him so he tried to fire again, to snap off shots at anyone nearby. But, incredibly, they were all misfires... that old gun failed to respond and the hammer clicked uselessly. Amazing that the Colt was faulty and the one shot that worked was the one that killed Wild Bill.

With Harry Young and others edging forwards, McCall turned on his heel and rushed for the door. Out in the street he spotted a horse hitched to a nearby rail and tried to vault into the saddle, but the cinch strap was loose and the saddle turned under the horse's belly spilling McCall unceremoniously in the dust.

By now, Captain Massie had staggered out, clutching his bleeding wrist and yelling that Wild Bill had shot him. Other witnesses from inside were soon correcting that statement, blurting out what had happened to passers-by and pointing frantically at McCall as he scrambled to his feet and took off down Main Street in a panic.

A more level-headed man might well have made his escape in the confusion of the moment, but McCall created such a mad fuss in his desperation that he was soon caught. Fleeing, some say, into a butcher's shop, he was cornered by a mob of pursuers and roughly taken prisoner.

Word spread like wildfire. All through the town and in the surrounding camps as riders galloped out to give the news. Inevitably, the first reports were garbled and inaccurate, some versions even claiming that Wild Bill had gone crazy and was shooting up the town. It was quite some time before the initial pandemonium calmed down and most of Deadwood's inhabitants took in the truth that Hickok was dead and his assassin locked up.

When Doctor Ellis Pierce was summoned to the murder site, he was to remark that he found the dead man lying next to the poker table, his knees drawn up near his chest in the position from where he had toppled over. The cards he was holding had fallen from his crimped hand, stirring another legend about what these cards actually were. Black aces and eights with a possible jack of diamonds, it was said, a run which would from then on be known as the *Dead Man's Hand*.

Doc Pierce also said that Wild Bill's corpse was the *"prettiest I have ever seen"*, resembling a wax figure having bled out so quickly.

***

Reaction to Hickok's death was a mixture of grief and elation. To his friends it was a shocking tragedy, but there were plenty in Deadwood who welcomed it, glad to be rid of his unnerving presence.

Calamity Jane relished the sheer drama of it, drawing attention to herself with loud histrionics and quickly spreading a false yarn about how she had personally captured Jack McCall whilst wielding a meat cleaver.

Colorado Charlie claimed the body of his friend, prepared the corpse for burial and arranged the funeral for the very next afternoon in the town's hillside cemetery. Wild Bill was buried in a fine coffin, paid for by Charlie, dressed in a suit of black broadcloth with his Springfield rifle by his side.

There was talk of forming a lynch mob to dispense swift frontier justice to the killer but, surprisingly for such a lawless community, order took precedence and it was decided to hold a trial. This was arranged without delay and actually convened at 9.00am. the following morning in the McDaniels Theatre.

It was an unofficial miner's court, the twelve jurors having been drawn from a heap of worker's names thrown into a hat. There was nothing legal about it because Deadwood was not even a recognised community in the eyes of the US government, but in the spirit of frontier justice an effort was made to proceed properly. The judge was a former president of the Wyoming Stock Grower's Association and prosecution and defence representatives were selected from local men of importance.

McCall was brought into the makeshift courtroom and sat stooped over with his arms crossed, adopting an attitude of moody indifference to his predicament. That is until he was called to speak when he displayed desperate bravado, barking out his defence in what was described as a *"harsh, loud and repulsive voice"*.

There could be no doubt that this formerly undistinguished

character was guilty of killing Wild Bill with a backshot to the head. All the witnesses attested to that and he made no attempt to deny it. The question hinged on why he had done it and was it justifiable?

At first McCall claimed that it was an act of pure vengeance as Hickok had murdered his brother in Abilene. So he said, but, although the court would not have known it, McCall did not even have a brother.

So why did he do it?

Theories abound…

In court he was asked why he did not face Wild Bill to commit the deed rather than backshoot him in such a cowardly fashion, but McCall just answered that he had no desire to commit suicide; a logical explanation!

It was also suggested that McCall had been offered a bounty by certain criminal elements in town who wanted the worrisome ex lawman out of the way.

This is possible but, perhaps, the most simple explanation is that this loser of a man, who is only remembered historically because of this one yellow hearted act, acted on impulse. No plan, as such, just an opportunity, in his drunken state, to make a name for himself, tinged by the resentment and humiliation of losing at poker and by the great shootist patronisingly buying him breakfast.

McCall was not an obviously sympathetic figure. He was an ugly and pretty nasty character all round it seems, who came across as desperate and a tad pathetic. So there is a hollow feeling of irony in the fact that a giant of Western folklore like Wild Bill should meet his end at the hands of such a sad man.

However, to the consternation of Hickok's friends, the court would unbelievably find Jack McCall not guilty and he was permitted to go free. Somehow, the jury had sensed something sympathetic and excusable about him after all.

The assassin of Wild Bill could not believe his luck and cockily hung around Deadwood's saloons, almost crowing about his good fortune. That is until he realised that Colorado Charlie, and others, had marked him down for revenge of their own.

Jack McCall left the Black Hills in haste, heading for eventual retribution.

***

Old Woman Creek and other creeks with names like Mule, Robber's Roost, Red Cloud, Beaver and Cold Spring… so many emotive places as I motored north east on the Interstate 85, over seemingly endless miles of scrubby plains, the North Platte River gradually vanishing in my wake. Skirting Buffalo Gap and the Ogallala Grasslands, the famed Black Hills loomed ahead, the thick woodlands resembling inky dabs on the rolling heights of a broad landscape.

There followed a long winding drive traversing fabulous gullies, buttes and towering evergreens. It was early May yet wide patches of deep snow still lay on the lower slopes.

Once past Cheyenne Crossing and the small city of Lead, it is just another three miles before entering that deep gulch which cradles the legendary frontier town of Deadwood where I checked into a hotel called Hickok House. Where else?

On a baking hot, glorious day I walked the length of historic Main Street, basking in the fabulous old timey feel of the place, with its attractive period style buildings and the residents relaxing on their porches in the sunshine. Everyone seemed so welcoming, warm and friendly.

Of course, as great as modern Deadwood is, it is no longer the town that Hickok would have known. This is owing to the devastating fire which almost totally destroyed it back in 1879. It was in the early hours of the morning on September 26th. when a coal oil lamp was knocked over in a bakery, the flames quickly taking hold and raging through the highly flammable sap filled pinewood structures. When the inferno reached a warehouse stocked with kegs of gunpowder, it set off an enormous explosion which all but wiped the centre of the old town off the map. Amazingly, only one person lost his life.

The town was rebuilt, this time largely in brick and stone, and one can still visit the new Number 10 Saloon which claims to stand on the site of the original where Wild Bill died. In actual fact, it is quite a way from the genuine location but the interior has a terrific atmosphere, filled with Western artifacts which you can appreciate whilst sitting at a long marble counter consuming enormous ice creams! There is a traditional soda bar and a buzzing casino. High up on the wall, illuminated behind glass, is an ornate piece of period furniture which boasts of being "Wild Bill's Death Chair". Sadly, this cannot be so… not only because of that fire which would have frazzled everything, but also because the Number 10 is known to have had only stools for its seating arrangements.

That is not the only red herring in Deadwood. I dropped into the visitor's centre (which was once the railroad station) and was enjoying myself as I took in an array of interesting exhibits. Suddenly I was approached by an ebullient and unstoppable guide who immediately launched into a lengthy lecture about the town and its history. He was just doing his job, I know, and honed in on me as someone who appeared intrigued. His eyes were blank, staring straight ahead as he recited what was obviously a script he must blurt out like an automaton several times a day. Now, you might say that this is a good thing for the *education of tourists who will leave with a better understanding of what occurred in these Black Hills, BUT, what he said does more harm than good. Much of it was pure nonsense, as if it had been lifted straight from the pages of Nicholson and Buel. When he looked at me, straight-faced, and whined on that Wild Bill was known to have killed 117 men in face to face gunfights, I had to just shake my head and walk away...*

Mount Moriah Cemetery was another highlight, however. This is Deadwood's very own Boot Hill where many are buried on the wooded slopes above the town. It is a beautiful, sweeping spot, the most famous grave being that of Hickok himself. This is where his body was moved to, by Colorado Charlie, three years after his death. Several of his original markers were vandalized or taken away by souvenir hunters, but now there stands a permanent stone which displays his name, beneath which is a replica of the original "Pard" board erected by Charlie (see details of this in a few pages ahead...) The small area, about ten feet square, is surrounded by a low stone wall and a chest high sturdy steel and wire fence.

Not quite "buried next to Bill" as she requested, the mortal remains of Calamity Jane are placed on a slightly higher elevation just behind his memorial stone.

From here I stood on Lookout Point to appreciate a breathtaking view along the impressive gulch of Deadwood.

It was said that half a dozen men, strategically placed at the narrow entry into town would be able to hold the place against any hostile attack.

I could see how that could be so...

CHAPTER 12

LEGACY

So, Wild Bill Hickok, a famous somebody, had died by the hand of an unknown nobody.

A lifetime of adventure and narrow escapes, danger and derring do, snuffed out with ultimate low key simplicity.

Had he lived on, it is intriguing to speculate what course his future may have taken. How long would he have remained in Deadwood? Would he have somehow raised enough personal fortune to finance the future he spoke of with his new wife?

If no other chancer had managed to gun him down and he had rejoined Agnes in less risky surroundings, perhaps he would have embraced a radical lifestyle change after all.

The eye problems would have got worse, before long leading to almost certain total blindness before he was much older. What then? Presumably he and Agnes would have tried to retire to a place where they could melt into obscurity. She must have been aware of his looming fate so would have been prepared for a future caring for him, we can guess.

But Wild Bill as a helpless invalid? How would he have coped with that, to be dependant upon the assistance of others following a lifetime of fighting against the odds and riding high…

Well, whatever, his fate in Deadwood was, from an historical and legendary point of view, a more fitting one. He died young but with his dignity and status intact. Shot down by an assassin, cards in his hand, spared from an ignominious old age. One cannot help but wonder what he would have preferred.

As for Jack McCall, his initial good fortune was short lived. He made his way to Laramie, where he was heard by many, boasting about how he had killed Wild Bill and got away with it. This backfired on him as various officials began to mutter that justice had not been done. The Deadwood verdict could not be legally recognised and McCall would have to be retried in proper fashion.

To his great surprise, McCall found himself arrested again for murder and locked up in Yankton, South Dakota.

Word spread across the nation about Hickok's sad end, reaching his family in Illinois where his estranged mother took it badly. His brother Lorenzo, who had returned to Troy Grove from his life out West, made a point of travelling to Yankton so as to represent the family at McCall's trial.

The assassin languished in his jail cell for weeks, then months, before making a desperate bid to escape, but this attempt was foiled, knocking the fight out of him.

The trial lasted for six days during which McCall claimed that he had indeed accepted money from one of Deadwood's shady figures to kill Hickok, but this desperate attempt to turn state's evidence led nowhere.

Further facts disclosed by recalled witnesses proved overpoweringly against the accused and this time there was no doubt that he was guilty of murder.

Jack McCall's fate was officially sealed and on January 3rd. 1877 he was sentenced to death. Even so, there were still several attempts to commute that sentence, instigated by those who clung to the less savoury aspects of Hickok's reputation.

It was to no avail and McCall was hanged on March 1st.. The noose was so tightly embedded around his neck that he was buried with the severed rope still in place.

Wild Bill's wife, Agnes, managed to visit his grave the year after his death and eventually had a monument erected in his honour. She remarried but it was a union which did not last long and she returned to work in John Robinson's Circus until 1880, after which she lived a more settled life with her married daughter, Emma. For the last decade of her life she struggled on as an invalid, passing away at Emma's home in 1907. She was buried alongside her first husband, Bill Lake, in Cincinatti.

Colorado Charlie Utter was deeply upset by the loss of his friend for they had grown quite close during their final short relationship. Having arranged the funeral of Hickok, burying him with his rifle, Utter moved on from Deadwood to open saloons and dance halls across the West. He returned to the infamous Gulch, however, in 1879, just in time to establish another dance hall and set himself up as a theatre manager before a devastating fire tore through the town totally destroying most of it.

Despite all the chaos of that trip, Charlie moved Wild Bill's body to another location; the Mount Moriah cemetery on the slopes above the town. This had proven necessary because the town was expanding and the existing cemetery was in the path of progress. The opportunity was taken to take a look at the corpse which was found to be in a quite remarkable state of preservation, calcified by some process in the soil. His features were still distinct and those present remarked how peaceful he looked, even showing the traces of a benign smile. Hickok's long, lustrous hair remained in perfect condition and a lock of it was taken for posterity. The rifle was also removed and before the coffin lid was replaced, Charlie took one long final look at his old friend.

And so Wild Bill endured his second burial, and there he rests, with a heartfelt sentiment on his marker (even though Charlie spelled his surname incorrectly) ...

"Wild Bill J.B.Hickock killed by the assassin Jack McCall in Deadwood Black Hills, August 2nd. 1876. Pard, we will meet again in the happy hunting ground to part no more. Goodbye, Colorado Charlie, C.H.Utter."

Charlie went on to diverse business interests and ended up opening drugstores as far away as South America. He died in Panama in 1915 and is buried there.

Calamity Jane got considerable mileage out of her questionable connection with Wild Bill and no doubt held court about it in numerous barrooms for years to come. That said, she did have a kind heart when pressed and the caring, selfless work she did looking after victims of the Deadwood smallpox epidemic is remembered fondly. In later years she may have owned a ranch in Montana before Buffalo Bill employed her in his Wild West extravaganza where she excelled as a flamboyant storyteller. Her alcoholism was her downfall, however, and, in 1903, she fell ill following a characteristic heavy drinking bout on a train to Terry, South Dakota, where she died, aged 51.

Her dying request... *"Bury me next to Wild Bill"* was granted... almost.

Buffalo Bill Cody became an enormous international star. Parting with Texas Jack Omohundro in 1877, they both went on to tour separate productions but Bill was by far the more successful. Texas Jack founded his own acting troupe but died of pneumonia, aged just 33, in 1880.

Cody was very ambitious and worked hard to fulfil his dream of bringing the Wild West to the world. As he built it up, he would often still return to the frontier inbetween seasons to maintain his authentic life as a real scout for the army. In 1876, following the defeat of Custer's 7th. Cavalry at the Little Big Horn, the fight against the Plains Indians had gone into overdrive and the army were pursuing the hostile bands with a vengeance. That same summer, Cody was present at Warbonnet Creek where he claimed to have killed and scalped the Cheyenne chief Yellow Hair, waving the bloody trophy in the air as he declared that he had taken the *"first scalp for Custer"*. This is an incident which he would replay, to great dramatic effect, in his future shows.

Founded in all its glory in 1883, Buffalo Bill's Wild West touring production was a sensation wherever it went, featuring spectacular displays of cowboy skills and re-enactments of exciting events from the frontier. It had a huge, energetic and colourful cast and would often include appearances from the likes of sharpshooter Annie Oakley and even the Sioux Chief Sitting Bull, Custer's legendary final opponent.

In 1887 the whole caboodle was shipped across the Atlantic at the invite of Queen Victoria to celebrate her Golden Jubilee where it enjoyed a six month run in London. Come 1889, it was touring Europe and Cody even had an audience with the Pope.

Buffalo Bill's incredible efforts were responsible for creating the image of the Wild West which laid the groundwork for Hollywood and the distorted glamourisation of cowboys, Indians and all the sanitized stuff so many of us grew up with. But people loved it. In 1894, Edison Studios shot thousands of feet of film to immortalise it all, but, sadly, much of this was lost. What remains are some wonderful emotive moving images (albeit black, white and silent) of how it must have been.

As mentioned earlier, Buffalo Bill established the town of Cody, Wyoming, in 1895, building a grand hotel there and naming it after his daughter, Irma.

But even the great Buffalo Bill had to grow old and his health began to fail, even though he struggled to remain in the saddle to front his shows.

As mentioned earlier, he had been awarded the Congressional Medal of Honour for his bravery in actions against the hostile tribes, but just before he died, in 1917, there was, sadly, a campaign to revoke the award for non military recipients. This churlish action was endorsed by Congress and Cody, along with many other scouts and technically civilian heroes, had their medals taken away from them. Fortunately, the legendary old scout and showman died just before this was made official so he at least never heard of the indignity.

Cody's family were outraged and they, and many others, fought for years to have the honours restored. It was quite a battle but, in 1989, the arguments were recognised and Buffalo Bill, and others, had their medals reinstated.

Buffalo Bill Cody is buried, as he wished, on Lookout Mountain, overlooking the Great Plains.

General George Armstrong Custer (whose actual rank at the time of his death was Lieutenant Colonel, but usually referred to by his brevetted Civil War rank of General) had played a quite significant role in Wild Bill's career and had certainly helped to solidify his fame. The pair lost touch mainly after Hickok's violent troubles with the General's 7th. Cavalry in Hays City, but Custer always seemed to retain a soft spot for the scout he continued to admire and praise in print.

Known as *Long Hair* to his enemies, the Sioux and Cheyenne, Custer's reputation as an Indian fighter grew throughout the 1870s although, apart from his attack on a village at the Washita in 1868, his only pitched battle with them was his final one, on the slopes above the Little Big Horn River in Montana on June 25th. 1876 when he and five troops of the 7th. were famously wiped out. (I have written about that in detail in my book *From Crockett to Custer*.)

On the day of Custer's disaster, Hickok was in final preparations for his expedition to the Black Hills with Colorado Charlie, but he surely would have learned about it when he reached Deadwood.

The fellow card player who shared the same bullet with Wild Bill at that final fatal card game found a separate infamy for years after the shooting.

Captain Bill Massie had taken leave from his renowned position as a river boat pilot to try his luck in the Black Hills Gold Rush, although, like Hickok, had been distracted by the lure of the card table. The Captain was very experienced on his river runs between St. Louis and Fort Benton. McCall's bullet which had ripped through Hickok's head, exiting through his right cheek and burying itself in Massie's wrist remained there, or so Massie claimed. (Some said he had it surgically removed.) Nine years after the incident, in 1885, the Captain caused quite a stir when he showed up in Bismarck, prompting the local *Daily Tribune* to run a story headlined *"The ball that killed Wild Bill arrived in the city yesterday…"*

Massie led a colourful life anyway, but sharing that ball ensured his lasting fame. Maybe he really did always carry it with him and into his grave when he passed on, in St.Louis, in 1910.

Of course, Hickok encountered all manner of characters and desperadoes during his adventurous life and it would not be practical to list them all, but I will grant a final mention to a couple…

Ben Thompson, for instance, who outlived Wild Bill by quite a few years. Despite surviving lots of gunplay and dangerous situations, he was finally ambushed and killed in a fusillade of bullets, alongside his friend King Fisher, in a theatre box in San Antonio in 1884. His younger, trouble making brother Billy made it all the way to 1897 before dying of natural causes; not the usual exit for men of his calibre in the West.

And Wes Hardin who had experienced those dalliances with Hickok in Abilene. Following his flight from town, aged just eighteen, he relished a career which underlined his reputation as a psychotic killer who really did seem to enjoy putting bullets through people. He was involved in many gunfights and random killings which were largely the result of his evil temper and tendency to take offence easily. Involved in the Sutton/Taylor feud of 1875, Hardin claimed to have gunned down approximately forty men before being jailed for twenty years in 1878. He actually served seventeen years during which time he studied and obtained a licence to practice law, as well as writing his auto-biography.

Released in 1895, he made his way to El Paso where he got in a further argument with lawman John Selman. This confrontation expanded to include Selman's father, John Sr., who apparently took it to heart. The day after their row, Hardin was playing dice in the Acme Saloon when Selman the elder burst in and shot him through the back of the head, ending his life in an almost carbon copy of Hickok's death.

***

This has been a condensed telling of the tale of Wild Bill Hickok; a tale which has been told many times since his death, ensuring his immortality for as long as interest in such colourful and fascinating characters exists.

I have done my best to keep to the verifiable facts, only embroidered by personal observations of what I have learned through my own respectful research.

Resisting going into too much detail has been a challenge, but you can find that extra information in a wealth of publications. I would just advise caution when choosing which sources you might peruse. There are many, but, confusingly, and sadly, most are deceiving... mishmashes of fact and fiction. The legend of Hickok was embellished to a ridiculous degree, starting with Nichols' flowery *Harper's* article but then getting blown out of all proportion over the decades that followed.

J.W.Buel, one of Wild Bill's earliest biographers published his so called definitive life story of Hickok in the 1880s and it is largely fiction. The problem is that so many writers, and would be historians, have since then used Buel's material as a source of studious knowledge and this is where so many of the stories have blurred between pure fantasy and what really happened.

This is a shame because I have always felt, since making a serious study of Hickok's life, that the simple truth of what we can be pretty sure he did is fascinating and exciting enough without any need for all the absurd embellishment. Why mar it all and give cause for doubt when the facts will more than suffice?

My interest in Wild Bill was stirred when I was a child, initially by films and television, like so many of my generation. I was fascinated by history in general, but particularly the Wild West. One of my very first delves into a serious appraisal of an historical figure was when I found a paperback copy of Richard O'Connor's *The Life and Times of the West's Greatest Gunfighter: WILD BILL HICKOK*.

I loved this book and devoured it almost at a single sitting. It is very well written, stirring, exciting, filled with details, dates and a factual style which is highly convincing... to a novice. However, having spent years believing that these pages contained the truth about this incredible figure, I eventually realised, following my own gradual increase in historical knowledge, that the book is at least 50% false. It came to me that O'Connor was a writer, not a serious researcher or historian, who had relied almost entirely on material he had gleaned from the likes of Buel, then coloured by a fanciful imagination which painted his own view of the West.

Many other writers, though well intentioned, fell into a similar trap, regurgitating that same false information and even adding their own embellishments. The result was that Hickok emerges as one of the most confusing and hard to pin down figures of the whole genre.

By contrast, we can thank one man whose diligent research and dedication to the subject has unearthed a wealth of verifiable fact, much of it gleaned from his long association with Hickok's descendants. And he was an Englishman... Joseph G.Rosa (1932-2015). Now, he was a proper researcher whose lifelong passion for the true details of Wild Bill's life led to the publication of several intriguing books which separate the "man from the myth". Rosa's thirst for knowledge and determination to get to the very roots of everything that can possibly be discovered about his subject is quite mind blowing. He spent over fifty years turning every Hickok story inside out and would accept nothing until it could be proven, with intelligent analysis, beyond reasonable doubt.

Balance that against most of the other material and it is "no contest".

That said, there are still reams of writings which are worth delving into but, in my experience, Rosa is the one to fully trust.

There are several social media sites devoted to Wild Bill too and they are worth becoming a part of, once you get used to some of the more eccentric and misinformed contributors. Overall, it is positive and does help to broaden one's view!

Wild Bill has featured in many Western films since the earliest days of motion pictures. Cecil B. DeMille's *The Plainsman* (1936), starring Gary Cooper as Hickok is an enjoyable romp but forget the historical truth. Just about every other portrayal of Wild Bill on the screen has been just as fictional, if not worse, but interest in him as a character, right up to the time of writing, never seems to wain. The excellent HBO television series *Deadwood* was rather good, with a gritty realistic feel, featuring many genuine real life figures from the period. Keith Carradine's Wild Bill was fairly convincing, but the best for me, to date, was by Jeff Bridges in Walter Hill's *Wild Bill* (1995). Bridges is great in the role, looks virtually perfect and succeeds in recreating Hickok's vibe in many ways. Such a shame that the plot is absurd, including a ridiculously good looking Calamity Jane who Hickok happily canoodles with. Hmmm... I don't think so!

The real Wild Bill lives vividly in my imagination. Unlike many of the characters of the Old West, Hickok left us with many photographic images of himself, dating from the early 1860s right up to just a few months before his death. These portraits show him in several different guises... the plainsman, the dandy, the gunfighter and the showman, so we are fortunate to have a pretty good impression of how he looked during each phase of his career.

I can really picture him, and hear him too... soft spoken, courteous in mixed company, those who knew him said... yet more than capable of meeting the rough and savage elements of frontier society when called upon to do so.

He was streetwise and tough but his wily intelligence shines through the numerous accounts which have been handed down to us.

Out of all the Old West figures whose legend still survives, I think Hickok is my favourite. There is something unique about him, a special quality which, to me, qualifies him in a league of his own. It's not just the undeniable physical impressiveness of the man, nor the verifiable character traits which seem to me to prove that he possessed an inherent basic decency, a backbone of honesty and fairplay, as well as unshakeable courage. True, his ego must have been rather pronounced, and yet at the same time there remained an undercurrent of modesty, even elements of shyness. He was a killer, for sure, but always, as far as we know, for a justifiable reason... the result of upholding the law or in defence of his life.

He certainly would have been a man you would have wanted in your corner during a sticky situation when the chips were down.

Wild Bill Hickok... maximum respect.

PART TWO
BILLY THE KID

CHAPTER 13

FIRST BLOOD

Saturday, August 17th. 1877... Atkins Saloon, Bonita, South East Arizona.

"*Pimp...*" snarled the burly Irishman near the bar.

It was not the first time that he had hurled this inappropriate, yet deliberately wounding, insult at the youth known as Kid Antrim.

Sixteen years old, young Henry (his actual name) was a target for a blustering bully like Frank "Windy" Cahill. Windy, who was about twice the boy's age, was the blacksmith up at the nearby army post of Camp Grant, and he had earned his nickname from loud personality traits such as being a "blowhard" who sounded off about everything. He was a big character, weighing a solid 200 pounds or so. A tough, swaggering fellow from a tough job of fire and steel, confident of throwing his considerable weight around.

Cahill was a long way from his birthplace in Galway, Ireland, but the American Western frontier had long been his home.

Kid Antrim came from a very different mould, though he could also claim Irish ancestry. Evidence does seem to strongly suggest that his parents were immigrants from across the Atlantic Ocean, who spent their earliest times in the New World surviving the slums of New York City where Henry was likely born sometime between September and November 1859. His mother's name was Catherine and she was married to a man named McCarty, but he disappeared early on, though the details are lost. It was during the Civil War years, so maybe he died in the conflict, or just left his family, or... who knows?

Anyway, Catherine soon travelled inland, winding up in Indiana with Henry and his brother Joe (there have been doubts about him being senior or junior to Henry, but he was probably the latter). Catherine, a widow alone, undoubtedly struggled to support her boys so she must have been relieved to team up with war veteran and drifter William Antrim around 1865, even though he was about a dozen years younger than her. Along with so many other pioneers of the time, they drifted further west in search of a living and it appears they found it in Wichita, Kansas, in 1870, where Catherine established a successful laundry business, known locally as a *"jolly Irish lady"*. They bought land and put down roots until Catherine's tuberculosis forced the family to yet again push west in pursuit of drier, healthier climes.

Via Denver, Colorado, they swung south into New Mexico, delving deep into remote and wild areas which had not yet been reached by the ever expanding railroad. The beautiful yet starkly raw mountains, plains, forests and deserts of New Mexico could certainly be viewed as a land of opportunity, but it needed pure guts and foresight to establish oneself there. This vast area had become part of Mexico in 1821 but the Mexican/American War had resulted in it being ceded to the USA in 1848 although it did not officially join the Union until 1912 when it was granted the status of the 47th. American state.

That was all way off in the future, however, so the Antrims found themselves in a land fraught with numerous dangers, not least of all the risk of marauding Apache Indians and roaming bands of outlaws who viewed travellers as easy prey. Initially, they sought refuge in the biggest settlement... Santa Fe... which already had quite a history behind it. The town was centred around the ancient square, dominated by the long established Palace of the Governors which had stood there for close on three centuries... the oldest state capital in the country. It was a bubbling hive of activity, a focus of comings and goings into and out of the wild frontier... buckskin clad mountain men, ox trains, huge wagons, cattlemen, half breeds, traders, gamblers, prostitutes, characters of every description, mostly mounted and armed to the teeth and ready to protect their interests at the slightest provocation... the epitome of the Wild West indeed.

Yet the vast majority of the populace were predominantly Hispanic, overseen by a small Anglo elite of businessmen, lawyers, opportunists and those who could spot a chance to exploit any loophole. A sharp eye and a ruthless temperament created a Mafia like circle which became known as the *Santa Fe Ring*. The tentacles of this mob spread far and wide across the territory, as we shall see later.

Maybe this was all too much for the Antrims because they moved on yet again, but not before William and Catherine finally got married, in the town's First Presbyterian Church, on March 1st. 1873, with the boys Henry and Joe as witnesses.

So now it was south, down the course of the Rio Grande, past Albuquerque, a couple of hundred miles before turning west to Silver City, a mining town where William had his sights, hopefully, on a rich strike.

The area was strewn with fertile soil, so there were many farms dotted all over the valley, and the town was quite eastern looking compared to the other places they had lived in of late, with two storey brick buildings nestling alongside squat little adobe structures and narrow, shaded streets. Unlike Santa Fe, the population here was mainly Anglo. The family settled into a log cabin at the head of the stream bed, known as the Big Ditch.

Despite all this moving around and shaky settlement, Catherine ensured that her boys were educated. Henry, in particular, was, by all accounts, a good student, well schooled and pleasant according to his teachers at the time. From very early on, associates spoke of him as having a delightful personality, always smiling and good humoured, and willing to help. He was generally popular and people welcomed his company, a trait which he maintained for the whole of his short life. He was literate too, devouring books any chance he had, also the widely read dime novels which were all the rage in his day, and copies of the Police Gazette (which must have opened his eyes to the world of law and order). Having spent a lot of time mixing with the Hispanic community, he made it his business to learn their language fluently and willingly mix with them. Unlike most white folks, it seemed that he had a natural affinity in the world of the Hispanics and they quickly grew to love him for it.

Another passion of the teenaged Henry proved to be in entertainment. When he was about fourteen, another older associate described him as *"a scrawny little fellow with delicate hands and an artistic nature"*. He helped found a minstrel troupe in which he was regarded as the "Head Man of the Show" when they put on performances at Morrill's Opera House in town. Little Henry Antrim really loved to sing and dance, one of his favourite songs being the current hit *Silver Threads Among the Gold* which had become immensely popular throughout the land since its composition by Danks & Rexford in 1872. Ever the showman, one can imagine his rendering of this mournfully sentimental ballad with its meaningful lyrics of love and aging, especially from one so full of the sparkle of youth. When being more lively, he particularly enjoyed dancing to reels like *Turkey in the Straw*, and he really knew how to move, it is said.

So, it would seem that young Henry and his brother may have been destined to live a pretty respectable life had fate not dealt them a cruel hand. Their mother Catherine's tuberculosis had been steadily worsening and throughout several months, in 1874, she was bedbound, finally passing away in mid September.

Following a funeral service in the cabin, the loss of Catherine's steady and caring influence had a dramatic effect on all the Antrims.

Old Bill's response was to almost immediately distance himself from the boys. Before long he had taken off for the Arizona strikes, effectively abandoning them and forcing them to fend for themselves, lodging with whoever they could in exchange for odd jobs. They were actually separated from each other at this point, living apart in different places.

This was a baptism of fire and they needed to adapt quickly in order to survive.

Losing his mother at such a tender age must have been traumatic for Henry and it can be easily imagined how the tragedy was complicated by his abandonment. However, he and brother Joe were resourceful, even though they no longer had the authority of parental guidance to keep them in check. They trod their own very different paths. (Just out of interest, it is known that Joe was not like his brother, neither physically nor in temperament. Apparently he was quite broad in build with a somewhat dull personality. When he and Henry drifted apart, he hung around Silver City for a while, not pursuing anything in particular, then spent his life aimlessly eking out a living from gambling. Sadly, no one ever troubled to interview him properly about his legendary sibling who morphed into Billy the Kid… a wasted opportunity if ever there was one… and he died penniless in Denver in 1930.)

Unsupervised, young Henry (as he was still known then) found work in various outlets, but he fell deeply under the influence of Silver City's underworld, enjoying excitement and activity within the town's unsavoury elements of society. A drunken tearaway known as Sombrero Jack (named, obviously, for his distinctive Mexican style headgear) became something of a hero to the boy and he took to following him around. Jack was an habitual thief and ne'er do well and he was happy to enlist the help of this sycophantic youth, off loading much of his dirty work onto him.

In September 1875 (around the anniversary of his mother's death) following several near misses which included escapes, Henry finally had the law catch up with him. At Sombrero Jack's urging, young Antrim assisted in stealing clothes from the Chinese laundry of Sun & Chung, after which Henry was persuaded to hide the booty at his lodgings. When his landlady discovered this, she quickly evicted him, then turned him in to the local Sheriff. Locked up in a cell, Henry took the wrap alone as the local paper reported that Sombrero Jack had *"skinned out"*.

Hardly being the crime of the century, it is recorded that the Sheriff's intention was to do nothing more than keep the boy incarcerated for a brief period without charge, to teach him a lesson, but Henry did not delay in demonstrating his determination and resourcefulness. Slender, wiry and flexible, he soon found an opportunity to wriggle his way up the chimney and onto the jailhouse roof and, from there, a stolen horse and freedom.

Henry presumably saw himself as some kind of arch villain because he used this minor misdemeanour as an excuse to vacate the territory in great haste, leaving his old life behind to seek new pastures.

It is at this point that his activities melt into obscurity because his whereabouts for several months are lost in the mists of time. Although we do know that he headed west, across the border into Arizona where he turned up the following year in the vicinity of the military post at Camp Grant.

Just south of the parade ground, within a mile or two, a scattered settlement had sprung up to furnish the needs of the civilian element which inevitably attaches itself to the army. Buildings began to dot the flatlands with a hotel, a general store, saloons and outlets of many descriptions. These places and the surrounding land brought work options for Henry and he took advantage of several of them. He herded sheep, drove wagons as a teamster, toiled in a sawmill, even worked in Woods Hotel, but it was being taken on as a ranch hand which really suited him... or so he thought. It was on the vast ranch of Henry Hooker which supplied beef to several military posts, including Camp Grant, as well as the lucrative contract at the San Carlos Indian Agency.

Henry Antrim took to this work with renewed passion and relished picking up the basic skills of cow punching, tending horses, riding, roping and all things cowboy. Also, for the first time, and with the encouragement of his fellow wranglers, he was able to concentrate on learning all about firearms, a skill which he embraced keenly. Very soon he became quite a marksman with pistol and rifle and, no doubt, acquired his own weapons.

Despite such enthusiasm, the ranch foreman did not see things in quite the same way and was not impressed by Henry's obvious youthful lack of experience. Although he was proving himself to be a fast learner, the slim, baby faced youth was dismissed from Hooker's employ and found himself rootless again.

Never one to remain idle or self pitying, Henry soon found another *compadre* to ally himself with, but, once more, it was a new friend of dubious character. Scotsman John Mackie, ten years Henry's senior, was an ex cavalryman and Civil War veteran, but he was also something of a hoodlum.

He and Henry were soon indulging in petty crime which quickly transformed into outright theft, mainly of stable accessories, bridles, saddles and so on, along with the occasional stolen horse.

On at least one other occasion, he was arrested but slipped his shackles over his small hands (not for the first time) and *"skeedaddled"*.

Henry also began to run with gangs of rustlers, a boy in a man's world who proved himself able and was thus accepted by them. Indeed the cowboys at the Hooker ranch and the rustlers he rode with taught him the rudiments of range life by learning on the job. They began to call him Kid Antrim because of his beardless, boyish looks, but at the same time they respected him as one of the boys.

His wiry, slim frame had been toughened by hard, outdoor work in and out of the saddle. Narrow shouldered but growing muscular, standing about 5 feet 7 to 8 inches tall, he had a long neck, surmounted by an oval shaped face. Clear blue eyes shone out from a wavy shock of blondish, brown hair. Then there was his small mouth and thin lips, which were usually parted by that pair of slightly protruding front teeth which, some said, gave him a vaguely squirrelish appearance. That said, virtually all surviving descriptions portray him as an attractive young man, uniquely handsome and always ready to laugh good naturedly. (The one truly verifiable photograph of him, the famous faded tintype, is not flattering and everyone who knew him said it was not a good likeness.) Good company, popular, warm and friendly... this was the side of the Kid which his many friends knew, with the added advantage of being literate and fairly well educated in a world where most of his contemporaries were not.

It was thus that Kid Antrim matured quickly, in experience and attitude if not in appearance. *"The Code of the West"* now came naturally to him and he took to the culture of gunmanship and horses with gusto. He also gave much attention, as he had always done, to all things Hispanic, spending much time with the people and improving his already strong knowledge of their language to the extent that he could speak it like a native.

This, and the qualities mentioned previously, endeared him to many, who also recognised in him a superior intelligence, quick wit and lightning fast reactions. He was a big hit with the young senoritas too who appeared to adore him even beyond the grave, as we shall see later on in this story.

Apart from all this, Kid Antrim's other big passion was saloon life. Although he barely drank much alcohol himself, he thoroughly enjoyed the atmosphere within these rough establishments, surrounded by inebriated toughs from all aspects of the Old West. Cowboys, gamblers, whores... he fitted within this world on his own terms. He also loved the card tables and spent much time at them, becoming an accomplished poker player and, eventually, a skilled Monte dealer.

Any excuse to dance or sing and he could well be the first to take the floor.

So, this was how he found himself in the situation which opened this chapter; facing the daunting prospect of another clash with the bullying blacksmith Windy Cahill.

Cahill was a rare soul in that he did not like young Antrim. Most people could not resist the boy's charms, but Cahill was not only naturally aggressive but also probably jealous of such youthful popularity. The Kid's cheery nature likely sank into darkness whenever Windy was around.

They were both present in George Atkins Saloon on that particular Saturday evening. Whoever arrived first is not recorded but I think we can assume that the Kid did not welcome the big man's presence. Cahill could never resist picking on the smaller youth and had done so regularly, ruffling his hair, slapping him and throwing him to the ground amidst a torrent of abuse... always when a crowd was present to achieve maximum humiliation. In addition, Cahill was known to have knifed the servant of an army officer.

It is said that Antrim had purchased some new clothes and that Cahill scoffed at this fresh look. One witness described the youth as looking like a *"Country Jake"*, wearing shoes instead of boots, and "store pants" with a pistol stuck in them, either waist band or pocket. Being August, it was probably a warm evening so he likely wore no coat or jacket. Cahill eventually called him a pimp. The Kid was many things, but I think we can be sure that an agent for prostitutes he was not, so it was a peculiar accusation.

It seems this was an insult too far and Antrim's response was to call the bully a *"son of a bitch"*, which was a pretty standard Western insult.

Cahill flared up at this and, in front of all present, went for the youth, arms flailing. They tussled back and forth, but the Kid had little chance against the solid beef of the big man and they soon fell to the floor with Antrim's meagre 135 pounds pinned beneath Windy's 200 or so.

Cahill sat astride the boy, spluttering with rage, as he commenced his slapping routine again. The Kid struggled but could not shift the smothering bulk which held him captive.

Whether Windy was armed is not recorded but young Antrim, wriggling like crazy, managed to free one arm for long enough to reach for the pistol in his pants. Grasping the handle, he pulled the weapon clear, slid it around to waist level, cocked it and pulled the trigger.

The big man must have jerked with the shock of being hit by a sledge hammer. Immediately relaxing his grip on his victim, he went as loose as a hanged man, slumping sideways to the wooden floor as he clutched at the gaping wound in his belly.

Kid Antrim straightaway jumped to his feet, the pistol still smoking in his hand. He looked around at the stunned witnesses then sprinted for the door.

Outside he found a tethered horse, vaulted into the saddle and was away like the wind.

It is not clear if he actually disappeared in that moment. Some reports say he was arrested and locked up in the Camp Grant guardhouse… if so, he manufactured yet another of his habit forming escapes for he was soon gone, this time a fugitive from his first killing… not at twelve, as the legend says, but at sixteen.

As for Windy Cahill, they took him, in agony, to the fort's infirmary where he lingered, groaning, until the following day.

He dictated a statement declaring who he was, where he was from, a description of his two sisters who lived at different sides of the country, and an account of the fight with Henry "Kid" Antrim. *"I did not hit him"* he whined defensively, but the witnesses remembered it differently.

Ultimately, it did not really matter for Windy because he died before nightfall.

A coroner's jury declared the shooting *"criminal and unjustifiable"* but the shooter was gone.

Ironically, had the Kid remained to face the music, in the circumstances and in the loose letter of the law of those days, he almost certainly would have been cleared by the territorial jury on the grounds of self defence, and his popular life could have carried on. Nobody would really miss Windy Cahill.

For Kid Antrim, matters had escalated to another level. Stealing clothes and saddles, rustling a few cows, even the odd horse theft… it all paled into insignificance now.

He had taken a life and could now truly regard himself as an outlaw.

***

September 2004… on the road, heading east along Interstate 10, crossing the state line into New Mexico. Turning north at Lordsburg (with memories of

John Wayne's gunfight there in his movie STAGECOACH) the 90 drives on into the Gila National Forest where the country gives way, obviously, to densely wooded hills. And then came Silver City, where Billy spent his early teens.

Booking into the old Palace Hotel, on Broadway in the centre of town, the heart of what is known as the Historic District, this seemed like the place for me...

Historic indeed. The buildings all have the flavour of the late 1800s, but everything was so quiet, almost like a ghost town. It was early evening, but the streets were eerily silent, not even any traffic to speak of. I even had to drive back out of town to find somewhere to eat.

The next morning was not really any more lively. Exploring the area, there was still hardly anyone around. The atmosphere was sleepy and slow paced but soon took on a charm of its own. I walked along the Big Ditch, the site of the city's original Main Street before it was washed away by the floods of the 1890s. This would have obliterated just about all that Billy would have recognised, in fact only one of the original buildings survived. I crossed the bridge over the pretty creek and found the log cabin which film director Ron Howard donated to the park here. It was used in his film THE MISSING and is a reasonable replica of the cabin Billy would have dwelt in with his mother, stepfather and brother.

Not much to see at Bonita either. The site of Atkin's saloon, where Billy tangled with Windy Cahill, is a modern store now. Likewise Camp Grant which is located on private land. It is barren and overgrown with cactus and mesquite. The rubble of the scant ruins is barely visible.

A winding and steep road took me up towards the Gila cliff dwellings and hot springs, reaching the rather quaint little hamlet of Pinos Altos. The deserted Buckhorn Saloon and Opera House were well worth the visit, wonderfully preserved.

The road grew heavily wooded with many sharp curves and steep inclines, a beautiful drive but intense and somewhat torturous, forty miles of it, then back the same way. No other cars, just solitude. I could not help thinking of how these gorgeous surroundings would have once been a no go area for a lone traveller.

Renegade Apaches dominated this land back in the mid 1800s when men like John Joel Glanton roamed around, leading his pack of merciless scalp hunters. Glanton was a vicious brute of epic proportions who savagely exploited the governor's policy of paying reward money for Apache scalps; man, woman and child. Glanton's gang hunted down and massacred all the dark haired people he could find, even innocent Mexicans whose scalps he could pass off as Indian. When the authorities got wise to this, Glanton turned total outlaw, carrying on with his murderous crimes until he and his gang were overcome by a vengeful tribe of Yumas, finally suffering a taste of their own medicine.

South of Silver City, the country gradually becomes much flatter, giving way to the Chihuahuan desert region. Eventually you find yourself approaching what at first appears to be an almost mirage-like vision in the far distance. It actually resembles a modern skyline of skyscrapers looming up out of the wilderness until closer proximity reveals it to be what is known as the City of Rocks. This is a unique natural phenomenon; a square mile feature formed by the eruption of a volcano over thirty million years ago. Huge, naturally sculpted rock formations tower as high as forty feet, smooth columns divided by the erosion of time which has created pathways like lanes and city streets. Stunning to behold and like something from another world.

This was the West of Henry Antrim, the Kid, and much of it is still exactly as he would have experienced it...

CHAPTER 14
APPRENTICE OUTLAW

So, how was Kid Antrim feeling as he rode away from the scene of his debut as a killer?

Scared? Panicky? Regretful?

Judging by what we know of his nature, probably none of these things... certainly not for long anyway.

On the contrary, he was most likely elated to be forced out of a growing rut. True that apart from his clashes with Cahill, his life in Arizona was fine. He was well liked, busy and enjoying what he was continuously learning, but where was it heading?

This new drama gave him purpose, albeit that it made him a fugitive. However, the chances are he basked in that role. Now he could honestly identify with all those figures he had read about in dime novels and the Police Gazette. He could regard himself as special as he entered the next chapter of his life.

Picture him as he cantered along, slouched easily in the saddle of yet another stolen horse, kicking up dust in the yawning landscape which stretched away on every side, back across the border into New Mexico again. He could feel safe in the knowledge that the Arizona authorities would not bother making the effort of trying to follow him into another territory.

His conscience was clear. Cahill had got what was coming to him and the Kid could justify what he had done in terms of doing the community a favour. All alone and taking the trail east to an unspecified fresh adventure, he was doubtless smiling away to himself, whistling merrily and not giving a damn.

And he was well prepared for whatever lay ahead. In his short life to date he had packed in a lot of experience, having travelled many hundreds of miles across the Continent, lived in several diverse places, immersed himself in numerous cultures, honed necessary skills.

He was ready.

First of all, he headed for refuge with a friendly rancher he knew in the Burro Mountains, south west of Silver City, but he did not remain there for long. These were familiar surroundings for him but he knew he had to keep moving.

That said, he took the time to cautiously look up a few sympathetic faces from the past, including his brother Joe, but it would be the last time they would ever see each other.

The Kid had found yet another shady character to identify with...

one Jesse Evans. Evans had arrogance, ruthlessness and a penchant for criminal behaviour. Having come up from Texas in 1872, this hard figure, with bandit leadership qualities stamped all over him, had initially been in the employ of cattle baron John Chisum. Chisum's empire spread for thousands of acres of prime New Mexican grassland and he could use men like Evans. Mescalero Apaches regularly descended from their mountain reservation to decimate his cattle herds so, in retaliation, Chisum would send his own roughnecks... men like Evans... to take back what was his.

A seasoned rustler, Evans drifted further west, teaming up with a kindred spirit named John Kinney who owned a ranch near Mesilla. Together, Evans and Kinney took the outlaw trail and began to indulge in all manner of nefarious past times. Evans formed his own gang, known as The Boys, who roamed all over southern New Mexico, causing havoc and occasionally using Kinney's ranch as a refuge.

Evans was soon on the wanted list for several killings.

These are the men who Kid Antrim teamed up with, initially in the Burro Mountains where it seems he helped them to steal some horses before heading back east. Apart from Evans, the bandit group included one Frank Baker who would shortly play a significant role in the Kid's destiny.

For two months Kid Antrim rode with The Boys and their company had a huge influence upon him.

Rampaging around, the Evans gang left trouble in their wake. A pursuing posse was driven off in a sharp gun battle, and an attempted stagecoach robbery was only foiled because the driver convinced Evans that they carried nothing of value. They rode on brazenly and loudly, stopping at road houses to eat and drink their fill before leaving without paying. It seems no one had the backbone, or suicidal tendency, to try and stop them.

Riding through the mountain passes, they entered Lincoln County where in the small town of Tularosa, they got roaring drunk and commenced to *"hurrah"* the place... that is they shot it up with wildly aimed gunfire, terrorizing the inhabitants... particularly a man who had informed on one of their gang members. They terrified this fellow and his family, riddling his house with bullets, uncharacteristically sparing him but executing his dog.

One night they danced around a bonfire, singing and carousing as they declared the right to take whatever they wanted because, *"The public is our oyster!"*

Jesse Evans was proclaimed to be their Colonel and they fed the fire with a copy of a local newspaper which had written scathing things about them. Whooping and hollering, the drunken outlaws stomped in a wild procession around the flames before heading down towards the lower Pecos and the area known as Seven Rivers.

How much of this Kid Antrim was actively involved in, we can but guess, but he surely observed it all and must have been chewing over the thought of whether or not this kind of life was actually for him.

Yes, he was seeking stimulation and adventure but did he really want it in this rootless, aimless fashion? Essentially, The Boys were just proving themselves to be pretty mindless thugs and the Kid probably felt he was better than that.

For now, though, he went along with it, that is until mid October when the bulk of the gang holed up for a while at the ranch of a sympathiser. The Kid decided to make himself scarce and stayed instead at the home of a family called Jones whom he had befriended. It seems that this was a deliberate act of wanting to separate himself from The Boys, at least for a while.

He made the most of his sojourn with the Jones's, taking it easy and spending his time on target practice with his Colt revolver and Winchester rifle. Indeed, he was becoming exceptionally proficient as a marksman and general fancy handling of weapons. So much time in the saddle had made him an expert horseman too, and not just in a practical sense. He rode for pleasure and liked to show off to any available womenfolk. One wrote of his skills... of how he could pick up a cloth from the ground whilst riding at speed. He could also duck down alongside his mount at the gallop, firing from beneath its neck *"like an Apache"*. Young Lily Casey, a visitor, described him as being *"as graceful as a cat"*.

Kid Antrim's few weeks with The Boys had forced him to evolve to yet another level of maturity.

It had been a hard school amongst rough men and he had gleaned a great deal from it, absorbing lessons which would serve him well in what lay ahead.

Still only seventeen (or maybe just eighteen) years of age, he carried the bearing of a much older veteran whilst still retaining his boyish charm. That good nature and ready smile still shone through, but one was always left with the impression that his mood could turn in an instant if he felt it necessary. A hair trigger temper bubbled beneath the surface at all times, and it was one that could be backed up by swift and unhesitant gunplay.

His image was that of a genuine cowboy by now. He did not

particularly favour fancy attire, his garb was practical; dark frock coat, vest, pants tucked into knee high boots and a brightly coloured scarf around his neck. The most elaborate adornment was the wide brimmed sugar loaf sombrero which he liked to wear, but that was quite typical for the land he frequented.

Of course, on his hip, his high holstered six gun... either a Colt single action .44, known as the *Frontier*, or what became his favourite later on, the more compact Colt double action, self cocking .41, known as the *Thunderer*. He possessed impressive dexterity with any revolver, but his real expertise, and favour, lay with his Winchester '73 rifle which he could lever and fire with speed and accuracy.

His young features were still unmarked by the lines of passing years, yet a long term outdoor life on the range, battered by the elements of wind, rain and sun had resulted, naturally, in some effect of slightly leathery bronzing. Those small hands also bore the hallmarks of a working man.

Any attempt to grow a beard at this stage had merely resulted in some light downy fluff on his chin and cheeks, but his top lip usually sported a silky fuzziness of growth. At a short distance, you would not even notice it.

And his voice... we can only make an educated guess at how he would have sounded. He had grown up under the influence of his mother's Irish accent so that would have left its mark, but he had also mixed with all manner of people during his travels. Therefore the Hispanic brogue would have been evident too as their language came so easily to him. His early education would have been in contrast to what he absorbed once he began associating with the rougher side of society, resulting in a colourful blend of coarse sophistication. He was intelligent enough to probably act accordingly depending upon what company he was in.

Then there was one thing that Kid Antrim had seriously adopted since leaving Arizona... a new name. He was now William Bonney... or Billy Bonney. Where this had come from, no one is sure, but he made it clear that this was now how he wished to be addressed. He also still answered to Kid, but the title of Billy the Kid still lay in the future and would not be attached to him until the last few months of his life.

Billy's options were pretty open during this period. He was taking his time, pondering on where life might take him next, which hopefully would not be back alongside the Evans contingent.

A widow and her four children driving cattle to Texas stopped briefly at the Jones place and Billy, with his customary friendliness, had soon attached himself to them. He even asked if he could join them on their journey but his request was denied. It does show, however, that he was willing to try anything.

However, something was to happen which would draw him back to The Boys, temporarily.

Back in September, Jesse Evans and Frank Baker had purloined some horses from the ranch of Dick Brewer, who was also in the employ of an English born rancher named John Tunstall, as ranch foreman. (Both of the latter were to play a big role in Billy's future.)

Brewer was swiftly on the trail of these horse thieves but gave up having trailed them all the way to Mesilla, only to return to the Pecos, where he knew they were laying low, but this time with a sizeable posse of about fifteen men. This posse was supported by the Lincoln County Sheriff, William Brady. Catching up with the thieves, there was a brief exchange of bloodless gunfire before the fugitives surrendered. Evans and Baker, along with their *compadres,* Tom Hill and George Davis, were taken back to the town of Lincoln and thrown in jail.

Well, one could say jail, but Lincoln's only means of holding prisoners was a hole in the ground. This had come about following Sheriff Brady's unsuccessful bid to the County authorities for the funds to construct a proper holding area for miscreants. The minimal finance he had been awarded was only enough to throw together this unsatisfactory pit, about 10 feet deep, 30 long and 20 wide. It was lined with logs and separated into two cells with bars and rudimentary adobe covering across the top; lit by candles and with a trap door and ladder for access. Latrine facilities must have been disgustingly primitive. Not exactly secure, therefore escapes were not rare.

Billy was called upon to take part in liberating Evans and the others. About thirty of The Boys gathered on the Rio Ruidoso, just south west of Lincoln, and rode menacingly into town just before dawn on November 17th. 1877.

Now, this was a complicated situation... Lincoln County was on the brink of a melting pot of trouble which would soon explode into a full scale war between rival business factions. Sheriff Brady was very much on the side of one of these factions and had merely gone through the motions of arresting the Evans quartet for appearance's sake. The so called Lincoln elite wanted these potential mercenaries freed so that they could play a part in the pending conflict. Therefore, when the mob handed Boys rode in, the scene was set to make it very easy for them to "escape". The token resistance of a lone guard was a joke.

With Evans reunited with his small army of roughnecks, they cantered back down to the Pecos, Billy amongst them, but not for long. When the gang rode on from the Ruidoso to the lower Pecos Billy did not ride with them.

He was making new connections, the kind who appealed to him more than the Evans gang. Anglo ranchers with Hispanic wives or partners, settled civilized folk, many of whom might just be willing to step outside of the law if there was mutual benefit in it. Billy was soon in cahoots with many of them.

He received a particularly warm welcome at the ranch of Frank Coe who took an instant liking to him, describing Billy as good humoured, full of fun and a great story teller. Frank and his cousin George, who were both impressed by the youth's skill with guns, would also feature heavily in Billy's life. Strangely, Frank did not give the Kid the work he was seeking so he moved on further up the Ruidoso in search of gainful employment.

Before long, he found it.

CHAPTER 15
LINCOLN COUNTY

Billy's connection with Jesse Evans had introduced him to the territory which was to dominate the rest of his life.

Lincoln County is an enormous expanse of land covering some 30,000 square miles of south east New Mexico. To the west it is mountainous country, criss-crossed by a network of rivers, with the sprawling staked plains further east where the vast empire of cattle king John Chisum, centred near Roswell, held sway.

Dotted across the county, with daunting distances between them, lay the towns and smaller villages which were to feature in Billy's coming adventures. Las Vegas to the north (not be confused with the very different Nevada gambling city) and Fort Sumner on the Rio Pecos, White Oaks, Puerto de Luna, Anton Chico, Seven Rivers and Las Cruces.

Central to all this stood the small town of Lincoln, a few miles south of the slopes of the Capitan Mountains, it lay parallel to the banks of the Rio Bonito. With a population of less than 500, the settlement was originally founded by Mexican settlers in the 1850s and was known as *La Placita del Rio Bonito* which translates as the *The Place by the Pretty River*. The name was changed in 1869 with the creation of Lincoln County, in honour of the assassinated President Abraham Lincoln.

Lincoln in the late 1870s was a single dirt street stretching for a mile or so, on each side of which were a series of spaced out largely flat roofed adobe buildings. The slope roofed Murphy/Dolan Store at one end of the street was one of the larger, more imposing structures, almost opposite of which stood the hotel and restaurant owned by Sam Wortley. Near the far end of the street lay that hole in the ground which served as the jail, whilst in the centre of this metropolis one could find (and still can) the circular, two storey stone fortification known as the Torreon, which had been built by the first inhabitants as a defence against Apache raiders. By 1877 it had fallen into disrepair and was starting to crumble.

Opposite the Torreon was a large single roomed adobe inhabited by aging "Squire" John Wilson who served as Justice of the Peace. The district judge, based in Mesilla about 100 miles south west, would pay a couple of visits a year to Lincoln to preside over a makeshift courthouse.

Sheriff Brady had an office close to the jail pit, but he actually lived with his wife and children on a ranch beside the river four miles outside of town.

Just a few miles to the west stood the military base of Fort Stanton, named after an officer who had been killed in a skirmish with Apaches in 1855. It was garrisoned by the 9th. U.S. Cavalry, the troopers of which were entirely black African Americans, although, in keeping with the segregated values of the time, the regiment's officers were all white. The Fort itself had quite a dominating influence on the surrounding area.

The situation surrounding Lincoln and the simmering tension which was soon to escalate in the form of the Lincoln County War was complex, involving a tangled web of corruption, greed and a host of characters but, for the purposes of this condensed history, I will try to keep it as simple as possible.

For the full, detailed version, there are numerous excellent sources to be consulted, but, basically, it can be explained thus…

This raw, largely untapped territory was ripe for the taking, leaving it wide open to opportunists, and none took more advantage than Lawrence Murphy. He was an Irish immigrant from County Wexford who served in the Civil War before being mustered out of the army from Fort Stanton in 1866, aged about 35. Settling in the area, he quickly began to involve himself in nefarious deals such as selling land he did not own and securing dodgy contracts for supplying the military, the result of which was that he founded his business, L.G.Murphy and Co., in 1869.

In 1873 he met and quickly employed, as a clerk, another Irish immigrant (from County Galway), one James Dolan who was also a Civil War veteran. Dolan, in his mid twenties when he met Murphy, was a smooth faced, villainous sort, who was referred to as having *"an evil look"*. It seems he lived up to this reputation by his general behaviour, often drunk and *"cutting loose"* with the more unsavoury elements of Lincoln County, brandishing firearms and acting recklessly. However, he was obviously wily and industrious because he impressed Murphy enough to make him a partner in the business by 1874. Together they founded a banking and mercantile operation which was soon highly profitable, mainly because they had no competition and were able to demand outlandish prices from the locals, thereby causing much resentment.

Although he was in a potentially respected position of authority and commerce, Dolan did not withdraw from his wild ways. He took a shot at an army officer which brought trouble for the company from

Fort Stanton, plus he knifed a Mexican to death but was somehow able to wriggle out of any charges. From this moment on, he would hire men to do his killing for him.

The Murphy/Dolan partnership became known as *The House* and they centred their activities on the imposing building which dominated one end of Lincoln town.

Murphy and Dolan had many allies in their pockets, and they could well be considered to be part of the *Santa Fe Ring*, that all powerful group of politicians, economists and social manipulators who oversaw the territory with a blend of undisguised corruption... men like the Attorney General of New Mexico, Thomas Catron, who was the biggest land owner in the territory. From the same mould came the territorial governor Sam Axtell, territorial judge Warren Bristol, District Attorney William Rynerson and a host of others.

Lincoln Sheriff William Brady was deeply in the pockets of Murphy and Dolan, one of the main factors being the fact that the three of them, and other local countrymen, were all of the same heritage and obviously held a national affinity and understanding as Irish Roman Catholics.

Brady was the eldest of the trio, born in County Cavan in 1829, and his life leading up to Lincoln was eventful and action packed. His father having died young, he struggled to help his mother and siblings survive during the devastating potato famine which drove so many Irish families across the Atlantic. He made the journey himself, aged 21, joining the US army and attaining the rank of sergeant as he fought in campaigns against the Apaches and Navajos throughout the 1850s.

In 1859 he was assigned to the remote outpost of Fort Union, New Mexico, and then, at the outbreak of the Civil War soon afterwards, was transferred to Fort Craig as part of the defence of the territory against invading Confederate forces. He fought in the Battle of Glorietta Pass (1862) when the Confederacy were defeated. Brady's commanding officer said of him, *"A brave man and an honest and gallant soldier"*.

Reaching officer status, he eventually served as acting commandant of Fort Stanton where he led further operations against the Apaches before being discharged from the army with the brevet rank of Major. As stated previously, Brady settled down to ranching with his wife and children a few miles outside of Lincoln on the banks of the Rio Bonito, but he was elected Sheriff for the first time in 1869, taking office the following year. Although he lost his seat, he was a well respected figure in the community and was re-elected in 1876. By the time Billy Bonney was around, Brady was well established and working alongside the activities and ambitions of The House who not only controlled the Sheriff but also the courts and all aspects of business.

So this was the lay of the land in the late 1870s, and Murphy, Dolan and Co. must have been comfortably confident in their position, with every reason to believe that their domination would continue indefinitely.

But that was before John Henry Tunstall arrived.

Tunstall was an Englishman, born in the East End of London in the borough of Hackney. His family were considered upper middle class, because his father had become moderately wealthy through various business interests in Britain and abroad. Being a self made man, Tunstall senior and his family were looked down upon by the upper echelons of society; such was the character of the class system in the Victorian era.

The younger Tunstall was restless and ambitious and was unable to settle in the confines of the family business, so he took off to Canada in 1872, aged nineteen, to work as a clerk in a store part owned by his father in Vancouver. He declared that he then suffered a miserable few years pushing paperwork around, and writing home, *"the road to riches does not lie in the mercantile world"*.

Not short of energy, nor the optimism of youth, John Tunstall had his one eye (an accident robbed him of sight in the other one) on an escape route from the boredom which had crossed the ocean with him. He was also an agnostic with little time for established religion and convention.

Finally, he broke out of the rut in 1876 and travelled down into the USA, a bone jarring, week long coach journey to Santa Fe, where the frontier surroundings were quite a culture shock for him. His attention was grabbed by the potential of this embryonic country, and a chance meeting in a hotel was to seal his fate.

The man he met was 39 year old Alexander McSween, a law school graduate of Scottish descent, although born in Canada. McSween and Tunstall immediately connected and soon recognised their mutual ambitions could be of benefit to one another.

Tunstall paid close attention as the Scotsman outlined the many opportunities which were still available in the heartland of New Mexico, for those with the intelligence, courage and acumen to seize them.

And McSween should know, for he was working as a lawyer (the only one in Lincoln) for Murphy and Dolan in The House.

Tunstall was convinced and he followed McSween back to Lincoln. No doubt helped by his father's money, the young Englishman purchased his own ranch on the Rio Feliz, about 30 miles south of the town. Becoming a simple cattleman was not enough and before long he was in partnership with McSween (who had forsaken The House). They established their own stores and bank in direct competition to Murphy and Dolan thereby earning them the enmity of the Santa Fe Ring.

Tunstall was tall, handsome and refined. He spoke French and his distinctive English tweeds and accent were attractive to the residents of Lincoln who were charmed by his manners, intellect and affable nature. They also liked what he offered them… cheaper prices. Obviously, the McSween and Tunstall stores in the centre of town were soon doing great business and this had a disastrous effect on the Murphy/Dolan enterprise down the street… banking loyalties were switched too. To make things worse for The House, the gigantic figure of the greatly respected John Chisum was showing his support for these newcomers. Chisum even agreed to lend his name as president of their new bank.

Tunstall triumphantly, and somewhat cockily, put a letter in the post to his father back in England boasting that he intended to unseat Murphy and Dolan and become so successful that *"half of every dollar made in Lincoln County will end up in my pocket…"*

Naturally, this infuriated the Irish contingent and they could not allow it to go on. The natural historic enmity between Irish and English only stoked the fire, adding to the already seething resentment. This upstart Englishman and his treacherous Scottish lapdog daring to take them on like this? It was unthinkable…

With their profits rapidly dwindling, the formerly unchallenged House immediately started to look at ways to put these rivals out of business. There seemed to be no way this could be done fairly or conventionally so darker notions began to fester.

But Murphy's health was rapidly declining… alcoholism and cancer ravaged him and he began to withdraw leaving Dolan to lead the opposition… and Dolan still had powerful friends and the iron will to fight back.

To back up his plans, Dolan needed some extra "muscle". He was not shy of gunplay himself, but he made sure that there was a strong contingent of hired weaponry on call. With Jesse Evans conveniently sprung from jail, the Dolan faction could rely on quite an army, the nucleus of which could be The Boys.

***

As an Englishman, and for the benefit of any readers who may not be familiar with John Tunstall's roots, I will write a few lines here about the London Borough of Hackney where he was born in 1853.

It is an area I am rather familiar with because although I was born and raised some miles south west of London, in the county of Hampshire, I actually got married in Walthamstow which is literally down the road from Hackney. Consequently, I lived in the region for several years.

Hackney features in historical records dating right the way back to the 1100s. It was a tiny rural village then, and the name derives from the word "ey" meaning a raised piece of land in a marsh, which was the marshland surrounding the nearby River Lea. A Dane named Haca apparently owned this land, hence Haca's land, which transformed over the years into Hackney.

Up until the late 1700s, Hackney remained rural, dominated by small dwellings and farmland, but throughout the Victorian period of the later 1800s, as a direct result of the booming population which swarmed towards the work which could be found in the nearby metropolis of London, the area underwent a dramatic transformation. Many houses were built and for a long time Hackney was considered to be a fine area to live. Wealthy merchants settled there, in grand homes, and such was the case for the Tunstall family.

By the 20th. century, circumstances changed. The area deteriorated, many of the grand houses grew to be overpopulated slums and the moneyed folk moved out, mostly to the west of the city. By the 1980s, Hackney was largely considered to be one of the poorest areas in the country. Things appear to have come full circle since then, however, and by the second decade of the 21st. century Hackney once again became a trendy and desirable place to be.

CHAPTER 16
ROOTS OF WAR

Leaving the hospitality of the Coe cousins, Frank and George, Billy drifted through the Ruidoso valley, making friends amongst the farming and ranching community. His presence was well known and his easy going, affable personality shone as he brightened up the lives of these hard working souls. He was especially popular with the Hispanics, not only because he could converse with them fluently but he was also willing to give them his time; something that many Anglos did not bother with. As mentioned earlier, he certainly appealed to the girls and drifted from one *querida* (lover) to another. They adored their *Bilito* and presumably preferred to overlook his lack of loyalty. But he was young, carefree and open with his charms, so it seems he was easily forgiven once he flashed that disarming smile.

Still only eighteen years old, after all...

During this period, Billy never laid his head in one place for long and was in no hurry to settle down. No doubt still indulging in the odd foray into cattle rustling and horse theft to make ends meet, he maintained the connections he needed to stay in the scene whilst now avoiding Evans and his gang.

His new friends were a step up the social scale... men like Charlie Bowdre and Doc Scurlock, both more than a decade older than Billy and better educated than most in the area. Family men too who both ran their own small spreads. Doc even had some medical training behind him and Charlie too was fond of books. Even so, they both harboured a fiery, violent side when called upon. Doc had been in a gunfight which resulted in his front teeth being shot out.

Bowdre's future wife, Manuela, was Hispanic and so Billy could communicate with her better than Charlie himself could. One cannot help but wonder if Charlie fully trusted "Mrs." Bowdre when in company with his young *"lothario like"* pal. Actually, that observation is probably a tad unjust, but it's a tempting thought... whatever, friend or not, Charlie was apparently irritated by this closeness.

The Ruidoso valley folk, and those in the vicinity, did work hard, so, consequently, they also liked to party. *Bailes* (dance gatherings) were a regular feature in any venue which suited. Lively, happy occasions they surely were, with the locals dressed in their finery (as best they could muster!), the senorita's colourful skirts swirling as they spun to the *fandango* style of *guitarras, huiringua* and also the hoedown fiddling of the Coe cousins. Billy was a great hit at these sessions and was always twirling partners across the floor.

The Kid was probably already acquainted with 26 year old Dick Brewer through the various cattle dealing affairs he had been involved with since arriving in Lincoln County. Brewer himself was not a regular rustler, as such, but he was most likely on the periphery of the seedier side of what was going on. He was actually a well respected figure; good looking, imposing, well built, he handled guns and horses with easy skill. An air of authority and leadership defined him, qualities which would prove of use in the months to come.

Brewer was well and truly allied with John Tunstall, acting as his ranch foreman and right hand man on the range. With Dolan gathering hired guns around him, Tunstall realised he must do the same and gave Brewer the job of finding them.

Brewer could see how things were stacking up. He must have still felt resentment at the way Evans, Baker and co. had been so casually broken out of jail following their theft of his horses, and now to see Evans' Boys recruited as Dolan's strong arm gang... it was pretty galling.

Under the pretext of ranch hands, Brewer employed a series of men who he knew to be capable of handling themselves when it came to a shootout. Bowdre and Scurlock were swiftly snapped up, along with known gunmen such as Henry Brown, only nineteen but an ex buffalo hunter with at least one man killing to his credit. He had previously worked for Dolan but left over a wages dispute, giving him cause to square up to The House.

Then there was John Middleton, a mature 23, with his dark looks accentuated by a gigantic black moustache. Tunstall described him as the most desperate looking fellow he had ever set eyes upon.

Of a similar age was Fred Waite, part Chickasaw Indian. For a while, he and Billy Bonney grew particularly close and had even begun to talk of acquiring a ranch together, that is until shattering events put paid to everyone's future planning.

Billy, following his own brief incarceration in the pit jail, had been taken on by Brewer at the end of 1877, convinced of Billy's dexterity with pistol and rifle, regardless of his youth.

Indeed, they were all so young...

Into the new year of 1878 a kind of unsettled peace lay over the bubbling tension, but everyone knew it was just a matter of time before it all blew. In the meantime Dolan and Co. and the Tunstall/McSween faction kind of manouvered around one another, prodding and seeking out possible weaknesses in each other's armour.

With Tunstall and McSween going from strength to strength, their businesses starting to boom, Dolan felt desperation setting in. He was not far from bankruptcy if things did not change in his favour soon.

What happened next kicked the conflict into a dramatic phase of action, but it was a highly complex chain of events which I will not detail here.

In essence, it involved a life insurance policy which McSween, in his lawyer role, had collected from a deceased foreign partner of Dolan's. Refusing to hand over the money in lieu of his fee (which appears to have been in some kind of dispute), McSween found himself facing a charge of embezzlement.

Summoned to Mesilla in early February, accompanied by the ever supportive John Tunstall, McSween stood, with looming dread, before Dolan sympathizer Judge Warren Bristol. The case was deferred until April when it would be heard fully in Lincoln, but the bail conditions were harsh. Judge Bristol ordered that the value of McSween's property be seized.

In triumph, Dolan sped back to Lincoln ahead of his rivals to ensure that this attachment was enforced. It was an ideal opportunity to score a huge blow against them.

Enlisting the willing assistance and authority of Sheriff Brady (who was always on hand to help The House), Dolan explained the terms of the attachment, adding his own assumptions. He wrongly came to the conclusion that McSween and Tunstall were officially a partnership, therefore he was entitled to include the contents of Tunstall's store in with that of McSween's. The total of the amalgamated goods would quadruple the amount needed to cover the bail conditions, but Dolan persuaded Brady to push ahead with a full inventory.

An outraged Tunstall got back to this scene a couple of days later to find Brady and his posse taking charge inside his store, methodically listing all of his stock.

Billy Bonney and Fred Waite happened to be in town, possibly planning to put their ranching ambitions into action, but Tunstall ordered them to follow him as armed backing when he faced Brady.

They marched into the store and Billy and Fred stood in the doorway, cradling their Winchesters. Tunstall had left a man named Widenmann in charge of things whilst he was away and there he was loudly, but uselessly, berating Brady and his men who were totally ignoring him.

Tunstall joined in the protest demanding to know what they were doing with his property when the judge's order only applied to McSween. Brady merely shrugged, reluctantly conceding to release half a dozen horses and a couple of mules, but the inventory continued and Tunstall, Billy and Fred backed off. In effect, the McSween and Tunstall stores were locked down.

McSween had also returned, frustrated by this blatant confrontation, but he was a man of words, not violence. He had to step back and bite his lip whilst his wife, Sue, reminded him that she had always advised against going up against these ruthless men. True, she had never wanted to open the store and accurately predicted trouble.

Matters escalated swiftly.

By the next day, Sheriff Brady had decided, mistakenly, that under the terms of the judge's order, he would be able to include all cattle and horses held on Tunstall's Feliz ranch, deputizing House member Jacob Mathews to lead a posse to carry out the job. This posse included John Hurley, Manuel "Indian" Segovia and, once past Blazer's Mill, the addition of George Hindman and Andrew "Buckshot" Roberts.

Riding on, they ran into Jesse Evans and his ever present sidekicks Hill, Baker and Davis. When Mathews explained their mission, Evans said they would unofficially tag along because Billy Bonney had a horse which belonged to him and he intended to retrieve it.

Tunstall remained in Lincoln for now and Billy, Waite and Widenmann returned to the Feliz with the mounts released by Brady.

Mathews' posse arrived at the Tunstall ranch early on the morning of February 13th.. Brewer and Widenmann stepped out onto the porch, the rest of their men concealed inside with guns at the ready.

At Brewer's command, Mathews' reined his riders in well away from the building before trotting forward a few yards to read out his orders; that he had come to attach the livestock of Alexander McSween.

"McSween has no livestock here!" he was emphatically told.

This being true, Mathews became agitated and confused. Following a lengthy argument, during which Evans mocked Widenmann over an alleged arrest warrant he carried, the two men exchanged threats. At one point Frank Baker drew his pistol, cocked it and pointed it at Widenmann. A tense moment, but Brewer managed to defuse it. In return, Mathews agreed to return to Lincoln to get instructions from Brady as to what he should do next.

Inside the ranch house, Billy's finger was most likely itching on the trigger of his Winchester but instead, along with Waite and Widenmann, he rode out with the hostile posse under an uneasy truce, because the Kid also needed to get an updated insight from Tunstall. Evans and his companions kept their distance from Billy and remained in the vicinity of the Feliz ranch.

Back in Lincoln, an impatient Sheriff Brady confirmed that the posse should return to the Feliz to seize *Tunstall's* livestock, so back they went. Dolan had already sent word to his cattle camp manager, Buck Morton, at Seven Rivers that he should assemble more men to add to the existing posse. This was done and they rendezvoused at Penasco, a few miles south of the Feliz. Dolan met them there, effectively taking charge and bringing the strength of the posse up to over twenty, including Evans and his Boys.

On hearing the latest forboding news, Tunstall agreed that his ranch should be defended at all costs, sending Billy, Waite and Widenmann back with that strict instruction. In preparation, Dick Brewer ordered grain sacks piled against the walls and gun ports chopped into the adobe.

The stage was set for one almighty firefight... except it didn't happen... not yet...

Tunstall had rethought his strategy. After dark on February 17th. the Englishman returned to his ranch and glumly told his followers that the ranch was not the place to make a stand. He felt they had insufficient strength in numbers to successfully take on Dolan's growing posse. One of Tunstall's hands was a man named Bill McCloskey and he had friends on the Dolan side. Tunstall instructed him to ride up to the Penasco without delay to inform Dolan and Mathews that he was willing to give up the cattle as per the attachment order.

Any disappointment felt by Brewer and his men could be offset, intimated Tunstall, by the notion that they could all live to fight another day.

***

Just before 7.00am., with the first tinges of light clearing the eastern sky, John Tunstall and his men were ready to hit the trail.

It was Monday February 18th. 1878, a cold morning, but they were anxious to get going and not be around when that aggressive posse turned up at Ranch Feliz to carry out the attachment order. Facing them alone, to oversee matters, would be a harmless old German man who tended the kitchen, Godfrey Gauss. Tunstall was determined to avoid a conflict at this stage.

Heading north towards Lincoln, the Englishman had several of his gunhands with him.

They were leading nine riderless horses, including those that Brady had handed over a few days before. Tunstall no doubt wanted to keep possession of something. The party kept together for a few miles before deciding to take a shortcut, a route which was fine for those on horseback but too rugged for Fred Waite who was driving a buckboard. He carried on alone.

The Dolan/Mathews posse were surprised to be met at the Feliz by the solitary representation of Old Man Gauss. Disappointed too, because essentially they were spoiling for a fight. When Gauss told them that Tunstall was heading to Lincoln with that string of horses, Dolan saw it as an opportunity to take things to the next level, insisting that the mounts must be included in Judge Bristol's attachment order.

With orders to overtake the Tunstall party before they reached town, a revamped posse of fourteen men was assembled, this time with Buck Morton in charge. As they galloped away, Jesse Evans and his men followed but not in an official capacity. His excuse was that he still wanted to reclaim that horse from Billy Bonney. Mathews was not keen on them being part of what might happen but Morton egged them on, making intentions clear by loudly, and ominously, crowing, *"Hurry up, boys… my knife is sharp and I feel like scalping someone!"*

With the sky darkening as dusk descended, Tunstall and his strung out group, with the horses tethered behind them, entered a narrow gorge which led down to the Rio Ruidoso. Dick Brewer and Widenmann, riding in the lead, came across a flock of wild turkeys which fluttered across their path. The birds scrambled, gobbling and squawking as they flew away, the two men giving chase up the steep slope on their left, hoping to bag a couple for supper.

Tunstall was left a little way behind, leading the horses. Billy and John Middleton were well in the rear by several hundred yards and it was then that they heard the drumming of hooves along the trail they had just covered.

Turning in their saddles, the Kid and Middleton were startled to see a large group of horsemen, the new posse, galloping fervently towards them.

Outnumbered, there was nothing to do but flee and try to warn their friends.

Billy dug his spurs into his mount's flanks and took off towards Brewer and his turkey hunt. Middleton galloped towards Tunstall crying out a warning.

Morton's posse topped the rise. Spotting Billy, Brewer and Widenmann, half of them broke off in pursuit, opening fire on their prey as they did so. The trio of Tunstall men galloped up a bare slope, desperately aiming for some trees and boulders at the top of the hill in which they could take cover.

A bewildered and excited Tunstall wheeled his horse as Middleton caught up with him, not breaking stride as he yelled, *"For God's sake, follow me!"*

Tunstall was mounted on his favourite horse, a good mount, but the panic of the moment fazed him.

"What, John? What, John?" he cried out repeatedly, but Middleton had to concentrate on saving himself, spurring his horse to join his friends in reaching cover.

The posse reined in at the crest of the hill, turning their attention down towards the lone Englishman who was still on the trail below with his horses in tow. Quickly he vanished into a dense thicket of brush with Jesse Evans, Buck Morton and Tom Hill in pursuit. Within moments, they were out of sight too and, soon after, the crackle of gunfire echoed across the landscape.

Billy and his two companions, hunkering down in the rocks and scrub, looked at each other.

"They've killed him…" muttered Middleton.

And so they had, the only question being, *"Why?"*

Out of sight and with only the killers as witnesses, the story they told was a highly unlikely one.

As the posse gathered up the horses which were being led, Morton appeared from the thicket with his version of what had happened. He said that he and the others had confronted Tunstall with the writ of attachment and had demanded that he throw down his weapons. Tunstall had apparently responded by drawing his revolver and firing two shots, which was an absurd explanation.

Why would he have done that? It would be tantamount to committing suicide.

Whatever, Morton, Evans and Hill opened up on him with their Winchesters or revolvers and Tunstall was blasted out of his saddle with bullets in his head and chest. Maybe out of sheer spite, they even killed his horse.

The posse members crowded around the murder site and probably not even any of *them* believed Morton's tale. This killing bore the hallmarks of an execution pure and simple, not a gunfight. Tunstall's pistol had indeed fired two shots, but I think we can safely say that it was not the Englishman who pulled the trigger. Rumour soon spread that Tom Hill had done it to plant false evidence.

As an added, disrespectful insult, Tunstall's corpse was dumped unceremoniously alongside his dead horse, as if they were sleeping together, the Englishman's overcoat beneath his shattered head and his hat beneath that of his horse.

Killed resisting arrest would be the official story from Dolan's side... one a deputy and the other two who should not even have been part of the posse. It just did not hold weight.

This posse felt they had done enough for now. One of their main protagonists dead and the horses they were after seized. With their other targets entrenched in a strong defensive position they pulled out.

Jesse Evans was even said to have scoffed that Tunstall deserved to be killed, yet later on, giving testimony, he denied that he was even present.

As darkness fell, Billy and his concealed companions felt it was safe enough to make their way back down the hill. Hastening on to Lincoln, they arrived at McSween's house where a crowd had already gathered. Most of them were men who had responded to Tunstall's earlier appeal for help, and now they were being told he had been murdered.

It was shocking news which infuriated the majority. Tunstall had been a popular figure within the community, if not with everyone then definitely for those who had benefitted from the competition he had brought to town. He may not have been quite the saint he is often portrayed as being in the fantasies which grew up around the coming war, but his support was strong. Ambitious, quite ruthless in a business sense, there was never-the-less much sympathy regarding the callous brutality of his death.

Tunstall's body was retrieved the following day and taken to his store in town where it was laid out in the back room.

The popular and generally accepted belief that Tunstall was a close friend and father figure to Billy Bonney is simply untrue. For a start, Tunstall was only 24 years old himself. Billy worked for him, one of quite a gang, and their association had lasted less than two months. There is no evidence to suggest that they had any kind of affinity beyond boss and hired gun. Despite what the movies, television, and some books and other pieces, may tell you, Billy was not even found by the Englishman. Dick Brewer could take credit for that.

Yet the death of his employer had a profound and life changing effect upon the Kid. Maybe it was the abrupt way their relationship ended, just when Billy was starting to feel he was beginning to belong.

And perhaps there was an element of guilt too… after all, Billy and those who rode with Tunstall that fateful day were supposed to be there for his protection. Chasing turkeys, hanging carelessly back on the trail, fleeing for their lives and leaving their boss to face his killers alone… in effect, they had let him down, and now he was gone.

It all seemed so unjust.

No one had seen the Kid quite like this as he approached the lifeless form of John Henry Tunstall in that darkened, lamp lit room. Billy's almost ever present laughing smile was concealed by a deep frown, an air of serious resolution overlaying that youthful vibe.

It was as if he knew the dead man could hear him as he stared into the pale, waxen face and whispered, *"I'll get some of 'em before I die…"*

And so he would.

***

There is an official historical marker commemorating the site of John Tunstall's murder.

It is situated in the area of Glencoe, New Mexico, located about four miles off of Interstate 70. Reaching it is not easy in a vehicle because it is along a very rocky trail. There is a place to park then you need to walk down a hill between gullies and through peaceful woods.

The marker itself can be found in a clearing and, with a finely tuned imagination, it is possible to sense the grim scene which took place here back in February 1878, even though the vegetation would have significantly changed since then.

CHAPTER 17
REGULATORS

The battle lines were now well and truly drawn and the tension within Lincoln town must have been tangible.

Billy Bonney had been swiftly elevated to prominence and was very vocal about wasting no time in getting justice against the killers. Many agreed with him and were itching to get to it, the Tunstall avengers numbering in excess of forty armed men.

McSween was now their leader, but he was a lawyer, not a gunfighter. His immediate response was to call for reasonable calm as he sought legal means to attain their goals.

On the face of it, the law favoured the Dolan side, with Sheriff Brady making no secret of his loyalty to his Irish countrymen. The House was strong with their own formidable army, but McSween cleverly found avenues to hit back without resorting to out and out violence.

The law in Lincoln, argued McSween, could be sliced like warm butter. Brady was the Sheriff but he did not hold every strand of authority. Old Squire Wilson was the Justice of the Peace and, as such, held the power to issue arrest warrants of his own. McSween wasted no time in getting to him and by the day after Tunstall's death he had persuaded Wilson to take his side.

Billy, Brewer and Middleton were called into the Squire's office where they swore affidavits naming the murderers of John Tunstall. Prominent on this list were Evans, Morton and Hill, naturally, but also Jimmy Dolan and Frank Baker who were not even present at the murder site (though guilty by association). That also applied to quite a few of the others because the warrant included most of the Mathews posse, not just the ones who had ridden under Morton's leadership.

Taking full advantage of the dithery Wilson's compliance, McSween pushed for another warrant, this time against Sheriff Brady himself. It was a wily technicality but the Scottish lawyer knew how to manipulate the law. Brady's men were still occupying Tunstall's store, an intolerable situation, but they had used the dead Englishman's stock of hay to feed soldier's horses from Fort Stanton who Brady had called in as protection against any possible attacks from Tunstall supporters. This was a convenient excuse for McSween to charge Brady with larceny for taking private property. Brady and his men were forced to vacate the store and appear before Justice Squire Wilson who bound them over to appear in court when next assembled.

This was unexpected and humiliating for Brady and he would not forget it.

Emboldened by this pair of legal documents, Billy and the McSween faction quickly indulged in a series of outward provocations the length and breadth of Lincoln town over the next few days. Threats flew back and forth, guns were levelled and the powder keg drew close to the fuse's end. If it had not been for the presence of troops from Fort Stanton, who did their best to stand between the opposing forces, a bloodbath would have erupted for sure. That said, the army could not get involved with any bias in a civil dispute but could only act in keeping the peace.

Responsibility for carrying out the arrest warrants fell upon the local constable Atanacio Martinez and he was not happy about the notion of arresting the Sheriff and his men, that is until Billy threatened him with death. Martinez then acted with the support of the McSween gunmen and the Tunstall store was back in their hands.

Brady and his followers returned to the Dolan store where the bulk of Dolan's men had gathered to brood about the building situation.

To complicate matters even more, Rob Widenmann, who held the post of a U.S. deputy marshal, had his own separate federal warrant against Jesse Evans and others for horse theft. This warrant allowed for the backup of soldiers and Widenmann used them in a show of force by searching the Dolan store thoroughly. Brady could not argue with the presence of the military but it must have enraged him, even though Evans was not to be found.

Constable Martinez used this opportunity to his advantage. Swallowing his previous reluctance, and no doubt reacting to Billy's persuasion, he pushed his way into Dolan's store as the soldiers withdrew, Billy and Fred Waite at his side.

Brandishing his arrest warrant, he confronted Brady and several of the men who were on it, but this time, with the soldiers gone, the Sheriff was not willing to comply. Before Martinez could speak, the muzzles of several pistols and rifles were pointed in his direction and Billy and Fred froze.

Brady had the three men disarmed before demanding to know what business they had with him. Martinez read from the warrant, naming those he intended to arrest, but Brady soon stopped him, accompanied by a torrent of abuse from those around him, many of whom found it amusing.

"*No one is going to arrest these men,*" declared the Sheriff, "*… they are* my posse and, anyway, I do not recognise the authority of your Squire Wilson."

Silenced and disarmed, insulted and humiliated, Martinez, Billy and Waite were placed under "House" arrest, literally. Martinez was soon released, without his weapons, but the other two were held for quite a while, victims of Brady's vengeance for his own recent humiliation.

Over the next day and a half, efforts were made to peacefully secure the release of Billy and Waite through go-betweens but Brady was not having any of it. Asked why he was holding the pair he merely said that he *"had the power"*. He also refused requests to revoke the attachment order which had been the root of all the recent problems.

With over thirty hours having passed, Brady finally let Billy and Fred go, but he kept their guns, much to the fury of the Kid who had been determined to keep hold of his rifle. It was another proverbial kick in the teeth from the Sheriff who felt he had scored a big win over the upstart, cocky youth. Billy seethed and walked away but Brady had made a big mistake in underestimating the teenaged killer, especially as the incarceration had made the Kid miss Tunstall's funeral.

The original embezzlement charge against McSween still stood and The House was determined to use it. District Attorney Rynerson was an unashamed supporter of Dolan's activities and was more than happy to enforce any means to bring down his opponents. McSween was now suffering financial difficulties himself and was therefore unable to raise the required cost of the bond required to ensure his liberty before the next available court session. Several powerful friends joined forces to cover the cost but Rynerson, completely unreasonably, refused this. The alternative was that McSween would have to spend weeks in Brady's hell hole of a jail which would conveniently remove him from the scene.

McSween was not prepared to face this so he left Lincoln and disappeared for quite some time leaving his supporters leaderless.

But, those that remained still retained passion for their cause, vengeance being the essential motivator. They chose a new leader… Dick Brewer, who was appointed special constable by Squire Wilson. Wilson also issued a fresh warrant, reaffirming all those whose names had appeared on the first one, eighteen in all.

A hard core of tough supporters rallied around Brewer as deputies. None were higher on the list than Billy Bonney whose firm resolve to spill blood on behalf of Tunstall was no secret. Then came Fred Waite, John Middleton, Doc Scurlock, Henry Brown, Charlie Bowdre, Frank and George Coe, all pulling together in a brotherly cause. Essentially, they numbered about a dozen of Anglo extraction, but their strength was supplemented by quite a few Hispanic sympathizers and others who drifted in and out of the force over the next few months.

Powerful cattle baron John Chisum still gave his name to the McSween/Tunstall cause... he was their bank president, after all, but that was the limit of what he was prepared to do, drawing the line at actually becoming actively involved in any conflict. Some of those on his payroll, however, were willing to play a bigger role... men like Big Jim French and Frank McNab, whose job had been to track down the rustlers who preyed on Chisum's vast herds. Many of those rustlers were Dolan men who specialized in converting the Chisum brand from a long rail shape to the arrow shape of Dolan.

Under Tunstall, his warriors had been promised a daily rate of pay but now they would be paid nothing, other than a vague promise that reward might eventually come from Tunstall's far distant father.

What held them together was something much deeper than the loose, materialistic scruples of mercenaries. It sounds dramatic but it appears they did quickly form a brotherly bond, united by that single focus of justice and revenge.

That is why they called themselves *The Regulators*.

CHAPTER 18
VENGEANCE

Dick Brewer's Regulators, numbering about a dozen on this occasion, hit the trail on March 2nd., determined to make a concerted effort to track down their prey.

Following up on a few leads, they rode towards the lower Pecos where they had heard that the more prominent names they wanted were likely to be found.

On March 6th. they struck lucky when, by pure chance, they came across five men resting their horses in a clump of trees, one of whom was at the very top of their list... Buck Morton, the leader of the posse which had cornered Tunstall, and one of the three who had actually murdered him.

Morton and his companions immediately leapt into their saddles and were away at speed. The chase was on, taking the form of a classic Western style scene.

They galloped for several miles exchanging gunfire. Scores of shots were fired between the two parties, Morton and his men blasting back over their shoulders at their pursuers who responded with their own fusillade of bullets.

But such rapidly moving targets were elusive, and none of these shots found their mark. Before long, the pursued decided to split up, veering off in different directions. Two of them were ignored and managed to get away because the entire posse stayed on the tail of the others, the trio which included Morton.

Riding with him was Frank Baker, another prominent name on the list, even though his presence at Tunstall's killing had been cut short by his horse giving out before he could take part. Never-the-less, he was a wanted man.

The other rider with Morton and Baker was a cowboy named Lloyd. He fell behind as his horse also gave out, but Brewer's posse galloped on past him, determined to nail his companions.

Morton and Baker whipped their mounts desperately as their pursuers bore down on them. Before long the overridden animals could take no more... they began to flag, finally slowing and giving out almost simultaneously as the relentless posse rode across their hoofprints.

Morton and Baker abandoned their horses and ran into the safety of a shallow, brush covered gulley. The posse reined in and quickly surrounded them, cutting off any avenue of escape.

The trapped men must have been terrified but they tried to

negotiate. Brewer called out to them to throw down their weapons and emerge from cover with their hands up. Understandably, they were reluctant to do this, knowing that they were putting themselves at the mercy of an angry mob of vengeful gunmen, but when Brewer threatened to set fire to the brush that concealed them, they had no choice but to surrender or die in an outmatched shootout.

They chose the former. Warily stepping into the open, they were disarmed by the Regulators who were in no mood to do them any favours. Billy Bonney was particularly aggressive and wanted to shoot them out of hand, it is said. Even Brewer told them that he was disappointed they had given up because he had no desire to take them alive.

Baker was described as being rough and *"gorilla like"* in appearance with a *"brutish"* countenance, but he must have been severely humbled by his present predicament. Morton, just 22 years old, came from a good family, was well educated and had been known as a good sort, though *"wild and reckless"*. However, his scalping knife remark, enthusiastic rustling activities and willing participation in Tunstall's murder says most about him.

The plan was to deliver their prisoners into custody in Lincoln, or so they said.

None of the Regulators were keen on that idea because it would mean handing them over to Sheriff Brady who, though a Dolan enthusiast, was still the official chief lawman. Brady could hardly be trusted to hold them until a court could be convened, and even then it would be overseen by a biased judge.

So Morton and Baker had every reason to be more than worried about their safety. What motive did Brewer and his men have to deliver them alive?

At a leisurely and thoughtful pace, closely watching their captives, the Regulators rode up the Pecos, tethering their horses and stopping for a rest at John Chisum's South Spring ranch where they were warmly received.

On the way there, they had been joined by Bill McCloskey who was also on his way to Lincoln on business of his own. They all knew him, of course, because he had worked for Tunstall, but also for Dolan and the Seven Rivers cowboys.

Therefore, Brewer, and most of the others, Billy included, did not trust him. He was known to be a good friend of Morton's and his sympathy for the desperate, captive was immediately apparent.

Whilst the Kid took distraction from vengeful thoughts by going fishing with Chisum's young nephew, Morton was permitted to write a letter to a friend of his back east in Virginia which he sealed. It contained his deeply held and justifiable concerns about whether or not he would make it to Lincoln.

Already rumours were being heard about Dolan assembling a force to rescue the prisoners so Brewer decided that they must push on.

On March 9th., they took a diversion into the small hamlet of Roswell where Morton was allowed to post his letter. Here he expressed his worries to the postmaster, Ash Upson. McCloskey also confided in Upson that he too was concerned for his friend's safety, even going so far as to say that he would support and protect him from any threats against his life. *"It won't be done as long as I live..."* vowed McCloskey, with uncanny prediction.

The following day, the Regulators, with McCloskey in tow, carried on riding the main road to Lincoln but then, suspiciously, left it to take a rough trail towards the Capitan Mountains along Blackwater Creek. The excuse would be that they did this to avoid any clash with a House rescue committee but their intentions were almost certainly more sinister.

The truth of what happened next is lost in history, but there were several versions.

Frank McNab took the news to Roswell that evening whilst Dick Brewer related the same story to McSween in Lincoln.

They solemnly said that, inexplicably, along the trail, Morton had suddenly grabbed McCloskey's pistol from his holster and shot him through the head, then he and Baker had spurred their horses in a hopeless bid to escape.

The Regulators had then had no alternative but to pursue the fugitives and shoot them from their saddles.

Exactly what did occur, leading to those three deaths, I think we can safely assume that the Regulator's official version was pure fantasy.

Once again, as with Tunstall, and in the spirit of divine retribution, these were executions.

Morton shooting McCloskey with his own pistol... his only ally and friend in the party? Why would he do that?

There are several possible scenarios but when the evidence is considered, the most likely one is that they took the Blackwater Creek trail to deliberately dispose of their prisoners. When it came down to it, McCloskey probably objected and ended up shot through the head for his trouble by a Regulator... maybe trigger happy Billy who had been itching for any excuse.

Knowing they had nothing to lose now, Morton and Baker might have tried to make a break for it, or perhaps they just accepted their fate as their captors opened fire on them, none more enthusiastically than the Kid.

Whatever, it is a sobering fact that McCloskey had but one bullet in him whilst Morton and Baker's bodies were riddled by multiple slugs each... which was conveniently at least one for each of the Regulators present.

If that was not suspicious then what on earth was?

***

McSween had arrived back in Lincoln on March 9th., the day before Brewer's posse disposed of their prisoners. Although he had made himself scarce, the Scots lawyer now felt that he should return to face the music rather than skulk in hiding.

As it happened, things had really turned against him and his cause.

On that very same day, Samuel Axtell, the Territory's Governor, had also arrived in town to see for himself what was happening and it was no surprise to find evidence of his total bias in favour of the Dolan faction.

He was only in town for a few hours, but in that time his written and verbal proclamations changed everything, starting with his declaration that Squire Wilson was not legally holding the position of Justice of the Peace. There was now no question of challenging the authority of the county law which in Axtell's view was in the hands of Judge Bristol and enforced by Sheriff Brady.

Therefore, when Dick Brewer arrived at McSween's house the following evening, with news about the latest shootings, there was dismay all around. Brewer and his Regulators could no longer claim to be acting within the law and now, with their warrants deemed unlawful, they had potential false arrest and murder charges against them.

McSween, with his strong willed wife Sue away visiting friends on the other side of the country, was completely demoralized and certainly not in the frame of mind to make plans and resist. At this time, all he could suggest was that all those in his camp disband and lay low, keeping out of the way until the court convened on April 1st. where, perhaps, they could get a fair hearing. Some chance of that with Judge Bristol presiding...

The news of Morton, Baker and McCloskey's deaths spread quickly and Dolan urged Sheriff Brady to act on it. In actual fact, Dolan had not been entirely happy with Brady's lethargy when it came to forcing his hand against McSween and Co.. It was true that the Sheriff was in the pocket of the Irishmen, being one himself, who apart from long friendship and business interests was also in considerable debt to Dolan's partner Murphy, but Brady was an older and considerably wiser man than his contemporaries. He was tough but acted with an element of patient caution, believing that McSween was sensible, and fearful, enough to present himself on the court date without the need to lock him up.

However, the latest drama of the killings moved things to another level.

McSween did not want to take the chance of Brady imprisoning him where, understandably, he thought the Sheriff might look the other way whilst a Dolan led assassin dealt with him. Instead he took off to the sanctuary of Chisum's South Spring Ranch where he was to spend the remainder of the month.

The Regulators temporarily disbanded, as suggested, mostly going back to their homes with a watchful eye on any approaching riders. Billy Bonney and Fred Waite decided to lay low amongst their Hispanic friends in the village of San Patricio, a tiny place consisting of a few strongly built adobe dwellings with high gun ports in the strong walls, constructed by the original inhabitants for defence against Apaches, all in a single dusty street.

Billy was most welcome and the local populace would have supported him and his friend happily. He and Fred probably had a good time there until the end of March, pampered by the girls.

It was then that they received word, along with the rest of the scattered Regulators, to attend a meeting at Chisum's ranch. Sue McSween had returned and rejoined her husband, apparently spurring him into action again.

The meeting was also probably instigated by the appearance of another unexpected visitor at the Chisum ranch that week; none other than Sheriff Brady, of all people. The Sheriff must have been feeling extraordinarily relaxed, confident and somewhat courageous to turn up in such a hostile environment, but, of course, he considered himself the official, one and only, law enforcer.

Informing a doubtful McSween that he was trusting him to present himself in court on the appointed date of April 1st., Brady rode away, but the Scots lawyer was not convinced. When they were both in Lincoln, what would this House lawman do, once McSween was in his clutches?

And so, with his wife urging him on, McSween gathered his supporters, Anglo and Hispanic, around him once more, ostensibly to make a plan for future movements.

McSween was worried. So much had happened to derail his intentions and he seemed to be losing much of the local sympathy he had previously enjoyed. Now that he no longer had any official legal backing, he was at a loss, although he did still have considerable armed strength to call on, if he just had the nerve to use it. After all, his Regulators were considered outlaws now.

We can only guess what exactly was said at that ranch meeting, as they all sat around listening to various viewpoints. Billy Bonney's conviction to act positively and without further delay was a certainty, and he was not alone.

The straightlaced McSween would surely not have openly condoned any violence, as such, but what little evidence that survives from that fateful meeting does suggest that he implied that his survival depended upon the removal of Sheriff Brady… and that could not be by any legal or peaceful means. One witness even stated that a reward was offered.

Whatever, it was enough to convince six of the Regulators that McSween had made his wishes clear. If it was planned or a spontaneous action is open to debate, but it is a fact that these men gathered at the Tunstall store in Lincoln overnight on March 31st. into April 1st.. They were Billy Bonney, Fred Waite, John Middleton, Frank McNab, Henry Brown and Jim French. Rob Widenmann was there too, although he was to immediately deny that he was involved in what took place that morning.

***

Sheriff William Brady was 48 years old. Far senior to just about anyone else involved in all this trouble, with the exception of John Chisum and the ailing Lawrence Murphy.

The Sheriff was respectfully referred to locally as Major Brady, in deference to his brevet army rank. He was a family man and ranch owner with many interests in local business, and it is fair to say that he was firm and competent in the role of lawman which he had held for quite some time.

His long experience in overseeing Lincoln produced a man who was comfortable in his job. Most people looked up to him but the events of the last year or so had upset the *status quo* and Brady had been forced to openly take sides. That position had affected his popularity somewhat.

The morning of April 1st. 1878 dawned with drizzle and a few snow flurries in the air. Moist slush would have been covering much of Lincoln's single long street, but the townsfolk would be going about their business, regardless of the tension brought on by the events of just a few weeks ago and the continuing concerns of where it would all lead.

Around 9.00am., Sheriff Brady left the Dolan store at the far end of town with four of his deputies; George Hindman, John Long, George "Dad" Peppin and Jacob Mathews (he who had led the original posse to enforce the attachment order against Tunstall back in February). With a chill in the air, their coats were buttoned with rifles lodged in the crooks of their arms.

Today, Monday the 1st., was supposed to be the appointed date for the long awaited district court convention, but there had been a clerical error in the announcement which should have read April 8th.. Brady and his men were on a leisurely mission to the courthouse to amend the notice. Carrying out this routine task in force and fully armed must have been an indication that they were being cautious in view of what had been happening lately.

Were Billy and the Regulators in the Tunstall House expecting Brady to be taking a stroll at this time? Were they tipped off? Who knows... but in any case they would have observed the Sheriff and his deputies making their way down the busy street, as Brady stopped to exchange a few words with a woman he knew before tipping his hat and hurrying on to catch up with the others.

Seizing up their Winchesters, the six assassins filed out into the corral which backed onto the Tunstall House, taking up positions behind the shoulder high adobe wall which extended from the east of the building. Across the street was the modest home of their erstwhile demoted ally Squire Wilson who was at that moment obliviously attending his garden. Widenmann later said that this was when he went out the back door to feed the late Tunstall's dog, his supposed alibi which had him labelled from then on, with contempt, as the *"dogfeeder"*.

Brady's party carried on the short distance to the courthouse opposite the Torreon where they pinned the notice on the door. With no reason to tarry, they turned back the way they had come, probably perceiving a largely uneventful day ahead.

Crouched behind the adobe wall, Billy and his *compadres* saw this as their opportunity. Multiple clicks as they cocked the levers of their rifles would have gone unheard by the intended victims as they drew level with the ambush site...

Simultaneously, in one swift movement, the Regulators levelled their barrels over the top of the wall and opened fire *en masse*, all aiming at the hated Sheriff, repeating the fusillade even as he fell.

Brady was hit at least a dozen times, the range being short.

Even so, he was not the only victim. Whether intentional or not, Deputy Hindman was also hit, probably from a shot which had passed through Brady first and who had been killed instantly. (That said, Frank McNab did harbour a grudge against Hindman.)

Another bullet had found its mark through the buttocks of the unfortunate Squire Wilson, innocently hoeing his onion patch. He lay there bleeding and shocked, but he did survive.

The other deputies, momentarily stunned, soon realised the danger and sprinted for the cover of the nearest house.

As the Regulators ceased firing and a thick pall of gunsmoke drifted from behind the wall, a deadly silence dominated the scene, punctuated only by the groans of the wounded Deputy Hindman.

"Water..." he cried feebly, *"Bring me water...."*

The street had emptied but Ike Stockton came hurrying out of his nearby saloon to help the stricken man. As he reached him another shot rang out and Hindman died on the spot. Whoever fired it, it was a purely malicious and unnecessary act... and the evidence seems to point to it being Fred Waite.

More stunned silence, but suddenly there was action again.

Billy Bonney recklessly vaulted over the wall and rushed to the riddled body of Brady, followed closely by Big Jim French. This was either sheer bravado or madness, exposing themselves to the returning fire of the Sheriff's deputies, but they did not seem to care.

Billy stooped over the lifeless Brady and took hold of his rifle. Was this an act of retribution to reclaim the weapon which had been confiscated by the Sheriff weeks before, or one like it, at least? Or maybe Billy also intended to reach into the dead lawman's coat where he was likely to find McSween's arrest warrant and that *goddam* attachment writ.

From the house across the street where he had found cover, Jake Mathews seized the chance for some payback. His aim was true and a single bullet winged Billy's thigh but carried on to cause a more intense injury in the same area of French's body.

This was enough for them to vacate the scene. Billy dropped the rifle and he and French limped as fast as they could back to the wall and through the gate to safety.

A stalemate followed. The townsfolk were shocked, obviously, but the gunfire subsided. No one seemed keen to leave their homes and a young girl who had been playing in the Torreon was the first to venture out and approach the corpses of the two lawmen.

Billy's wound was superficial but probably still caused him discomfort. French was in a worse state but he received treatment from Reverend Ealy, a medical missionary, next door in the McSween House.

No one did anything about prolonging the gun battle and a forboding stillness took over the town. It was quite a while before the assassins decided to leave and when they did it was without haste as they rode towards the distant hills.

A few of Brady's surviving deputies made a half hearted attempt to pursue them, firing at the distant figures from a useless long range. John Middleton was the only one of the Regulators who returned fire, but it was a pointless gesture.

The Regulators had to leave French behind as he was in no fit state to ride.

The Reverend had drawn a silk cloth through his wound and dressed it as best he could, but, now he was alone, French would need to be concealed from the deputies' vengeance.

Dad Peppin had unofficially appointed himself Brady's replacement and he straightaway authorised a search of the McSween home to which a trail of blood led. Luckily for French, he had allies who had cut a hole in the flooring beneath a bed where they placed him on a blanket with a pistol in each hand. It must have been an uncomfortably painful few hours for him, but that night his friends were able to smuggle him out of town.

With the assassins gone and Peppin taking charge, Lincoln bubbled with activity again as everyone passed their view on the tragedy and excitement of the morning. At Peppin's request, Fort Stanton sent a detachment of cavalrymen in an attempt to restore order.

Mr. and Mrs. McSween also turned up in a carriage with John Chisum, accompanying his friend as moral support in the expected court hearing which they had every reason to expect would take place that day. Surprised to hear that the hearing was now not happening for another week, and also shocked (or was he?) to hear of Brady's assassination, McSween thought it best to keep clear of his house and sought refuge instead at the home of his friend Isaac Ellis.

Peppin immediately followed him there and, as soldiers stood by, attempted to arrest McSween on the strength of the warrant which Brady had been keeping for the last few weeks. No doubt Peppin and his men were also pretty certain that McSween had more than a little involvement in the Sheriff's murder.

Feeling that it would be suicide to turn himself over to the rough justice of the Dolan faction, McSween argued that Peppin had no authority now that the Sheriff was dead. The officer in charge of the soldiers recognised the lawyer's dilemma so, to keep him safe until the court finally convened the following week, he agreed to keep him in custody at Fort Stanton.

Once again, the escalation of events had really tipped the balance. All the sympathy for McSween's cause had now been deeply damaged. From a popular crusade against unfair prices and domination by the Murphy/Dolan *"House"* and the outrage surrounding the murder of Tunstall, the tables were turned.

The deaths of Morton, Baker and McCloskey were regarded as highly suspect and now the outright brutal slaying of the county Sheriff and his deputy in broad daylight... it was beyond the *"Code of the West"* and had entered the realm of pure crime, as far as the average inhabitant of Lincoln County could see it.

Add to that the fact that the Regulators had now had their legal status revoked and could not claim any lawful justification for their actions... they had become nothing more than outlaws.

CHAPTER 19

BUCKSHOT

As far as Dick Brewer was concerned he still had warrants to be served, regardless of his authority having been lawfully removed by the actions of the Territorial Governor.

From Brewer's point of view, and those of his Regulators, they had right and justice on their side... and a passion for vengeance. This was a case of being morally justified in opposing what they saw as "bad lawmen".

They were intent on carrying out their avowed mission, seemingly oblivious to the consequences.

In the meantime, they were, in effect, hunted men, outlaws who were also hunters themselves.

Tunstall's murder still simmered in their minds and they felt that he was still not fully avenged, the main culprits remaining at large, along with many who also deserved to pay the price for their compliance.

Brewer carried the list of names and was determined to work his way through them. He and several Regulators spent the next couple of days following Brady's death roaming fairly aimlessly around the Ruidoso valley. Billy and the other assassins had rejoined Brewer for whatever may come up. Their drastic action in killing the Sheriff had certainly raised the stakes. Brewer must have approved because he was happily riding with Billy and the other shooters again.

They were all carefree, single minded and more than willing to kill without hesitation... hungry to find their next victim.

Acting on further tip offs, it seems, a bunch of them headed south west towards the Rio Tularosa and there they found that victim... though he was one tough *"son-uvva-bitch"* who made them bite off more than they could chew...

***

Andrew "Buckshot" Roberts was not looking for trouble but had unwittingly found himself in the midst of it.

He was a solitary soul of few words... stockily built but short in stature, exuding an aura of frontier toughness which warned people to keep their distance, to leave him alone. There was nothing outwardly hostile about him... he was affable enough in his quiet way but he was a mystery who made it clear that he was content with that.

Very little was known about his past although a few details had somehow slipped out. He was in his late forties and had obviously been around the West for a long time. It was known that he had fought in the Civil War as a sergeant, though as Union or Confederate, no one seemed sure…

There was also a strong rumour that he once served as a Texas Ranger, and had certainly been a buffalo hunter, acquainted with the legendary Buffalo Bill Cody. He got the name "Buckshot" because he carried a load of it embedded in his right shoulder; the result of some undisclosed fight he had been in at some time, probably one of many. This had left him partially disabled in that he was unable to raise his right arm above his waist, restricting him in his shooting skills. He could only shoot from the hip but could do so effortlessly with rifle and pistol.

Buckshot Roberts had the reputation of not being a man to tangle with.

By 1878 he was running his own small ranch on the Ruidoso where he was befriended by Frank Coe, alongside occasional work for Dolan at a store he owned on the Tularosa. Generally, Roberts minded his own business but, being in Dolan's employ, he found himself caught up, probably reluctantly, in Jacob Mathews' posse back in February when the attempts had been made to seize Tunstall's horses. He was not anywhere in the vicinity of the Englishman's murder but his name was on Brewer's list.

Roberts really had no interest in the war which was boiling up around him. He was just trying to make a living and keep to himself and was not partisan in any way.

It seems he decided to make himself scarce by selling his ranch and leaving the area completely. Finding a buyer, he packed up his things and was anxiously awaiting payment so that he could clear out and leave all these people to shoot it out amongst themselves.

First, he had to pick up his cheque and was hoping to find it in the keeping of the postmaster at Blazer's Mill.

***

Dr. Joseph Blazer had once been a dentist but, following the Civil War, he found his way to a pretty little valley on the Tularosa where the river narrowed and he established a sawmill, fed by the surrounding forested slopes. In time it became a compact but busy community, thriving on the materials it sent to places like Lincoln. Eventually the property was absorbed within the government's Mescalero Apache Reservation but Blazer welcomed this opportunity, leasing his house to the Indian agent, Fred Godfroy, although he still maintained an office of his own within. Blazer mainly lived with his family in a smaller house a short distance upstream.

The house itself was a two storied, solid adobe structure, a couple of hundred paces from the sawmill. It faced the gentle flow of the river which, at this junction, ran more like an idyllic stream. Godfroy's wife operated a restaurant and makeshift hotel here too.

On the morning of April 4th., Buckshot Roberts turned up at the main house. He was mounted on a bay mule whilst leading a pack horse. For some reason Roberts preferred to ride a mule rather than a horse.

His cheque had not arrived at the post station but the mail carrier was due that day so Roberts thought he would wait around a while, until Dr. Blazer advised him against it.

It was general knowledge that Roberts was included in Brewer's defunct warrant and a report was received that a group of mounted men had been spotted in the vicinity. If they were Regulators, said a concerned Blazer, he did not want the chance of any gunplay on his property and so he asked Roberts to leave. Buckshot agreed and rode away, taking a rugged trail off the main route. He was no coward but it made sense to avoid running into the men who were looking for him, and could always return when he knew how the land lay.

After a while, we can assume he looked back and must have seen the mail carrier's buckboard approaching Blazer's Mill. This probably would be carrying his cheque so he thought he might go back, collect it and leave all this trouble behind him, once and for all.

Not much of a risk. He most likely took a long look at the buildings from a distance and all seemed clear. No Regulators. Satisfied, he tied his packhorse to a tree and cautiously urged his mule back towards the big house.

Unfortunately for him, Buckshot Roberts was about to place himself smack in the middle of the trouble he was anxious to avoid.

It was just three days after the killing of Sheriff Brady. Tempers on both sides of the conflict were running high. Brewer and his party of Regulators were still spoiling for a fight whilst having the sense to keep away from Lincoln for now.

Approaching noon on the morning of April 4th. fifteen horsemen rode into the corral across the stream from Blazer's house, breaking the peace of the quiet little community. Their appearance was unexpected, being so far west of their normal haunts, but they did seem to be following a lead, perhaps...

It was also possible that they had another dramatic attack in mind. Murphy and Dolan certainly thought so. Pro "House" Judge Bristol would be making his way from Mesilla to Lincoln any day now to preside over his court hearings and would make an obvious target on the road. Having so blatantly murdered the Sheriff, surely the Regulators would have no hesitation in erasing the Judge and other officials too.

It was a rational summation, so much so that an escort of troopers from Fort Stanton had been sent out to meet the judge's party.

For now though, the Regulators were taking a break. Unsaddling their mounts, they stretched their limbs and wandered over to the house. Jim French would have been hobbling along from that nasty wound he had recently sustained from Deputy Mathews' bullet, the one which had also winged Billy Bonney.

Led by Dick Brewer, this group also included the Coe cousins (Frank and George), Scurlock, Bowdre, McNab, Waite and Middleton. They were hungry so they sat themselves down in the house and ordered lunch from Mrs. Godfroy.

As Buckshot Roberts rode his mule towards the house, he had no reason to feel he was in immediate danger. The corral was surrounded by a high, planked fence so the Regulator's horses were hidden from view, plus the men themselves were inside the house. All, that is, except John Middleton who stood guard outside on the porch. Roberts probably did not notice him at first, but Middleton was surprised to see the heavily armed man riding towards him.

Stepping cautiously aside, he watched as the rider dismounted, hitched his mule to a corner of the house and greeted one of Dr. Blazer's sons to whom he gave his name.

Middleton took this news into the house for Brewer who immediately got to his feet declaring that Roberts was on the arrest warrant. The other Regulators lost interest in their meals and made ready to follow Brewer who was making for the door, but Frank Coe had another idea.

He knew Roberts... they had been neighbours and were quite friendly... would it not make more sense to let Frank speak to Buckshot man to man rather than descend on him in force? Frank felt sure that he would be able to persuade him to surrender peacefully.

Impatient to get the business done, Brewer reluctantly agreed to give it a try but emphasized that he was not willing to wait long.

Frank Coe nodded and made his way outside just as Roberts was strolling towards the front of the house. Respecting Blazer's rule about sidearms on his property, Buckshot had hung his gun belt and holstered pistol across the pommel of his saddle but he still carried his short barrelled Winchester carbine.

He was pleasantly surprised to see his friend Coe and the pair shook hands before Frank took him aside, leading him to the door of Blazer's office where they sat down on the porch to talk. The revelation that there were another fourteen armed men inside must have come as quite a shock.

Gently, Coe tried to make Roberts see the sense of handing himself in, but the veteran gunman was having none of it. *"The Kid is with you and he will kill me on sight..."* argued Buckshot; such was Billy Bonney's growing reputation and the fear he instilled. Coe tried his best, assuring Roberts that he would personally guarantee his safety but, despite about half an hour of debate, Buckshot stubbornly refused to give in.

Frank Coe, when he spoke of this in years to come, always stressed how determined and calm Roberts was about his predicament, not at all *"excited"*, he said, adding *"... he was the bravest man I ever met..."*.

By now, Brewer's patience was exhausted. Presumably the Regulators, unlike Roberts, had not adhered to Blazer's rule because when Brewer gave the order for them to make the arrest, they were well heeled.

Appearing around the corner of the house, the Regulators confronted their prey, obviously meaning business.

Charlie Bowdre was upfront, pistol in hand as he barked for Roberts to throw up his hands.

Buckshot squinted as he casually rose to his feet, levelling his carbine from the hip as he did so.

"Not much, Mary Anne..." he murmured as both guns roared simultaneously.

Bowdre gasped and doubled over as the Winchester slug hit him square in the midriff, but incredible luck was with him that day. The bullet connected with Charlie's solid metal gun belt buckle, severing its connection to the leather and, almost comically, dropping it along with its holster to the ground around his ankles. But the round was not spent, ricocheting to the side and tearing into George Coe's right hand, mangling his thumb and totally blowing off his trigger finger.

The next few moments could have been lifted directly from a Hollywood Western, and has gone down in the annals as one of the only truly classic gunfights.

Bowdre's bullet had also struck home, but there was no belt buckle to save Roberts. A big puff of dust exploded from Buckshot's coat as the slug tore into his stomach, but it did not stop him. On the contrary, Frank Coe later claimed that he never saw a man handle a Winchester as fast as Buckshot Roberts did that day.

The other Regulators were spurred into action, over a dozen against one, but before they could return shots, the tough ex buffalo hunter was already levering his carbine and spewing out a withering fire.

John Middleton took one of the first bullets, directly in the chest, Scurlock was winged by another. Billy Bonney leapt aside between the wall and a parked wagon as a shot whistled just past him, followed a moment later by one which grazed his arm.

The Regulators were scattering like panicked chickens but Roberts, despite his serious wound, was cool as a cucumber. Billy alone remained in the fight. A Winchester carbine held a maximum of ten rounds and the Kid realised that Roberts had emptied the chamber. Jumping back onto the porch, Billy raised his own Winchester, but, as he pulled the trigger, the quick thinking Roberts used his empty carbine as a weapon, jabbing it sharply into Billy's stomach, winding him and deflecting his aim. Just in time, the Kid's bullet whined past Roberts, smashing into the door frame.

Doubled over and gasping, Billy drew back as Roberts somehow staggered along the porch where he all but fell through the doorway into Blazer's empty office. He must have been in terrible pain, weakened by that gut shot, but there was plenty of fight left in him yet. His carbine was empty but he quickly found Blazer's Springfield rifle hanging on the wall; a box of ammunition too.

Bleeding heavily, he took the weapon down, slipped a cartridge in the breech and prepared his defence. There was a bed in the room so he pulled the mattress from it and used it as a barricade across the open door before laying down to cover anyone who might dare to approach.

The Springfield was a single shot weapon but a few choice and well aimed blasts from it were enough to keep the Regulators scattered and taking cover wherever they could.

Nursing their wounds and reeling from the shock of the old warrior's courage and resilience, the Regulators were pinned down and reluctant to face Buckshot head on. Middleton was the most badly hurt and his friends did their best to treat his wound, a bullet lodged in his lung.

Dick Brewer was outraged. How could one man have decimated

them like this? Frustrated and determined to get his man, the Regulator's leader demanded that they gather themselves for an assault but no one seemed keen. When Dr. Blazer and Agent Godfroy turned up, Brewer ordered them to do something, to at least try and speak to Roberts as go-betweens and get him to surrender but nobody wanted to go near him.

Even Billy Bonney, who was usually game for anything, hesitated.

When even Brewer's threat to set the house ablaze failed to get anyone moving, he angrily declared that he would get the job done by himself. The others watched him as he clutched his rifle and set off across the stream, circling his way down towards the sawmill. To the west of the house, he found a position behind a pile of logs which gave him a good view of the doorway where Roberts lay.

Taking careful aim over the log pile, Brewer chanced a shot. It was close but flew over Roberts' head, smashing into the wall behind where he lay.

Buckshot was a wily and cool customer, badly hurt though he was. He must have noted the drift of gunsmoke snaking up from above the logs where Brewer was positioned.

Shifting his own position slightly, Roberts turned the barrel of Blazer's Springfield towards the log pile, cocked the weapon and sighted it.

He did not have long to wait. Brewer foolishly had not thought to move as he took the chance of raising his head above cover. Roberts' squeezed the trigger as soon as he saw that head appear and the big heavy slug whistled across 125 yards, ripping into Brewer's left eye and blowing a huge exit hole through the back of his skull.

Quite a shot.

From that moment, the Regulators decided that enough was enough.

No one would be so foolish as to try and get Roberts after that.

Dr. Blazer, though a dentist by trade, did what he could for the wounded and Godfroy loaned a wagon to transport them for further treatment. Everyone thought Middleton would not survive his chest wound but, incredibly, he did.

Brewer, of course, was beyond help.

As the Regulators left Blazer's Mill, attempts were made to persuade Roberts to allow someone in to attend to him but, still stubborn, he refused to believe that his enemies had gone. Eventually an old man who Roberts worked with at the Dolan store was able to get close enough to convince him but, by now, he was very weak.

The military surgeon from Fort Stanton had been summoned but there was nothing they could do for the gut shot old warrior and he died the next day.

Ironically, Buckshot Roberts and Dick Brewer were buried alongside each other on the slopes behind the Blazer House.

***

Sadly, and to my great disappointment, I was unable to locate the site of Blazer's Mill. Apparently, Interstate 70 runs right through the middle of the gunfight's location, which, I was told, can be seen from the road. Despite driving up and down several times, I just could not see anything which seemed relevant to me. I did spot a sign or two for "Mescalero", relating to the Apache reservation, but no entrance to an old road or historic markers. I was later informed that I must have been right on top of it. So near and yet so far...

On Youtube, one can find several videos of the area, shot by enthusiasts who managed to find what I could not. It seems you can park up and wander around but there are mixed opinions about how accessible it is. However, most seem to agree that what remains has been allowed to deteriorate needlessly. Very little remains of how it would have looked on the day of the gunfight in 1878. The New Mexican authorities, regardless of criticism, appear to be totally disinterested in making any effort to preserve this important example of their historical heritage.

However, there is at least a marker which gives a brief description of what occurred there and a cemetery with about fifty headstones. These graves contain the bones of a variety of characters... soldiers, scouts, local settlers and several members of the Blazer family, etc., but, the most famous are the neatly kept stones above the bodies of Dick Brewer and Buckshot Roberts, still lying side by side.

I also need to mention that Roberts was probably not known by his cool moniker of "Buckshot" whilst he was actually alive. More recent research appears to show that this name was attached to him long after his death in later accounts by writers who added colour to his tale. That in itself is a kind of disappointment too, because "Buckshot" really suits him.

For that reason, I hope the serious historians will forgive me for referring to him as such here.

CHAPTER 20
SIEGE

The gunfight at Blazer's Mill was another big setback for McSween's cause, yet it still retained much power, sympathy and support.

However, damage was done. Tunstall's murder had been largely eclipsed by the suspect killings of Morton, Baker and McCloskey and then, even worse, by the blatantly public broad daylight assassination of Sheriff Brady and Deputy Hindman.

And now, the death of Buckshot Roberts, whose incredible lone fight against huge odds was a source of great admiration in the frontier community.

This was slightly countered by the death of Dick Brewer who was a respected and popular figure locally. The bottom line, however, was the fact that all these encounters had not been fought out on what was considered *"fair ground"* (an important aspect of the "Old West code").

All these things were points in Dolan's favour, but he was by no means winning in the popularity stakes.

When the court finally convened at the Lincoln Courthouse on April 10th. (two days later than scheduled), presided over by Judge Bristol and overseen by District Attorney Rynerson, it lasted for most of the remainder of the month. Even with the authority and "House" bias of these two senior legal figures the sessions were somewhat chaotic. The selected grand jury listened to no end of witnesses to the dramas of the last few months, testimonies which clashed colourfully depending upon which side was being taken.

The circumstances surrounding all the matters on trial were confused and complicated but, at last, a few conclusions were reached.

McSween was cleared of his embezzlement charge (the jury being largely sympathetic to him helped with this, naturally). On the more serious murder charges, Buck Morton, Tom Hill and Jesse Evans were considered rightly guilty of killing John Tunstall but of the three of them, only one was still alive... Evans... and he was wounded and in custody at Fort Stanton. (This was the result of an unrelated shootout which had taken place early in March when Evans and Hill had attempted to rob a sheep drover who fought back, killed Hill and wounded Evans.) Dolan and Jake Mathews were accused as accessories to the Tunstall murder, even though not present for the deed.

Charlie Bowdre faced the charge of killing Buckshot Roberts, which was fair enough, and Fred Waite was indicted for the death of Deputy Hindman.

For the murder of Sheriff Brady, indictments fell upon Billy Bonney, John Middleton and Henry Brown, while the killings of Morton, Brady and McCloskey were not even on the agenda. The entire process was a mish-mash of hearsay and confusion.

Many who were known to be guilty of numerous misdemeanours seemed to escape scot-free whilst innocent parties were persecuted.

Along with his business partner John Riley, Jimmy Dolan's problems were worsening by the day and bankruptcy had finally caught up with them. At the beginning of the year, with financial pressures building, Dolan had mortgaged his store, the big *House* headquarters, to the all powerful Thomas Catron, New Mexico's District Attorney. It had now reached the point where Catron had the property seized and the Dolan store/H.Q. had to shut up shop.

The new Sheriff, John Copeland, Brady's replacement, was not good news for Dolan either. Slow witted and easily manipulated, Copeland was soon convinced by McSween to lean in his favour. Before long he was enjoying the company of the Regulators in their McSween House sanctuary which was ironic, because he now carried the arrest warrants for Billy and the others but made no effort to enforce them.

Despite all that was hanging over them, the Regulators appeared to relax and carouse with abandon. Sue McSween's piano could often be heard rattling out merry tunes as the tough cowboys sang along and whooped it up in the parlour.

The Reverend Ealy's wife, Mary, who often played for them, recalled how they stood around, draped with cartridge belts and guns, as they warbled, laughed and enjoyed themselves. None sang more loudly than Billy Bonney, but Mary fondly said they were all *"very nice and polite"*.

The ambitions of the Regulators had not been diminished in the slightest. To replace Brewer as their leader they had chosen the Chisum man Frank McNab and Billy Bonney's status within their ranks had also taken quite a leap.

Still barely out of boyhood in years, the Kid had done much to prove his worth during the violent escapades of late. Billy's courage and skill with firearms was beyond doubt and he could always be counted upon to be up front when the chips were down. His ruthless insistence on rough justice, particularly during the Morton/Baker incident, proved that he was decisive and callous when necessary. When the bullets flew he stood tall, as was seen during his fearless sprint to Sheriff Brady's body and when he confronted Buckshot Roberts.

The Kid seemed to live a charmed life too as bullets flew all around him, inflicting a graze or two but never doing serious damage.

By now he had been involved in several gunfights, returning fire with the best of them but, up until now, the only verified kill put down solely to him was that of Windy Cahill back in the summer of '77. However, along with others, he had certainly put bullets into Brady, Morton and Baker and, perhaps, some more...

Jimmy Dolan was still determined to see the recently appointed arrest warrants served on the Kid, Waite, Brown, Middleton and Bowdre, technical fugitives who the new Sheriff Copeland was openly socializing with. Losing patience, Dolan called upon Dad Peppin and Jake Mathews, who still considered themselves deputies on the previous authority of the dead Brady, to ride on down to Seven Rivers and form a posse from the cowboys there. The idea was that with a bunch of gunmen behind him, Copeland might be persuaded to act and do his job.

At Seven Rivers, the two deputies had no problem finding men who were willing to go up against the Regulators. Numbering about thirty, on April 29th., they were cantering towards Lincoln when they encountered a couple of their targets, Frank McNab (the leader) and Frank Coe with his brother-in-law, Ab Saunders. An immediate firefight brought down the Regulator's horses, wounding Saunders badly. McNab and Coe tried to escape up the channels of separate gullies but McNab was chased by Manuel "Indian" Segovia, one of Jesse Evans' "Boys", who killed him with a shotgun blast.

Coe ran into a dead end and surrendered.

The next day, when this posse reached Lincoln, they reoccupied the seized Dolan store and sent some of their number out to occupy positions around town.

Sheriff Copeland, relaxing with his Regulator friends inside the McSween store, received word that a posse had arrived to help him make the arrests, which must have been awkward for him, to say the least. The Regulators responded by taking up arms and filtering outside to meet this new threat.

Some of them made their way to the rooftops to take up firing stations.

George Coe, sitting with Henry Brown atop the Ellis Store, drew the first and only blood in what became known, over grandly, as The Battle of Lincoln. George must have been in discomfort, nursing the raw stump where his trigger finger had once been three weeks before, courtesy of Buckshot Roberts. Somehow he was still able to handle his Sharps rifle because he laid a keen eye upon a target which he could just make out as a man's shape, out in the open, several hundred yards away.

It was a long shot but Coe's aim was true and a posse man named Dutch Charlie was drilled through both legs.

This acted as a signal for both sides to open up on each other, and for several hours they blasted away from the rooftops and behind walls, making a lot of noise but inflicting no further human damage.

A bewildered Sheriff Copeland, unsure what to do, sent for help from Fort Stanton, and yet again a score of soldiers arrived to try and bring peace to the beleaguered town. Their lieutenant asked Copeland who, exactly, he wanted arrested to which the Sheriff replied, *"The whole damned business"*, whatever he meant by that.

This was interpreted as the attacking posse, the Regulators presumably being seen as defenders of Lincoln.

In the confusion, Frank Coe, who was being held prisoner in the old Dolan Store, managed to slip away and join his *compadres*.

As the firing petered out, the thirty or so possemen seemed to tire of the pointless battle but they were not going to surrender to Copeland. As a compromise, the officer in charge of the cavalrymen agreed to take them into custody at the Fort until things settled down. So that is where they went as the Regulators dispersed yet again, Billy, Bowdre and Middleton (miraculously recovering from his chest wound) heading for their preferred haunts in San Patricio which soon became a kind of secondary headquarters for all of the Kid's fellow riders.

Back at Fort Stanton a new commanding officer had taken charge earlier in the month. Lt.Col. Nathan Dudley was now saddled with thirty or so Dolan possemen in his custody and he really did not want the responsibility.

McSween had obtained a further warrant, this time from the Justice of the Peace at San Patricio, which called for the arrest of most of these possemen for the murder of McNab. This document was presented to Lt.Col. Dudley who really did not want to know. He disliked McSween and was angered by Sheriff Copeland's lack of impartiality. The short tempered Lt. Colonel instigated the creation of yet another warrant, from the Justice of the Peace at Blazer's Mill, for the arrest of McSween and several Regulators on a charge of "riot".

Within a few days, the bewildered Sheriff Copeland asked Dudley to release the Dolan possemen. The army was more than glad to be rid of them and they were too much for Copeland. Clueless as to what he should do with them, the Sheriff just told them to go home and stop making trouble!

Both factions now squared up to each other with renewed determination. One of the first things each side did was to recruit more Hispanics into their respective little armies, the idea being to embrace sympathy from the local community at large.

The Regulators had chosen Doc Scurlock to replace Brewer as their leader and he quickly proved to be decisive. In the middle of May, with a deputy's authority imposed by Copeland, Doc led his men on a raid on the Dolan cow camp near Seven Rivers. They rounded up horses and mules and sent the cattle scattering in panic across the plain, as well as capturing "Indian" Segovia, the Mexican who had killed McNab.

Indian was certain that his captors would kill him. Billy and Doc were overhead discussing the desire to do so. Hardly surprising then that the captive made a break for it, pursued by the Kid and the Hispanic's head deputy.

Indian did not get far and was shot down either by Billy, the deputy, or probably both.

The attack on what was thought to be Dolan's property was a fatal error because it all now belonged to the unforgiving Thomas Catron, following Dolan's bankruptcy. This complicated matters more than ever by stirring the wrath of the Santa Fe Ring.

Copeland was removed from his position as Sheriff, his place taken by Dad Peppin, so the official authority of the law was now very much back in the hands of the Dolanites.

Over the next few weeks, aside from a brief period of peace, during which the factions regrouped, there were several clashes, notably two at San Patricio and one at Chisum's ranch. There was a lot of gunfire and galloping around but, surprisingly, apart from a few shot horses and men slightly wounded there were no more fatalities at this stage.

As for Billy Bonney, he was now a seasoned warrior, much respected by the older men, not just for his riding and gun skills but also for his enthusiasm and courage.

With the carefree attitude of youth he was probably loving the thrill of it all. He was also infatuated with John Chisum's teenaged blonde niece, Sallie. She liked him too but we can only speculate as to how far their romance progressed. They had known each other for quite some time and spent hours sitting on the porch in the moonlight. They also liked to race horses together, and who knows what else?

Sometime during this period, Billy found another friend. This was

Tom O'Folliard (maybe just Folliard), a young, naïve Texan who had shown up at Frank Coe's ranch seeking work. He was tall with red hair and a likeable personality. Billy took to him straightaway and thought he had potential. Tom was soon taken into the Regulator fold.

O'Folliard hero worshipped Billy and became his constant companion. Billy taught him to shoot using a buffalo gun and Tom followed him around, even holding his horse outside places where the Kid was entertaining one of his senoritas. Devotion indeed... and maybe just a tad weird!

Warrants and counter claims flew around like confetti. Narrow escapes, threats and tension built to boiling point. Billy himself now faced two separate charges; the original territorial warrant for Brady's killing and now, the addition of the murder of Buckshot Roberts which was no longer just hung upon Charlie Bowdre. Because Roberts had been slain on the Mescalero Indian Reservation, this made it a Federal matter.

McSween felt that he had been on the run for long enough. Hiding out in the hills and living like a fugitive was not his style, so, on July 14th. 1878, he made a somewhat triumphant and challenging return, by night, to Lincoln at the head of around sixty men, Regulators included.

This formidable force spread out around the town, occupying McSween's house and the Montano and Ellis stores, knocking gun ports in the roof parapets. There were Dolan men stationed at the Wortley Hotel and a handful occupying the Torreon but they were greatly outnumbered. Most of Dad Peppin's men were out on the hunt for the Regulators so those in Lincoln kept a low profile for now.

It all changed the following afternoon when Peppin and his armed toughs cantered into town, reining in outside of the Wortley Hotel where they were soon updated on the situation. Many of them were veterans from the Mathews' posse, including Jesse Evans and his Boys. John Kinney and his Mesilla crew had joined them too.

Wasting no time, even though McSween had the advantage in numbers (by about sixty to forty), Peppin's men lined up alongside the nearby McSween house and commenced a rapid fire. The targeted building rocked as the shots smashed home, pocking the walls and shattering the window shutters.

It was a hot day but high winds were whipping up dust clouds. Into this, and alerted by the gunfire, Billy Bonney emerged from the Montano store at the head of a dozen or so supporters, rushing down the street and exchanging gunfire with the Dolan men in the Torreon. They reached the McSween house just in time to join those there in responding to the attack with volleys of their own.

Peppin and Dolan's men scurried for cover as Billy's group sought refuge in the house. And yet, with all these bullets zipping through the air there were still no casualties.

McSween himself was despondent. His strong willed wife, Sue, had returned from her trip out east but the Scotsman was far from happy about the way things had gone. He just wanted to find a way out of this mess.

Over the next five days, this new Battle of Lincoln was largely a stalemate as the opposing sides scoured each other's weaknesses, exchanging the odd pot shot but doing little damage. McSween's men were spread between several strongholds, so although they had the advantage of numbers, the Dolan/Peppin faction were able to concentrate their fire more intensely. In this way, they did succeed in killing one defender in the McSween house and seriously wounding another.

The McSween men also made the mistake of inadvertently firing upon soldiers who were bringing messages from the Fort. Although they did not actually hit any of them, this infuriated their hot headed Lt. Colonel Dudley who was also under pressure from constant pleas for help from the Lincoln townsfolk.

Dudley was supposed to be neutral, but his personal dislike of McSween prompted him to act. Under the guise of trying to keep the peace, to protect innocent citizens who were caught in the middle of this pandemonium, Dudley brought his troops to town.

On July 19th. he rode at the head of a column of cavalry and infantrymen, but they brought with them a howitzer and a Gatling gun.

This was an ominous sight for the McSween defenders, even though they knew that Dudley could not officially take sides.

Dudley's troops set up camp nearly opposite the Montano store and officers could be seen entering the Wortley Hotel to speak to those inside. This led to McSween's conclusion that the army had come to Dolan's aid and it created something of a panic inside the house.

McSween immediately wrote a note to Dudley demanding to know why soldiers were threatening his house and reminding him that he was with a constable who possessed warrants for the arrest of Peppin and company. Dudley's reply was dismissive and his actions were confrontational and worrying.

The howitzer was blatantly aimed at the Montano store. Dudley excused this in the interests of a "defensive measure". Understandably alarmed and fearing a twelve pound shell at any moment, the defenders vacated the building and ran across to the Ellis store to join their comrades there. Dudley reacted to this by ordering the howitzer to be retrained on the Ellis store instead... and he was supposed to be impartial!

This caused a mass evacuation of the store. Any attempts to make it to the McSween house were driven back by rifle fire from Peppin's men and they were forced to retreat across the shallows of the Bonito and into the hills.

Dudley was obviously intent on keeping these men out of the fight because when some of them tried to join McSween later on, he aimed the Gatling gun at them, persuading them to retreat again, this time for good.

This was a heavy blow to McSween and the Regulators because this supposedly neutral interference of the army had cost them about two thirds of their firepower.

McSween's hardcore of Regulators were left to defend his big, U shaped adobe house. Billy was there, along with Tom O'Folliard, George Coe, Henry Brown, Jim French and a fair gathering of other Anglo and Hispanic supporters.

Loyal Regulators like Frank Coe, John Middleton, Doc Scurlock, Charlie Bowdre and probably Fred Waite had been amongst those ousted from the Ellis store.

It was now impossible for the McSween house defenders to return fire on Peppin's men for fear of hitting Dudley's soldiers, so it had become a somewhat one sided contest.

Sue McSween courageously decided to do something, or at least try.

Marching out into the street she confronted Dad Peppin at the Torreon, who had just given orders to burn out the defenders. Sue observed these preparations with horror, yelling at Peppin as his men prepared the kindling to set fire to her home

Peppin was unmoved, telling her that the only answer was for her to persuade the Regulators and their followers to surrender.

Mrs. McSween carried on determinedly to the soldier's campsite where she angrily challenged Lt.Col. Dudley. Sue slung justifiable accusations at him of favouring the Dolan side plus pleading with him to save her husband, house and friends. But Dudley remained stubborn, insisting that he had no authority to interfere in civil matters, even though he so obviously had.

Frustrated, Sue made her way back to her house to find that Peppin's men had been working hard on progressing their intended arson. There were kitchens at the end of each wing of the building and one of them had kindling piled up against the door. A family named Shield occupied this part of the house and they were trying to remove furniture from the room before anything was lit but the posse men pushed more kindling through onto the floor, soaking it in coal oil.

The menfolk in the house saw this happening but did nothing to prevent it, probably worried that any resistance might trigger an armed response from the army. A pair of Peppin arsonists got the fire going and started to make their retreat across the backyard, but they were surprised by a burst of fire from the Tunstall store next door. George Coe and a couple more Regulators had positioned themselves there and the posse men ran for the closest cover... the open pit of the crude outdoor privy!

Knee deep in raw sewage, the arsonists were pinned down for hours by a constant fire from an amused George Coe.

The fire they set did not burn for long, probably extinguished by those inside, but in the kitchen of the other wing, more Peppin men succeeded. The flames from their efforts took hold by mid afternoon and, though it burned slowly, it was relentless and out of control.

The women and children were permitted to leave unmolested and they sought shelter in the Tunstall store. Sue McSween stayed with her husband for a while longer but Alexander was in a state of helpless despair. Sitting with his head in his hands, he merely agreed that his wife should make her escape while she could, and so she did.

McSween could no longer be considered the Regulator's symbol of resistance. He appeared to have given up hope. Billy tried to rally him, shaking his arm and saying that they would have to make a break for it.

With Doc Scurlock forced into retreat from the Ellis store and beyond offering help somewhere in the hills, all eyes turned on Billy Bonney. Eighteen years old but the only one present who was showing any gumption.

This moment was another turning point for The Kid, when his reputation took another turn upwards. For the first time, he naturally assumed the role of leader and he took to it gleefully. Apparently, in the midst of this deadly crisis he grinned, joked and whistled merrily, as if he had not a care in the world.

The flames were slowly but surely spreading from room to room and the house occupants, now all men and numbering fourteen, were forced to retreat. By about 9.00pm., with darkness descending, they were all crowded into the cramped space of the north east kitchen where the original fire had failed to take hold.

The back door of this kitchen was their only escape route and Peppin's men would be ready for them, weapons cocked.

Huddling together in the cloying heat, choking on the smoke, they all still looked to Billy. McSween was useless, a bundle of shaking nerves and Billy slapped him to try and bring him around, telling him that he needed to live for the war to continue after this night. Not fully responding, remaining in a daze, McSween answered *"Boys, I have lost my mind…"*

Billy turned to the others and outlined his plan. No point in dashing out in a blaze of glory, guns blasting. Although the raging fire was illuminating the night sky and much of the surrounding area, the backdoor itself and part of the yard leading to the gate were in darkness. The Kid asked for volunteers to break cover first, turning east for the Tunstall store, giving McSween and a few others the chance to dash north towards the river where they could hide in the cover of the trees, bushes and deep shadows.

Billy's volunteers were O'Folliard (of course), Big Jim French, Jose Chavez y Chavez and a non combatant named Harvey Morris. This unfortunate fellow, suffering from tuberculosis, was no Regulator but just happened to be visiting McSween studying law. He refused the offer of a gun, as did McSween who just clutched a Bible to his chest.

It was now or never. With the flames licking at their backs, Billy, with a pistol in each hand, led them through the door, stealthily treading their way across the yard. The gate was swung open, beyond which the alleyway was bathed in the orange light of the flames. Morris stepped through, an immediate target for Peppin's gunmen who opened up immediately. As Morris dropped, Billy and the others burst into action, running for the next building and shooting blindly into the blackness.

Dodging back and forth, the Kid and the surviving trio veered north away from the Tunstall store where Peppin's men were concentrating their fire. They found the sanctuary of pitch darkness where they continued running on down to the safety of the banks of the Bonito. Here they bumped into George Coe, Henry Brown and another Regulator who had also decided to make their escape from the Tunstall store.

The plan had fallen to pieces for McSween and those with him. As they tried to follow Billy's group, the Peppin posse were ready for them and a volley of shots drove them back towards the blazing kitchen, but the fire was too intense for them to re-enter. Instead they backed into the shadows of the outer wall, some of them crawling into a chicken shed in the corner.

Hopelessly trapped, McSween called out that he would surrender. Deputy Bob Beckwith, quoting the details of his arrest warrant, cautiously made his way across the yard just as McSween, clutching his Bible, stepped out of the shadows into the light of his burning house.

And then it all went crazy...

Someone, maybe McSween, suddenly cried out, defiantly, *"I shall never surrender!"*

This was the trigger for a rapid exchange of bullets from both sides. A perfect target, Beckwith took a round full in the face. As the deputy fell dead, McSween, fully exposed in the glare of the flames, and even more eye catching in his pure white shirt, took the full force of five shots. His body jerking with each impact, the lawyer pitched forward across Beckwith, dead before he hit the ground.

Flashes from numerous guns erupted from all points in the darkness, firing wildly at invisible targets. The chicken shed was literally shredded with shots and, inside, Regulators Francisco Zamora and Vincente Romero were riddled multiple times, killing them. Yginio Salazar was hit in the back, knocking him down, whilst another Hispanic Regulator made it down to the River, though wounded. A handful of others also got away.

Peppin's men were triumphant. With all resistance crushed, they stepped into the light. One of them wanted to shoot the wounded Salazar but was talked out of it and they left him where he lay. Salazar later managed to crawl to the safety of his sister's house as the sound of the posse's drunken celebrations rang through the night air.

Billy Bonncy's group of fugitives made their way along the bank of the Bonito, rendezvousing at the Ellis store where they grabbed a quick bite to eat. Ike Ellis was anxious for them to move on, understandably, and so they did, sleeping in the open that night before stealing horses and making for Frank Coe's ranch.

***

A ten mile stretch of achingly pretty hill country took me west into Old Lincoln which immediately struck me as a rather lovely and well preserved example of how things used to be. Just one main street still, laid out virtually as the Kid would have known it during the height of the Lincoln County War... with the exception of the modern road and motor cars, of course.

Many of the original buildings have been lovingly restored or recreated... the Ellis and Montano stores... the Torreon which stands as a vivid symbol to the town's colourful past. The Tunstall store too, inside of which you can experience the atmosphere of how it was in 1878, complete with shelves lined with accurate goods of the time. Nearby stands the Wortley Hotel which closely resembles the original, and across the street is the unmistakeable County Courthouse which I shall describe in detail further on in these pages.

Where McSween's house stood is just an empty lot now... a green lawn shaded by a line of trees, through which you can still wander down to the flowing waters of the Rio Bonito.. Following the fire, the house was never rebuilt. In the 1980s, a series of archaeological digs unearthed some interesting fragments which gave a few clues about the McSween's lifestyle.

John Tunstall and Alexander McSween are buried alongside one another, the former preceding his partner by several months. Tunstall at least had a reasonable funeral but, under the circumstances, McSween's was a somewhat rushed and traumatic affair, his body unceremoniously wrapped in a grubby blanket without a coffin. Both of them were interred in the yard on the eastern side of Tunstall's store but the markers were inaccurately placed several yards away, behind the store itself. Also buried with them are the bodies of Regulator Frank McNab and that unlucky law student/non combatant Harvey Morris who was in the wrong place at the wrong time.

CHAPTER 21
REGULATORS ADIOS

The reassembled Regulators remained a formidable crew but the Five Day Battle of Lincoln had, in effect, brought the Lincoln County War to a messy conclusion.

With Tunstall and McSween eliminated and Murphy/Dolan in the throes of bankruptcy what was left to fight over, apart from endless "tit for tat" vengeance?

A great deal of blood had been spilt over the last few months and this had inevitably led to resentment and much heartbreak. Ultimately, it had all proven to be so pointless.

Although Doc Scurlock still technically led what remained of the Regulators, his enthusiasm was obviously dwindling and his attention was being drawn back to his ranch and family. Billy had now really proven himself to be a natural leader and following the McSween house breakout, the older men were now looking at him with an even fonder respect.

Quick thinking and cool in a crisis, the Kid was now a man amongst the best of them; in fact he shone.

Licking their wounds at Frank Coe's place, Billy had no intention of growing idle or hiding away. Stirring up his followers, he quickly led them back to Lincoln, determined for a showdown, but the posse had dispersed. In the cold light of day, Dad Peppin had re-evaluated his position. Realising that the most dangerous of the Regulators were still at large, the Sheriff recalled the fate of Brady and sought refuge at Fort Stanton under the protection of his ally Lt.Col. Dudley.

Billy and his men spent a few days in town putting pressure on anyone who they perceived as having assisted Peppin and Dolan, but the main culprits had made themselves scarce.

In early August, the Regulators rode on to Blazer's Mill, frightening the Indian agent Godfroy who seemed to think he was on their hitlist. There was no tangible reason for him to be on it but it must have been quite intimidating when about a score of them rode in. In fact, the gunmen wanted to visit the grave of their late leader, Dick Brewer, but that was not the only reason for their presence. They were probably after horses... Apache horses... With Billy were the usual faces; O'Folliard, the Coes, Scurlock, Bowdre, Middleton, French, Waite, plus a similar number of Hispanics who were riding separately.

Near to the Mill, Billy's group trotted down to a spring to water their horses as the Hispanic party rode on up the main trail. Within moments shots rang out from the direction ahead. The Hispanics had confronted some Apaches and somehow the two parties had commenced firing upon each other.

By sheer misfortune, Agent Godfroy and his clerk Bernstein had ridden into this melee and Bernstein was shot from his saddle, dead. Godfroy spun his mount and galloped back to the Mill where he rallied some soldiers who happened to be present.

When they got back to the road, the first thing the soldiers saw was Billy's group down at the spring who by now were being fired upon by the Apaches.

The Kid and his men were taken aback by this. Billy's horse reared from where he had led it to drink and broke away from him. The Regulators took off but Billy was left on foot until George Coe cantered up alongside him, reaching down to help the Kid clamber up behind his saddle. As shots whistled around them they, double mounted, managed to get away.

Back at the Blazer's corral, Billy and three others who had lost their mounts chose unsaddled horses from an enclosure. The Kid threw a rope around one and rode it bareback away from the scene.

The killing of Bernstein, although nothing to do with Billy, seemed to start a trend which haunted the Kid for the rest of his life. Apaches or Hispanic Regulators had slain the clerk, probably inadvertently, but the killing was almost instantly blamed upon Billy Bonney. This was largely stirred up by the resentful Lt.Col. Dudley who called it a cowardly murder which *"excels the killing of Sheriff Brady"*.

Another crime on the reservation, a federal act which Dudley felt gave him the justification to hunt the Kid down with troops. All to no avail however, as Billy slipped away easily.

With the desire to place themselves out of harm's way, the Regulators put some miles behind them, heading up the Rio Pecos with stolen horses. Chisum had his original ranch at Bosque Grande and Billy and company arrived there in mid August. The big boss John was away on business in Missouri but his brothers, Jim and Pitzer, were there preparing for a cattle drive northwards.

The Regulators were warmly welcomed and Billy was pleased to find Sallie Chisum there. Jim was her father and she was accompanying him and her uncle on the drive. She and Billy had been exchanging letters for quite a while so they were probably expecting to meet up.

When the Chisums moved out, carrying on up the Pecos, Billy's Regulators tagged along, reaching Fort Sumner a couple of days later where they stayed over.

Fort Sumner had been established as a military post during the

Civil War but its purpose was to oversee a new Indian reservation. It was a brutal plan. The U.S. government waged war on the local Apaches and Navajos, destroying their homes, fields and livestock in an attempt to "civilize" them by forcing the tribes into farming and Christianity. Those who survived armed conflict were starved into submission and the area became a virtual prison camp for the tribes.

This attempt to *"anglocise"* these people was a total failure and by 1868 most of them were permitted to trek back to their original homes.

In 1870, the whole site was sold to wealthy land holder Lucien Maxwell who refurbished the deserted buildings and moved his family there.

Lucien eventually turned his interests over to his son Pete who was soon the patriarch of a pleasant little village centred around the old parade ground, mainly populated by Hispanics. Maxwell's fine house faced east onto the open space and the north end was decorated by an attractive peach orchard. The old barracks across from the Maxwell house had been converted into homes and small businesses. Beaver Smith and Bob Hargrove each operated a saloon at opposite ends of the village, Beaver to the south, Bob to the north.

The parties began almost immediately and carried on for a week or so, starting with a lively *baile* on the night they arrived; the Coes brought out their fiddles and the dancing commenced as the whisky flowed free. Mexican girls, cowboys and Regulators had a whale of a time, carousing merrily until the small hours.

Billy, as always at these occasions, was the centre of attraction but, popular though he was, it seems that his attention was firmly attached to Sallie. He bought her candy and other gifts and she responded affectionately. In her diary she wrote that he was always good natured, happy and pleasant and that he could be *"quite a dandy"*, sometimes wearing a bright flower on his coat.

It was a frivolous, freewheeling period for the Kid and his friends and they were making the most of it. Bidding their farewells to the Chisum party, who turned towards Texas, the Regulators carried on up the Pecos with no particular aim in mind. Reaching Puerto de Luna they indulged in a few more nights of partying with the locals before pushing on to another small village, Anton Chico, to recuperate.

Here, however, they encountered further potential trouble. About twenty miles north lay Las Vegas where the Hispanic Sheriff, Desiderio Romera, had received word that the "Lincoln County War Party" were in his vicinity, Gathering a heavily armed posse, Romera had taken the trip down to Anton Chico to investigate.

Billy immediately heard that this posse had established themselves in Sanchez's Saloon and he was keen to confront them.

Romera's men were Mexican toughs, bristling with weaponry, numbering half a dozen or more. They were all strung out along the bar, full of questions, as Billy entered the room, the Regulators spreading out behind him.

The Kid, without hesitation, strode straight up to Sheriff Romera, who must have been somewhat shocked by this unexpected appearance, especially when Billy brazenly declared that here was the "Lincoln County War Party" he was looking for and what did he intend to do about it?

The Regulators had command of the situation and Romera knew it. The Mexican posse's threat deflated in seconds and Billy flashed his engaging smile.

"Take a drink on the house," he said, pleasantly, but with meaning, *"then we want you to leave..."*

Romera and his men drank up swiftly and left town without argument.

A couple more days of celebration and the Regulators camped outside of town for a serious discussion about the future.

What exactly were they going to do? This aimless wandering could not continue indefinitely. Frank and George Coe had certainly had enough and wanted to ride away from the outlaw life, setting themselves up anew in Colorado.

Billy respected that decision but made it clear that he still felt that he needed to avenge all that had happened. All but the Coes agreed to support him and so they parted company amicably.

With his diminished band, and now the undisputed leader, Billy headed back towards Lincoln, indulging in some more horse theft *en route*. The plan was to herd them into Texas for sale to the numerous cattlemen there, it being the surviving Regulators only realistic means of income.

Doc Scurlock and Charlie Bowdre had not been with the others during the Fort Sumner adventure. Their enthusiasm for further outlawry had been dimmed following the killing of Bernstein at Blazer's Mill and they had chosen to return to their families on their respective ranches. When Billy and their other old friends showed up again, Scurlock and Bowdre were reminded of the danger which still hung around them in Lincoln County. Lt.Col. Dudley was making noises about them too, loudly saying that the "McSween Ring" was back in the vicinity, stock stealing and making trouble.

Doc and Charlie decided to uproot themselves, and their families, count their losses and head north with their ex Regulator pals. Billy was glad to have them along, even though he knew they were not rejoining him permanently. Driving the stolen horse herd, they returned to Fort Sumner where Scurlock and Bowdre settled down, finding employment with Pete Maxwell.

By now, only a small hard core of the Lincoln County War veterans still rode with the Kid... O'Folliard, Waite, Middleton and French... and they set off for the Texas Panhandle, pointing those illicitly obtained horses.

On the border, in late September, they caught up with the Chisum outfit again, so there must have been another joyous reunion between Billy and Sallie. It was to be their last meeting but she always spoke and wrote about him fondly for the rest of her life.

On the great sweeping plains of the Panhandle, Billy quickly offloaded his stolen herd to the stock buyers who were always on the lookout for good mounts. No questions were asked and the Kid and his followers made a tidy sum.

In Tascosa Billy Bonney made another, on the face of it, unlikely friend. The Kid and his pals were taking it easy again, enjoying the delights of Texan hospitality, when they met a young doctor named Henry Hoyt who was travelling around the frontier before settling down to what became a distinguished medical career.

Hoyt and the Kid hit it off immediately and the doctor soon became part of the Regulator's social circle. Like Billy, Hoyt did not really drink alcohol (like most Westerners profusely did) but they all took part in whatever other pleasures life had to offer... gambling at cards and other sports, target shooting, racing horses, dancing, singing, women... Billy loved all these things.

Hoyt later wrote quite profusely of his life at this time and much of it is most enlightening about Billy Bonney. One story, in particular, tells us a lot...

One fun filled evening, during a *baile* laid on by one Pedro Romero, Billy and Dr. Hoyt strolled out of the dance hall for some fresh air. Reaching the far side of the town plaza, they decided to race each other, on foot, back to the building. As they ran, neck and neck, Billy, in his excitement, stumbled at the doorway and sprawled face forward into the dancing crowd inside.

Face down on the dance floor, and no doubt a little stunned, surrounded by the partygoers, the Kid had not even raised himself to his knees before his friends were around him... O'Folliard, Waite,

Middleton and French... pistols cocked with their backs to their leader, a protective ring of threatening loyalty.

Romero did not allow weapons in his dance hall, but they had somehow managed to smuggle them in. Banned from future *bailes*, the Regulators had dramatically offered proof that they could be counted upon.

It was time for them to move on once more. As they prepared to say goodbye to Tascosa, Hoyt made a gift to Billy of a gold watch. Touched, Billy responded by presenting the doctor with a fine horse named Dandy Dick, which had actually belonged to the murdered Sheriff William Brady. The Kid must have stolen this animal at some point, but to verify the action he even supplied an official bill of sale dated October 24th. 1878.

Now what?

Waite, Brown and Middleton were keen to head east, leaving New Mexico far behind but Billy stubbornly refused to join them. They tried their best to persuade him but the Kid insisted that he was going to return to Lincoln for unfinished business.

And so they parted and it was *"Adios"*. The Regulators were no more.

Billy Bonney and his loyal pal Tom O'Folliard were all that remained.

CHAPTER 22
AMNESTY

Billy and Tom spent a few weeks back in Fort Sumner, in no hurry to move into the next phase of their lives.

They were amongst friends, feeling safe and enjoying themselves but, finally, the Kid pulled himself together and decided to see how the land lay in Lincoln.

He took a leisurely ride there, with Tom, in early December and was welcomed by more old friends, but the town was still inhabited by many erstwhile enemies.

Much had changed. Dad Peppin had failed to get re-elected so a new Sheriff, George Kimball, was in place. Since October, a new Governor too… ex Civil War General Lew Wallace, a colourful figure who, ensconced in his office in Santa Fe, seemed mainly pre-occupied in the writing of his epic novel *Ben-Hur; A Tale of the Christ* which eventually even outsold Beecher Stowe's *Uncle Tom's Cabin*, becoming an American literary classic. For now though, most folks failed to understand his artistic passion and felt he should maybe show more enthusiasm for the day to day business of his new appointment.

Also in October, in Santa Fe, Lawrence Murphy had succumbed to his ill health and was now dead and buried, leaving Dolan and Riley to pick up the pieces of the County War's aftermath.

Sue McSween had also recently returned to Lincoln, having spent a couple of months in Las Vegas plotting her revenge against those who she blamed for her husband's death. Top of the list was Lt.Col. Dudley.

Sue arrived in town accompanied by a lawyer named Huston Chapman whose services she had procured for the advancement of her case against Fort Stanton's commander. Chapman was an excitable fellow, disabled by the loss of one arm, and he pursued his cause loudly and with open accusation. Much of the sympathy for his support of Mrs. McSween was diluted by the fact that his methods and hostile personality made him generally unpopular.

Billy Bonney was tired of being an outlaw. He harboured hopes that now that the war was over, there might be a chance to settle any legal proceedings against him in an amicable fashion. After all, it did appear that no one else involved in the hostilities was going to face charges.

In fact, Governor Wallace had already made a move to draw a line under the troubles as he had no desire to inherit any messy residue from what had occurred before his time. Plus President Rutherford B. Hayes had appointed him specifically to restore peace, law and order to Lincoln County.

In this capacity, Wallace was willing to offer a general pardon to all participants in the conflict, provided they had not been indicted by a grand jury. Unfortunately, that then did not include Billy as he was facing two indictments; one territorial and one federal.

Even so, the Kid was determined to seize any opportunity to clear the air. Maybe coincidentally, maybe not, he took the huge and unexpected step of making his move on February 18th. 1879; exactly one year to the day since Tunstall's murder. On that day he sent a message to his enemies via Fort Stanton requesting a meeting to discuss the possibility of peace.

Dolan's faction must have been surprised by this but the majority welcomed the notion. By this time almost everyone who had been involved in the past year of bloodshed was tired of looking over their shoulders and were willing to find a solution so they could get back to some form of normality in their lives.

Most, that is, but not all.

As it stood, the opposing sides agreed to the arrangement of a parley in the main street of Lincoln that evening, but caution was the name of the game.

Billy and O'Folliard were virtually the only long standing hard core remaining of the Regulators, the others not even being in the Territory. That said, Yginio Salazar (a survivor from McSween's burning house) accompanied them on this peace mission, along with a handful of lesser figures from the Tunstall avengers.

Jimmy Dolan was still around and he conceded to accept the olive branch, backed by a group which included Jake Mathews (who had once wounded Billy and Jim French with a single shot) and the Kid's nemesis Jesse Evans. These Dolanites had a new face on board too, and he was a mean one... a fierce wanderer named Billy Campbell.

Understandably nervous to face each other openly, the two groups initially took positions on either side of the street in the shelter of adobe walls. As already stated, most present were not looking for any further gunplay but the first attempt at shouted negotiation did not start well.

Evans was belligerent from the start, calling out that Billy Bonney was not a character who could be reasoned with and that he should be shot on sight.

Billy, to his credit, must have made a huge effort to swallow his pride because he refused to take the bait; although knowing what we do of his nature it must have stuck in his craw. He replied calmly, shouting over the wall that he was there to speak peace, not open the negotiations with lead.

This did the trick as a few moments later the mood cooled and the opposing sides slowly began to emerge from their respective cover.

For the first time in many months, the Lincoln County War survivors faced each other in close proximity without cocked weapons. Views were exchanged, reasonable words were spoken and the basis of a treaty was agreed upon.

There was to be no further killing and everyone was to swear that no one present would testify against each other in court. To do so would be to violate the treaty and would be a target for a death sentence from the other signees.

A makeshift document was drawn up on the spot and this was signed by those that mattered, resulting in a huge relaxation of tension. Relieved grins were exchanged and hands shaken, but probably not between Bonney and Evans who most likely eyed each other darkly.

It is actually quite something that all these bitter enemies were able to bury the hatchet in this way, especially when it is viewed alongside all that had transpired between them during that long and murderous war. So many of those who had lived through it had emerged with no end of reasons to bear grudges and feelings of vengeance, yet on the evening of the treaty they found cause to celebrate. Maybe it was an uneasy alliance, but the men, numbering about a score in all, immediately embarked upon a tour of Lincoln's saloons and watering holes, sharing drinks like the best of buddies.

Before long, most of them were roaring drunk and making one hell of a noise, except for Billy (never one to indulge in such an alcoholic binge) and O'Folliard. They were along for the ride though and observed it all with interest.

In the latter part of the evening, as they staggered between hostelries, the crowd of revellers encountered someone who would have been much wiser to have kept out of the way that night. It was Huston Chapman, Sue McSween's unpopular lawyer, who had been making himself busy around town with his loud accusations and reminders of all the troubles these drunken gunmen were trying to forget.

Why Chapman presented himself in the middle of the street to encounter this bunch is anyone's guess, but, never the less, there he was, and the staggering crowd gathered around him in front of the courthouse.

The lawyer was a sorry sight, facing them with one empty sleeve pinned across where his missing arm should be, and a heavy bandage wrapped around his face to ease a raging toothache. He carried no weapon.

Billy Campbell looked him up and down and bluntly demanded to know his name, although he probably knew it.

When Chapman complied by stating his name, Campbell laughingly, yet menacingly, ordered him to dance, pulling his pistol and cocking it by way of persuasion. Presumably trying to defuse the situation and having no intention to dance for this drunken bully, Chapman responded by asking if he was addressing Mr. Dolan.

Jesse Evans, always eager to stoke the fire, interjected, *"No, but you are talking to a damned good friend of his!"*

With Campbell's cocked pistol pressed against his chest, Chapman froze, but a few feet away, a well oiled Jimmy Dolan, swaying drunkenly, drew his own pistol at the sound of his name being spoken and, for some reason, probably accidentally, discharged a shot into the street.

Startled by the blast, Campbell's unsteady trigger finger jerked the mechanism and Chapman was blown off his feet. The range was so close that the flash of the gunpowder caught fire to his clothing and he fell dead with flames licking up across his chest.

Momentary shocked silence from the witnesses was soon overcome by further inebriated ribaldry and the party resumed. The crowd staggered on, leaving the lawyer's burning corpse smouldering in the street as they rolled into the next drinking establishment to order supper. As a parting gift, one of them poured a splash of whisky onto the flames to boost the blaze,

Life was certainly cheap in Lincoln that year.

As the celebrants ate, it would seem that at least somebody gave a thought to what had just happened because it was suggested that perhaps a weapon should be placed in the dead man's hand so that, in the cold light of day, self defence could be claimed.

This was deemed a good idea by the indifferent killer. Billy Bonney had stood by, sober, and witnessed the whole thing. He offered to plant the weapon and the others agreed, but it was just an excuse to make himself scarce. Once outside, accompanied by Tom O'Folliard, the Kid left town in haste.

***

The new Sheriff, Kimball, even before Chapman's killing, had been made aware of Billy Bonney's presence in town and, regardless of the Kid's peace mission, was determined to apprehend him. Successfully appealing to Dudley at Fort Stanton, a score of troopers were sent into town to help achieve this, but when they arrived, close to midnight, they found Billy gone and the charred body of the one armed lawyer still laying in the street.

Word soon reached Governor Wallace in Santa Fe, spurring him into action amidst fears that violence was stirring in Lincoln County again. Putting *Ben-Hur* on hold (which must have been quite a wrench for him), Wallace and his entourage turned up in Lincoln on March 5th. to immediately make a show of restoring public confidence in his authority.

Blustering Lt.Col. Dudley was immediately relieved of his command of Fort Stanton and replaced by Captain Henry Carroll. Carroll's first duty was to make a concerted effort to seek out dozens of individuals who were wanted for various misdeeds carried out during the recent war. But, out of the many who were apprehended, almost all would plead that they could be freed under the terms of the new Governor's amnesty... and so they were.

The killing of Huston Chapman had put fresh emphasis on the situation, however, having occurred after the proclaimed amnesty. Plus, of course, quite a few of those on the wanted list were not eligible.

Wallace made a point of stating that he wanted all those present at Chapman's killing to be brought in for questioning. He meant business and soldiers were sent out to hunt down culprits and witnesses alike. Before long, the main players like Evans, Dolan and Campbell (who had fired the fatal shot) were locked up in Fort Stanton, but the hunt continued.

Billy Bonney and Tom O'Folliard were laying low, hiding out with friends at San Patricio as Governor Wallace wrestled with a delicate dilemma. Arrests had been made without warrants and local opinion was beginning to rise against such methods, even though the Governor was struggling to appease everyone. Many potential witnesses were remaining silent, in fear of retribution before courts could convene.

The Kid, always sharp, saw this as a situation he could exploit to his advantage.

Around the middle of March, Billy wrote the first of what would be a string of letters to the Governor. His words were succinct and intelligently expressed; not exactly a work of art but certainly evidence of a more than basic education.

Courteous and to the point, in a couple of paragraphs the Kid stated how he had *"no wish to fight anymore"* and was willing to broker a deal which would be of benefit to Wallace as well as himself. Billy made it clear that he was well aware of the indictments against him, but now that the war was over he had no intention of creating further trouble. He emphasized that many local people would be willing to come forward to verify his essential good character.

"I was present when Mr. Chapman was murdered and know who did it…" he carried on, offering to appear as a witness on the condition that Wallace would use his power to annul the indictments.

This would mean betraying Campbell, Evans and Dolan, but Billy obviously felt that he owed them no favours, regardless of the treaty they had all recently signed before Chapman's death. Those present on that fateful night had sworn to support each other, the penalty for betrayal being execution… however, most of the others were already under lock and key at Fort Stanton so Billy could feel safe enough, for now at least.

Anyway, it was a development which intrigued the Governor and he seized it immediately… a witness willing to speak out was just what he needed.

With Billy's whereabouts still a secret, Wallace sent his reply via the same tight-lipped courier. Yes, he was happy to meet the Kid. He suggested a private parley between them for the following Monday night (the 17th.) at Squire Wilson's house, insisting that Billy come alone under conditions of the utmost stealth and secrecy.

Billy was punctual. At 9.00pm. exactly, Governor Wallace and Wilson were sitting by candlelight in the shadowy surroundings of the Squire's home when the single arranged knock wrapped on the east door.

It was the Kid and he entered cautiously, a Winchester clutched in one hand and a Colt pistol in the other. Over his spectacles, Wallace studied the young outlaw with interest, a little taken aback by his youthful, trailworn countenance. By contrast, the Governor was mature and formal, his cheeks bare and framing a thick bushy moustache and chin beard which burst down over his collar.

The greeting was affable enough, but tense. Wallace and the Squire ushered Billy to a table which they sat around before the Governor spelled out his terms.

In his reply to Billy he had written that he had the authority to exempt the Kid from prosecution but, in fact, this was not true... only the District Attorney could do that, and the D.A. was William Rynerson who would never agree to such leniency for Billy Bonney the outlaw. What Wallace could do was pardon him, promising that he could go *"scott-free"* providing he cooperated in court and thus help convict Chapman's killer.

Billy was still concerned about reprisals, even with the source of his main threat under arrest, but Wallace said he was willing to arrange protective custody by staging the Kid's capture, all for appearance's sake.

It was still a risky venture, but Billy was content enough with the arrangement, shook hands on it and disappeared back into the night-time shadows.

Unfortunately, word came the next day that Jesse Evans and Billy Campbell had escaped from their lock up at the Fort and were soon lost in the wilderness of the mountains. They actually left the territory and headed out to Texas but Billy, thinking he was in immediate danger from their retribution, was not to know that at the time. At least Dolan was still in jail.

The Kid immediately wrote another letter to Wallace, assuring him that he intended to still keep his part of their agreement but that these escapes naturally placed him in unexpected jeopardy. He was not afraid to die fighting like a man, he wrote, but not *"killed like a dog"*. In other words, he was urging the Governor to hurry up and "arrest" him and added to be sure to send men *"that you can depend on"*. Billy also offered up some detailed advice about where he thought the fugitives, Evans and Campbell, could be found.

Sheriff Kimball took a posse up to San Patricio for an easy going and compliant arrest of Billy and Tom O'Folliard in their safe house. They were then taken down to Lincoln where Juan Patron allowed them to be placed under guard in his home. It was all very low key, next door to the Montano store where Governor Wallace was staying. When word got around that the Kid was back in town, technically under lock and key, some of the Hispanic locals gathered at the Patron house to serenade him with lilting ballads; such was his popularity.

Wallace, observing from his lodgings, found this astonishing and could not disguise his contempt. In a written report to a colleague, he referred to Billy as

"A precious specimen nicknamed The Kid..."

The Governor did have a lengthy meeting with the Kid however, and Billy proved to be exceptionally cooperative, basically sharing his extensive knowledge of the outlaw world of New Mexico; names, places, techniques, the lot. Yet again he had gone against the terms of the County War participant's peace agreement, but he had reached the point where he was only looking out for himself.

Wallace could have actually formally issued Billy's pardon before the pending court session of early April but he did not. By the time the court convened for it's Spring term on April 14th., the Governor was back in his Palace in Santa Fe to turn his attention back to writing *Ben-Hur*.

As Billy languished in his comfortable prison, along with his pal Tom, they were joined by Doc Scurlock who had been captured at Fort Sumner. Wallace's specially formed militia were also after Charlie Bowdre but he had managed to slip away.

Keeping to his promise, Billy willingly took the stand several times over the next few hectic weeks of court appearances and did not hesitate in naming those responsible for the killing of Huston Chapman, backed up by fellow witness Tom O'Folliard. No detail was omitted.

This resulted in the indictment of Campbell and Dolan for murder, and Evans for "incitement" to commit the deed. As Campbell and Evans were long gone out of the territory, this was an empty result and even Dolan was acquitted shortly afterwards.

No wonder when the District Attorney Rynerson and Judge Bristol were so biased. They had no intention of holding to the Governor's "promise" of a pardon for Billy Bonney, and now that he had testified against those they sympathised with, i.e. Dolan, they were determined to do all they could to bring him down.

Even so, there were scores of indictments to deal with, involving many men who had fought on either side of the recent war. Sue McSween still had a vindictive eye on Lt.Col. Dudley and succeeded in bringing him before the court to answer for what she saw as his significant role in her husband's death and the burning of her home. Even without the belligerent dead lawyer Chapman to back her, Mrs. McSween pushed her case to the limit and brought many witnesses forward, including a most helpful Kid, but Dudley's defence counsel fought back and succeeded in getting the old soldier off the hook.

Using every tactic they could to obstruct the proceedings, including a change of court venue to a different, more sympathetic county, Rynerson and Bristol got what they wanted and even Dad Peppin had the charges against him dropped.

In all, dragging on through May and June, the whole circus had been a total waste of time.

Billy, Tom and Doc, with Sheriff Kimball showing more than a little sympathy towards their situation, now had the run of Lincoln. No longer locked up, they wandered freely around town, kicking their heels and no doubt wondering why they were bothering.

But Rynerson and Bristol still harboured hostility and bitterness towards Billy in particular. They had not forgotten the charges against him and were very vocal about his territorial accusation of the murder of Sheriff Brady. In addition, Bristol convened his US government district court in Mesilla where the authorities for New Mexico were ordered to bring in the murderers of Buckshot Roberts; now named as the Kid and Doc Scurlock, to face that Federal charge, as well as the Territorial one.

Although he had long held out hope, Billy was beginning to realise that the Governor's promise did not furnish him with much protection, if any. There was no way he intended to stay around for another court appearance before the hostile Judge Bristol.

With no one willing to stop them, Billy, Doc and Tom simply saddled up and rode out of town, heading north to friendlier climes.

CHAPTER 23
MOVING ON

Las Vegas, New Mexico, was a spanking new railhead town which in early July welcomed the first locomotive of the Santa Fe Railroad. This event generated a lot of interest and the town buzzed with excitement and ribald activity which attracted the Kid and his pals.

Billy Bonney loved the atmosphere, especially as he was able to blend into the milling crowds of characters who flocked to the town in search of adventure and opportunity. It was a tough environment filled with every kind of frontier opportunist, male and female. Billy set up his own illegal monte dealership, it seems, for he was something of an expert at the game. He whiled away most of the summer making money at the tables, but was also pleased to bump into another old friend... Dr. Henry Hoyt, who was continuing his perambulations around the West by spending a spell as a bartender in one of Las Vegas' numerous saloons.

Enjoying each other's company again, Billy and the young doctor's socializing spawned an incident which is highly interesting. The only evidence which clarifies it is from Dr. Hoyt's book which he wrote many years later, but it is worth considering.

According to the doctor, he and Billy dined one night in a hotel just outside of town where the Kid was also in the company of a man he introduced as Mr. Howard. Hoyt did not think that much of this until Billy later told him that Mr. Howard was in fact the famous fugitive outlaw Jesse James, no less!

The Kid even said that Jesse, travelling in disguise, was trying to recruit members for a new gang of train and bank robbers he was hoping to form to replace the one which had been decimated in the disastrous James/Younger raid on the bank in Northfield, Minnesota, three years before.

Billy turned down Jesse's invite to join up with him, apparently, but what a pairing that would have been. However, Billy was not that kind of outlaw and he basically still longed for a route to go straight.

So was the tale true? It is an intriguing thought but, as I said, the only evidence is the account written by Hoyt in his autobiography *Frontier Doctor*, published in 1929. It was so long after the event that historians have cast doubts upon the story, but it is a fact that Jesse James did hide behind the name Howard during that period, plus the doctor accurately described the man as having a missing finger tip, just like Jesse.

After a few weeks dealing Monte and partying in Las Vegas, the Kid grew restless again and in early August decided to risk a trip to

Lincoln. He paid a visit to Sue McSween's new home where he found her dancing with a soldier from Fort Stanton. Frank Coe was playing his fiddle for them, for he too was making a low key visit to the town on some farming business.

Leaving Tom O'Folliard at the door holding the horses, Billy brazenly made his entrance. Sue and Frank were no doubt surprised, yet pleased, to see him; the soldier not so much. Billy squared up to the man, a sergeant, and asked his business.

The sergeant, totally unprepared, must have felt deeply uncomfortable. Technically, he should have tried to arrest the young outlaw but he was not going to attempt that. Instead he let Billy take over the dancing with the widow McSween.

Backing down, the soldier beat a hasty retreat as soon as he could while Frank Coe told Billy that he was being hunted and had best *"skin out"*.

Billy replied that he had been running for long enough and was keen to find a way out. He still had hopes that Governor Wallace would honour his promise but that avenue now seemed closed.

Sheriff Kimball had been made aware that the Kid was in the area again. His previous efforts to apprehend Billy had never been that serious, but now, with the cocky young desperado presenting himself so blatantly, the Sheriff was under pressure to act.

Summoning up the energy and willpower, Kimball enlisted the help of a troop of soldiers from Fort Stanton and they soon picked up the Kid's trail, tracking him down the Bonito to a shack where he was laying up for the night. The soldiers stealthily surrounded the place and settled down to make an arrest come daylight.

Quick witted Billy was no fool. He knew they were out there. In a repeat performance of his wily escape method from the Silver City jailhouse back in '75, he took off his gunbelt and shimmied up the chimney onto the roof. In the darkness he was able to slide down the side of the shack and sprint away to freedom.

So, now it was back to Fort Sumner, which lay conveniently on the southern border of San Miguel County.

Billy felt safe here, surrounded by friends and in a town which was almost totally devoid of law enforcement. The nearest Sheriff was based in Las Vegas, about 100 miles to the north, and Billy had already sent him packing before during that confrontation in Anton Chico. In any case, that Sheriff would have had more than his hands full dealing with local affairs in that wild town to worry too much about scouring the countryside for possible villainy.

The Kid was warmly welcomed by the Hispanic sheep herders and Anglo cattlemen, especially the former. He enjoyed spending time with them at their camps, grateful for their hospitality and genuinely relaxing in their company, singing and storytelling. The cattlemen respected him for the skills which seemed to defy his youth, plus he was as capable as the best of them. His easy going, affable nature was certainly infectious but everyone knew how he might react if pushed.

Doc Scurlock was no longer in the area. He really had taken his fill and returned to Texas to be with his large family. But Charlie Bowdre had returned to Fort Sumner with his wife Manuela and seemed pretty content to stick around.

Charlie had a regular job with a local stockman but it did not deter him from joining Billy in an increasing habit of cattle and horse theft. Rustling was an easy business in that vast country, with no shortage of illicit markets. Billy, Charlie and Tom even established a kind of ranch of their own, hidden by the huge rocks of Los Portales about 70 miles south east of Sumner. It was a perfect setting to conceal "lost" cattle.

Alongside all the potential market places for stolen stock, a new one arose that year when gold was discovered in the mountainous region of White Oaks, one hundred miles or so to the south west. The miners and camp followers flocked in, establishing a boomtown virtually overnight. Within a short time, at least ten saloons were doing a lively 24 hour business.

Billy and his *compadres* took to White Oaks without delay, selling their illegal beef and hitting the gaming tables. For The Kid, with increasing frequency, White Oaks became his second home, almost as much as Sumner. A popular monte dealer, Billy quickly established a reputation amongst the shady characters who populated such a raw environment.

Towns like Fort Sumner and White Oaks were a magnet for the criminal fraternity of the Old West. The railhead brought them in, many of them booted out of the neighbouring State at the point of Texas Ranger's guns. Situated on the edge of the vast cattle spreads, these hamlets that asked no questions seemed beyond the law, with safety in numbers.

The saloons in Fort Sumner, Beaver Smith's and Bob Hargroves', were favourite haunts for these desperadoes and Billy, Charlie and Tom mixed with them freely, no doubt falling under heavy influence. It was on this path that the Kid was quite rapidly drawn into an openly outlaw way of life.

Apart from the loyal companionship of Charlie and Tom, Billy attracted some new close members to what was becoming regarded as his gang.

One was Dave Rudabaugh, a stockily built, heavily bearded villain who is said to have had an evil disposition. He was eventually known as Dirty Dave because of his aversion to bathing. Rudabaugh was in his late thirties with a long history of stagecoach and train robbery behind him, as well as murder.

His tainted past included membership of the renowned Dodge City Gang during which period he had tangled with the likes of Wyatt Earp and Doc Holliday.

Always on the run, circumstances had brought him from Kansas to New Mexico by the spring of 1880.

With him came a burly Texan named Tom Pickett who had a past as a Texas Ranger (though not for long). In Las Vegas he at first served as a police officer but ran into trouble owing to his attitude so, from there, he befriended Charlie Bowdre who found him some ranch work. Ending up in Fort Sumner with Rudabaugh, hanging around the saloons, they teamed up with the Kid.

Completing the nucleus of Billy's tight group was a stern faced youngster from Ohio, a little younger even than the Kid. His name was Billy Wilson and he too was attracted to nefarious activities.

Billy Bonney always denied that he was the actual leader of a gang, as such, and this was true.

It was more a case of respect for his abilities. Seasoned veterans like Rudabaugh, for instance, would always act independently rather than take orders but the Kid's intelligence and personality would have made a mark.

Older men listened to him and went along with his ideas, and so this group rode together regularly throughout 1880 as leading lights in the rustling fraternity.

Throughout all this banditry, Billy never neglected his vibrant social life.

Of course, he gambled and generally mixed with the drifting toughs in the drinking holes of Sumner and White Oaks, but his lighter side regularly found him attending the dance events. These colourful, happy occasions were quite a contrast to the darker side of the communities.

Pete Maxwell's little sister, Paulita, wrote that Fort Sumner was a *"gay little place"* and of what an attraction it was to the pretty senoritas of surrounding hamlets like Santa Rosa, Puerto de Luna and Anton

Chico who would ride in by the buggy load to dance the night away.

"*Billy cut quite a gallant figure at these affairs...*" recalled Paulita, "*... he had a certain sort of boyish good looks... always smiling, good natured and very polite... he danced remarkably well and the little Mexican beauties made eyes at him from behind their fans...*"

Billy was not shy about responding to these *"little Mexican beauties"* and he shared his charms liberally without any sense of loyalty, it would appear.

And why not? He was young and free and enjoying his popularity like any nineteen year old.

Some of his romantic flings were more serious than others and it is reported that he fathered several children, although two of his daughters died of diptheria.

Paulita herself was one of his closer *queridas*, although she denied this in later life, probably out of respect for the man she married when Billy was no more. And there was also Celsa Gutierrez who the Kid was particularly fond of.

It is said that Celsa was the sister of Apolinaria who later on married a man who was eventually to play a prominent role in Billy's life; Pat Garrett... but at the time he was little more than an acquaintance. Garrett, from the deep south state of Alabama, was a former buffalo hunter who had arrived in New Mexico around the time the Lincoln County War ended. He was an exceptionally tall man, well over six feet, with a thin and gangly physique, towering over just about everyone. At first he worked for Pete Maxwell but then became a bartender at Beaver Smith's saloon which is where he would have come into contact with the Kid on a regular basis.

Legend has it that Garrett and Billy were close friends but there is no concrete evidence for this. They would have known each other during this period, for sure, but only as separate parts of the saloon crowd.

It was also around this time that Billy posed for the famous tintype photograph which is widely recognised as the only truly verifiable image of him. Many other pictures have emerged, with all manner of doubtful and absurd claims, but this is the only one that we can be sure of.

Paulita Maxwell remembered it being taken. A travelling photographer had passed through Fort Sumner around the early part of 1880 advertising his services, and the Kid must have been amused and attracted by the thought of preserving his image. Photography was still a novelty then and was growing in popularity.

We cannot be certain who actually took the picture but likely candidates are from the Las Vegas based studio of Furlong and Crispell who often travelled to extend their business. They also took the wedding pictures of Charlie and Manuela Bowdre.

Another possibility is the mobile photography operation of one Ben Wittick who carried a large collection of props with him... weapons, pottery, blankets, hats and clothes.

The strictly posed picture was taken in the street close to Beaver Smith's saloon against a sloppily erected backcloth. Billy was told to stand stock still, his head held firm by a clamp which was fixed to the back of his head. The corner of the stand of this clamp can actually be seen in the picture just behind his right foot.

The photograph is interesting and revealing in several ways.

Billy is dressed for the range in his working clothes, so it must have been quite an impromptu session. As Paulita said, the Kid was a dapper soul, fussy about his appearance as a rule *"dressing neatly and in good taste"* when in town.

It was probably a chilly day as Billy is wearing a thick oversized ribbed cardigan over his vest and a bib fronted shirt. The shirt seems to be decorated by anchor shaped embroidery. On his left little finger he is wearing a gambler's *"pinkie ring"* just where he is steadying the barrel of his Winchester carbine.

And then there is the question of the floppy, high crowned hat he is wearing. Films, pictures and artwork have since usually depicted him as wearing this dented "topper", presumably considering it to be authentic, but, actually, many accounts report that he favoured a sugar loaf sombrero, decorated with a bright green hatband. Maybe the sombrero was too large for the photographer's view and so could have been exchanged for the floppy hat which was just a prop?

I personally think that is much more likely.

High on his right hip is his .44 Colt revolver, holstered in a cartridge belt which carried the same shells as can be used in the carbine.

Exposure of a photograph was a laborious process back then. Photographic emulsion was applied to a thin sheet of metal which had been coated with a solution of light sensitive lacquer. The plate would be placed in a large and heavy box camera which had a cap over the lens. When the cap was removed to produce a uniquely positive image, Billy would have been instructed to hold his pose for up to ten long seconds and the awkward tension shows in his expression. His eyes are squinting, his smile lop sided and uncomfortable. Being outside, it looks like there is also a breeze blowing because his thick scarf is blurred from motion.

"I never liked the picture..." reminisced Paulita, *"... it makes him look rough and uncouth..."* whereas in reality he was *"boyish and very pleasant"*.

A pity then that his only photograph is not truly representative of what he was really like.

A session such as this would result in four virtually identical tintype images for a charge of twenty five cents. Only one of these originals survived and in 2011 it was sold to a private collector for $2,300,000.

Another anomaly which arose from this picture is the false story that Billy was left handed. This is because the image emerged in reverse format and shows his pistol mistakenly on his left hip. Later versions of the picture have been reversed again to show the pistol in its correct position on his right hip, but the left handed version is still the one that seems to get reproduced more often than not.

***

A veteran of many gunfights, Billy Bonney, also known as The Kid, was familiar with the crack of bullets around him. He had participated in lots of encounters where men had died, sharing the gunplay with others, so there is no doubt that he had put rounds through Morton, Baker, Sheriff Brady, Indian Segovia (probably) and quite likely other victims from the many shootouts of the Lincoln County War. Perhaps other incidents too that have been lost to history...

Apart from the undisputed claim he had to the demise of Windy Cahill back in the summer of '77, no other killing could be solely attributed to him alone... that was until Joe "Texas Red" Grant came to town.

***

White Oaks became a ghost town and is now just a shell of the vibrant place it once was. Following its boom period, when the Kid and his compadres enjoyed its pleasures, the intended railway link was rerouted, affecting the potential of its future. By the 1890s, the mines were played out and the town descended into a rapid decline. A few people still reside there, but generally the area is dotted with deserted old buildings from the era and a saloon with a sign at the door which declares "No Scum Allowed".

As mentioned earlier, Billy's Las Vegas, in San Miguel County, bears virtually no resemblance to its namesake much further south in Nevada. The famous sin city and adult playground is all about grown up fun but Las Vegas New Mexico (the name translates as "The Meadows") is a somewhat more sedate town, to say the least. Sleepy and historic, it is, in many ways, the personification of small town Americana. Centred around the old square, the buildings evoke the period of the Kid, emanating a striking atmosphere, if one is sensitive to such things. We booked into the imposing Old Plaza Hotel, right on the square itself and I loved it. My wife, Val, was not so keen, finding it dingy and depressing, but it was all part of the adventure, I felt, especially when we learned that the place is said to be haunted by the ghost of a past owner, Byron T.. The hotel was built in 1881 so Billy may well have seen the early rumblings of construction. It was quickly established as a hot spot and could soon boast that the gun toting dentist Doc Holliday and his girlfriend, Big Nose Kate, had stayed there.

I wandered the quiet streets with my imagination running riot, as it so often does. So many significant landmarks... on this very Plaza, in 1846, General Kearny made his official announcement that New Mexico had become a territory of the U.S.A.. Teddy Roosevelt recruited many of his Rough Riders here and silent cowboy movie star Tom Mix used our hotel as a unit base for the making of his Westerns. Val was not impressed. She wanted to know the location of the nearest Walmarts!

A relentless drive south of about 100 miles on the Interstate 84 crosses bleak flat plains en route to the next destination of significance. Yet again I was struck by these breathtaking distances of straight road, something we who are familiar with the British highway system are unused to. Travelling like this in a modern day car is wearing enough, but it is mind boggling to think what it must have been like in Billy's time, on rough trails by horseback or unsprung wagon.

Fort Sumner has become a modern town. The site of Old Fort Sumner, the one that Billy would have known, is located about six miles away, situated along a lengthy tree lined street with plenty of greenery; quite a contrast to the harsh vista we had just traversed. Much to my surprise, and some dismay, the old town and fort no longer exist... not a trace. No Pete Maxwell's house, no Beaver Smith's saloon, no old hospital, parade ground or walls... nothing... although where it all stood is largely marked out, at least. There are some graves, which I shall speak of later, and a museum which was interesting in its own way but devoid of any Billy related exhibits.

Closer to the newer town, we found the Billy the Kid Museum which is considerably larger and fascinating. Now, this place does emphasise the Kid and is overflowing with artifacts and information. Terrific atmosphere and so much to see, including what they claim is Billy's Winchester rifle and a lock of his hair, but I had my doubts about that.

The southbound Interstate 20 was even more relentless; an undulating straight line which stabs directly across seemingly endless scrubland, the heat haze shimmering in the far distance beneath a vast blue sky. Almost hypnotising, and, as we know, the Kid and his kind did it on horseback... routinely!

Such a relief to finally arrive at Roswell...

CHAPTER 24

GRANTED

Saturday January 10th. 1880... Fort Sumner, New Mexico.
"I'll bet twenty five dollars that I kill a man before you today!"

It was still early but Joe Grant was already drunk. The slurred boast was aimed directly at The Kid; Billy Bonney, who shrugged and barely acknowledged the pointless remark.

Billy had other things to do that day. Grant, a burly, slobbering Texan, had been making a nuisance of himself ever since turning up in Sumner shortly before. What his business was, no one was sure, but he was determined to get himself noticed. He was loud and obnoxious, confronting people and intent on making trouble.

When Billy was made known, Grant honed in on him as a target but the Kid was not up for being goaded or taking the bait, leaving town in the company of a pair of his less frequent outlaw *amigos*; Barney Mason and Charlie Thomas.

The trio spurred their mounts a few miles onto the plains where they encountered a small group of cowboys herding some cattle. It was Jim Chisum, a brother of boss man Big John, with his own triplet of hands.

Chisum and his men greeted the newcomers, as they did know them, but there was a hint of tension in the air. Jim had just rounded up these steers and it was noted that the Chisum brand on them had been crudely changed, so they were just reclaiming their stolen property. It was widely known that Billy Bonney and his crew were responsible for much of the rustling going on in the territory so were most likely the culprits here.

Billy, however, was his usual affable self, but he asked Jim if he could check the brands on these cows. The Kid would have known that he was under heavy suspicion but nothing could be proved. He probably thought such a brazen request was the best form of defence. Nobody wanted any trouble so Jim agreed.

When the façade of checking had been carried out, Billy remained openly friendly, maybe feeling a tinge of guilt. To soften any potential ill feeling, he merrily invited Jim Chisum and his boys to ride with him to Sumner for a drink.

"My treat!" he grinned.

This eased the atmosphere and the two groups rode together down to Fort Sumner as the late afternoon sun was beginning to set. The men were comfortable with each other now, exchanging some banter.

One of the Chisum hands, Jack Finan, even fired off a couple of practice shots from his fine ivory handled pistol as they cantered along.

The air was bitterly cold and the heavily bundled men were glad to get into the lamplit welcoming bar of Bob Hargroves' saloon. Warmth from the wood burning stove was like a mini heaven, alongside a few friendly, familiar faces.

Not everyone was quite so friendly, however.

As Billy ordered drinks for the newly arrived group, an unwelcome face of familiarity sidled up to him, unsteady on his feet and even drunker than he had been a few hours before. Joe Grant was in the Kid's face again.

Billy brassed it out, not ignoring the inebriated Texan but certainly not encouraging him. The Kid raised a glass with his friends and the snubbed Grant turned his gaze to that distinctive pistol in Jack Finan's holster.

Swaggering over to Finan, Grant snatched the weapon and placed his own lesser pistol into the empty holster, his hostile glare daring Jack to protest. Finan was not up for a fight and let it go.

Brandishing the pistol by its fancy ivory handle, Grant swung it back and forth as he looked around the room by way of a general challenge.

His attention grabbed, Billy seized control of the moment.

Grinning widely, the Kid sauntered over to Grant with the words, "That's a mighty nice piece you've got there, Joe... can I see it?"

The drunken Texan was disarmed in more ways than one and swayed back and forward as Billy inspected the gun. As he made a show of looking it over with a sigh or two of feigned admiration, the Kid recalled how Finan had fired a couple of shots during the ride here. There were spent chambers and Billy made sure to click the cylinder around so that the next attempt at a shot or two would discharge harmlessly.

(Whether or not Billy actually did this is subject to historical debate, but for the purpose of this account, let's assume he did.)

When the pistol was handed back to him, Grant suddenly became even louder and more threatening, craving full attention. He got that as he lurched behind the bar and began sweeping bottles and glasses off the shelves. As they smashed on the floor, Billy sought to distract him by joining in the destruction.

Everyone else in the barroom froze.

"*I'm gonna shoot someone...*" bellowed Grant, menacingly. As his rolling eyes locked upon the figure of Jim Chisum, he levelled his pistol at the cowman and snarled, *"I'm gonna kill you, John Chisum!"*

"Whoa... hold on Joe..." interjected Billy, *"You've got the wrong sow by the ear... that's Jim, not John!"*

In the momentary confusion, Grant lowered the pistol slightly and swung his attention back to the Kid, crying out, *"That's a lie!"*

The next part of Billy's plan was in play. Fully aware that Grant's next pull on the trigger would be harmless, he turned his back on him and strode towards the door. Sure enough, "Texas Red" Joe, infuriated by Billy's back, aimed at it, cocked Finan's pistol, wildly squeezed the trigger and was stunned to only hear an empty click. (Maybe it was just a misfire.)

Billy heard it too and that second or so delay was all he needed. Spinning around, the Kid's own Colt was in his hand as he fired off three shells in rapid succession.

Grant never knew what hit him, even though every round caught him in a small group just below the chin, lifting him off his feet.

Billy looked wistful as he holstered his smoking gun, looking down at the dead man as the dust still rose around his corpse.

"Joe," murmured Billy, coolly, *"I've been there too often for you..."*

Word spread rapidly of the Kid's latest victim and the name Billy Bonney became even more notorious.

"Justified" was the verdict of the local folk and it would not be enough to bring the Sheriff down from Las Vegas. The local newspaper, *The Optic*, barely gave it a mention.

Billy quietly basked in the glory. A short time afterwards, when asked about the shooting, he merely replied, *"Oh, it was nothing... just a game of two and I got there first."*

CHAPTER 25

ON THE OUTLAW TRAIL

Throughout 1880, Billy's descent into open outlawry deepened.

While still maintaining a latent desire to clear his name (mostly reliant upon that slim promise from Governor Wallace) his growing reputation for unlawful activity grew by the day. Apart from his blatant and busy rustling activities, other strings were now attached to his bow, including involvement on the periphery of the production of counterfeit dollar bills. This being a serious federal offence, the United States government flagged up interest and sent one of their special agents from the Secret Service, a man named Wild, to investigate.

Wild, working from his headquarters in Lincoln, soon established connections between the counterfeiting ring and the rustling gangs of Fort Sumner. Naturally, Billy Bonney's name arose regularly, putting him under high suspicion of circulating the fake notes.

Although, as far as we know, Billy did not make a habit of outright robbery... banks, trains and stagecoaches were not his thing... stock theft was, and he was inordinately good at it. That said, in the autumn, he was identified as one of a group of bandits who held up a buckboard carrying the U.S. mail near Lincoln.

The haul included a large sum of cash in the form of money being sent home to the families of troopers from Fort Stanton who had just been paid.

This was another serious federal offence which again put him in the frame as a high level offender.

In addition, Billy's popularity did not extend everywhere. As he spent more of his time in White Oaks, the mainly Anglo community there began to grow somewhat tired and irritated with his illicit beef trading and gambling activities and the way he was perceived as using the town as a kind of dumping ground for his darker pursuits.

New Mexico's Hispanic working folk, especially around Sumner, still loved him and the way he integrated with them so sincerely, but others were becoming wary.

Out of Texas, the various ranching victims of cattle theft formed the Panhandle Stock Association headed by Detective Frank Stewart who was tasked with putting an end to this out of control rustling. At White Oaks, amongst other things, he found hides and evidence which led directly to the Kid's involvement.

Wild also meant business and he set about it with an enthusiasm previously not embraced by the Santa Fe authorities. He had the support of one of the main figures in the land, Old John Chisum himself, who was happy to throw in with a force which seemed to promise to bring law and order to New Mexico at last.

The relationship between John Chisum and the Kid had deteriorated badly. Billy made no secret of his belief that Chisum owed him money from his active role during the Lincoln County War but the old rancher would not take responsibility. In one face to face confrontation Chisum vehemently denied ever having hired Billy's gun and swore that he owed him nothing, even offering the chance to take a bullet from the Kid. Billy responded with contempt, saying that the old man *"wasn't worth killing"*.

But the resentment and bitterness remained with Billy, and Chisum saw him as a threat now.

Wild and Stewart, regardless of their growing evidence, were facing a brick wall of silence from the general populace who feared the bandits who dominated all corners of the territory. To clean up Lincoln County and surrounding areas, things would need a major overhaul, one of the main objectives being the election of a new Sheriff.

In early November voting took place. The existing Sheriff Kimball was well known for his pro Billy sympathies and had long turned a blind eye to the Kid's crimes. The time had come for that to change.

Kimball's challenger, strongly supported by the likes of Chisum and other leading figures in New Mexico's hierarchy, was the lean and gangly figure of thirty year old Pat Garrett.

Chisum recommended Garrett for the job, persuading Governor Wallace that he was a man who ticked all the boxes when it came to cleaning up the land.

The idea appealed to Garrett. At something of a loose end in Fort Sumner, the long legged potential lawman was already known for his cool and resolute demeanour. He was soft spoken but his words carried authority. Obviously tough and courageous, he was also known to have killed when necessity arose.

His personal circumstances had also dramatically changed the year before following the mysterious death of his young wife, Juanita. She was a mere nineteen years old and they had only been married for a fortnight which must have been quite an emotional blow for even a tough character like Long Pat. In January 1880 he had married again, this time to Apolinaria, that sister of one of Billy's possible queridas, Celsa Gutierrez. This marriage would prove to be of long duration and they produced eight children.

It did not take much persuading for Garrett to relocate to Roswell where he wasted no time in starting his campaign to run for office.

As previously stated, Billy and Garrett were familiar with each other but not friends, as such, so the latter would have had no qualms about taking on what would amount to hunting down the Kid. Likewise, Billy openly favoured Kimball, but the election was a storming success for Garrett and he became Sheriff. What is more, he was also granted a commission as a Deputy U.S. Marshal which would give him the authority to hunt his prey across borders.

Following a brief period of transition between Sheriffs, Garrett was to take on the role completely and officially in January 1881 but even before the New Year, lanky Pat was already setting about his task in earnest.

Billy Bonney could no longer feel safe anywhere.

***

The Kid was now on the hit list of three separate enemies… the Government's Secret Service, the Panhandle Stock Association's deputies and the dogged determination of the new Sheriff Pat Garrett.

Increasingly alienated and mistrusted in White Oaks, where the locals had no interest in how much he was loved further north, Billy had begun to reevaluate his standing again. Matters grew complicated as the Kid made moves to negotiate with figures of authority once more, like the Governor and a scheming lawyer named Ira Leonard, who had been heavily involved in the spring 1879 Lincoln court sessions. Between them, a plot was hatched which might benefit all parties.

In cahoots with Special Agent Wild, Leonard proposed that they might be able to use Billy Bonney to their own advantage and the Kid himself was in agreement. Another deal… if Billy would cooperate in incriminating those counterfeiters known to him, then perhaps the charges against him could be diminished?

Yet again, Billy's fragile loyalties were tested and it seems he was more than willing to discuss these terms. However, a potential meeting never happened and the whole idea collapsed, and with it the Kid's last chance at redemption.

So Billy carried on rustling, gambling and increasing his outlaw reputation, making it more and more difficult for an already reluctant Governor Wallace to make any effort to save the boy.

Then came an incident which alienated Billy even further.

In mid November, the Kid and several of his cohorts, including

Dave Rudabaugh and Billy Wilson, stole horses from a rancher they knew near Puerto de Luna, driving them south, as usual, for sale in White Oaks. On the way, about forty miles from their destination, they called in at a way station owned by "Whisky Jim" Greathouse, who had earned that moniker from his habit of selling liquor to passing Indians. Greathouse bought four of the horses before Billy and company carried on to town in hopes of shifting the remaining dozen.

By now, Billy's outlaw gang stirred resentment in White Oaks just by showing up, especially when they stocked up on provisions which, it is said, they probably did not pay for. Camping outside of town, they nonchalantly turned up again the following day to finish their business, but were far from welcome. This time an old *compadre* of Billy's, one Barney Mason, had turned informer and was working for Pat Garrett and Agent Wild now. Mason immediately rushed off to inform the nearest law that the Kid and his gang were in town.

Deputy Sheriff Bill Hudgens sprang into action but by the time he assembled a posse, the outlaws had *vamoosed*. Following their trail to the abandoned camp, Hudgens' posse carried on, catching up with the outlaws at Coyote Springs.

Bullets flew. Billy and Wilson lost their horses while Rudabaugh and the others galloped away. The two Billys also managed to escape, but with more difficulty, on foot.

The fleeing outlaws reunited at the Greathouse Ranch to recuperate but at dawn on the 27th. an employee named Steck ventured out to be confronted by about a dozen men pointing guns at him. It was Hudgens' posse and they were already fanning out to surround the building.

Steck was given a note which he took back inside to hand to Billy. It was a demand for surrender and when Billy read it out, laughter rocked around the wooden walls. Steck was sent back out with a blunt refusal.

Hours passed with Billy and his men manning the windows which were being covered by Hudgens' trigger hungry posse. It was a stalemate until someone suggested that a member of the posse be sent in to discuss possible terms of surrender. That role fell to Jimmy Carlyle, a blacksmith from White Oaks, who was generally well thought of and trusted by all, but it was on the condition that Whiskey Jim come out in person and deliver himself to Hudgens as a hostage.

This was agreed and the two men passed each other near the front door.

The Greathouse Ranch had a well stocked bar and the outlaws were already taking advantage of it. By midday most of them were pretty much under the influence, except for Billy who did not indulge. Everyone was getting loud though, and the Kid was putting pressure on their prisoner Carlyle to imbibe.

Nervously, Carlyle downed the liquor and was soon as drunk as most of the others, but it did not calm him. As the half hearted negotiations rumbled on without result, Deputy Sheriff Hudgens and his posse began to lose patience, demanding that Carlyle be released.

Billy refused to comply and the mood turned sour. Carlyle was worried and felt that his life was in danger.

In a clumsy and ill advised attempt to break the stalemate, at around 2.00pm., Hudgens sent in a message that they would kill Greathouse unless Carlyle was released immediately. This did not help matters at all and Carlyle, even in his drunken state, was panicking, demanding to leave.

At that moment, a shot rang out from the posse. It was probably accidental, but it was enough to be the final straw for poor Carlyle who must have thought Greathouse had been executed. Losing control and in total desperation, Billy's prisoner leapt to his feet and dashed for the closed sash window, hurling himself headlong through it with a smashing of glass and woodwork.

In the next few confused seconds shots rang out and Carlyle was hit several times, tumbling outside and sprawling to the ground.

This triggered a fusillade from both factions which riddled the building and outside barricades. When the ceasefire came, and a pall of thick gunsmoke drifted skywards, Carlyle's crumpled and bleeding body had breathed its last, lying about ten feet from the demolished window.

The debate around who actually killed him has never ceased. Perhaps it was bullets from the posse who might have thought an outlaw was trying to escape, or, more likely, could it have been the outlaws inside whose natural reaction was to shoot their fleeing hostage?

Billy always denied responsibility and totally blamed the posse, but a different recollection was to come from Dave Rudabaugh who admitted putting a bullet into him, as did Billy Wilson, he said, whilst the Kid had plugged him twice.

On reflection, that does seem the probable scenario and, if true, would increase Billy's growing body count.

This dramatic turn of events demoralised the posse at a stroke, plus they were cold and craving food and drink. Reinforcements had already been summoned but Hudgens and his men were spent. They quietly withdrew and by early evening, when Billy's gang realised the threat was gone, they also slipped away.

Hudgens' posse, now increased in number, appeared again the following morning. They cannot have been expecting Billy and company to still be there waiting for them but they took their anger and frustration out on Whisky Jim's ranch, burning it and the outbuildings to smoking timbers and ash. Such was his punishment, they said, for harbouring murdering outlaws.

***

This was the moment when Billy's fame took a quantum leap and began to take on the legendary status which is now emblazoned in the annals of the Old West, although he still had a way to go.

Billy Bonney, known as the Kid, was already fairly notorious within outlaw circles and to those who feared them. But, he was by no means the leader of the many gangs which operated all over New Mexico. This covered an area from Las Vegas down to Seven Rivers and across the vast expanses, from the mountainous Arizona border to the sweeping staked plains of Texas. Yes, he had influence with them, especially his own tight circle, but there were as many as fifty known bandits operating separately in their own groups whilst occasionally pooling resources.

However, Billy's name was prominent amongst them. News of the popular Carlyle's death spread like wildfire and word went out that the Kid was responsible. Letters of indignant complaint were sent to Governor Wallace demanding that something be done to curb the wanton reckless lawlessness of these feral bandits who were affecting the progress of civilization.

In early December, the widely read, and influential, newspaper, *The Las Vegas Gazette*, ran a lengthy piece explaining the situation, denouncing the lawbreakers and describing them as *"the off scourings of society, fugitives from justice and desperadoes by profession"*. It went on to claim that the leader, *"a desperate cuss"*, was Billy the Kid.

This was the first time that William H. Bonney, alias Kid Antrim, alias Henry McCarty, had been named thus and it stoked the imagination of editors and writers countrywide. Stories of Billy the Kid's exploits, true and imagined, began to fill publications, even way out to the east coast where a New York paper printed their extended version of the adventures of the *"amazing outlaw chief"*.

Billy was probably as horrified as he was flattered. This new notoriety would bring him no end of problems, not least his fast dwindling hope of leniency.

In desperation, he rattled off another long letter to Governor Wallace in which he denied accusations of being a bandit leader and that he was not involved in any criminal behaviour, claiming instead that he made his living from gambling. These untrue stories, he wrote, had come from the maliciousness of John Chisum! Explaining his involvement in the Greathouse incident, Billy said he was only present because he was on his way to White Oaks, at the lawyer Leonard's invitation, to try and *"straighten things out"* but had been attacked by a posse. Cornered at Whisky Jim's, the Kid said he dared not surrender to what he thought of as a *"mob"* as they had no official warrant for his arrest. He stressed that the posse were the ones who had killed Jimmy Carlyle and that it was nothing to do with him.

Unsurprisingly, Wallace was not impressed by this rather clumsy and mostly fictional tirade and he passed the letter on to the *Gazette* to use in a further article. It was all too late anyway. Billy's trial by newspaper was the final stamp the Governor needed to absolve himself from any lingering thoughts of helping the young outlaw.

On December 13th. he authorized his posting of a reward ... $500 for the apprehension and delivery of Billy the Kid to any Sheriff in New Mexico.

***

I covered a lot of ground during my research, crisscrossing New Mexico and the border areas of neighbouring states in a hired Pontiac. From Denver, Colorado, it was down the Interstate 70, turning onto the 25 past Castle Rock, through Colorado Springs then Pueblo with the majestic Rockies on my right. Walsenberg and Trinidad and across the border into New Mexico, through the Raton Pass which had been established by the noted mountain man Uncle Dick Wootton. Dick's name never became as familiar as some of his contemporaries, like Jim Bridger and Kit Carson, but he certainly made his mark, establishing the quaint little township of Raton and selling the pass to the railroad.

Further on and turning west onto the 64, the country grew pretty wild and remote on the Santa Fe Trail before reaching Cimarron, a truly historic town, but kind of rundown. Here I explored the wonderful St. James Hotel. Built in 1872, it retains its Old West atmosphere and can genuinely boast one hell of a history. Bullet holes still perforate the ceiling of the restaurant which was once the saloon where, it is said, the notorious Clay Allison danced naked on the bar.

Jesse James favoured Room 14, and many other legendary names of the era frequented the hotel, including Wyatt and Morgan Earp (who booked in en route to Tombstone), Buffalo Bill, Annie Oakley, Bat Masterson and Black Jack Ketchum.

The St. James was the scene of numerous gunfights and murders. Little wonder then that the building is rich with tales of mysterious and quite hair raising hauntings.

Heading for Taos involved a long, winding ascent and descent of the Sangre de Cristo mountains, a stunning journey which took in the splendour of the Carson National Forest. Taos itself is a really lovely town, filled with colourful adobe structures nestling in a cocoon of bushy trees. Art galleries, bistros and trendy bars abound and many arty types live there. The area in general emanates a New Age feel.

The famous scout Kit Carson settled in Taos and his old house is now a museum dedicated to him and filled with artifacts he owned. He established a Masonic Lodge here with Charles Bent. Bent served as Governor for a brief period until 1847 when a mob of Hispanics and Pueblo Indians attacked his home, protesting about American domination of their way of life. Bent stepped out onto his porch in an attempt to reason with them but they shot him full of arrows and scalped him as he lay dying. His wife and family, and some friends, retreated into the house and managed to dig their way through the wall to make their escape. One can still view part of their frantic work, along with the poker and big spoon which they used as tools.

The Kit Carson Gardens and Cemetery where Kit is buried alongside other members of his family is worth a visit for Western enthusiasts. Very peaceful.

It is also worth making a slight diversion across the plains out to the gigantic Rio Grande Gorge Bridge. Hundreds of feet high and wide, spanning a yawning, rocky gorge with the Rio Grande flowing far below. Quite a stomach churning experience to peer over the rail, but so spectacular.

Tucked attractively beneath the mountain slopes is the Taos Pueblo, the historic home of the Pueblo native Americans in their ramshackle adobe dwellings. It is fascinating to wander amidst the crumbling alleyways where the poverty is still most apparent, even though, at the time of my visit, they were charging $10 a head for entry, plus another $10 for the right to use a still camera and camcorder. Down one deserted path, an ancient crone peered malevolently from a window and growled, "You takin' pictures?"

"Some..." I cautiously replied, to which she thrust out a gnarled, bony hand and, with a toothless grin, demanded cash.

Lots of restrictions too, regarding where you can wander. But that is understandable, I guess. Following Bent's murder, the U.S. army descended upon this place in force and massacred many of the inhabitants in vengeance. My impression was that most of these Pueblo are not very friendly. They resent being gawped at but reluctantly accept what they regard as necessary.

I was amused by the sign which declared reserved car parking for the War Chief!

Santa Fe I found to be a far cry from its 19th century reputation. Back then the town echoed with gunfire and rowdy behaviour, every other doorway being a saloon, brothel or gambling house. It seemed rather sedate to me, certainly in the midweek afternoon sunshine, the biggest problem being finding a place to park the car. Although rich with history, the town has become a haven of cheesy shops, pseudo art galleries and rebuilt streets. Pleasant enough but not overly inspiring to a hungry pilgrim like me. But it was good to see the Old Palace of the Governors (established in 1610) on the central plaza looking pretty much intact, and I enjoyed a tour inside. A large archaeological dig was going on behind the building, which looked intriguing... and any reservations were swiftly mellowed by a hearty lunch in the Sleepy Dog Saloon.

CHAPTER 26
THE NOOSE TIGHTENS

Now with a price on his head and with the newspaper's branding as New Mexico's "Number One Outlaw", Billy Bonney was firmly outside of the law whether he liked it or not.

He was now carrying far too much baggage for one so young.

Even so, he retained his youthful energy and optimism and continued to enjoy himself within the confines of his regular haunts in Fort Sumner. Sumner was now the refuge where he spent most of his time, along with regular forays in the surrounding areas where he could always count on the hospitality of the supportive and friendly Hispanic population.

But he was still elusive and forever wary of the forces which were on his tail. A network of devoted informers always seemed to keep him one step ahead.

Yet again, Billy found himself at a crossroads in life. Constantly on the run, watching his back… he realised that such an existence could not go on indefinitely.

So many of his former friends and allies had deserted him in the name of self preservation, leaving the territory for far flung destinations countrywide. Those few that remained were advising him to follow suit… maybe a new life in Mexico.

The two closest to him were still O'Folliard and Bowdre. Tom would stick by the Kid regardless of anything, but even Charlie was now putting out feelers in an attempt to save his own skin. The main difference for him was that he had concerns for his wife, Manuela, unlike Billy and Tom who only had themselves to worry about.

Since moving up to Sumner, Charlie Bowdre, whilst retaining loyalty to Billy, had been doing his best to distance himself from any outlaw activity. He became ranch foreman for a nearby cattleman named Tom Yerby. Tom Pickett also found work there. But the Kid liked to use the Yerby ranch as one of his safe houses, a situation which was making Charlie increasingly uncomfortable.

Billy must have seriously been considering the possibility of leaving the territory altogether, but with bad influences like Dave Rudabaugh and Billy Wilson still hanging around, it must have been difficult. The Kid's strong ties to all he knew were holding him firm.

By November, Billy's pursuers were really putting on the pressure, sweeping the country in a concerted effort to bring him and his *compadres* to book, aided by information supplied by the likes of

Barney Mason. Pat Garrett was riding in the company of men such as "Pecos Bob" Olinger who was to play quite a role in the Kid's future.

Dodging this strong and relentless posse was a full time occupation and there were several near misses. At one point they almost caught a lone Tom O'Folliard who narrowly escaped, following a running, mounted shootout.

Bowdre was growing anxious and was able to arrange a secret parley with Garrett to discuss his options. The long legged Sheriff/Deputy Marshal listened with sympathy to Charlie's concerns but was firm in his response. Bowdre was still facing a murder charge but if he could cut his connections with Billy and cooperate with the law, Garrett assured him that he could be helped out of the mess he was in. Charlie wanted to go down that route but simply could not outwardly betray his friends. He promised to try his best but felt he could not refuse Billy hospitality when he needed it.

Garrett's steely glare said it all as he told the Kid's pal that he had best make up his mind very quickly before he fell victim to the law which was closing in on them all.

Garrett's posse swept through Fort Sumner but Billy was just ahead of them. Frustrated, and with a couple of minor outlaws under arrest, they rode on to Las Vegas to plot their next move.

As soon as they had gone, Billy slipped back into town where his many friends updated him on the latest developments, not least of all Charlie Bowdre's change of heart. The two friends must have discussed this and Billy presumably understood Charlie's reasoning because they remained on good terms. It was at this point that Bowdre left the Yerby ranch and relocated Manuela and her mother into some rooms in the old military hospital building in Sumner.

Billy and his bandit pals stayed in the same building whenever they were in town.

By mid December, with snowstorms ravaging the whole area, and the prospect of a bleak future, it seems that Billy and those closest to him had made the decision to uproot themselves and head for Mexico. Bowdre had written to a lawyer expressing his desire to go straight, also mentioning that he believed Billy Bonney was heading for pastures anew.

They were all well aware that Garrett and his posse were closing in on them again. The Sheriff's spies were doing a fine job of keeping tabs on the Kid's movements, but, likewise, Billy had his own informers and he knew that Garrett, aided by the Panhandle Stockman's Association and emboldened newly recruited deputies, were close by.

Travelling on the snowbound roads was difficult, but Billy and his men made the journey out to a nearby ranch to stock up on provisions for their retreat to old Mexico.

In the pre-dawn darkness, snow was falling heavily as Garrett, at the head of dozen or so men, rode cautiously into Fort Sumner only to learn that Billy was absent again. Frustrating... Garrett was pedantic when following his leads and he was well aware that the Kid's sharp wits were keeping him just ahead in the game.

The posse fanned out through Sumner, probing, questioning, but it was hard to find anyone who was willing to turn on *Bilito*... hard, but not impossible.

Garrett was going to need to use some wily methods to net his prey. Eventually he managed to find a couple of youths who were persuaded to play a part in the planned trickery. False notes were written and allowed to be intercepted by Billy, which gave the impression that Garrett's posse had yet again withdrawn, defeated, from Sumner.

Billy was no fool but he became convinced that it would be safe to return to Sumner, unaware of the trap.

It was late in the evening of December 19th. and snow was falling lightly now on the already thick white carpet. The moon shone brightly through scudding clouds, and fog wound its wispy way across the plains and slopes as six horsemen picked their cautious path through the snow drifts.

Ahead lay the muted lights of Fort Sumner, the nearest building being the north east corner where the old Indian hospital was located. Here the frozen, numbed riders would find the welcoming shelter of the Bowdre's quarters.

Billy and his *compadres* rode bunched together, the breath of men and animals steaming in the crisp, bitterly cold air. Anxious to get out of this cold, there had been some banter along the trail, along with repeated talk about how they should have followed Garrett, caught up with him and maybe taught him a lesson or two. But no... they were too fatigued and shivering and were in enough trouble already. Scores could wait...

The Kid spurred his horse slightly ahead of the others but Tom O'Folliard quickly came level with him. Billy's eyes were locked on the dark shape of the hospital in the near distance. It was then that something made him pull on the reins and turn his horse's head. Intuition? Self preservation? The sixth sense of a man permanently on the run?

Whatever... the Kid wheeled around and slowly merged with the other riders bringing up the rear... Rudabaugh, Wilson, Bowdre... leaving Tom Pickett to hasten forward to trot alongside O'Folliard. Billy continued to stare beyond at the ever nearing building with the dark shadows beneath its outside overhung portal.

Pat Garrett and his men were waiting. Warned of the rider's approach, they had abandoned their poker game inside the hospital; the haven they knew would be the Kid's destination.

Crouching in the blackness of the portal, Garrett cocked his Winchester, his posse following suit.

O'Folliard was in the lead now, Pickett a short length behind, the other four getting closer as Tom, the tall Texan, rode right up to the building, so close that his horse's head began to nuzzle beneath the overhang.

Garrett barked out the order to halt, his voice emerging from a shadowy void, and O'Folliard, startled, instinctively reached for his gun. The Sheriff's rifle, along with that of the posseman by his side, roared simultaneously and this was the signal for the entire group of lawmen to open up with a rapid fire.

O'Folliard's horse reared high on its hind legs as Tom yelped sharply with the pain of the bullet which had torn into his chest. Pickett was not hit but screamed as if he had been, his own mount whirling around half circle and galloping off at speed back along the trail. Billy and the others followed him at speed, the posse's bullets whistling all around them until they disappeared into the night.

O'Folliard bent double over his saddle, one hand clutching at his heart, as his mount trotted away in the direction of his friends. Before long, only a few dozen yards, and maybe at Tom's urging, the horse turned again and slowly walked back towards the building.

Garrett and the posse swiftly surrounded the stricken young man and helped him down.

"I'm killed..." gasped O'Folliard as they carried him into the building and laid him on a blanket in the lamplight.

A quick examination of his wound assured everyone that it was fatal. The possemen nonchalantly went back to their card game leaving Garrett to listen to Texas Tom's curses which included calling him a *"long legged son uvva bitch"* and cursing him to hell. Garrett, hard, calm and blunt, told him that it was probably best not to talk that way as he would soon be dead.

O'Folliard, through gritted teeth and suffering terribly, asked for water. He managed to swallow a little before his anguish seemed to ease slightly. In his final moments he apparently wondered if it was possible that he must die... but he did, aged just twenty one.

The following day, the possemen and townsfolk furnished a coffin and buried Tom O'Folliard in the hard, icy ground before Garrett turned his attention upon those who had escaped.

***

Billy Bonney and his three companions, Wilson, Rudabaugh and Bowdre, rode hard in their flight, but Rudabaugh's horse had been hit by one of the posse's shots and soon collapsed and died. Dirty Dave jumped up behind Wilson's saddle and the quartet carried on, heading for the shelter of their safe haven at the Wilcox/Brazil ranch.

Tom Pickett had fled blindly into the wilderness, galloping in panic for several miles before his beleaguered mount gave out and he was forced to struggle on by foot. He joined the others several hours later at the ranch.

The outlaws did not tarry for long at the ranch for fear of Garrett wasting no time in tracking them there. They briefly pulled out to the shelter of the nearby hills, returning only to discuss their thoughts with the ranch owners Tom Wilcox and Manuel Brazil.

Wilcox and Brazil had been helpful allies of Billy in the past but were now, secretly, growing nervous of any friendly connection with the young outlaw and his gang. Harbouring them now out of previous loyalty, they were beginning to find it difficult to hide their reluctance and their assistance was now based more in fear of the Kid rather than sympathy.

Sharp minded Billy must have picked up on this and his own doubts grew. Out of the two of them, the Kid felt slightly more trust for Brazil and decided to send the rancher into Sumner to check out the situation.

On the 20th., the morning after O'Folliard's killing, some of Garrett's posse had attempted to follow the fugitive's trail but they only found Rudabaugh's dead horse half covered by the newly fallen snow. This snow had also erased any tracks left by the outlaws so they returned to Sumner.

The following day, Manuel Brazil arrived and was more than willing to cooperate with Garrett, presumably to get himself off the hook. Between them they came up with a yarn for the rancher to take back to Billy. He was to say that the Sheriff was still sheltering in Sumner, accompanied by only a single deputy and scared to take to the road for fear of ambush.

So, on the 22nd., Brazil relayed those words to the Kid who was convinced by this treachery. A dangerous bluff but it worked. Billy, hoping O'Folliard had been captured but now having heard of his death, was keen to ride back to Sumner for a reckoning with Garrett. Charlie Bowdre was very much against that idea, however. Still caught between his loyalty for Billy and his desire to find a way out, he wanted no further trouble.

Eventually, it was decided that the most sensible course of action was to pull out of the area... in fact it seems that the trail to Old Mexico was beckoning more than ever...

Refreshed, remounted, well fed and supplied, the outlaws saddled up and headed east to pick up the southern trail... Billy, Bowdre, Rudabaugh, Pickett and Wilson.

As soon as they left, Brazil, not wanting to waste a moment, excitedly galloped off into the freezing night back to Sumner to tell Garrett the news.

It was midnight but Garrett ordered his dozen men into the saddle. They took off without delay, Brazil riding ahead but returning to report that the outlaw's tracks could be clearly seen in the snow, illuminated by a brightly shining moon.

The long legged Sheriff had a pretty sure idea of where they would be bound.

CHAPTER 27
CORNERED

Stinking Springs was located only about three miles east of the Wilcox/Brazil ranch, so named because it stood by the site of a polluted water hole.

The remote, single building was a crumbling, flat roofed rock house, built long before as a shelter for sheep herders. Measuring only about 30 feet by 20 feet, it was windowless with a single doorway, the actual door of which had rotted to nothing some time ago.

They had not travelled far since leaving the ranch, but Billy's party were frozen already. The site of the crude shelter, primitive though it was, must have appeared too tempting to pass by. Would it really harm to hanker down within those comforting stone walls for just a few hours before pushing on?

It did not take much persuading. The outlaws quickly dismounted but there was no fire or warming coffee... just scant shelter within those bare stone walls as they wrapped themselves in their blankets, laid down on the rough earthen floor and did their best to catch some fitful sleep. They hitched three of their horses outside but took the other two inside to try and garner a little more warmth. One of these was Billy's favourite, his bay coloured mare with the white star on her forehead; the mount which was renowned throughout the territory as one of the best.

Like Brazil had said, the outlaw's tracks in the snow were clear as day.

Garrett was aware of the Stinking Springs rock house and sensed they would be heading that way... the tracks were confirmation.

By the time they reached it, around 3.00am, the outlaws were apparently all asleep. As Garrett's men spread out and silently approached the structure they could hear snores emanating from within.

Frank Stewart and his stockmen were part of the group, along with Jim East. Lee Hall, Tom Emory and the treacherous Barney Mason. Garrett at first wanted to rush the place, catching the fugitives napping, but Stewart persuaded him that it would be best to sit out the night and take them at dawn. They were not going anywhere.

The Sheriff nodded and carefully positioned the possemen in the surrounding arroyos, covering every side of the rock house. Wrapping themselves up as snugly as they could, they settled down in the snow, guns at the ready.

Garrett had briefed everyone on what to expect, especially the likely appearance of the Kid himself who would be recognisable in the gloom from the big wide brimmed Mexican style hat he generally favoured.

The night wore on and everyone was glad to see the first tinges of light opening up the eastern sky. New Mexico is renowned for its uniquely stunning sunrises and this one seemed to promise another beauty.

Suddenly there was movement in the dinginess of the empty doorway. A figure was emerging, hunched up against the cold, and he was wearing a wide brimmed hat just like Garrett had described.

The Sheriff had already decided that he would take no chances, and that included not giving Billy the Kid the slightest hope of escape. Garrett knew that the young outlaw would not submit easily, always preferring a shootout to surrender.

The possemen had all raised their cocked weapons; one eye on the figure, the other on Garrett who probably did not utter a word. Instead, his raised arm was the signal and rifle blasts ripped through the dawn silence.

The heavy .45 slugs tore into the stonework around the door frame, but at least a couple found their mark in the chest of the huddled figure who was all but blown back through the doorway and out of sight.

But the figure was not Billy. It was Charlie Bowdre who was in the act of taking a bag of oats out to feed the horses. On the way, he might have mistakenly donned the Kid's headgear in the darkness.

Charlie fell back against the inside wall clutching his chest, his eyes wide with shock as blood began to well into his mouth. Billy went to his friend, gently pulling his arms away to survey the damage as best he could in the dim light. It was bad…

Billy Wilson was the first to call out to the surrounding posse.

"You've hit Bowdre," he shouted, *"He wants to surrender."*

"Then tell him to come out with his hands up…" responded Garrett.

Inside the house, Billy's usual cheeriness had turned stern and sober. Looking his pal square in the eyes he stoically said, *"They've killed you, Charlie, but you can get revenge. Go get some of 'em before you die!"*

Spinning Bowdre's gunbelt to the side so that his holstered pistol hung down between his legs, Billy then took the dying man by the shoulders, turned him around and shoved him unceremoniously out of the door.

If this sounds callous and harsh, then maybe we should try to put ourselves in the boots of a desperate outlaw in New Mexico's 1880.

Charlie staggered forward, bent over with his arms stretched out in front of him.

Garrett got to his feet, lowering his Winchester as the stricken outlaw stumbled towards him. All but falling into the Sheriff's arms as he gasped his last words, *"I wish... I wish..."*

What did he wish? Anyone's guess...

Poor Charlie... caught between a rock and a hard place. He just wanted out, but not like this.

Others stepped forward to help but by the time they laid him down, Charlie was gone.

If this was going to be a siege, Garrett was prepared for the long haul.

The possemen settled down again and a lengthy period of silence ensued, that was until Garrett caught sight of more movement from the doorway.

Those three horses were still tethered to the fixings outside the rock house. Having been spooked by the recent gunfire they were now settled again, but a rope was strung from the head of one of them that stretched into the house. This rope had slowly begun to grow taut as someone from inside was gradually pulling the animal towards the doorway.

Garrett levered a shell into the breech of his Winchester and took aim. He had no intention of allowing the outlaws to get a third mount into their shelter so that they could attempt a breakout.

The Sheriff waited until the horse was well into the opening when he opened fire with a shot which took the animal directly in the heart. With a snort, the horse fell in the doorway, blocking the opening. There was now no way that the trio of remaining outlaws could attempt a mounted escape. Even on the two horses they had left inside, they would be unable to leap over the fallen one. There would simply not be enough headroom.

And Garrett was not finished. He aimed again, this time at the ropes which secured the remaining two mounts, proving himself to be quite a marksman as he severed those tetherings with a couple of well placed shots. The horses jerked free and trotted away into the hands of the waiting posse. At least that is what Long Pat claimed.

Not long after this, Billy's bay mare and the other horse inside the house were ushered out, just able to leap over the dead animal in the doorway. The Kid, Rudabaugh, Wilson and Pickett realised that there was no way they could use them now. They were probably also not too keen on sharing that confined space with the natural habits of those fine beasts!

The posse quickly caught those horses too and added them to their little growing herd.

Regardless of their pretty hopeless predicament, the Kid's good humour and merry temperament did not falter.

He and Garrett indulged in a long session of almost jokey banter, calling out to each other as the morning progressed.

The Sheriff asked how they were doing in there, inviting him and his *compadres* to come on out for the breakfast they must be wanting. Billy laughed and replied that they were too busy to be so sociable, with no time to *"run around"*.

Garrett spelled out that he had a dozen men surrounding the place and that there was no way out, but the Kid just invited him to *"come on in and get me... it'll be easy!"*

The Sheriff went along with it all, no doubt amused and impressed by the youth's spirit. Over and over Garrett calmly invited the Kid to surrender but Billy gleefully sang back, *"Go to hell, Pat!"*

Every now and again Garrett or his men would place a shot around the doorway, just to remind those inside that they were well and truly pinned down... not that they really needed reminding. Hours passed and eventually the sounds of scraping and chopping could be heard from inside the house. The outlaws were trying to dig their way out! East and Emory were swiftly placed in a position overlooking where the sounds were coming from and their bullets ploughing into that section of the outside wall soon silenced the digging.

During this time, Garrett had taken half of the posse back to the Wilcox/Brazil ranch for breakfast and on their return had sent the others. When they were all reassembled, it seemed that they were in for a long wait. Inside the house, the outlaws must have gone over every possibility of their chances but what hope could there be? Billy's famous reputation for keeping cool and cheerful in a tight fix must have helped but this was stretching things beyond limits. With the deaths of Tom and Charlie, the Kid really had lost his last close friends and it must have affected him deeply as he crouched in that cold, dark, stinking shelter. He was literally the only one left now from the old *camaraderie* of the Regulator days... his remaining companions, Rudabaugh, Pickett and Wilson, were no true replacements.

At around 4.00pm., with the winter sun low in the sky, Manuel Brazil turned up in a wagon loaded with supplies, in anticipation of the expected long siege. A fire was quickly built, coffee brewed and bacon cooked.

Inside the house the aroma of this tempting feast was the final straw for the famished, freezing outlaws. Rudabaugh was the first to crack. He tied a soiled rag to a stick and waved it through the opening, calling out that they were ready to surrender.

Garrett raised his Winchester and called on his men to make ready.

"Alright," he said, cautiously, *"Come out with your hands up."*

Rudabaugh did as he was told but came out alone. He certainly looked like a man who had spent a long, hungry, freezing night in a filthy pit.

Surrounded and searched, Rudabaugh spoke for those still inside when he told Garrett that they would be willing to come out if the Sheriff could assure their safety. Dirty Dave, in particular, had concerns about being turned over to the Las Vegas authorities where he knew they had a grudge against him for past misdeeds. He wanted a promise that they would all be taken to Santa Fe on the federal charges where it was felt they would get fairer treatment.

That seemed reasonable to Garrett and he allowed Rudabaugh to go back inside to pass on the agreement. Soon he came out again, this time with Pickett and Wilson, all with their hands raised high and immediately surrounded.

Probably playing it for maximum dramatic effect, Billy left it for a few agonizing moments before he too emerged, grinning away like he was at one of his *bailes*. Gun muzzles covering him, the Kid sauntered forward, raising just one arm and then slowly lowering it as he raised the other. He was mocking his captors, still determined to maintain some control over the situation.

Billy's eyes hardened and locked with the nervous glare of the traitor Barney Mason who raised his rifle threateningly, barking out that they should kill the *"slippery son of a bitch"*. Mason's fellow possemen, East and Hall, who regarded the man as a trigger happy troublemaker, turned their guns on him, warning that if he dared fire a shot, they would cut him down. Backing away, and realising there was respect and admiration for the young outlaw, Mason lowered his weapon and fell silent.

Garrett was anxious to get away from Stinking Springs before dark so he quickly broke camp, handcuffed the prisoners and had them escorted back to the ranch where Mrs. Wilcox prepared a much appreciated dinner for the whole party, about a score in all. Brazil's wagon was sent back to retrieve Charlie Bowdre's body which would stay well refrigerated in the cold night air.

They spent the whole night at the ranch, all of them exhausted from the previous day's efforts. Billy was in unbelievably good spirits; cheerful and talkative as if he was in the midst of a celebration. Even

Rudabaugh seemed relieved and calm, but Pickett and Wilson were morose and nervous.

Garrett gave strict orders that the four of them were to be closely watched, at gunpoint, all through the night, and he added his approval that they could be shot if they caused provocation.

At first light, they were off again, this time with the prisoners in the wagon and the stiff corpse of Charlie at their feet. The posse members rode alongside in tight formation all the way to Fort Sumner where they arrived close to midday causing quite a bit of excitement. Billy was very popular here and there was much concern to see him in captivity *en route* to an unknown fate.

Garrett was aware that he would have to extend extra watch over the Kid in Sumner. Billy had been very communicative with the Sheriff ever since his surrender, chatting easily, accepting his fate and seemingly bearing no ill feeling. But Garrett knew only too well that the Kid was a master at luring folks into a false sense of security. Never let your guard down with Billy Bonney, no matter how friendly he seemed...

One of the first tasks was to get the blacksmith to fit leg irons on the captives. Billy and Rudabaugh were shackled together; likewise Pickett and Wilson. The Kid laughed and danced a little jangling jig to show his indifference.

They all enjoyed another hearty meal and Billy increased his popularity by making gifts to a couple of his captors who he had befriended in the past. Frank Stewart was generously given the Kid's coveted bay mare, which was quite something, being Billy's most valued and virtually only asset. Jim East also had a soft spot for Billy from happier days and the Kid rewarded him with his treasured Winchester rifle. East was quite touched by this gesture but, later on, grouchy old Beaver Smith, behind the bar in his saloon, learned of this and led off angrily about how the Kid was in debt to him... so much so that East gave in and presented the gun to him to shut him up.

Many of the locals wanted to see *Bilito* before he was taken away, not sure if they would ever get the chance to see him again. There were many tears and the Navajo woman Deluvina Maxwell was one of the most insistent. Deluvina was not a Maxwell by blood. She had been kidnapped as a child by Apaches and kept as a slave until old Lucien Maxwell had bought her. Since then she had been a loyal servant to the Maxwells and had become an adopted member of the family. Lucien was long dead but his widow, old Mrs. Maxwell, sent a message to Garrett through Deluvina, who adored Billy. The widow Maxwell, mother of the current patriarch Pete, and his younger sister Paulita, asked if her daughter would be able to see *Bilito* one last time.

The Sheriff consented to this and it was arranged that Billy be taken up to the rather grand, multi roomed Maxwell home which dominated the west side of the old parade ground. Awkwardly, Billy was still shackled to Dave Rudabaugh so they had to attend as a pair and under the watchful eye of their guards Jim East and Lee Hall.

The teenaged senorita Paulita was overjoyed to see Billy and even though, as stated earlier, she denied ever having been one of the Kid's *queridas*, Jim East was a much quoted witness to what occurred between them. They requested time alone, but that was not practical, so under the eyes of armed guards and what must have been a very embarrassed Dirty Dave, Billy and Paulita embraced and shared a lingering and very intense kiss. East added that they had to be almost *"pulled apart"*.

Earlier, poor Jim East had been through another ordeal. When the riders and wagon had first drawn up outside the old Indian hospital, Garrett instructed East and another man to carry the frozen corpse of Charlie Bowdre into his quarters.

Charlie's wife, Manuela, was understandably distraught at the site of her dead husband and immediately flew into a grief stricken rage. She ranted and screamed, attacking Sheriff Garrett, kicking and punching him and hurling curses. The towering Garrett held her off with ease, tiny woman that she was, but it was an awful scene and she also had to be firmly led away, sobbing.

As respectfully as possible, East, and a man named Bousman, carried Bowdre's body into Manuela's room but she assaulted them with a branding iron, striking East across the head and forcing the pair to drop his body.

In an attempt to make some kind of amends, Garrett arranged to pay for a new suit for Charlie to be buried in. He also covered the cost of a grave digger and by the afternoon the procession of prisoners and guards were on the move again.

It was Christmas Eve.

***

Christmas Day and the captive laden wagon, still guarded on every side, rolled into the quiet little hamlet of Puerto De Luna, which charmingly translates as *Gateway to the Moon*. They pulled up outside of a long, porticoed building which they knew well... the well stocked store of an ex priest, a Polish man named Alex Grzelachowski. Billy had enjoyed many dealings with Grzelachowski, both legitimate and not, including having recently stolen a bunch of prize horses from the man.

This could have led to a difficult situation, but the Pole greeted them good naturedly.

"Hey Kid... what'd you do with my horses, eh?" he laughed, "Maybe you'll leave me alone now, eh?"

Billy chuckled in return, taking customary advantage of the ex priest's forgiveness. It was not easy for most people to stay angry with Billy's natural charm for long and his chatty *bonhomie* soon won over almost all present.

Grzelachowski had a big family and they had just all been about to sit down to a sumptuous seasonal dinner. A gigantic wild turkey, surrounded by festive trimmings, sat in the middle of a broad dining table in the back room of the store. The Pole happily invited the new party of travellers to join them as he said there was enough for everyone.

No one was going to argue with that. Garrett and his possemen, with their four shackled captives wedged in the middle, keenly took seats at the table and a merry time was had by all. Quite a bizarre turn of events on the road to justice with poor Charlie Bowdre still barely cold in his grave.

Billy was very much the centre of attention at this jolly meal, comfortably holding court alongside the killers of his friend.

The Kid certainly possessed the ability to move on quickly in any situation.

Late in the afternoon, with their bellies full and bodies warmed, the travellers were ready to hit the trail again, just as flurries of wind driven snow stung their faces. Before long the wagon broke down... a cracked axle or some such... and they were forced to make camp in the open whilst two men rode ahead for assistance. A replacement wagon arrived during the night and they staggered on, making laborious progress but eventually arriving for breakfast at a ranch a few miles south of Las Vegas, their next destination.

This did not go down well with Dave Rudabaugh. Garrett had promised him that they would avoid this town and push straight on to Santa Fe. Rudabaugh knew he would receive a hostile reception in Vegas because he was facing a murder charge there for the killing of a popular local deputy. Now the plan was to carry on to Santa Fe by train and Garrett assured the brooding, dark faced outlaw that he would be safe.

Their reception in Las Vegas was a mixed one. Word had been received that Garrett was on his way in with his celebrity prisoners, so on Boxing Day afternoon there was quite a crowd thronging each side of the slushy main street calling out a heady mix of cheers and boos.

Billy revelled in the attention and played to the crowd, hat pushed back, sitting up in the wagon, waving and smiling, cheerily recognising faces he knew with words of greeting and humour. Generally speaking, the townsfolk were happy and excited to see him. For all his notoriety, the Kid was still a popular figure to most in this part of the territory.

Not so Dave Rudabaugh who sat slouched over, his face grim and his hat pulled low as he tried to ignore the abuse thrown at him by the mob on every side. Pickett and Wilson tried to melt into the wagon's woodwork too. Billy was speaking, and acting, for them all.

Sheriff Romero must have felt some satisfaction with the Kid's plight, no doubt thinking back to the time when Billy had humiliated him and his posse in the saloon at Anton Chico over two years before. The cocky young outlaw was now in his town and at his mercy but Billy infuriatingly still performed as if he did not have a care in the world.

Locked securely in the town jail, the outlaws briefly had their shackles and handcuffs removed the next day so that they could put on the new suits which had been brought in for them. Their trail clothes, worn for days, must have been pretty shabby and Garrett wanted his captives looking presentable for the next stage of the journey.

That same day, Romero and Garrett agreed to permit a reporter from the *Gazette* to interview Billy, an opportunity which the Kid took to with joyful enthusiasm.

Happily answering all the questions put to him, Billy staged quite a performance. The jailhouse front door was wide open and the prisoners stood in the passageway, gawped at by a large, neck straining crowd.

Cosgrove, the reporter, put it to Billy that he seemed to be accepting his predicament with ease, to which the Kid grinned and responded by saying, *"What's the use of looking on the gloomy side?"* He went on to boast about there being so many people gazing at him, adding that he thought maybe they might consider him human now and not *"some kind of animal"*.

Pat Garrett was anxious to move on from Vegas. The hostility against Rudabaugh was tangible and an ugly mood in town grew to the extent that the formation of a lynch mob was more than likely.

Fearing an attempt to seize Dirty Dave, Garrett and his men remained alert all through the night of the 26th. with their prisoners under armed guard, for their own protection as much as anything else.

Sheriff Romero was also putting pressure on Garrett, demanding that he hand over Rudabaugh into local jurisdiction, to face separate murder and robbery charges. The steely resolve of tall Pat would not falter and he refused. In his position as a U.S. Deputy Marshal, Garrett was holding three of his prisoners on federal charges which would need to be pressed at their next destination, Santa Fe. Territorial charges aside, Billy was facing a murder indictment for the killing of Buckshot Roberts, Rudabaugh for U.S. mail robbery and Wilson as a counterfeiting accessory. The only concession was for Tom Pickett, whose main crime was mere horse theft. He alone would remain in Vegas.

In their new suits and reshackled, Billy, Rudabaugh and Wilson were hastily bundled onto a buggy and driven over to the railroad depot in the new part of town, Garrett and his men surrounding them protectively.

The steaming engine stood on a sidetrack next to the platform, held up until another train could pass by. Garrett ushered his prisoners into the passenger carriage as he turned to face the angry mob which had followed them. Romero was there too, at the head of a large posse. The deputies guarding the captives now, all seated in the carriage, were Stewart, East, Emory, Mason and a new man; Jim Bell... another figure who was to feature heavily in Billy's eventual legend.

A group from the Romero posse ascended the platform steps, marching up to Garrett who stood immovable. Long lean Pat was an imposing figure and he faced them down. Their demand to give up Rudabaugh was met by a calm, but firm, request to step down... and they meekly did. However, a growing crowd was pressing against the carriage and their mood was getting uglier.

Not one to be intimidated, Billy leaned out of the carriage window and opened another conversation with the reporter Cosgrove who he spotted in the mob.

"*If only I had my Winchester,*" he hollered, "*I'd lick the whole crowd!*"

The crowd surged forward threateningly and the Kid boldly chose the moment to proclaim his innocence, also declaring, "*I wasn't the leader of any gang... I was for Billy all the time!*"

At this point, the guards shoved up the windows and told their prisoners to lay down on the carriage floor out of sight. At last, following further attempts by Romero's men to hold the train, including turning their guns on the fireman and engineer, the stalemate was broken and the tension eased a little. At one point, things had become to seem so desperate that Pat told the Kid that if the mob made a move, he would arm the prisoners.

Billy loved that thought. *"All I want is a six shooter, Pat…"* he grinned.

But it never came to that. Garrett stepped up onto the locomotive as it began to shunt forward, wheels spinning in the operator's rush to leave.

At last, the engine picked up speed and they were on their way.

Romero's men and his mob of supporters were left dumbfounded and frustrated, glaring and shouting after the vanishing train.

But Billy had wriggled out of yet another scrape.

***

The location of Stinking Springs is on private property in a very remote spot some fifteen miles or so east of Fort Sumner. It can be found by dedicated souls but there is very little to see; just a ground level indication of the stone foundations where the rock house once stood. Souvenir hunters have devastated it over the years. However, in September 2024, the wonderful Billy the Kid Historical Coalition erected a permanent monument on the site. Maximum respect to them.

Another remote spot of interest to me was Fort Union which lies quite a stretch off of the Interstate 25. In the middle of windswept plains, much of the old fort is very much still in evidence, and I was anxious to take a close look behind those walls. After all, it was a place of great significance during the height of the Apache Wars and Lt. Col. Dudley took command there after his ousting from Fort Stanton.

Unfortunately, I was running behind schedule and only reached the site about thirty minutes before closing time. Rushing up to the entrance, there appeared to be no one around apart from a grumpy and grizzled old timer who did not appear overjoyed to see me. A bit breathless, I smilingly offered my dollars to get in and the old timer scowled, "Too late!"

Taken aback, I took a deep breath, maintained my smile and tried to explain that I was all the way from England on a pilgrimage around the Western sites of my dreamy childhood and I would not hold him up…

It cut no ice. "Rules is rules!" he growled.

And so they were and I had to content myself with a slow trek around the outer perimeter. The old timer glared at me suspiciously the whole time as if I was a marauding Chiricahua buck. He probably fought them back in the day and still bore a grudge!

I found a much more satisfying experience some time later and far away in

Colorado at Bent's Old Fort, located on the other side of the Comanche National Grasslands near La Junta.

The pioneering brothers Charles and William Bent, along with their partner Ceran St. Vrain, built the fort in 1833 on the north bank of the Arkansas River and for several years it was the most important settlement along the Santa Fe Trail. That was until its destruction in 1849, an act which may have been carried out by William Bent to avoid giving up the fort to the army.

The fort has been brilliantly reconstructed with what is considered to be 99% accuracy. Adobe walls, wooden walkways, furnished interiors; it has all been painstakingly recreated. I arrived just in time to join the tour of an excellent period costumed guide, David Newell. Not only did he really know his stuff, he presented it very well, taking us around the many rooms, stores, dining areas, kitchen, hospital, gentlemen's club, etc., explaining it all in glowing detail.

Afterwards, I spent a long time exploring the rest of the fort on my own. I was most reluctant to leave.

I digress from Billy's story a little here, but I just wanted to give a further impression of the wonders to be found in these areas of the American south west.

More Billy based sites, turning onto the Interstate 54, can be found around Tularosa, where the Kid first met and hung out with his good friend Dr. Hoyt, then from there, mile upon mile of arid land flanked by the stunning Sacramento Mountains. Pushing on from Alamogordo we entered the fiercely beautiful desert of White Sands National Monument. The self drive loop is a unique experience, unless you are a camel, I guess! Fabulous… we took the chance of pulling up and leaving the car to risk wandering a short distance over a rise, finding ourselves in a seemingly endless wilderness, horizon to horizon of pure white gypsum sands and rolling dunes. It was kind of hypnotizing and I quickly realised that it would be very easy to lose one's bearings. It all looked the same… a few steps in the wrong direction and you would never find your way back to your starting point, so we swiftly remedied that.

Later on in this mammoth trip, on the road to Albuquerque heading back to Santa Fe, we drove for many miles alongside the terrifying vista of the Jornada del Muerto, named by the original Spanish conquistadors as "The Journey of Death". And so it turned out for countless souls who underestimated this waterless desert basin, their bleached bones lost forever.

CHAPTER 28

IN CHAINS

The Santa Fe reception was somewhat different to what Billy had become used to in his few days as a celebrity captive. It had been less than a week since his capture but the laborious journey thus far, though eventful, seemed like an age.

There was a much smaller group meeting them at the station and any adulation was reserved for Garrett who was heartily congratulated for cleaning up the territory. By the next day the local newspaper, the *New Mexican*, was hailing him as the *"hero of the hour"*.

Sheriff Pat immediately handed his prisoners over to Sheriff Silva who, acting on behalf of the federal authorities, bundled them unceremoniously into the county jail. Relieved to be rid of the responsibility, Garrett and his men made straight for the old Exchange Hotel for a celebratory meal.

It was quite a contrast to the treatment meted out to Billy, Rudabaugh and Wilson. Crowded into a grim, dank cell that evening they were at least looking forward to some dinner. This had been ordered by Garrett and sent in but it had been eaten by the jailers!

This was just the beginning of the rude awakening Billy was to suffer over the next three months of captivity.

Santa Fe was a busy, chaotic hub of a town, bustling with the comings and goings of frontier life. Too much was happening for there to be much interest in the presence of who, to the general mobile populace, was nothing more than yet another common outlaw. Here, Billy the Kid was a small fish in a big pond of indifference.

The jailhouse stood just to the south of the famous central plaza which was dominated by the ancient Palace of the Governors. Billy knew this was the headquarters of Governor Wallace who he still hoped might be able to help. On New Year's Day 1881 the Kid scribbled a one line note to Wallace asking if he would take the time to come and see him.

Unfortunately, the Governor was not in residence. Only the day before Billy's arrival, Wallace had left town on an extended trip out east to Washington.

It was going to be a long wait before Billy and Wilson were sent down to Mesilla for trial. Rudabaugh was to be extradited back to Las Vegas but was already fighting his own separate legal battle. Dirty Dave had friends working on his behalf, old contacts from his days within the Dodge City Gang who were in town. They apparently raised money for their *compadre* and hired the services of a lawyer, one Edgar Caypless, who took on the case.

Billy was not so fortunate. He was penniless. When he turned to Caypless for help, the lawyer was willing to take him on, but not for free.

The Kid's only tangible asset had been his fine bay mare which he had given to Detective Frank Stewart at Stinking Springs. This had been a hasty gesture in the heat of the moment, probably part of Billy's theatrics, but he was regretting it now. He told Caypless that he was welcome to the valuable animal if something could be done to get it back. The lawyer felt some sympathy for the Kid and agreed to try but his enquiries found that Stewart had already passed the horse on to the wife of a Las Vegas hotel proprietor. Caypless started an action to question ownership but it was potentially a long legal battle… time that Billy did not have.

In the meantime, Garrett, resting on his laurels, turned his mind to the $500 reward which he was entitled to for the capture and delivery of Billy the Kid.

With the Governor absent, the acting Governor and his minions dithered and leaned upon technicalities to delay payment, but gratitude to Garrett from other local dignitaries resulted in them raising the money themselves and advancing it to him. Satisfied, his work done for now, Long Pat relaxed and concentrated on his new appointment.

Although he had been doing the job for quite a while already, January 1st. 1881 was the date he actually officially took on the role so he now had other pressing concerns. $500 was a lot of money in 1881.

The captives were having a totally miserable time in their oppressive jail cell. At one point it is said they were even chained to the floor.

Billy was alone and completely isolated in this friendless town; not what he was familiar with at all. Such a free spirit as he must have gone through agonies of frustration, boredom and discomfort during those long weeks cooped up away from everything he knew and held dear.

By February, with no tangible hope on the horizon, the three prisoners attempted to dig their way out, burrowing away at the base of the cell wall. Apart from anything else, it gave them something to do during this maddening tedium and they became creative in finding ways to conceal the dirt and stones which they loosened and brought up.

This occupied them for quite a few days until near the end of the month when an informer shopped them and the deepening hole was discovered. The result of this was that more iron was clamped upon them and they were even more heavily guarded.

Within a day or two of this, in the first week of March, Billy heard that Governor Wallace had returned to his office in Santa Fe.

Straightaway he rattled off another letter, the tone of which would just add irritation to Wallace's attitude of indifference to the Kid's problems. This time Billy could not resist a thinly veiled threat of blackmail…

"Dear Sir… I wish you would come down to the jail and see me… it will be much to your interest to come… I have some letters which date back two years and there are parties who are very anxious to get them… but I will not dispose of them until I see you… that is if you come immediately… yours respect Wm. H. Bonney"

Obviously, the Kid was impatient and desperate but it was naïve of him to think that Wallace would respond to such a missive. The Governor was probably quite incensed by the young outlaw's audacity and brushed it aside.

Whatever promise he made all that time ago back in Squire Wilson's office was now ancient and irrelevant history. Billy had got himself too deeply ensconced in outlaw activity since then for any consideration of clemency to be taken seriously. Add to that the determination of powerful men like Attorney Rynerson and Judge Bristol to bring the Kid down and Billy's hopes were totally scuppered. Governor Wallace had washed his hands of him, his attention centred upon getting a more desirable appointment well away from New Mexico.

Two more days of anxious and fruitless waiting and the Kid wrote again, on March 4th.. This time he expressed his disappointment at the lack of response, complaining about his treatment and appealing to the Governor's sense of justice, reminding him how promises had only been kept on his side. He signed off with the indignant demand *"I will expect to see you sometime today"*.

Still nothing, and nor would there be. Wallace probably barely glanced at the words.

The month dragged on. Rudabaugh was taken first, transferred to Las Vegas to face his own problems, leaving just Billy and Wilson fast approaching the date when they would make the journey to Mesilla for their trials.

On March 28th., with the stuffing finally knocked out of him, a desperate Billy made one final effort but he must have known it was hopeless…

"Gov. Lew Wallace... Dear Sir... for the last time I ask. Will you keep your promise... I start below tomorrow. Send answer by bearer. Yours respt. W. Bonney"

Manacled together, the pitiful pair of captives were taken to the rail depot. It was a low key affair with no fuss and they were guarded by just two deputies.

The only glimmer of hope for the Kid was that he would be accompanied on the train ride to Mesilla by the lawyer Ira Leonard who would be acting as his defence attorney, appointed by the court for the federal charge as Billy did not have a cent to his name.

The locomotive rattled its way south down the Rio Grande, not a straightforward run as the group had to switch trains and zig zag between various stops *en route*, just adding to the stress of the elongated ordeal.

At a stop just north of Albuquerque, there was to be a welcome diversion when an old friend appeared. The incident only comes from the autobiography of Billy's close *amigo* from the Tularosa days; Dr. Henry Hoyt, but there is no reason to disbelieve it.

Hoyt, who had not seen the Kid for a long time, and was certainly not expecting to, was waiting for the train at a small hamlet called Bernanillo. When the locomotive pulled into the station, Hoyt was surprised, but delighted, to spot Billy through the window of the rear carriage seated dejectedly between armed men.

The young doctor hurried inside and was shocked to find the Kid weighed down by the heavy manacles and leg irons, shackled to Billy Wilson.

Across from them sat the two deputies. One was Tony Neis and the other was, according to Hoyt, none other than Pecos Bob Olinger who had a long history of enmity with Billy. Olinger was a big, burly brute with a pock marked face. It is well recorded that he hated the Kid and relished any chance to try and rile him, so it must have been a painful trip. Pecos Bob sat with a double barrelled shotgun cradled in his lap.

But it was a warm greeting between the two young friends who had shared such good times together in what seemed like another life.

Pleasantries exchanged and with Billy encouraged to brighten up with a tinge of his old self, Dr. Hoyt asked the young captive if there was anything he could do for him.

"Sure Doc," smiled Billy, adding a chuckle as he said, *"just grab Bob's gun and hand it to me ..."*

It was a moment of levity which even amused Olinger as he gave a dark and threatening grin. *"Kid,"* he murmured, *"you had best tell your friend goodbye. Your days are short."*

Billy's face lit up with his old cheeriness. Maybe he slipped Hoyt a wink too as he poetically answered, *"Oh, I don't know… there's many a slip 'twixt cup and lip."*

It was a fond final memory for Hoyt. The deputies made it clear that he was outstaying his welcome and indicated that it was time for him to move on down the car.

"Good luck, Billy…" said the doctor, affectionately patting the Kid's slim back, then he turned and hurried away.

It was a brief and much appreciated little break in what must have been an interminable journey. But the Kid was not defeated yet.

***

The rest of this relatively short train trip was quite eventful as word spread of who was on board. At Rincon and Las Cruces separate mobs had gathered to make threatening moves against the prisoners but, to their credit, the deputies stood up to them. Billy did his part too, boldly displaying the best aspects of his carefree humour when someone menacingly wanted to know which one of the party was the famed Billy the Kid.

Standing in the carriage doorway with his entourage around him, the Kid firmly rested his hand upon the lawyer Leonard's shoulder.

"This is the man…" he declared, with mock seriousness.

At Mesilla, Billy and Wilson were locked up in the old stagecoach stop across the dusty plaza from the one storied adobe building which served as the courthouse. It was another squalid experience for the pair.

The Kid, longing for a change of scene, probably welcomed his first appearance before the vindictive Judge Bristol when the session opened on March 30th.. It was a rough and primitive room with a host of spectators crammed onto the wooden benches.

Billy was led, still chained, to the makeshift stand and the federal charge of the murder of Buckshot Roberts was formally put to him. Although present at the famed Blazer's Mill shootout, it was absurd that this indictment was brought against Billy as it was common knowledge that Charlie Bowdre's single bullet had dispatched the tough old warrior nearly three years before. Attorney Leonard claimed several technicalities to question this charge and, following about a week of legal jargonise, Judge Bristol dismissed the case on April 6th..

So far, so good…

However, Billy was immediately rearrested on Lincoln County's territorial charge of the murder of Sheriff Brady. Wearing different official robes, Bristol was also to preside over this case too. Leonard was replaced by a new defence team, an ultra hostile prosecutor was selected and the all Hispanic jurors were no fans of the Kid. It seemed obvious that this was a set up which planned to nail Billy Bonney once and for all.

It was a predetermined verdict no matter what defence was offered up. As part of the gang which had shot down Brady on that April day in 1878, it made Billy liable for the charge of premeditated murder in the first degree, no matter how many others had taken part. That said, it is pretty much without question that at least one of the dozen or so bullets which had struck Brady would have originated from Billy's Winchester. He alone was to take the full wrap.

Witnesses were brought forward to attest to the fact of Billy's presence and active involvement, one of them being Jake Mathews, an old rival, and the one who had grazed Billy and Jim French with a bullet on that fateful day.

The trial felt very rushed, lasting only two days, April 8th. and 9th., and the entire process was a formality, it seemed, nothing more. As for the jury, they came to their decision with unseemly haste and returned a verdict of guilty. Under New Mexican law, this could mean only one sentence.

This was delivered to the Kid at 5.15pm. on Wednesday April 13th. as he stood before a stern, but doubtless cockily joyful, Judge Bristol, who informed him that he was to be handed over to the Sheriff of Lincoln County and held in custody until May 13th.. It was recorded that the defendant said nothing in response.

Reading from the court's written records (which actually spelt the Kid's name wrong) the judge declared...

"That on the day aforesaid, between the hours of nine... in the forenoon and three... in the afternoon, he, the said William Bonny, alias Kid, alias William Antrim, be taken from such prison to some suitable and convenient place of execution within said County of Lincoln, by the Sheriff of said County, and then and there on that day and between the aforesaid hours thereof... he, the said William Bonny... (etc., etc.) be hanged by the neck until his body be dead."

So it had come to this... the ultimate penalty of the law. How ironic that out of all the men involved in the criminality and murders of the Lincoln County War and all those squashed indictments, young Billy was the only one to actually find himself sentenced. If he had possessed the money to finance an appeal, the verdict would almost certainly have been overturned.

Doubtless he was the scapegoat, the solitary representative of so called justice which had ultimately led to this travesty.

There were far worse villains than Billy roaming the territory but he had somehow come to symbolise the elements of the Old West which "progress" was desperate to eliminate. In the eyes of the powers that be, the Santa Fe Ring, the cattle barons, authority in general... he was admired and liked by far too many people... the glamorous *"Boy Bandit King"* needed to be knocked from his pedestal.

***

La Mesilla, where Billy was tried and sentenced to hang, is an attractive little hamlet, centred around another typically cosy historic plaza. Nicely preserved old structures abound, including what is, they say, the oldest adobe structure in New Mexico.

The highlight of the plaza is a garish bright pink building. Single storied and flat roofed, like so much of the territory's architecture, this place once housed the Capitol of Arizona and New Mexico, but it later became the local courthouse. So, it was in here where Billy stood in chains to hear his fate read out by the dour Judge Bristol. How different to step inside now, through the wooden batwing doors, and wander around an array of tacky gifts relating to its connection with one of America's most notorious outlaws. Above the entrance, framing an almost lifesize facsimile of his portrait, are the bold black letters of the Billy the Kid Gift Shop.

For some reason, and quite unusual when being on the road in the West, we had trouble finding a good place for breakfast. Finally settling down in an adequate fast food outlet, entertainment was supplied by an interesting little drama we saw played out through the window. Three cops were frisking a young black guy who had attempted to hide in the well of a parked truck having evaded paying for his food. They were not being gentle with him, but, eventually, presumably without any charges being pressed, he was pointed down the highway, a long, straight stretch into the hazy distance, and told to keep walking! He set off, looking back in disbelief as the trio of lawmen watched him trudge away until he became a tiny speck en route to Arizona...

CHAPTER 29
ESCAPE

Now the journey continued with Billy as the solitary prisoner. Just three days after the sentencing, on April 16th., the Kid was led out of his cell and past his long term confederate Billy Wilson. A brief wave of manacled hands and they were parted forever.

It was nearly ten at night when they put Billy Bonney in the wagon which was to transport him on the long rickety trail back to Lincoln, chained to the rear seat. To avoid any slim possibility of a "necktie party", or maybe even a rescue bid, word had been deliberately spread that the condemned young outlaw was to be transported the following week.

This after dark excursion was a clandestine effort to move the Kid with the least possible fuss.

There was a heavy guard of seven men to accompany him, three as outriders and four surrounding the shackled Billy himself; one upfront driving the horse team, of course. The Kid had not been out of those chains for months.

Probably a deliberate choice, nearly half of those guards were deputies who held grudges against the Kid; men who would not hesitate to shoot him down given the slightest excuse.

One was Jake Mathews... another John Kinney... and the third none other than the bitter and ruthless Bob Olinger. The three of them sat around their prisoner and it must have been intimidating ... not that the Kid would show it. By all accounts, Pecos Bob really had it in for Billy. Apart from anything else, he held him personally responsible for the death of his friend Bob Beckwith who had been killed during the breakout from the burning McSween house.

Olinger was six feet tall, bull necked with a barrel chest. It was said he had fists like sides of ham. Bushy eyebrows framed piercing dark eyes, his hair hung long and shaggy and his unruly moustache barely hid a cruel grimace.

Despite his build, he was agile and quick with his guns, never shrinking from a fight. He made no secret of the fact that he detested Billy. Along with Jake Mathews, the pair of them must have given the Kid a pretty rough time with their caustic remarks and goading on the trail. The Kid could handle this kind of thing well, shrugging off their intended provocation with his carefree wit and easy smile. This probably infuriated and frustrated them even more.

It was over 100 miles heading north east from Mesilla to Lincoln, crossing all kinds of country. Fording the Rio Grande and through the

San Agustin pass to a long stretch across the desert of the Tularosa basin and beyond. It was an arduous though familiar journey for those involved and it would take five days. Therefore, *en route*, they made several stops, usually retaking the trail later in the day to avoid the intense spring sunshine. One of these stops was at Blazer's Mill which would evoke intense memories for Billy. Even so, the recollection of losing his friend Dick Brewer there did not openly affect him as, over dinner, he dramatically replayed the gun battle with Buckshot Roberts and other incidents.

On April 21st., they reached Fort Stanton where the prisoner was formally handed over into the custody of Sheriff Pat Garrett again for the short final leg of the journey into Lincoln. It must have been a strained reunion but, by all accounts, Billy did not appear to bear a grudge. He and Garrett went back quite a way and had an understanding of each other. No malice, just a mutual respect. They chatted easily, with the Kid making it clear that Old Pat was just *"doing his job"*.

Garrett acknowledged that those four months locked up in dark cells had done nothing to diminish Billy's bright spirit. His humour and optimism remained intact. The only visible change was in the white pallor of the Kid's complexion, having been out of the elements for so long.

It was to be another three weeks before the death sentence was to be carried out and Garrett wanted to be sure that his captive was held securely.

Incarceration in Lincoln's inadequate pit jail was out of the question. All the locals knew that it *"leaked prisoners like a sieve"*. The old Murphy/Dolan store, the one time *House*. which had been acquired by Tom Catron, was now in the hands of the Lincoln County commissioners who had recently purchased and transformed it into the County Courthouse. The imposing adobe structure was still officially the biggest building in the county with its multiple rooms and sloping roof, and Garrett had his office on the second floor. It was decided that Billy would be held under constant armed guard, until his execution, in the room next door, access to which was only possible through the office itself.

This was the northeast corner room and its windows looked out onto Lincoln's single main street. The side window gave a good view of the Wortley Hotel on the other side of the street and also looked down on the gate which opened onto a fenced pathway. This path led down to a large rear yard and vegetable garden which was surrounded by a high wall.

Garrett's office had a doorway which opened onto the long balcony which dominated the front of the house.

Billy's prison room contained a cot, a small table and a couple of chairs for his use by the east wall. On the west side was another table and pair of chairs for his guards. The room was divided by a line scratched in chalk across the bare boards of the floor and the Kid was solemnly advised that he was never to step over that line without permission from his guards.

And there were to be the two same guards assigned to that task all the way to May 13th. ... doomsday. One was Jim Bell, a good natured and fairly mild mannered fellow who had grown, it seems, to quite like Billy. By contrast, the other one was Bob Olinger who had most likely been selected by Garrett because of his hatred of the prisoner. Pecos Bob would not shy away from shooting Billy if the need arose.

The difference in attitude between the two guards was probably seen as a formula of workable balance over the next tense fortnight.

Billy's only brief liberty would be permitted trips to the outhouse in the back yard, which meant awkward jaunts in leg irons through Garrett's office, along the hall and down a flight of stairs with a bend at the bottom before exiting another doorway out to the privy. Garrett quickly responded to Billy's discomfort during these necessary trips. The leg irons were way too short for negotiating the stairs so the Sheriff considerately had the blacksmith pay a visit to rivet on a longer chain.

Olinger and Bell were often together overseeing Billy, but they also took regular shifts alone. When it was Bell's turn, things must have been much easier for the Kid. They chatted and played cards and got on pretty well, but when Olinger had time alone with the prisoner the atmosphere took a nose dive. Pecos Bob took great delight in reminding the condemned young outlaw how his time on Earth was running out. He even pinned a large calendar to the wall and made a daily ritual of crossing out the date before turning the page to circle May 13th. with an evil grin on his face.

Billy made a point of never giving the big man the satisfaction of seeing his captive affected by this intended mental torture. The Kid would shrug and grin in return, at most responding with a cheery witticism which must have really riled the frustrated bully.

It is said that at one point Olinger even deliberately left a pistol on the table within Billy's reach, a temptation which the Kid had the sense to avoid. He was biding his time, never betraying what was really going on inside his calculating mind.

Olinger had a history of killing, all of the incidents surrounded by unsavoury circumstance, including the back shooting of a friend of Billy's named John Jones. The Kid, therefore, had many reasons to bear a grudge against Pecos Bob.

During Bell's shift, Billy was permitted the concession of occasional visits from his many local friends but Garrett eventually put a stop to this, feeling that it was too risky. However, out of compassion, Bell did still allow regular chats with the old German Godfrey Gauss who had once worked as the cook at Tunstall's Feliz ranch and was now the caretaker here at the courthouse. Residing in a shack in the backyard, Gauss would often appear in the doorway of the makeshift prison room, when Olinger was not around.

Billy and Gauss had much in common with a heap of shared memories. The Kid enjoyed listening to the knowledgeable old fellow's broken, heavily accented English as he brought him up to date with news about the characters they mutually knew and who Billy had lost touch with.

Garrett was generally busy with other duties but he regularly looked in on his prisoner, spending time in easy conversation. Deep down he probably maintained a soft spot for the likeable youth, but duty came first and Billy understood that. They both knew that whatever affability existed between them, neither would hesitate to put a bullet through the other should the chance and necessity arise.

The Kid had been occupying his prison room for one week when Garrett announced that he needed to leave town on business. It would be to collect taxes on the way to White Oaks where he would be ordering the lumber to be shipped up to Lincoln for the construction of the gallows. This grim structure was due to be erected in the big open space behind the courthouse. The noise from the work would be well within Billy's earshot, adding to the psychological torture. What is more, the execution would be open to the public.

Garrett made a point of telling Olinger to lay off so much goading of the Kid but as soon as the Sheriff was gone, Pecos Bob upped his game.

On the morning of Thursday April 28th, Olinger went to the closet which served as the lawmen's armoury at the top of the stairwell. He took out his shiny new Whitney 10 gauge shotgun and carried it triumphantly into Billy's room. Opening the breech, with the Kid's eyes on his every move, he slowly slipped two big brass shells into the twin barrels.

Snapping the weapon shut, he tauntingly hissed, *"There's eighteen buckshot in each of those barrels, Kid. The man who gets one of those loads will feel it."*

Billy smiled and replied, *"I expect he will, Bob, but take care you don't get a load yourself."*

Olinger glared back at him before propping the weapon in the corner by the north wall, well within the forbidden area of the chalk line. Later he returned it to the armoury.

The day wore on... sleepy and uneventful. Warm sunshine bathed Lincoln in an ambience of New Mexican weather at its best. Late in the afternoon, around 6.00pm., Olinger told Bell he was going to take the other prisoners over to the Wortley Hotel for dinner. Apparently there were five of them, minor offenders who were being held in another part of the courthouse.

Billy watched from the side window as Pecos Bob ushered the group across the street. It was now or never... Garrett was miles away, Olinger was out of the building... just Bell to contend with and he was looking over confident and careless...

Were the Kid's next movements spontaneous or long planned? We can only speculate, but he certainly acted with cool determination. He knew he had reached the end of the road. There would be no last minute reprieve, no appeal... the time had come to change his own destiny, or die trying.

Once Olinger and his party had entered the hotel, Billy told Bell that he needed to visit the outhouse. The easy going deputy was happy to comply and he took him down the hall, down the steps and out into the pleasant heat of the yard.

Chains rattling, Billy entered the privy and shut the door while Bell lounged patiently outside, turning his face up to the warmth of the sun. The deputy was relaxed. He knew and trusted the Kid by now... nothing to worry about... he was actually beginning to feel real sympathy for the boy's plight...

Billy emerged from the outhouse and made his way silently back towards the door with Bell following. If anything, the Kid had seemed a little more preoccupied today, quieter than usual, as if something was playing on his mind. He was making his way back into the building with unusual haste and the deputy stirred to keep up with him.

Billy took the three steps to the small landing, then turned sharply right to ascend the main flight of stairs. Although burdened by his leg irons, the Kid took hobbled leaps up these stairs, taking more than one at a time with Bell hurrying behind. He must have wondered what the boy was up to.

There is more than one theory about what exactly happened next but for me personally, having looked at the conflicting evidence, I think this is how it played out...

Maybe Billy already had a pistol concealed in his shirt which had been hidden for him by a friend in the outhouse. Whatever, as Bell reached the landing, he looked up the stairs to see the Kid vanish around the corner to the right at the top of the flight. Alarmed, Bell rushed up the stairs, maybe drawing his own pistol as he did so, knowing that the armoury closet was located there.

It all happened very quickly. It seems that Billy pulled his small hands, large wrists trick, because he had managed to wriggle out of one of his cuffs. As Bell reached the top of the stairs, the Kid swung the chain with its freed manacle like a medieval mace, viciously connecting with Bell's head and opening up an ugly gash. The deputy staggered but was still conscious as Billy jumped on him and they tumbled to the floor, half sprawled across the top of the staircase.

Now Billy, as I said, may have already had a pistol, either from the outhouse or maybe he had managed to quickly grab one from the armoury. Or, maybe, in the struggle as he wrestled with Bell, he succeeded in taking the deputy's six shooter... although that is doubtful because it was later said that Bell's weapon was still holstered after the fight.

However he managed it, Billy was armed but Bell managed to wrestle his way free, scrambling to his feet and bounding back down the stairs.

Billy was still on the floor as he shouted after the fleeing guard, begging him to stop. The panic stricken Bell ignored him and careened on down as the Kid, prone on his stomach, loosed off a single shot. It missed its target but ricocheted off the left hand wall, catching the deputy under the left armpit and ploughing on into his chest cavity.

Sheer momentum and desperation enabled him to carry on, stumbling as he turned down the short flight and back through the door into the sunlit yard.

Old Man Gauss, who had been working on his vegetable garden, heard the shot and was making his way cautiously towards the house. Startled to see Bell burst through the door, he hurried forward to catch him as he collapsed into the caretaker's arms. Gauss laid him down on his back just as he breathed his last.

Over at the Wortley Hotel, Olinger had also heard the shot. He and his prisoners immediately left their half eaten meals and went back to the street. Pecos Bob's first thought was that Bell had shot the Kid.

Billy, however, knew he needed every second to prepare for

Olinger's return. Hobbling back to the armoury he seized up Pecos Bob's fully loaded shotgun. As he clanked his way back to his prison room, the feel of the gleaming weapon in his hands must have been especially satisfying. Positioning himself in that east facing open window and seeing Olinger making his way cautiously across the street, pistol in hand, Billy swiftly made himself comfortable as he raised the weapon. One can imagine a wry smile crossing the Kid's smooth face as he basked in the sheer irony of the moment ... *"... Bob... take care you don't get a load yourself..."*

Gauss, leaving Bell where he lay, was hurrying around to the same east side of the building, aware that he must raise the alarm. He reached the spot on the path immediately below Billy's window just as Olinger opened the gate and stepped into the narrow yard between the wall and fence.

Olinger froze as Gauss gasped out to him, *"The Kid has killed Bell!"*

"Yeh..." murmured the burly deputy marshal, his eyes drawn up to the window above, *"and he's killed me too..."*

"Hello Bob!" exclaimed Billy cheerfully, the barrels of the Whitney steadied on the window sill just a few feet away from the doomed man. The powerful gun roared as the Kid pulled one of the twin triggers and Olinger was struck by that full load of eighteen buckshot, just as Billy had predicted. His head and chest shredded, Pecos Bob fell dead by the gate.

Still moving with difficulty, Billy rushed as fast as he could back across the room and into Garrett's office. Wanting to see the immediate lay of the land, he carried on through the door which led to the front balcony. The shocked townsfolk were keeping out of sight but it would not be long before they started to emerge. Olinger's prisoners were rooted to the spot at the door of the hotel, dumbfounded by what they had just witnessed.

Billy made his way to the east corner of the balcony where he could look down at the mangled corpse of Olinger. To seal his satisfaction to the full, he could not resist leaning over the railing, taking aim and letting the late Pecos Bob receive that second full load of heavy buckshot.

In triumph, Billy raised the smoking gun above his head, clutching the barrels with both hands as he brought it down with all his might on the wooden porch railing. The impact smashed the stock and he hurled the pieces down at the bloody, lifeless body of the man he hated.

"Take this too, damn you..." he cursed, the fury marring his usually pleasant face, *"You won't follow me no more with **that** gun!"*

Billy then shouted across the street to those who were beginning to reveal themselves, telling them to not come any closer. He had no intention of harming anyone who stayed out of his way. Then he returned to the armoury and picked out a loaded Winchester and a Colt revolver, along with a holstered cartridge belt. Through the rear window at the end of the hall he spotted Gauss and called to him to find something he could use to remove his leg irons; a file or similar.

The old German could only come up with a miner's pickaxe but Billy used the strong, thin point to work away at the rivets. It took a while but he succeeded in freeing the chain from just one of the anklets. Gauss most likely found keys, maybe in Bell or Olinger's pockets, for the handcuffs, but Billy was probably able to slip his hand through the remaining one anyway.

The chain of his leg irons hung loose but Billy made himself more mobile by looping the broken end into his belt, the other end still attached to his ankle.

By now quite a crowd had gathered at the front of the hotel but Billy insisted that they keep their distance, even though it was obvious that no one present was intending to do anything to stop him.

He was in no hurry and he seemed happy and relaxed enough to stay on the balcony, holding court, for about an hour after the killing of the deputies. Billy explained to them that he was sorry he had been forced to kill Bell. He had not wanted to do it but the deputy attempting to flee had left him no choice. As for Olinger, he had no similar regrets to voice. He added that he was now *"standing pat against the world"*.

At last, almost reluctantly, he seemed ready to take his leave. Walking out of the back door, he paused with sorrow beside Bell's body and mumbled an apology for having to kill him. Around the corner, just inside the gate, Pecos Bob's corpse merely received a curse and a nudge with the toe of his boot.

Billy demanded a horse and the first one available belonged to a clerk of the court; one Billy Burt. The animal was quite skittish, probably spooked by the dangling chain flapping around the escapee's midriff. Billy was a good rider, but he had some difficulty mounting this one. At last, he managed to swing into the saddle, loaded down with extra weapons.

He had even taken the trouble to shake hands with several of those who had gathered to see him off. Many of them were no doubt happy to see him gain his liberty again.

Thanking Gauss for his help and promising to send Burt's horse back into town as soon as he could, the Kid pulled on the reins and cantered west out of town into the glorious colours of the setting sun. Some said he was whistling a happy little tune.

Now if that is not an image straight from the most Hollywood of Western films, then I sure do not know what is.

***

As mentioned earlier, Lincoln itself is a true gem and probably the most essential and authentic destination on the trail of Billy the Kid.

The old courthouse is an icon of historical significance in this story and can boast a preserved atmosphere which is second to none.

Stand across the street in front of the Wortley Hotel (also nicely preserved) and one can let the image sink in of what was the Murphy/Dolan store where so much happened in the dark days of the Lincoln County War.

The building itself, apart from some cosmetic modification, is virtually unchanged from what Billy would have known. Just one major addition really, in the form of the wooden stairways which run down from either side of the front balcony. These stairways were not there when the Kid enacted his famous breakout.

Apart from that, one can really get the feel of how it must have been, especially when entering the building where it is permitted to walk freely around.

Upstairs, where Billy was held, walls have been taken down, so it is much more open plan than it was, but the area which was the north east corner room is intact. A board stands there which tells the story of the escape, along with Billy's manacles on display. And I was thrilled to be able to sit in the window which was Billy's view of the world for a week before he made his move. One can indeed get an excellent sighting of the Wortley Hotel from that window, where Billy would have watched, with satisfaction, as Bob Olinger came hurrying over to his death. Slightly to the left of that window a plaque now stands on the ground marking the spot where Olinger fell. The fence and gate are no longer there.

Walking along the corridor leading to the stairs where Billy struggled with Jim Bell, I could really picture the scene. Traces of blood have been found on the floor here, almost certainly from Bell's head wound when he was struck by those manacles. At the foot of the stairs, at almost head height over the small landing, there is a jagged perspex cover protecting a hole in the wall which claims to be where the bullet which killed the deputy ended up. This impressed me at the time, but I have since found out that this was apparently established in the 1950s for the benefit of tourists. (It really annoys me when things like this are done… I have too much respect for history to condone such flippancy.)

Downstairs, amongst other historical displays, is a lifesize replica of Billy's famous tintype photograph from Fort Sumner. Immediately outside the back door, situated in a pleasant grassy area, is a plaque marking the spot where Bell died in the arms of Godfrey Gauss.

I got talking to a lot of interesting and friendly people in Lincoln, but none more so than a delightful old lady named Beverley Hammond. She told me she was aged 83 (this was in 2004) and she was the official guide when I visited the house of Dr. Woods. Although this house is on the list of New Mexico's historic buildings, it does not really have any connection to the Kid, having been built in 1882… but it was the work of Dad Peppin, who, being a mason by trade, built many of the structures in the area. Dr. Woods became a local celebrity and important figure but that was decades after Billy's time.

Beverley had a lovely smile and most pleasant manner, and, boy, could she talk! But it was all brilliant stuff and I was totally fascinated by what she had to say about her life, all of which she had spent in Lincoln.

She was a really positive, humorous soul with a wealth of stories, but, best of all, she had personal recollections and knowledge of people who had actually known Billy.

As a little girl she attended parties where she had enjoyed George Coe playing his fiddle. She even had a vivid recollection of someone taking exception to his playing and cutting the fiddle strings as he sawed away. Well, that tough old Regulator must have really mellowed by then if he let the cutter get away with that!

She also knew Yginio Salazar, another Regulator and Billy's friend who helped him after his breakout. Salazar was fond of telling stories of the old days and Beverley heard them as a child. And to this day she was familiar with the descendants of Sheriff Brady, many of whom still lived in the area.

Conversing with this lady and hearing her stories was a true highlight for me; a real living connection with history.

CHAPTER 30
FREEDOM

Billy's initial mood as he galloped out of Lincoln must have been one of pure elation.

Weapons in his hands for the first time in nearly four months, a horse under his control and the undiluted path of freedom ahead.

The Kid was back in his element and he was enjoying it to the full. Whatever concerns lay in the future, this moment was his; riding alone and free.

But Billy was intelligent and his natural state never strayed far from analysing his situation.

Right now, the ball was in his court. He felt confident that he had a good head start on any possible pursuit. Garrett would not receive the news until well into the next day at the earliest. No one left in Lincoln would instigate getting after him... he was sure of that... the town was still pretty much in a state of shock from the sudden and bewildering turn of events.

Yes, Billy the Kid was at large again, but this time he had really taken the plunge. Already a convicted murderer, condemned to death, Billy had found himself in a corner with nowhere else to turn. In those long weeks of captivity, especially since his sentencing, he had little else to do but mull over what options remained for him.

Those options were basically limited to two things... wait to hang or escape. No other choice and, once his decision was made, it was then just a question of watching and waiting, to formulate his plan. When the moment was right, he would strike, and so he did... with great effect.

The slaying of his two guards was the final straw. There could be no way back for him now and the hunt would be intensified, an essential target for the authorities who would need to save face by bringing this upstart outlaw down. As it stood, he was making a fool of so called civilization.

As he would explain, his original intention had been to handcuff Bell, wait for Olinger to return, then cuff him too. Chain them together, maybe gag them and make his bloodless escape. That would have resulted in a very different predicament to what he now found himself in.

Billy's flight would have been humiliating for Garrett, the deputies and authority in general, but perhaps that would have been the catalyst to leave him alone. If he had shown mercy and just embraced his freedom, would much effort have been put into tracking him down again? Would he have been allowed to just quietly disappear?

Having killed his guards so ruthlessly, Billy had entered the realms of unforgiving retribution. He was now a badman of the first degree and there was no way he could be allowed to get away with it.

The Kid genuinely regretted shooting Jim Bell and his remorse was for real. The deputy and the outlaw had grown to mutually respect and like one another. One wonders if, during that desperate struggle on the stairs, Bell felt sure that his pleasant young captive would not actually pull the trigger. He took a gamble and lost, having made the mistake of underestimating what that Kid was actually capable of when cornered.

Billy strongly felt that Bell had left him no choice. He had to stop him. If the fleeing deputy had managed to make it to Olinger, the two of them, and maybe others, would have besieged the courthouse. Billy might have been able to outgun them and hold them off, but it probably would have led to his death or recapture.

No, it had been sad but necessary… and once done, with Bell dead, the Kid had nothing further to lose. The decision to blast Pecos Bob with his own shotgun was instantaneous and welcome. Billy and Olinger's hatred was mutual and the Kid took pleasure in killing the man. In a way, he gloried in the opportunity.

Right now he was raising dust on the main road to Fort Stanton just a few miles ahead. The last thing he needed was to run into a troop of soldiers so he took the first possible trail to the right which led him up through a gap in the Capitan Mountain range. He was very familiar with the hilly country beyond which was dotted with little farms and hamlets where dwelt numerous friends.

The first one he stopped at, as darkness descended, was the home of Jose Cordova who arranged for a neighbour to come over with tools to knock off the remains of the leg irons. This would have been an immense relief to Billy, who had been dragging them around for months. A heaped plate of hot chilli and black beans, along with a stack of warm tortillas would have gone down well too.

Next stop was at the Las Tablas home of Yginio Salazar who was surprised but pleased to welcome his old friend from the Lincoln County War experience. Salazar had narrowly escaped death during the breakout from the McSween house, lying wounded in the yard as certain parties argued about shooting him again where he lay. The Kid could not risk sleeping at Salazar's place so he hid out in the hills by night before arriving by day to eat and talk. During this time, Billy Burt's horse, which had served the Kid well, got loose from his tethering and made his way back to Lincoln, trailing a long lariat behind him. The townsfolk were amused by this... Billy had kept his promise to return the "borrowed" animal.

So it was now necessary to steal another mount, which was no problem for the Kid. He found a good mustang at a local ranch and galloped east towards Roswell where, just to the southwest of the town, on the Rio Penasco, he turned up at the cabin occupied by another old pal, John Meadows.

Meadows and Billy's friendship went back a couple of years to the time when the young wandering Texan had turned up in New Mexico desperate and suffering badly from sunstroke. The Kid had shown him kindness and helped him recover, so Meadows always remembered that and, as an old man, left us with valuable first hand memories of their relationship.

Meadows was cooking supper with Tom Norris, the man he shared the cabin with, when Billy appeared at the door. They knew nothing of his escape so it was quite a shock. Having not seen Billy for quite some time, Meadows was unsure what to expect.

"Well," said the Kid, *"I got you, ain't I?"*

Meadows answered cautiously, *"Well, you have... so what are you going to do with us?"*

"I'm going to eat supper with you!" smiled Billy, and so they did.

They talked long into the night with Billy telling of his adventures in full detail. The Kid even spoke of having a good feeling for Pat Garrett, saying how the Sheriff may have *"worked pretty rough to capture us"* but that he had treated them well during captivity.

Meadows made it clear that he was happy to help Billy, saying how he never forgot a kindness. Asking the Kid what he intended to do now, Meadows, like Salazar, said that his advice would be to get out of the territory as quickly as possible before Garrett tracked him down. He must keep heading south and hide out in Old Mexico where he could start a new life.

Billy shook his head and wondered what he could do in Mexico without money. He would need to raise some funds before he could make that move and Fort Sumner was the place where he could do that.

"Go to Sumner," muttered Meadows darkly, *"and Garrett will get you for sure, or you will have to kill him..."*

Billy was unaffected by this thought, saying how he would be amongst many friends in Sumner who would look out for him. He believed that Garrett would not try to get him there and he would stay just long enough to find the money he needed for Mexico.

Indeed, the lure of the warmth and security of Fort Sumner was strong. It was the closest thing Billy had ever known as home, certainly since losing his mother anyway. The circle of friends and lovers up there was tempting. He was confident that it was the only place he could feel safe.

Leaving Meadows' hospitality, Billy took a leisurely pace northwards in the direction of Sumner, sleeping under the stars and paying a string of visits to anyone he knew, and trusted, *en route*. A host of welcoming Hispanic working folk, the simple peons who adored him, were always on hand to shelter and feed their *Bilito* in their little sheep camps or farms.

There were a couple of adventures and near misses on the Kid's cautious journey. At one point he almost got into a confrontation with a bunch of cowboys who bumped into him by chance, spooking his horse and leaving him on foot again. Billy stole another mount from a rancher who sent some men in pursuit, one of whom was Barney Mason; he who had been instrumental in getting the Kid captured.

They caught up with Billy resting in a shack with a few Mexican allies. Not realising that the thief they were tracking was actually the famed fugitive outlaw, these men were somewhat surprised when the Kid stepped out to meet them cradling his Winchester. Mason's reaction was to turn his horse's head and ride hell for leather.

Billy found this funny but went on to talk pleasantly with the rest of the rancher's posse, telling them that he would return the horse, or pay for it, as soon as he had the means. The men nodded in agreement and turned away, leaving Billy to disappear into the hills again.

Billy the Kid made it to Fort Sumner on May 7th., nine days after his dramatic escape from Lincoln courthouse. It was a cautious comeback and he slipped into town without any fanfare. There were quite a number of locals who he could count on and, as he reacquainted himself, word quickly spread that he had returned, news which caused an excited stir, especially with the girls he knew. Paulita Maxwell was one, of course, and Pat Garrett's sister in law, Celsa Gutierrez too… and Deluvina… others as well. The Kid's presence in Sumner was the worst kept secret in the west! Everyone wanted to see him but he knew he must not let his guard down.

Making himself too comfortable would have been easy but far too risky. He was taking a big enough chance just being in the area so he rarely spent the night in town, tempting though it was. Dropping into Beaver Smith's and Bob Hargroves' was unavoidable but it must have been hard to relax. He even attended some of the *bailes* which took place, dependant upon his numerous friends who would keep watch for him and give warning of any suspicious presence in town.

But it was only a matter of time before Garrett would show his face again.

***

Sheriff Pat Garrett did not receive news of the Kid's escape until late on the night of Friday April 30th., well over 24 hours after the event.

Most of the locals in Lincoln were in no hurry to make it known, partly out of sympathy for Billy and partly out of fear. After all, he might be out there waiting on the road, to gun down anyone who he thought might be riding for help. Eventually, however, someone got word to Fort Stanton from whence a messenger was sent galloping to White Oaks.

Garrett was stunned but not in disbelief. It had been his greatest fear since Stinking Springs. He knew Billy Bonney and respected his cunning. Time and again long legged Pat had gone over every detail of the Kid's captivity and had felt as sure as he possibly could that there was no way out. As long as he was watched, and not given a moment's grace…

At sun up on Saturday morning, Garrett, grim faced and determined, rode the forty miles east to Lincoln where he viewed the stiffening corpses of Bell and Olinger, laid out in one of the outbuildings in the courthouse's back yard.

Not exactly surprised that no one had so far made a move to follow the fugitive, Garrett enlisted the help of a couple of men and straightaway rode out in the direction Billy had headed on the previous Thursday evening. They got as far as the gap in the Capitans but the trail was as cold as his dead deputy's bodies. Unsurprisingly, everyone they questioned, all those peons and travellers who dotted the land, knew nothing. They all shrugged their shoulders, shook their heads and looked blank when asked if they had seen *Bandido* Billy in the area. It was hopeless and Garrett and his men soon gave up.

They returned to Lincoln and Sheriff Pat retreated to his ranch just north of Roswell, to the comfort of his wife and their firstborn baby. He needed to think.

Was further pursuit pointless? Surely Billy would head for Mexico without delay. He must have learned his lesson and was probably across the border already, way out of the reach of official retribution.

As the days slipped by, word spread around the land that Garrett was doing nothing to track down the Kid. Why was he not scouring Billy's known haunts? Garrett knew them well. Was he afraid?

It was true that Pat's spirit had taken quite a knock. After all the effort that had gone into capturing the Kid and the slippery youth had managed to cheat the noose at almost the last moment. From being the hero of the hour, Garrett had made a rapid descent into being a figure of derision and harsh criticism.

In the meantime, newspapers nationwide, from the west to the east coast, were making a meal of this latest Wild West drama. Billy's notoriety hit the headlines with a refreshed savagery, portraying him as a *"widow maker"* and personification of evil.

Governor Wallace offered a further $500 dollar reward for the apprehension of Billy the Kid and this was made widely public throughout May. It was virtually Wallace's final official act, because by the end of the month he gave up his position and left New Mexico for good, glad to see the back of this "God forsaken wilderness" no doubt, as he declared, *"I have spent enough time in this place"*.

And still Billy remained glued to the comforts in and around Sumner. May morphed into June… the days were long and hot, the nights cool and romantic as the Kid drifted from sheep camps to farms to sleep and then made regular unannounced appearances for his friends in town.

He was shown the newspapers and kept informed of any activity which might arouse suspicion. In the first few days, even weeks, he was most likely serious in his wish to light out for Old Mexico as soon as possible, but as time went by, and no sign of trouble came his way, he was gradually lulled into a false sense of security. He got word that Garrett was inactive and began to feel that maybe Old Pat had had enough. Surely, if he meant business, he would have shown up by now…

But he could not deny the fact that he was on the run, and would remain so as long as he stayed in the jurisdiction of the United States and her territories. Right now things seemed fine… the heat was dying down, and he could relax, a little, accordingly. His *amigos* and *queridas* were looking out for him, watching his back, always protecting…

In time he probably would need to head south to create that new life, but why the rush? It would be hard to drag himself away from all he knew and those who loved him. And who exactly were his actual lovers? Well, it seems that from what history tells us, we cannot be exactly certain… but we have many clues.

The senoritas whose names are lost are numerous, but, as we have already seen, they existed for sure. Celsa was close to him, and Paulita Maxwell, who left glowing descriptions of his appearance and personality. Read between the lines and you can recognise her dewy eyed affection. And then there is that lingering kiss described by

Deputy Jim East from back when Billy and Paulita had to be practically *"pulled apart"* the previous December during his captivity. I think such tactile intensity proves that there was more than mere friendship between them.

On the face of it, Pete Maxwell, Paulita's elder brother and Sumner's unofficial patriarch, was a long standing *amigo* of Billy's. Living in his big, dominating house, *Senor Pedro* was well thought of as he oversaw the little empire which had been created by his late father Lucien. The Kid was well known to him, a familiar, smiling face in Sumner for a couple of years, at least. Pete acknowledged the young outlaw's popularity but there are signs that maybe he had grown to resent it slightly. He would not openly show it, although maybe it was natural for him to feel some sibling protection for his little sister. Did he approve of her close attachment to a bandit, a convicted killer on the loose? What future was there in that for her, foolish girl?

Whether or not Pete was instrumental in sending word to Garrett about Billy's whereabouts we cannot say for sure, but it is a fact that the Sheriff was beginning to receive quite regular information.

For weeks Long Pat had begun to give up hope of any solid leads which might make a renewed search worthwhile. There was no point in just turning up in Sumner, where he was well known, in the hope of bumping into his quarry. No one was going to turn the Kid in. What he needed was information, something he could cling to so that he could formulate another secretive plot which might lure Billy out of hiding.

Such detail was slowly filtering through. Reports of the Kid from here and there, in and around Sumner, sparking Garrett's old tenacious spirit again.

Manuel Brazil, whose ranch was close to Sumner, had his ear to the ground, although he kept well out of the way of any possibility of running into the Kid. It was definitely in his interests to have Billy apprehended again, having been an integral cog in the machinations which had brought him down the previous December. Brazil had no desire to be on the vengeful end of a bullet from Billy. Garrett wrote to the rancher in June, asking if he had any news. Brazil wrote back to say that he was sure the Kid was around although he was avoiding him. Garrett found this helpful.

The new chief detective of the Panhandle Stock Association, replacing Frank Stewart, was an ex buffalo hunter named John Poe. He was already doing a good job and had impressed Garrett enough to have employed him as a deputy sheriff of Lincoln County. Approaching mid July, Poe received a hot tip about Billy's whereabouts and took it to Garrett in Lincoln. Evidence was mounting that the Kid was definitely still hanging around Fort Sumner and making regular visits.

At last Garrett was nudged into action. This was the time, with enough information now to make an expedition north worth it.

Still unable to comprehend just why Billy would be careless and foolish enough to remain in such an obvious refuge, Pat realised that this was an opportunity that he dare not miss. Calling for the support of another lawman, Kip McKinney, Garrett made quick preparations and secretly headed for Sumner accompanied by his two deputies on July 10th.. They travelled by night using backtrails, arriving in the vicinity of the old fort under cover of darkness on Wednesday July 13th..

This was a hit or miss affair and very much a gamble on whether or not they might run into the Kid. Of course, they could not make themselves or their mission known and obviously there would be virtually no chance of finding someone who would be willing to help them.

Being a well known face in Sumner, Garrett would be unable to show himself, so it was decided that Poe, who no one would know, should pose as a stranger passing through town; a disgruntled miner from White Oaks who was making his way home to Texas.

Once in town during the day of the 14th., Poe was viewed with immediate suspicion, as was any stranger. He played it cool as he ate and drank in Beaver Smith's saloon, trying to engage the locals in conversation. The atmosphere was tense and the mainly Hispanic clientele clammed up as soon as he made a passing reference to Billy Bonney. A visit to a nearby rancher who it was thought might throw some light on the situation proved equally fruitless. No one was going to rat on the Kid.

Downcast, Poe reported back to Garrett and McKinney who were laying low in the surrounding hills. It was dusk by now as the trio of lawmen debated their next move.

It was beginning to seem like they were wasting their time, like looking for a needle in a haystack, but Garrett felt a strong hunch that it would be worth creeping into town when night fell. They could try staking out a few of the places where Pat knew Billy had connections... the homes of *queridas*... It was a long shot but worth a try.

CHAPTER 31
THE RECKONING

Billy the Kid had been at large again for seventy seven days.

All his youthful life he had been on the run, homeless and with no plans or hope for any kind of settled future. What was his state of mind now that he had reached probably the biggest crossroads of his 21 years?

Well, regardless of all he had been through and the many hard lessons, he was still very young. He retained all the optimism and carefree attitudes of youth, underlined by his natural confidence and solid belief in his ongoing luck.

He could look back on his eventful life and the many dangers he had survived with a sense of satisfaction. It had been a charmed existence, tinged with tragedy, but although he had lost many *compadres* and close *amigos* and made numerous enemies, he remained intact. And many friends and lovers were too.

It could be argued that he had lived an empty life. What had he actually achieved apart from a reputation as an outlaw and killer?

But, what did that matter beyond the moral high ground of those that judge?

Billy's conscience was clear, with the one exception of his regrets over having to kill Jim Bell, and even that he could justify. Everything else he had done did not trouble him.

All he wanted from life was to be left alone to pursue the things he enjoyed… friends, lovers, laughter, dancing, singing, racing horses, dealing monte, riding the high country with the wind in his face… As long as he had his Colt on his hip, his Winchester within reach and enough food in his belly, what more did he need? As for the future, he lived for today.

He knew he had stayed around Lincoln for far too long. Everyone was making the most of his company but all were advising him that he must leave for his own safety. Deep down he knew they were right, but on the surface he laughed off their concerns, insisting that all would be fine.

However, it had reached the stage where the Kid was growing tired of hiding out in the hills, making the most of swiftly grabbed visits to town, snatching trysts with his lovers, heeding warnings, taking advice… when all he wanted to do was live freely. Old Mexico beckoned… it was time…

The night of Thursday July 14th. 1881 was like so many others he had enjoyed during these last few weeks. A typically gorgeous and panoramic New Mexican sunset gave way to a brilliantly bright moon which cast a beautiful yellowy blue ambience over the tranquil hamlet of Fort Sumner.

As usual, Billy had ridden to the outskirts of town, hitching his horse and making his way cautiously to whoever awaited him on this occasion. Following on from the intense heat of the day, the evening was much cooler, but still pleasantly warm with the scent of wild flowers in the air. The Kid was in white shirt sleeves and a dark waistcoat, his sombrero pushed back high on his brow and his Colt "Thunderer" holstered on his right hip.

Around 9.00pm., Garrett, Poe and McKinney reined in their horses on the outskirts of town, keeping themselves well concealed as they unsaddled their mounts in preparation for what might well be a long night. From here they carried on by foot, making their way into the peach orchard which lay on the north side of the old parade ground. The pretty trees made good cover and the lawmen squatted down with their eyes on the silhouettes of the buildings just beyond. Very little was happening ... a few distant sounds from the saloons, the odd figure moving across the open space of the parade ground.

It was approaching midnight when Garrett expressed concerns that maybe their vigil would prove to be pointless. That said, he felt certain that the Kid was in the vicinity. He suggested that they go on over to Pete Maxwell's house. Pete would probably be in bed, but Pat felt he knew him well enough to rouse him and ask about Billy.

As they got to their feet and began to leave the orchard, they suddenly heard feint voices from somewhere in the shadows of the trees. They froze and crouched down again to listen. The voices were talking in hushed whispers, in Spanish, but were too far away to be understood. Straining their eyes, the lawmen could just about make out a figure some way away in the deep shadows of the trees, a man rising up from the ground. The figure was indistinct but they could see he was wearing a white shirt and a broad brimmed hat.

It was probably Billy, but Garrett did not suspect that at the time as he watched the figure step over the low adobe wall and make his way towards the buildings which ran alongside the compound.

So who had the Kid been with, laying down or sitting beneath the branches of the peach trees? Intimate and peaceful. Could it have been Paulita? If so, she would be making her way back to her bedroom in her brother's house.

When the man had disappeared into the porch shadows of the old barracks, Garrett and his deputies moved again, taking a circuitous route around to the west behind Maxwell's house. A gated picket fence ran along the east facing of the building and Pat knew that Pete's bedroom was located on the south east corner. As they reached it they noted that, owing to the heat of this high summer night, all the doors and windows had been left wide open.

Pausing at the gate, Garrett took a long, careful look around before instructing Poe and McKinney to wait here on the corner. He then took his long legged gait silently up the few steps onto the porch heading for the doorway of Maxwell's bedroom.

In the meantime, Billy had made his way to a room somewhere in the locality of what had once been the fort's quartermaster's store. Various accounts survive from those who claimed to know what he did, but they inevitably contradict one another. Some say he was with Celsa Gutierrez, or with *amigos* like Jesus Silva, Paco Anaya and others. He was relaxed by now, late at night in the company of friends, but he was weary, hot and hungry. They sent for beer from Beaver Smith's but the Kid, as usual, preferred coffee. He asked if there was any fresh meat as he fancied a steak. That morning, he was told, Maxwell had butchered a yearling and the carcass would be hanging from the porch of his house. Why not go and slice yourself a nice cut of meat and *"we'll fry it for you"*, someone suggested.

Billy had not been expecting to venture out again for a few hours and had removed his boots. His sombrero and waistcoat (vest) were strewn over a chair along with his gunbelt. The Kid took his Colt from the holster, tucking the weapon into the waistband of his trousers, a habit which was like second nature to him. He had learned to never stray far unarmed even when in such cosy surroundings.

The moon was so very bright. It was truly a lovely night. Billy picked up a butcher knife for the task ahead and made his way, in stockinged feet, out past the dance hall which stood on the corner of the parade ground, walking softly alongside the picket fence which ran up towards Pete's house.

It was all so peaceful, quiet and rather wonderful... maybe he was thinking, *"Do I really want to leave this?"*

***

Pat Garrett entered the darkness of Pete Maxwell's bedroom and strode over to the sleeping figure. Pete sat upright in his bed, as the tall Sheriff whispered his name and maybe shook his shoulder. Pat's eyes were slowly adjusting to the gloom but he could more or less make out what surrounded him.

It was a pretty rude awakening for Maxwell and he was startled and probably none too pleased about it. After all, who would welcome being woken from their dreams by the overpowering sight of a gangly, mustachioed lawman looming over them?

Garrett sat himself down at the head of the bed, right alongside Pete's pillow, and it was straight to business. With the minimum of formalities the Sheriff was soon asking about the Kid. Was he around? Had Pete seen him lately?

Half asleep and struggling to collect his thoughts, Maxwell mumbled that he knew Billy had been in the area but was planning to leave. Whether he had gone yet, he did not know... or so he said...

A few feet away outside, Deputy Poe was seated on the porch; McKinney was leaning on the other side of the fence by the gate.

Billy was approaching them, probably enjoying the pleasant sensation of the soft earth beneath his stockinged feet. Although the moonlight was illuminating everything in the open, the dark shadows cast by the overhanging porch were obscuring what lay within. Poe and McKinney were totally unaware of the Kid until he was almost on top of them, likewise Billy who suddenly halted and glared at the unexpected shadowy figures.

"*Quin es?*" he exclaimed, startled. ("*Who is it?*") Backing away and stepping up onto the porch, Billy pulled the .41 from his waistband with his right hand, the butcher knife still in his left.

The two deputies were startled too. Neither of them knew the Kid by sight and this sudden encounter had bewildered them. Poe rose to his feet and moved towards the young outlaw, answering in Spanish as he tried to assure the newcomer not to worry, all was fine. McKinney was frozen to the spot, his eyes on the muzzle of the Kid's Colt which wavered between him and his partner. At this point neither of them realised that they were facing Billy the Kid.

Billy must have been knocked out of kilter. This was such an abrupt turn of events. One moment he had been strolling leisurely in the glow of the moon, basking in the sheer tranquility of this beautiful night, anticipating the steak he would soon be eating, and suddenly this... strangers... who could they be? The Kid was renowned for his quick thinking and acting positively in a crisis but his hesitation was understandable. He had the drop on both of these men but did not pull the trigger... maybe they were guests of Maxwell's...

Billy walked backwards along the darkened porch, his pistol covering these strangers. "*Quin es? Quin es?*" he repeated, having still not received a satisfactory reply. Nervously he backed into the open doorway of Maxwell's bedroom, correctly assuming that the owner of the house would be there. He could give an answer, surely...

Once inside, Billy peered over towards Pete's bed, his eyes unaccustomed to the deeper darkness inside the room but aware of a figure under the bedclothes.

The Kid trusted Maxwell and probably relaxed momentarily, stepping across the carpet as he asked, *"Pedro, quines son estos hombres afuera?"* ... *("Pete, who are those men outside?")*

At this moment, it seems that Billy suddenly realised that there was another figure present… a tall one, sitting alongside Pete at the head of the bed… they had both been motionless at first, but now the tall one was beginning to move. It was all so dark… what was going on? The Kid raised his pistol again and backed away rapidly, *"Cat-like"* explained Garrett later, but still he hesitated…

Garrett and Maxwell had barely commenced their hushed conversation when they had heard the dialogue between Poe and Billy on the porch. Seconds later they turned their attention to the doorway as a silhouette appeared there, hastening into the room, anxiously delivering his question.

"Quin es?" asked the Kid, yet again.

"That's him!" hissed Maxwell but Garrett had already recognised that familiar voice. Even in the gloom, he could see that he was facing the barrel of Billy the Kid's deadly Thunderer, and the trigger was likely to be squeezed at any second.

It was now or never. Garrett reached down for his own six shooter, pulling and cocking it in one motion and sending a shell coursing towards the widest part of the dark body mass before him. The powder flash briefly brightened that small section of the room as Garrett threw himself sideways to his left, firing again, more blindly this time.

The next few moments were chaotic. Garrett felt sure he had hit his target but was about to fire a third time when he heard a gasping groan as the dark shape toppled forwards.

Maxwell had already leapt from his bed, scrambling for the door in his panic to escape, the bedclothes tangled all around him. Garrett was ahead, dashing through the door and almost bumping into Deputy Poe who was on the porch with his pistol drawn. Seeing the terror stricken Maxwell bringing up the rear like some maddened ghost, Poe pointed his gun at him but Garrett knocked his hand down, snapping, *"Don't shoot!"*

The tall Sheriff was agitated and in a slight state of shock as he told his deputies that he had just killed the Kid. Poe shook his head in disbelief, saying it could not be and that Pat had shot the wrong man.

Garrett was insistent. He knew Billy's voice too well and was certain it was him lying in that room.

The gunshots which had split the still of that moonlit night had woken most everyone in Fort Sumner. In a short time quite a crowd had gathered and word was already spreading that *Bilito* had been gunned down in *Don Pedro's* house.

The Maxwell family were the first to be roused, spilling out of their respective bedrooms... Pete's mother, Paulita, Deluvina... they all came to the porch, filled with anxious questions. The townspeople too, all wanting to know what had happened.

There was an understandable reluctance to enter the room. What if the victim was still alive and waiting in the darkness, gun in hand? Garrett, Poe, McKinney and Maxwell stood outside by the door debating their next move. Conflicting accounts describe the next few minutes. Some said that Maxwell gingerly held a candle up to the window and, by the dim light, could see the body of a young man lying motionless on the floor. Deluvina swore that she and Jesus Silva were the first to enter the room and, by the light of a lantern, saw the body lying face down on the carpet, his pistol in his right hand and the butcher knife in his left.

Gently turning the body onto its back, Deluvina burst into floods of tears as she stared into the lifeless, much loved face of her *chiquito*. Storming out onto the porch, the Navajo woman launched into a savage verbal attack on Garrett, calling him a *pisspot* amongst a torrent of other colourful insults.

Tall Pat took it in his long legged stride. He was getting used to this.

Garrett and others then entered the death scene to see for themselves. By candle light they examined every angle so that everyone could agree upon what had taken place. Billy had been struck by Garrett's first shot, the bullet tearing into his chest just above the heart. It had killed him almost instantly. The second shot had missed, ricocheting off the wall and narrowly missing Maxwell as it buried itself in the headboard of his bed. A lot of witnesses testified that they had heard three shots, but that last one would have just been the retort of the ricochet.

Garrett commandeered Billy's .41 pistol as they searched the body. He had nothing in his pockets; not a peso nor a dime.

The crowd outside had grown into a mob and the mood was beginning to get ugly. Womenfolk stood in a small knot of weeping souls... Deluvina, Celsa; shocked, shaking... alongside several others who had their own varied personal reasons to mourn their *Bilito*. Paulita stood blankly staring at her lover's corpse for quite some time, numb with grief, before she finally broke down and wept like the others. Their wailing echoed through the night air as the menfolk began to murmur in a more sinister fashion. Some of them were brandishing weapons, shouting and shaking their clenched fists at the lawmen, Garrett in particular. No one could deny Billy's popularity in Sumner… this was akin to slaughtering a favourite son in the front room of his home during a family party.

No explanation about terminating the career of a murderous outlaw would suffice in this situation. Garrett quickly realised that he was in danger of becoming a victim himself and the decision was taken for he, Poe and McKinney to barricade themselves in Maxwell's house for the night. The Kid's body was left to lay where he had fallen.

It was a long, fraught and worrying vigil before that glorious sun rose again in the eastern sky. Garrett and his deputies had dared not sleep and kept their weapons in their hands all through the night with the mob menacingly remaining close by.

By daylight, Garrett was determined to ensure that there could be no doubt that Billy had died by his gun and he set about procuring evidence. Already people were arriving from surrounding districts, word having spread like wildfire. Typical of human nature, as many as possible wanted to be part of the action.

With the death scene observed and recorded, Garrett agreed to the women's request to collect Billy's body and take it for burial preparation. Gently, the Kid's slim frame was carried over to the carpenter's workshop on the far side of the parade ground and laid out on a sturdy wooden bench. The clothing was removed, his ugly chest wound plugged and the senoritas solemnly made a complete job of washing down his cold body.

During the morning a coffin was hastily built by Silva with assistance from others who cared. Garrett donated $25 to buy a beige coloured suit for Billy to be buried in and by midday, the late Kid had been dressed and placed in the box with lighted candles at his head and feet. A short wake commenced in Beaver Smith's saloon, as a long line of sombre mourners passed by to view the young outlaw for the final time. Garrett also made sure that he obtained written declarations from many of them that he had got the right man. In the end, he collected over thirty signed notes from individuals who had known Billy well and who swore that they had seen his dead body. These declarations still survive for those who doubt.

The actual burial was scheduled for that very afternoon and

questions have been asked as to why everything was so rushed. Well, apart from the fact that it was customary to get bodies buried quickly in Hispanic culture, one has to remember that it took place at the height of the New Mexican summer with extreme daytime temperatures. There were no refrigeration facilities so how long could a dead body be kept in that heat without beginning to unpleasantly turn?

Another repetitive query that arises with tiresome regularity is, if Garrett was so keen to get evidence of his kill, why did he not arrange to have a photograph taken of the Kid's corpse, as was often customary, at the time, when outlaws fell to the justice of lawmen's guns? Well, the answer to that is blatantly simple. The nearest photographer would have been located in Las Vegas, well over a hundred miles away, which was one hell of a round trip by horseback or wagon. Yes, Billy had once had his picture taken in Sumner, but this had been a rare visit by a travelling photographer, the process of which was a complicated and cumbersome business back in 1881. What was Garrett to do? Send for a photographer or take Billy's body on a long journey of three or four days in that blistering heat? What kind of portrait would that have made?

Sheriff Pat also welcomed, and insisted, that there be an official coroner's report. The local Justice of the Peace was summoned and a jury swiftly assembled. It was a formality to come to the conclusion that the act had been "justifiable homicide" and that Pat F. Garrett was due the "gratitude of all the community"... plus, more pointedly, the reward.

That afternoon, Friday July 15th. 1881, Billy's coffin was sealed and placed on the back of a rickety wagon which took him over to the old military cemetery. Almost everyone in Fort Sumner, close to 200 souls, mostly Hispanic, attended the ceremony as the mortal remains of Billy the Kid were lowered into his grave, alongside the bodies of his close pals Tom O'Folliard and Charlie Bowdre.

So ended the ultra short yet highly eventful life of the Boy Bandit King, but the legend was yet to blossom.

***

The cemetery at Old Fort Sumner is a bleak spot but when I was there the sun was shining brightly, the sky a vivid blue. It was all so quiet and peaceful with no one else around. After all, there is generally no real reason to go there unless you are interested in the fate of Billy.

Over the years, the Kid's gravestone was stolen at least a couple of times, but eventually it was secured by chains, ironically echoing the way he was manacled for so many months in the last year of his short life.

In the early years following his death, wooden markers disappeared or disintegrated and on two occasions, 1889 and 1904, severe floods washed away everything on the site. It is possible that the human remains were scattered too so maybe Billy's bones are not even beneath where his headstone stands today. But he has a fine, heavy white granite monument now, surrounded by an iron cage. Carved into the top of this stone is the single word PALS, and underneath TOM O'FOLLIARD DIED DEC. 1880… WILLIAM H. BONNEY ALIAS BILLY THE KID DIED JULY 1881 and below them CHARLIE BOWDRE DIED DEC. 1880.

Either side of the headstone has had a lot of the detail chipped away by ghoulish souvenir hunters, hence the iron cage.

I stood and stared for a long time. It was one of those moments that resonates with me when I find myself in the presence of meaningful historic sites. As a passionate, empathic historian, you either get that or not…

I do not fully understand why but I was overcome with a deep feeling of melancholy, almost as if I had known the Kid personally.

Maybe I did…

CHAPTER 32
REQUIEM

And what of some of the other key players in Billy's story who lived on beyond his death?

Pat Garrett received the further $500 reward money for terminating Billy the Kid, but it was a troublesome process. He did not seek re-election as Sheriff, largely because of growing unpopularity in the territory, and even nationwide, for the way he had gunned down the young outlaw in the dark. Billy remained a kind of hero to many in New Mexico and Garrett swiftly became a figure to despise. The Kid's killing was big news all across the United States, and even reached the newspapers in London. Although Billy's legend grew out of proportion and he was widely and inaccurately demonized, Long Pat's reputation suffered and he was now generally regarded as a back shooter and coward.

As the months passed and rumours grew, Garrett became increasingly concerned by the way that night in Pete Maxwell's bedroom was impacting on his life. It seemed he could not go anywhere without being cornered on the subject of Billy's death.

Eventually he decided to do something about it and got together with part time journalist and Roswell postmaster Ash Upson to write a book and put the record straight. Unfortunately, the end result, published as *The Authentic Life of Billy the Kid* in 1882 (within a year of Billy's demise), was not anything of the sort. Upson himself had known Billy too, but he chose to embellish his section of the tome with absurdly outlandish and totally fictional elements of the Kid's early years which many readers were to accept as the truth. The last few chapters have the obviously more serious stamp of Garrett's influence because much of it is actually believable and verifiable, long Pat himself having been a big part of the tale.

However, on publication, the book was nowhere near as popular as had been expected and did not sell well at all. In due course, many years later, it was to become something of a classic, a collector's item, but at the time it failed to swell the author's bank balances by much.

Disappointed, and still dragging Billy's legacy in his wake, Garrett moved with his family to Texas where he very briefly served as a Captain with the Rangers. From there it was back to Roswell and various failed investments in ranching and irrigation and the odd foray back into serving as a law officer again. In 1899, he shot and killed his last man whilst assisting in an arrest.

Financial problems dogged him for the rest of his life and he simply could not get ahead. Somehow he gained influence with President Teddy Roosevelt who, in 1901, appointed him Collector of Taxes in El Paso, Texas, but this was an unpopular decision and he was dismissed.

Struggling on with various failed business ventures, often drunk and in terrible debt, Garrett became involved in a dispute over a lease. On February 29th. 1908, somewhere on the roadside between Las Cruces and San Augustin, he was shot in the back of the head whilst urinating. It was never fully confirmed who had actually delivered the bullet. Pat, at 6 feet 5 inches tall, was far too long for a conventional coffin and a specially built one had to be brought in from El Paso for his burial.

John Chisum died at the age of sixty in 1884. Surgery to remove a facial growth had led to complications which killed him. In his will, he left half a million dollars to his brothers. He also bequeathed a considerable sum to his two illegitimate daughters who, being unmarried, he fathered with his slave mistress. A big dramatic statue of him on horseback, challenging a raging bull, still dominates the centre of Roswell town.

James Dolan, having been cleared of all potential charges against him, eventually served as the Lincoln County Treasurer and in the territorial senate. Ironically, he was to acquire all of his enemy John Tunstall's former land and property and gained respectability from the people he had once conned so mercilessly. Like so many of his kind, he became an alcoholic and died in 1898, aged just 49.

Governor Lew Wallace enjoyed the fruits of his enormously successful book *Ben Hur*, although none of the other works he authored achieved anything like the same accolades. From his position in New Mexico, and by way of a huge contrast, he was appointed United States minister to the Ottoman Empire, a position he took up with relish in Constantinople (later to become known as Istanbul).

Lt. Col. Nathan Dudley, having been disciplined and removed from his command at Fort Stanton, was transferred to oversee Fort Union. Throughout the 1880s he was involved in quite a bit of Indian fighting against Apaches and an uprising on the Crow reservation. Reaching the high rank of Brigadier General, he died in 1910, aged 84.

The Kid's friend, Dr. Henry Hoyt, led an adventurous life. Following his eventful travels around the Wild West, he went back east to complete his medical studies. Once fully qualified, he was employed as a surgeon for railroad companies before serving in the U.S. Army as Surgeon General in the Spanish/American War and the Phillipines insurrection, where he was wounded. Awarded the Silver Star for gallantry, he wrote a fascinating autobiography which includes details of his experiences with Billy the Kid. Once retired, he set off on a long seaborne vacation but was taken ill on board ship and died on the shoreline of Japan in 1930, aged 75.

Rob Widenmann, the "dog feeder" who played a cautious and peripheral role alongside the Regulators, fled New Mexico and made his way to England where he met up with John Tunstall's family. He remained nervous about his safety, always feeling that his past would catch up on him, but he reached a ripe old age, dying in New York in 1930.

The surviving Regulators dispersed far and wide, but the Coe cousins, Frank and George, had returned from Colorado to Lincoln County by 1884.

George started an enterprise known as the Golden Glow Ranch at which he exploited his colourful past. Above the entrance he erected a sign which boasted *"He rode with Billy the Kid"*. Gladly he would speak of the old days to any visiting interested parties and even wrote a book, *Frontier Fighter*, about his Lincoln County War experiences. And, naturally, he was always proud to show off the stump of his right hand trigger finger which had been shot off in the Blazer's Mill fight with Buckshot Roberts. He made it to 85 years of age, the last of the Regulators.

His cousin Frank raised six children and killed his last man in 1898, his 16 year old daughter's boyfriend! However, he managed to get himself acquitted and died in 1931, aged 79.

Doc Scurlock reached a good age too, down in Potter County, Texas, where he became a pillar of society running the mail station. Apparently he never liked to talk about his gunslinging past.

John Middleton had miraculously survived the bullet he had taken square in the chest from Buckshot Roberts' Winchester in 1878 but he never fully recovered from it. When he left Billy, he made his way to Kansas, it is said, where he worked as a cowboy. By 1885 the effects still felt from that shell fatally caught up with him.

The Kid's one time close *compadre* Fred Waite made his way back to his native Chickasaw country where he was to raise a family. Fred's life turned around as he went from rancher to serving as an Indian policeman. Involving himself deeply in tribal politics he emerged as a senator before achieving the notable rank of Attorney General of the Chickasaw nation.

Big Jim French vanished but Henry Brown went on to achieve his own notoriety, first as a respected U.S. marshal, then as a bank robber.

Captured with his accomplices in a failed robbery which had resulted in fatal shootings, Brown was killed in 1884 attempting to make a run for it from a lynch mob, almost torn in two by blasts from both barrels of a shotgun.

Yginio Salazar lived until 1936 having become an honest farmer and rancher, while Jose Chavez Y Chavez ended up serving eleven years in prison for other crimes, released in 1909 and then living a quiet life until his death in 1924.

Dad Peppin, the Sheriff who had ordered the burning of the McSween home, never left the area until his death in 1904. Ironically, through his main profession as a mason, he had actually, over the years, overseen the building of that very house, along with the Murphy/Dolan store (later to be the courthouse from which Billy had escaped), the town's notorious pit jail and parts of Fort Stanton.

Ex deputy Jake Mathews managed cattle and became another character from the Kid's saga who served as Roswell's postmaster, also passing away in 1904.

Barney Mason, who Billy would undoubtedly have taken pleasure in putting a bullet through, must have been relieved to hear of the Kid's death. He then alternated between twin careers as a lawman and outlaw, alongside some irrigation and ranching projects, before serving some prison time. At the age of 67, he ended his days in California.

When Jesse Evans and Billy Campbell escaped together from Fort Stanton, they hightailed it to Mexico where they got into a gun battle with Texas Rangers. Captured, imprisoned, escaped again, recaptured... and sent to Huntsville Prison in Texas. Released in 1882, Evans disappeared into the mists of history and, presumably, so did Campbell.

Once separated from his cellmate, the Kid, Dave Rudabaugh received a 99 year jail sentence for mail robbery which was superseded by his conviction for the murder of a Las Vegas lawman. For that he was to hang, but he managed to break free and cross the border into Arizona where he joined the infamous Clanton gang in their feud with the even more famous Earp brothers in Tombstone. Surviving that, he carried on down to Mexico, indulging in more rustling and general misbehaving. In 1886, it is said, but not totally verified, that he got into a gunfight with locals in Chihuahua, shooting three men, two of them fatally. He fled but returned to the scene of the shooting for some reason, where vengeful Mexicans were waiting for him. He was gunned down from ambush and decapitated. His head was then paraded around town on the point of a tall pole; a scene that was photographed.

Billy Wilson, the Kid's other long term cellmate, was convicted of counterfeiting but he also escaped, from his jail cell in Santa Fe. In Texas, he settled down to raise a family. Becoming respectable and living under his birth name of David Anderson, he enlisted the willing help of Pat Garrett, of all people, and, in 1896, succeeded in achieving a Presidential pardon for his past crimes. He was serving as a Sheriff in 1918 when he was ambushed and killed.

Tom Pickett also ended up doing his bit as a deputy marshal and lived to a ripe old age.

The two deputies who accompanied Garrett on the night Billy was killed also suffered from the notoriety of having helped to end the Kid's career, but not to the same extent as Pat.

John Poe became the Sheriff of Lincoln County eventually and Kip McKinney served the U.S. Army as a scout leading wagon trains; also in the Spanish/American War as a guide. As the years went by, McKinney gave more than one version of what he had seen on that fateful night at Pete Maxwell's in Fort Sumner.

Billy's probable sweetheart, Paulita Maxwell, married Jose Jaramillo, just a year after the Kid's death. She was still only 18 years old and she went on to have three children. As stated earlier, Paulita began to play down the extent of her relationship with Billy, but that was probably in deference to her husband. Never the less, she always spoke fondly of her *Bilito*. In the 1920s, she was interviewed by Walter Noble Burns when he was researching his book *The Saga of Billy the Kid*. She said quite a lot which became valuable to subsequent historians, but when she became aware that Burns was going to reveal her feelings, she threatened to sue him. That is probably why Burns changed the written emphasis of Billy's love interest to the married Celsa Gutierrez who had died by the time of publication. Paulita passed away in 1929.

Deluvina, Maxwell's adopted Navajo woman, truly adored her *chiquito* Billy, her "little boy", and devotedly placed flowers upon his grave for many years. She continued to harbour an intense hatred for Garrett and his deputies. Before passing on in 1927, she often said, *"I am glad I have lived long enough to see them all dead and buried"*.

Another flame of Billy's had been Sallie Chisum, albeit briefly. Sallie was widely regarded as the cowboy's dream... it seemed that every man in boots and chaps from the Rio Grande to the Staked Plains was in love with her. But Billy caught her eye. With her family influence she was off to a good start in life, but she used it well and became a successful and wealthy cattle rancher in her own right. She remained in Roswell, revered and powerful before her death in 1934.

And Sue, the widow of Alexander McSween. Following all her legal battles she received help from John Tunstall's English family and became the executor of his estate. She remarried and showed considerable business acumen in building up her own cattle empire to the west of the Mescalero reservation... a 1,500 acre ranch encompassing about 8,000 head, one of the largest holdings in the entire territory. This made her exceedingly wealthy but she decided to sell up in 1902. Thereafter she settled in White Oaks which had become a pale shadow of the boom town it had been some twenty years before. Her money dwindled away and she died poor in 1931, aged 85.

Billy the Kid made a huge mark on these and the countless others who passed through his tragically short span on this Earth.

What would he make of all this attention and fascination so long after he's gone? Indeed, what is it that makes him, and just a few more, stand out from a long list of outlaws, desperadoes and gunmen of the brief period known as the Wild West?

There really were so many others who, arguably, achieved more, killed more (not that such a record is admirable), were more vicious, more dashing even... yet Billy the Kid has emerged as one, if not *the* most recognisable icon and symbol of the era. His youth? Well, no, not really... there were lots of very young drifters toting guns... many of whom were also tagged with the moniker of "Kid". It does seem that his personable nature and ability to make friends easily certainly made an impression, alongside his intelligence, quick wit and natural leadership qualities. Plus, following the ending of the Lincoln County War, he stuck around and made a name for himself in all quarters. And his well received affinity with the Hispanic community, the way he understood their ways, blended in, gave them time, spoke their language so fluently.

Although he had already achieved that reputation as the Boy Bandit King, with dime novels making a fantasy of his exploits, the one thing which really put him in the frame of true fame was his final dramatic escape from captivity.

Without that, would he still be remembered in the 21st. Century?

Garrett's book was the first step, and then the one by Burns in the 1920s, although that was also a highly colourful and largely fictitious rendition of the Kid's life. *"Killed a man for every one of his twenty one years"* and such similar tripe which people grew to accept as fact.

And then came the films, and television shows... some of them even made a reasonable stab at taking the subject quite seriously although the casting is eye poppingly ridiculous in several cases.

Kris Kristofferson as the Kid? Really? Too old, too big, too 1970s... although, to be fair, Sam Peckinpah's version (*Pat Garrett and Billy the Kid*) is enjoyable and entertaining. I just wish it hadn't pretended to be history. That said, it contains a beautiful scene which has become a classic moment in Western films... when a gutshot Slim Pickens shuffles mournfully down to the riverside to take his last breath in the rays of the sinking sun, accompanied by the plaintive Dylan song *Knocking on Heaven's Door*. Wonderful...

I rather liked *The Left Handed Gun* starring Paul Newman, which had its moments, and Gore Vidal's *Billy the Kid* with Val Kilmer in the titular role, although its absurd acrobatic final death scene annoyed me. And one called *The Kid* which seemed fairly promising until its over emphasis of a fictional sub plot rendered it all rather pointless.

John Wayne's *Chisum* (1970) is another entertaining romp over facts and credibility, in fact the plot is pure fantasy, alongside a totally ridiculous portrayal of Billy.

So many others, including a television mini series which is a total waste of a great opportunity. I also have a pretty vivid memory of a T.V. show from the 1970s, the title of which escapes me, the premise of which was to cast well known actors portraying iconic figures from history getting interviewed as if having appeared in modern times. Richard Dreyfuss, the right age then, portrayed Billy very realistically and I remember thinking at the time, wow, he should get the role in a proper movie. Sadly, Westerns were not popular at the time and those that were made just seemed to reflect the political rebelliousness of the era. One of those was the appalling *Dirty Little Billy*, featuring Michael J. Pollard, which absolutely stank.

Emilio Estevez's highly popular *Young Guns* films (1988 and 1990) injected fresh blood and energy into the Kid's story and certainly brought it all back into the arena of interest for the youth of the time. All very welcome good news, and the films were fun and actually rather good... although not from an historical point of view. It was really just the Brat Pack playing cowboys with a slim grasp of authenticity.

A major disappointment for many of we Billy the Kid enthusiasts and historians was the basic theme of the second film which gives credence to the doubtful boast of Brushy Bill Roberts, an old timer who, just after World War 2, claimed to be the Kid. His story was that he had survived that fateful night in Sumner by making a deal with Garrett to disappear. Another man had been killed and buried in his place and he had gone on to a full, but secret, life. A third *Young Guns* film is going to explore this theme even further, I am told...

Roberts even applied for the reassessment of the pardon given to "him" by Wallace some 70 years before. Well, I am not going to take up space in my book with a wordy assessment of his claims and the arguments against them; suffice to say that it does not convince me at all.

Other seemingly well researched (but incomplete) sources have made outlandish claims which apparently "prove" that Billy lived on. For instance, a detailed string of accounts which name a lookalike of the Kid named Billy Barlow who, we are told, accompanied our Billy in his last days. Barlow (who is mysteriously missing from most versions of the tale) resembled the Kid in height, build and general looks, though being part Mexican was darker skinned. Some say it was Barlow who entered Maxwell's bedroom and was shot in error. The following cover up was arranged to mask Garrett's humiliating mistake and the populace of Sumner went along with it so that their *Bilito* could make his escape and disappear. Far fetched in the extreme and a theory full of holes, surely.

As far as I am concerned, and most Billy-philes would agree, the Kid ended his days in the darkness of Pete Maxwell's bedroom, July 14th/15th. 1881, courtesy of a bullet from Sheriff Pat Garrett.

Before I leave the subject of films, at the time of writing, I am reliably informed that a major new production is in the planning stages, starring that charismatic young Irish actor Barry Keoghan as the Kid. I have high hopes for this movie because all the signs, so far, are that the whole subject is being taken very seriously, for the first time. This could be the one.

Nowadays there are several social media sites and forums dedicated to the study and fascination surrounding Billy. I have taken an active part in several of them and it is good to share thoughts and information with like minded souls.

The worldwide interest in the subject is truly enlightening, people of all ages and nationalities posting literally anything Billy related. It is a very mixed bag, and one has to scroll through an endless *potpourri* which includes topics from art, theories, new evidence, appraisals of known facts, appreciation and nostalgia through to absurd and foundless claims of previously unseen photographs (this is particularly tiresome), pure ignorant laziness, ridiculous remarks from those who have not bothered with any research at all before spouting nonsense, and blinkered Brushy Bill fanatics.

Sadly, all this quite often leads to conflict from keyboard warriors which results in out of proportion rudeness. However, I am pleased to say that there is enough sensible and pleasantly interesting interaction to make it all worthwhile.

And so many books... scores and scores, and now mine to add to the growing pile. Many writers of varying qualities have offered their take on Billy's story and it is worth wading through them to absorb every angle. Some really stand out as rather special and, for me, that would include the intelligent, entertaining and diligent work of Frazier Hunt, Robert Utley, Fred Nolan and James B. Mills.

So, as I asked before, what *would* Billy himself make of all this?

I pause for a moment and close my eyes, and I swear I can see him reining in his frisky bay mare, pulling on the halter with one hand as he pushes back the wide brim of his sombrero with the other.

His blue eyes flash and he charms us all with that warm, buck toothed smile.

All this attention on a simple young cowboy... he wonders who that can be...

"*Quin es ese hombre?*" he laughs, before turning and galloping away into the sunset.

PART THREE
WYATT EARP

CHAPTER 33
BLOOD FOR BROTHERS

Friday, March 24th. 1882... Iron Springs, Cochise County, Arizona.

Wyatt Earp was a man with a mission.

Determined and focussed by nature, Wyatt had his mind set on a straight path. There were complicated circumstances, but his ultimate goal could be summed up in one word... Vengeance.

That was the way it had been for months now. Wyatt and his brothers were close, in appearance as well as that lifelong family bond. They had each other's backs... loyal...

Now two of them were victims... one crippled, another dead, gunned down from ambush by back shooting sons of bitches... and Wyatt knew who they were.

He had sworn to make them pay.

Some already had but the list needed whittling down some more.

Vendetta was all that mattered now to Wyatt Earp. Much of his adult life had been spent wearing the badge of a lawman but things had grown deeply personal. Justice went beyond legal statutes for the Earp family and Wyatt wanted instant results not technicalities. If that meant taking the law into his own hands he would not hesitate to do so.

With his younger brother dying in his arms, Wyatt's steely resolve went into overdrive. Not one to outwardly express emotion, the elder Earp was overcome in that moment, hands and sleeves soaked in his sibling's blood as he watched his kin's life ebb slowly and painfully away. It is said that the last words the dying man heard were that of his elder brother promising to get his killers.

Wyatt had wasted no time in putting his words into action.

Despite warnings from various authorities not to do anything illegal, he ignored them and called on the support of his trustworthy friends and remaining brothers. His own personal posse formed, Wyatt set off at the head of his Vendetta Ride following obvious leads and armed to the teeth.

Another brother, the second eldest of them, had previously fallen to the same group of assassin's guns. Miraculously he had survived but one arm would remain useless for the rest of his life forcing him out of the picture and leaving Wyatt to seek payback.

With a loved brother now dead, Wyatt led his posse ruthlessly to obtain swift results. They managed this within days, two of their prey quickly found and killed in retaliation.

But Wyatt was a long way from total satisfaction. There were several names on his death list and a couple were particularly in his sights.

The Vendetta posse rode with purpose but they needed continuing finance to operate. Wyatt called upon another friend to furnish them with a tidy sum as a loan to tide them over. Now hunted by a faction of the law for the killings, Wyatt was forced to be cautious, therefore he arranged for the money to be brought to a specific, remote location way outside of town... a quiet little spot called Iron Springs, a muddy little watering hole on the low slopes of the Whetstone Mountains.

In actual fact, there were two posses on the trail of the Earp posse. One officially instigated by the county sheriff to bring them in and another formed by the very men who Wyatt was hunting. The latter's motive was self preservation and their own version of vengeance.

It was an exceptionally hot spring day when the Earp posse rode at a leisurely pace towards the rendezvous. The men were uncomfortable in their saddles but Wyatt, his usual anxious self, was trotting purposefully ahead of them. Alongside him rode his friend Texas Jack Vermillion, a long haired, tough hombre who had sworn allegiance to the Earp cause.

Wyatt's stern, unwavering gaze peered over his big, sweeping blonde mustache, the crown of his wide brimmed hat shading his features from the glare of the sun. He may have been thinking it best to remove the long tailed coat he was wearing, but his twin pistol-ed cartridge belt had already caused him enough irritation to make him loosen the buckle a few notches. It was a relief to let those holstered guns sag a little down his waist.

The trail to the Springs forked into a narrow, rock strewn canyon, and the horses picked up the scent of nearby water. Quickening their pace, the lead riders began a sloping descent, following an arc around large boulders and onto a wide shelf of sand. A grove of cottonwoods lay ahead, shading the shallow bank of the waterhole.

Wyatt had already begun to experience a feeling of unease, a premonition that something did not seem quite right... His suspicions soon proved valid...

Suddenly, from out of the shade of the trees, a group of figures began springing to their feet. It seems they had been relaxing by their campfire and the unexpected appearance of riders had startled them.

A frozen moment was instantly shattered by the drawing of weapons followed by a fusillade of rapid shots from the resting group.

Wyatt and Texas Jack reined in as bullets flew towards and around them. These men were familiar figures, nine of them, and Wyatt instantly recognised their faces. One in particular, burly, freckle faced and curly haired, stood out and made Wyatt's hackles raise. This cowboy was at the head of the list...

Texas Jack's horse was hit and went down with a piercing whinny. It fell dead, pinning Vermillion's leg, trapping him. As Jack struggled to free himself, Wyatt quickly dismounted, wrapping his horse's reins around his left hand as he reached for the shotgun he carried across his saddle.

The curly haired cowboy had already levelled his own shotgun and let fly but Wyatt's luck, as was so often the case, was with him and the lead pellets just ripped through and peppered the tail of Earp's long coat. Wyatt responded by raising his weapon and giving the cowboy both barrels, the heavy charge striking him fully in the midriff and throwing him down at the waterhole's rim.

Tossing the empty, smoking shotgun aside, Wyatt now reached for the Winchester rifle tucked in its saddle scabbard, but the constant firing had spooked the terrified horse so much that it was rearing and twisting around, desperately trying to pull away. Earp struggled to control the animal, his efforts confounded by his loosened cartridge belt which had worked its way down over his thighs, almost pinning his legs together and severely restricting his movements. His pistols had slipped around towards his back, but giving up on trying to grab the rifle, Wyatt now managed to reach one of the pistols which he was able to draw and bring into the fight.

All this with bullets whining on every side. It was a matter of seconds but must have seemed like an age. As he cocked that freed revolver, Wyatt had become aware of the rest of his posse high tailing it in the opposite direction in a cloud of dust. His partner Vermillion was still desperately trying to drag himself free of his stricken mount so, in that moment, Earp was alone and facing the remaining eight opposing cowboys who were blasting away at him from just a few yards away.

Fortunately, either their aim was poor or Wyatt's luck held firm, as he returned fire, dropping another cowboy with a slug to the body. Yet another one he shot in the arm. Quite a scene, but the odds were still way against him and he realised he had best make a run for it.

There followed an almost comical sequence as Wyatt struggled to mount his rearing horse, grasping the saddle with one hand and trying to pull up that restricting cartridge belt with the other. At one point he was stretched at an angle across the animal's back, a cowboy's bullet striking the saddle horn between his nose and hand, almost unhorsing him. Then another shot struck his boot heel, sending a tremor through his foot and up his leg making him feel that he had been hit. At last he succeeded in settling himself properly in the saddle just as Texas Jack fought free from under his dead horse.

With bullets still flying around them, but miraculously not finding any further marks, Vermillion scrambled up behind Wyatt, clinging tight as they galloped away in the direction they had come.

They soon caught up with the rest of their posse who had reined in to take stock further back along the trail.

Although they were all relieved to find one another, Wyatt must have wanted some satisfying answers as to why he and Vermillion were left to face the music all alone. They were told, maybe a little sheepishly, that the fire upon them had been so heavy they had no choice but to withdraw and could only assume that Wyatt and Texas Jack were following behind. To hear of the ensuing gunfight must have been something of a surprise, especially what a close call it had been.

Wyatt's leg had gone numb from the strike of that bullet on his boot heel but he was relieved to discover that he was not damaged. Likewise, the sight of his shredded coat tail must have been sobering.

Some of the posse now found renewed courage and were all for riding back to face the remaining cowboys but Wyatt ruefully declined.

"*If you fellows are hungry for a fight, you can go and get your fill…*" he said, no doubt feeling he had done more than his share for the day. He mounted up and rode away in the opposite direction.

A fine blow had been struck for his brothers and another day lay ahead.

As it stood, what became known as the *Battle of Iron Springs* would add to the growing legend of Wyatt Earp.

CHAPTER 34
WANDERING THE WEST

Wyatt's father, Nicholas, was a big, imposing man who made his mark controlling a large family.

The Earps were of English, Scots and Irish descent, the first of them arriving in Maryland in 1674.

Raised in Kentucky, as a young man Nicholas fought in the 1831 war against the Blackhawk Indians. His first wife Abigail gave birth to a son, Newton, in 1837, but she died two years later and Nicholas married again, the following year, to Virginia Cooksey. Two more sons followed, James (1841) and Virgil (1843) before the family moved to Illinois, just in time for the outbreak of the Mexican/American War. Nicholas enlisted and became a sergeant in the Illinois Mounted Volunteers under Captain Wyatt Berry Stapp, but his military career came to an abrupt end when he was severely injured by the kick of a mule.

Returning to Illinois with the status of a wounded veteran, Earp senior became a farmer, but this was just one of many occupations he was to pursue during his long and active life; jobs which included cooper, teacher, harness maker, justice of the peace and even some trouble as a bootlegger.

Settled briefly in Monmouth, a further addition to the family came along on March 19th. 1848 in the form of another son who was grandly named in honour of Nicholas' former commanding officer... Wyatt Berry Stapp.

Always restless and on the move, Nicholas uprooted his brood again, this time taking them to Pella, Iowa, where a further two sons were born... Morgan (1851) and Warren (1855). There were sisters too, but for the purposes of this account I will not complicate matters by detailing them here. All of the sons, with the exception of half brother Newton, were to play a big part in what follows.

The Earps all had a strict but fair upbringing, although farming was certainly not a vocation for young Wyatt. He was restless and anxious to break away from his humdrum existence plough pushing and carrying out mundane chores. A chance came with the outbreak of the Civil War but Wyatt was still only thirteen and unable to partake. Watching his elder brothers, Newton, James and Virgil, march off to join the Union Army just added to his frustration.

More than once, Wyatt ran away in failed attempts to enlist, for his father always tracked him down and dragged him back to the farm.

The three elder Earps saw action in various theatres of war out east and the savagery was brought home when James' left shoulder was shattered by a musket ball putting him in hospital for over a year.

When James finally made it back to his folks to recuperate, Nicholas decided that he wanted to put as much distance as he could between the war and his family. So, yet again, the Earps were on the move, this time all the way to Southern California with Nicholas heading a train of forty wagons.

It was 1864 and Wyatt had by now, at sixteen, grown into a strapping youth, tall and robust in build. He loved this new adventure and distinguished himself on the trail, which took several months, hunting game and, on a couple of occasions, helping to fend off attacks by hostile Indians. This practical apprenticeship for manhood included Nicholas' encouragement that his remaining sons should learn to read and write during the long, tedious sections of the trek.

However, it is worth noting that the diary of a fellow traveller recorded that Nicholas Earp was a *"foul and uncouth person"* whose engagement as wagon master was a source of regret!

When the Earps established themselves in San Bernardino County, Wyatt was reluctantly plunged back into farming work which, having experienced some adventure, he hated more than ever. Nicholas took on a role as Provost Marshal responsible for army recruitment but still kept his son out of uniform.

When Virgil returned from the war, Wyatt was keen to join his brother when he set off for fields anew. Together they travelled around Utah and Arizona working for freight companies. Wyatt originally would have taken on menial tasks such as loading and unloading wagons but he soon progressed to driving the teams. By now he was really clocking up some experience in the ways of the west and had more than begun to fit in.

Even so, he found himself with the family again when they moved back to Iowa in 1868, then on to Missouri. In the summer of 1869 Wyatt had wandered over to Bearstown, Illinois, where, some accounts say, that he indulged in his first gunfight. Apparently, a railway worker began deriding the young Earp with insults such as calling him "California Boy" which was a jibe used to rile those who it was thought had gone west to avoid the War. This was unjust as Wyatt had done his best to join up but was simply too young. The confrontation led to a fight in a hotel which resulted in Wyatt throwing his abuser out of the building where guns were drawn. Both men opened fire and Wyatt emerged the victor by wounding his opponent in the hip. The whole incident was hushed up and Wyatt returned home again, this time to the quiet little town of Lamar, where his father was just ending his tenure as a constable to take on the role of Justice of the Peace.

Wyatt replaced his father in the role of constable, his first engagement as an officer of the law, but it was a mainly peaceful job in comparison to what he would eventually face on the frontier.

In Lamar his duties tended to be no more dangerous or exciting than arresting the odd drunk, along with a highlight which involved a dispute about the free running of hogs.

In early 1870, Wyatt courted Urilla, a hotel owner's daughter and they got married, buying a small property and some land. However, within a year, Urilla suddenly died, maybe whilst pregnant, or perhaps from typhoid; the facts are vague. Whatever the cause, this was a huge blow to the young lawman and he was to sell up and anxiously move on leaving the tragedy behind him.

Before he left, Wyatt, perhaps as a result of his grief stricken state of mind, became embroiled in some controversy which has never been fully understood. For some reason, and it remains a mystery, Wyatt and his brothers James, Virgil and young Morgan (only about nineteen) ended up in a pretty savage street fight with Urilla's brothers Fred and Bert Sutherland, who were supported by their friends the Brummett boys, also brothers, Granville, Lloyd and Jordan.

This multi-brothered brawl was quite a dust up, leaving them all battered and bruised but it appears to have cleared the air.

When Wyatt left town it was under suspicion of fraudulently forging a court document and suspected theft. His father was dragged into the controversy and also moved away before any official hearing could take place, which does tend to be somewhat suspicious.

Wyatt found his way to Indian Territory (which later became the state of Oklahoma) where he wound up in further trouble when he and a couple of companions were charged with horse theft. In March 1871 a warrant was issued for the arrest of the three accused, and the charge even involved an accusation of a murder threat.

As it turned out, Wyatt never went to trial and he put distance between himself and such potential trouble. There are also reports that he and brother Morgan were arrested for pimping and living off immoral earnings. Records from that dark period of his life are unclear, even largely non-existent, but it does cast a cloud over the Earp reputation. Wyatt himself always refused to discuss that time and so, I guess, we will never know what actually occurred.

From there he rode wild and free throughout the winter of '71, down along the Arkansas River hunting buffalo for a government surveying team. It was during this time that he met fellow hunters the Masterson brothers, Ed, Jim and Bat, who were to become close friends (especially when they all became lawmen) over the next few years.

By this time, with the cattle trade expanding and booming, the original cowtown of Abilene was falling out of favour with the big trail drives which had now pushed on to make Ellsworth their new receiving and shipping hub. With all the trouble and mayhem that accompanied the lucrative business generated by the influx of fun seeking Texan drovers, lawmen were needed who could bring some kind of order to what had now become routine chaos at a trail drive's end.

For Ellsworth, this came in the form of Marshal "Brocky" Jack Norton and his somewhat corrupt crew who were overly aggressive in dealing with the town's ongoing problems. The drover's felt more affinity and showed respect for the county sheriff, Chauncey Whitney (a veteran of the famous Indian fight at Beecher's Island in 1868) but as sheriff his main duty was to oversee the overall situation in the wider area of the county. With his pockmarked face "Brocky" Jack and his deputy "Happy" Jack and crew basically held sway in town.

Considered unnecessarily heavy handed with the boisterous yet open handed paying customers in the saloons, gambling houses and other dens of fun, conflict was inevitable. It was mid cattle season 1873 and the notorious Thompson brothers, Ben and Billy, were in town enjoying some gambling. An argument broke out between them and fellow player "Happy" Jack in Brennan's Saloon and it spilled out onto the street where a few threatening shots were discharged into the air. Men from each faction were sizing each other up and it was getting ugly.

Ever the diplomat, Sheriff Whitney, by good fortune, happened to be present and he stepped in to try and soothe things. Approaching the Thompsons, the sheriff spoke calmly, imploring the Texans to calm down and talk it through over a drink. As they made their way back to Brennan's, according to later recollections from witnesses, "Happy" Jack suddenly appeared again, provocatively brandishing a pair of six guns. This was too much for the hot headed Billy Thompson. His brother Ben had already drawn his pistol and taken a potshot at Jack as he ducked behind a wall, but Billy levelled his shotgun and, in his inebriated state, let loose. Unfortunately, he totally missed his target and hit Sheriff Whitney instead, fatally wounding him.

Everyone around was shocked to see the popular lawman fall, none more so than Ben. Horrified, but always with his wayward sibling's welfare as his first priority, Ben kept his gun in his hand as he urged Billy to leave town without delay. Cocky as ever, Billy arrogantly mounted up and made a delayed show of riding out, as if inviting someone to dare try and arrest him.

Supportive Texans quickly and defensively surrounded Ben as those who supposedly represented Ellsworth law stood by, unwilling to act. It was left to the town mayor to approach Ben and demand that he give up his weapons and surrender.

Years later, a legend would spring up and gain unwarranted credence about Wyatt Earp's role in what happened next. This was owing to the swift spreading of wild rumours which grew in the telling, but mainly due, in the 20th.century, following the publication of Wyatt's hugely exaggerated biography, which we shall explore later.

It was widely believed that Wyatt, who happened to be present, faced down Ben Thompson and all those armed Texans, fearlessly confronting him with steely nerves and forcing him to surrender.

Highly unlikely ... in fact, rather ridiculous.

An old and experienced shootist like Ben would never have succumbed so meekly. Judging by later accounts from the likes of Bat Masterson and Wyatt's common law wife, who shared the probable truth with him in his later years, the facts were much less dramatic.

It is much more likely that in the standoff of the moment, Wyatt just ambled over and managed to speak reasonably to Ben who was probably looking for a way to save face in such an awkward predicament. His first priority had been to cover for his brother and now he wanted no further trouble. Wyatt probably suggested the reasonable solution of Ben offering to voluntarily surrender, thereby avoiding further violence. It was giving him a way out which he took in affable fashion, resulting in a minor fine instead of bloodshed.

The mayor was impressed and offered a lawman's job to Wyatt. "Brocky" Jack and his cohorts were instantly dismissed for their woeful behaviour and lack of response to the crisis.

The incident was a major hike in Wyatt's image as the Chinese whispers spread about what he had achieved in Ellsworth.

That was the day the Earp legend began.

CHAPTER 35

LAWMAN

The rail lines moved on relentlessly across west Kansas and Wyatt soon followed. As matters slowed down in Ellsworth the 26 year old ambitious Earp felt the need to keep abreast of the action.

His next stop was Wichita.

This latest focus of cowtown enterprise and high jinks had been growing rapidly from its modest roots as a dusty little trading post since 1872. Within two years it was a veritable hive of wild activity as the cattle trade embraced all it had to offer. Buildings sprouted from the prairie grass on both sides of the Arkansas River, the more respectable citizenry being located on the east bank whilst the less savoury elements were concentrated on the west in a suburb known as Delano. Here is where the inevitably numerous forest of saloons, brothels, gambling houses and iniquitous dens of ribald entertainment blossomed like cactus flowers. As was the pattern with all these towns, the Texan cattle boys were soon painting it red.

The attitude of most east bank residents was to tolerate the sinful ways of the west bank, provided that is where they remained. As long as they kept to themselves and their money rolled in, all was well.

Wyatt took to cowtown life with ease. It was a scene he understood and enjoyed, where he could relax amongst the kind of crowd he identified with, especially at the gambling tables where his growing skill at monte, faro, poker and other games was being honed by regular attendance.

He had arrived in town in 1874 in the company of his elder brother James who brought his common law wife Bessie with him. As Wyatt earned his living by runs of luck at the gaming tables, James became a bartender. Bessie brought in further income as a prostitute. Records also show that Wyatt took up with a woman named Sally who did the same.

Now, for some in today's climate of moral high ground, it can be an easy option to pass judgement on such lifestyles but one needs to put it all in the context of time and place. The western frontier of the 1870s held very different values to the society most of us operate in. Largely lawless, rough, dangerous, limited options, the cheapness of life through necessity… all these factors must be considered when observing historical circumstances through the distance and knowledge of hindsight. Some would say it was no excuse, but there was not a great deal of opportunity for women in that man's world, unless they were willing to sell their bodies. Prostitution in the Old West was not actually considered outrageously scandalous. It was a necessary way of life, fulfilling a need where men outnumbered women by a huge percentage.

That said, a Westerner's attitude to the female sex was paradoxical. An average drover, buffalo hunter, bullwhacker, railroad worker, mule skinner, soldier, etc., was well used to the idea of buying a woman's charms and would regard that lady accordingly. Yet, at the same time, many, if not most, of these rough, hardened men were capable of deferential and sincere courtesy to ladies… tipping their hats and displaying manners to the wives of storekeepers and their ilk.

Officially, even in Delano, prostitution was illegal but if it was kept on the far side of the bridge it did not tend to raise too many eyebrows. Even so, the Earp women and others paid regular fines for their activities.

Wyatt had a way about him which stood out. At around six feet in height, he towered above most of his contemporaries who, on average, measured several inches shorter. In addition he possessed a naturally athletic physique, well proportioned and strong. Fair haired and handsome with fashionable finely groomed mustachios, the young Earp cut quite a dash. His bearing was described as solemn but dignified, cool and quick witted, a man of few words yet with nerves of steel. Nothing seemed to faze him. It was said he rarely cracked a smile.

It is interesting to note how much Earp and Hickok's lives mirrored each other in many ways.

The town marshal, Bill Smith, observed Wyatt's demeanour and recognised qualities which he felt could be useful to him. He needed deputies with intelligence and the right attitude to be able to keep some semblance of control over the fun loving, tough Texan drovers. High handed thuggery as practised by "Brocky" Jack's bunch in Ellsworth had proven to not be the solution. The contradictory nature of Wichita's predicament needed balance… a police force which could temper the wildness of good times without alienating the cattle bosses. As was often expressed, dead or broken drovers were bad for business.

Taking on the duties of a deputy marshal, Wyatt soon proved that he was suited to such a role. He displayed just the right blend of firmness and diplomacy when faced with trouble. His physical presence, determination and calm, solid manner was enough to diffuse most situations, which were usually based in drunken bravado.

On the odd occasion when things got out of hand he was most capable of dealing with it decisively. That usually involved a lightning fast smack over the head with a pistol barrel… "buffaloing" as it was then known.

Although there is much evidence that Wyatt served in law keeping duties throughout that year, he does not appear in official records as a deputy marshal until April 1875.

It is possible that his appointment was casual, even part time, as his name does crop up as an officer in newspaper reports during that period. Brothers Virgil and Morgan both visited Wichita in '74, coming and going, with Virgil at one point acting with the special reserve police force alongside Wyatt.

Whatever the reasons, Wyatt did find the time to take on other activities including a spell at debt collection when a cattle company departed town leaving behind a pile of unpaid bills. Earp tracked them for miles and retrieved the owed amount at gunpoint.

There was also an occasion which could have led to mass bloodshed had it not been for Wyatt's people skills.

A complicated string of circumstances involving money and threats made for a potentially dangerous confrontation on the bridge which spanned the river between Delano and the main town.

On the western side, an armed bunch of about fifty belligerent cattlemen had gathered under the leadership of Mannen Clements, a cousin of the notorious Texan killer Wes Hardin. Wyatt and other officers, plus supportive townsfolk, positioned themselves on the eastern side to meet the threat.

Guns drawn, Clements and his men rode their horses noisily onto the boarding of the bridge as the opposing side spread out nervously. All but Wyatt and a small group who boldly stepped across from their side to meet the horsemen near the middle of the bridge. It was a classic stand off with neither side showing any sign of backing down. Anything could have triggered a bloodbath.

Wyatt stood firm and called upon Clements to holster his gun and withdraw. It was a tense moment as Earp spoke again with soft spoken but meaningful assurance. The tone of his voice was confident. At the same time there was no doubt that he meant business, but such was his way with people that Clements and his men decided that they could withdraw without losing face.

Wyatt scored many more points of respect that day.

So, during '74, his part time law enforcement activities were sporadic but notable. Come the spring of '75 and an election was looming for the Wichita marshal's job. Bill Smith was in the running again, his main opponent being Mike Meagher who had held the position from '71 until Smith's appointment. Meagher was keen to serve again and proved a popular choice, scoring far more votes than Smith. The new marshal quickly appointed Wyatt officially as one of his deputies.

The 1875 cattle season was hectic, as such periods always were, but there was very little in the way of serious crime. Smith's team remained in control, always swift to act firmly and with the minimum of force. The vast majority of any troublesome incidents were almost always based in drunken behaviour which Wyatt, in particular, seemed particularly adept at dealing with. His methods backed up by his height and build tended to calm the waters. People were impressed by his "quiet way" of diffusing problems... until "buffaloing" became that last resort.

However, the reality of the town's policing duties were, in the most part, far less dramatic, exciting or romantic than has been portrayed in public over the years. Packs of wild dogs were a nuisance around town and the law keeping force were expected to round them up. Repairing sidewalks too, inspecting clogged chimneys even... all in a day's work for a Wichita deputy, when not smooth talking drunken drovers or cracking them over the head.

I cannot quite imagine Hugh O'Brian carrying out such duties during scenes from the TV series which made an icon of Wyatt!

But Wyatt's name did make the papers several times that year, usually in the *Wichita Beacon* which reported various arrests. For instance, when he cleverly exposed a horse thief and stopped his escape with a warning shot instead of dropping him in flight. On another occasion, Wyatt confronted a drunk and disorderly man in the street and escorted him to the jailhouse for the night. The man awoke the next morning, probably with an aching head, but with his roll of $500 intact in his pocket. The locals were impressed by Wyatt's honesty in resisting any temptation to lift such a wad of notes.

Yes, Wyatt's track record as a policeman at this time was pretty sound, but the one stain on his dignity did arise when, in early 1876, he was seated in the Custom House Saloon. Leaning back in his chair, his revolver slipped out of its holster, hit the floor and discharged a ball which narrowly missed wounding him!

A lesson indeed. That is why most experienced gun toters would keep the hammers of their pistols resting on an empty chamber, plus usually clipping the weapon securely into place in its holster.

Wyatt remained in this role right through until April 1876 when he made the mistake of getting involved in the backroom politics of the next election.

Bill Smith was trying again for the marshal's job. Smith and Earp were not on the best of terms by now and the former was resorting to all kinds of tactics in his attempt to oust Meagher and get re-elected.

Apart from James Earp and his brothel connections, brothers Virgil and Morgan had also been showing up in town at various times and Smith seemed to resent what he presumably saw as a kind of sinister family takeover. Smith needed an issue to base his election campaign on if he had any chance of beating Meagher, who was still the favourite. Bad mouthing the Earps and attempting to create suspicion around them could possibly work, as Smith apparently spread word that if Meagher carried on as marshal, he would employ the entire Earp brood as deputies.

Word of this got back to Wyatt who was incensed at such underhanded behaviour. Meagher took his young deputy aside and advised him to ignore such talk, calm down and keep well away from his rival, but Wyatt was too riled.

Seeking out Smith, Wyatt confronted him. It turned physical and Meagher was forced to pull Wyatt away before he succeeded in dishing out a severe beating.

Wyatt's unblemished Wichita record was now in jeopardy. Meagher had to arrest him for disturbing the peace, as well as firing him from the job he did so well.

As it turned out, Meagher won a landslide victory over Smith and he was keen to employ Wyatt, regarded as an "excellent officer", again as his deputy. However, the damage had been done and despite Meagher's best efforts, the town council could not be persuaded to reconsider. Wyatt Earp had lost their trust and it was time for him to move on again.

***

As it happened, Wyatt was ready to take his talents elsewhere anyway.

The usual pattern had caught up with Wichita which had had its day. The previously lush prairie pastures for cattle were now being rapidly settled… fences and farms were springing up all over the surrounding landscape and the railroad was pushing on.

A new route, the Great Western Cattle Trail, had now branched off from the Chisholm Trail, pushing south west to another small settlement on a bluff on the bank of the Arkansas River. The Texas

Longhorn cattle were guilty of infecting other stock at settlements with a peculiar tic, outraging the farming community, and the Kansas State Legistature responded by shifting that quarantine line further west.

The latest cattle trade hub was now centred around what was originally a bar in a tent, established to satisfy the thirst of soldiers from Fort Dodge, but it was growing rapidly. When the railroad arrived, the stockyards sprung up and Dodge City became the latest maze of saloons and gambling, whoring and hurrahing.

The importance of Abilene, Ellsworth, Wichita and other places soon became consigned to memory as Dodge took on the mantle of "Queen of the Cowtowns", a crown she would wear for quite a while.

Founded by liquor dealers, the town's politics, such as they were, relied upon a handful of shady characters such as Jim "Dog" Kelly and Mayor George Hoover, rivals whose influence held sway in all of Dodge's early elections. The enormous bulk of Larry Deger, of German descent, was a leading figure appointed town marshal by Hoover. He found himself overseeing a police force which was notoriously weak, standing toothless as the town ran amok.

In May '76, Hoover made a move to bolster the power of the law when he received word that Wichita's much admired deputy marshal, Wyatt Earp, had been dismissed and might be looking for a job. True, he was.

Wyatt gladly accepted the position of "assistant marshal" to Deger whose position was more political than practical. In effect, Wyatt ran things his way and was permitted to commence his proven methods for keeping order just as the new cattle season, Dodge City's first major one, got going.

Insisting on the right to choose his deputies, Wyatt took on board another of his friend Bat Masterson's brothers... Jim, and together they established a good level of law and order. Bat himself arrived in town soon after.

Records become quite scarce regarding the details of Wyatt's movements during this time, but he seems to have turned up in Deadwood, South Dakota during the fall of '76, when the murder of Wild Bill would have still been hot news. Morgan was with him, apparently, and they made a healthy profit selling firewood that winter. Wyatt also said that he was taken on, in mid summer '77, as a shotgun guard for a shipment of ore coming down from the Black Hills.

By July, according to a newspaper, Wyatt was gladly welcomed back to Dodge City. It was a most complimentary report in which the hope was expressed that he would accept a law enforcement position once more, being as *"He had a quiet way of taking the most desperate characters into custody…"*

Bat's other brother Ed was assistant marshal of Dodge by this time and there is no clear indication that Wyatt was taken on officially in any kind of such capacity. It does seem quite likely, however, that he would have gladly assisted his friend if called upon, and probably did.

As the summer wore on, Wyatt would undoubtedly have been spending time as a dealer at the gaming tables, a pastime he could always turn his experienced hand to. One incident which stands out is of a confrontation he had with a muscular woman of the night named Miss Frankie Bell. Whatever the source of this row, it can be imagined that Wyatt's known patience was stretched to the limit by Frankie's profane insults because it is said he silenced her with a slap, a night in jail and a consequent $20 fine.

With the fall of '77 looming, Wyatt appears to have been employed freelance as a bounty hunter, a most perilous and solitary occupation. A known case for him involved the chasing down of train robbers, one of whom was none other than Dave Rudabaugh, whose name has featured heavily before in our Billy the Kid section.

It was a long and arduous hunt which took him across country into Texas where he wound up in the small town of Fort Griffin, at the bar of a saloon owned by an old friend, one John Shanssey.

Chewing the fat and reminiscing, Wyatt got around to the subject of his business. He asked Shanssey if he happened to know anything about this outlaw named Rudabaugh. Shanssey suggested that another man in the bar might have information and he pointed to a card game taking place in another part of the room.

One of the players looked frail and quite gaunt. He was slim, almost emaciated, in build with eyes of deep blue and fair hair and mustache similar to Wyatt's.

His name was John Holliday, better known to most as "Doc".

CHAPTER 36
DODGE

John Henry Holliday had started life with the makings of a southern gentleman.

Born to a distinguished family in Georgia in 1851, his father was the mayor of Valdosta. Young John received a good classical education at the town institute including a strong grounding in languages such as Latin and Ancient Greek.

When in his early teens, Holliday lost his mother to the ravages of tuberculosis (or consumption as it was then known), a savage lung disease which was also to kill his adopted brother.

Too young to fight in the Civil War, John was never the less surrounded by its effects as the conflict raged all around his home. Most of the male population, including his father, went off to fight for the Confederacy.

Destined for a professional career, John opted to study dentistry. Some students of the west have claimed that he never actually graduated with a proper qualification, but it seems pretty clear to me that he did attend the Pennsylvania College of Dental Surgery, completed his course and emerged at the age of 21 with his Doctor of Dental Surgery degree.

Taken on to assist at various dental practices, he moved to Atlanta, living with an uncle whilst he aimed to open a practice of his own. It was during this time that an incident may have occurred which set the tone of the course his life would take. Unverified but often spoken of in later years, John, who was to become known as Doc, went to a swimming hole on his uncle's land with some friends and was outraged to find a group of young black skinned soldiers using it. Presumably well steeped in the southern attitude to race which was so prevalent at the time, Doc flew into what was to become one of his characteristic rages, levelling either a shotgun or pistol at the bathers. Reports vary, but some claim he fired over their heads as they scrambled to escape, others actually state that he killed two of them.

Whatever the truth of this tale, Doc did leave the area, moving on to Dallas, Texas, where he partnered a dentist friend of his father's. Together they worked successfully, even winning the accolade of three awards in their profession for medical excellence. This led to Doc opening his own practice in town in 1874.

By this time, Holliday was suffering quite badly from the effects of the same disease which had taken his mother. Whilst still a student, his tuberculosis diagnosis caused some concern, even a warning that he would probably not live long. He was advised to move west to a drier, hotter climate which might help to prolong his life for a while.

His uncontrollable, hacking cough was not favourable when treating patients and, understandably, had an effect on business. He began to struggle financially as paying customers stayed away, forcing him to seek other forms of income.

As it happened, outside of dentistry, Doc found he had a talent, and liking, for gambling, making enough money from it to live comfortably. This being illegal in Dallas, he, and others, were under pressure from the authorities and so he moved again, all the way to Denver, Colorado, where he set up shop as a faro dealer.

This was just the beginning of Doc's zig zagging journey across the booming frontier towns, a far cry from his origins yet suiting him perfectly. He quickly grew to love the smoky, ribald saloons and gambling dens, thriving on the excitement and thrill of the chase. His temperament complemented such a life. Quick witted, smart, sassy and clever in his dealing, it was inevitable that he would attract trouble for he was capable of violence when needed. He could be good humoured, playful even, but his mood often turned in an instant to dark fury.

This was aggravated by the heavy drinking habit he had now adopted, the alcohol being a refuge and temporary relief to his painful symptoms and shredded lungs. Regularly coughing up blood into a handkerchief, Holliday defied the reality of his condition and soldiered on.

Years later, Bat Masterson, who respected Doc but did not really get on with him, wrote colourful descriptions of the man, stating that he was physically weak and *"... could not have whipped a fifteen year old boy..."* Holliday was well aware of this, said Bat, and that is why he was *"so ready to resort to a weapon whenever he got himself into difficulty... hot headed and impetuous... drinking... quarrelling... no qualities of leadership... unable to keep out of trouble for any length of time..."*

This does seem to be a pretty fair analysis of the deadly dentist who habitually attracted problems in his wake. By the time he arrived in Fort Griffin, Texas, in 1877, he was dragging along a mean reputation as a dangerous, unpredictable man. Stories were already attached to him which spoke of killings... a couple of Mexican victims... gunfights... and of a fellow gambler whom he had opened up with a knife.

In Shanssey's Saloon, where he first met Wyatt Earp, Doc had established himself in a game which had been joined by Dave Rudabaugh just a few days previously. All Doc knew was that he thought Rudabaugh may be headed back to Kansas. This started a long conversation between Doc and Wyatt and it appears the two of them hit it off well. Doc was full of questions about the lively scene in Dodge City, his brain ticking over with the potential of him making it his next port of call.

Wyatt took his leave and the pair parted amicably, destined to meet again and leading to dramatically historic consequences.

Doc was in a volatile relationship with a larger than life woman named Big Nose Kate Harony who partnered him on the road and in his bed. Hungarian by origin, Kate was a match for him in many ways and their fierce, violent quarrels were legendary.

She was intelligent and strong willed and it is said that Doc had once remarked that he felt she was his intellectual equal. Kate did as she pleased, including occasional sessions as a prostitute.

Not long after Wyatt's departure, Doc got into another scrape with a gambler and guns and knives played their part, resulting in Doc being hunted by a lynch mob. Once again, facts get foggy, including a colourful version wherein Kate started a fire in a shed to divert the mob's attention. She then, it is said, brought weapons to the lightly guarded Holliday who, at gunpoint, made his escape with her, mounting horses which she had hitched in a back alley.

Maybe… but whatever the circumstances, Doc and his Hungarian lover were now headed for Dodge.

**

The railroad track ran directly down the middle of Dodge City's Front Street, splitting the town into a pair of very separate worlds. The north side was deemed respectable with its stores, markets and general buzz of civilized comings and goings, whilst south of the tracks lay a "haven of sin". This was the usual layout for the western cowtowns and, with the river at its back, the red light district, condensed into a fairly small area, never slept, reserved to entertain those ever thirsty, ever lusty, ever fun hungry Texan drovers.

Here lay a dense establishment of the essential saloon trade, brothels and dance halls, along with bawdy theatres such as the highly popular Comique (French for "comical"), known more popularly as the *"Commy-Kew"*. With law enforcement under the loose control of Marshal Larry Deger, the drovers were having a ball during the '77 season with very little being done to bring them to heel.

Deger's assistant, Ed Masterson, did his best but it was a formidable task.

By the end of the year, with the season done, Deger was replaced and Masterson became marshal of Dodge, his assistant becoming one Charlie Bassett whose tenure as county sheriff had just expired. The role of sheriff was now taken by Ed's brother Bat.

Ed, the eldest of the Masterson brothers, was a determined lawman who had the odds stacked against him. Whilst still assistant to Deger he engaged in a gunfight in the Lone Star Dance Hall. It was a classic kind of western duel. Ed was shot in the breast, disabling his gun hand but he managed to switch his pistol to his other hand enabling him to down his opponent.

Recovered from his wound and in his position as marshal, Ed determined to enforce the city's newly appointed, strict policy of ridding Dodge of street violence. These rules included the banning of gun carrying.

Ed really had his work cut out. By this time, the drovers were pretty used to running wild and they resented this fresh heavy handed approach. However, Ed was courageous and meant business.

On April 9th. 1878, Ed was pacing out his round south of the tracks when he confronted a pair of armed drunks spilling out of a dance hall. His attempt to disarm them led to a close range shot being discharged into Ed's stomach, the muzzle flash igniting his clothing. Game as ever, Ed managed to pull his own pistol just as his brother Bat rushed over to join in the melee. Bullets flew and Ed staggered away, his shirt smouldering, leaving the two drunks in the dust, both peppered with bullets. One died the next day but the other survived.

Some said that Ed had managed to shoot both of them but it is more likely that the intervention of his brother Bat could claim responsibility.

Ed made it to a nearby saloon where he sank to the floor and died within the hour.

Charlie Bassett was immediately promoted to step into the now vacant role of marshal and word was sent to Wyatt Earp that his services were required again.

Wyatt responded to this request and hurried back to Dodge and a deputy's badge. The local press made much of this and heralded his return with exaggerated acclaim, but Wyatt soon lived up to his reputation as an effective lawman, supported by the surviving Masterson brothers, Bat and Jim.

With this new team in the field, the drovers quickly got the message that out of line behaviour would not be tolerated. Sure, they could have their fun… Dodge wanted and needed their dollars… but there was a limit. It did not take long for Wyatt to establish his authority as he had before. Usually, his presence alone was enough to curb potential trouble but, as always, when defiance reared its head, Earp and Co. were swift to administer a pistol barrel across it!

The police records of the time are filled with accounts of the arrests made by Wyatt for disorderly behaviour. On top of his monthly salary, he received extra payments for court appearances.

Doc Holliday and Big Nose Kate arrived in Dodge by early June. Alongside his drinking, gambling and penchant for trouble, Doc was still drawn to his dentistry skills and he wasted no time in setting up a practice in his hotel room. An advertisement he placed in a local newspaper offered his services, along with a guarantee of money refunded to patients if not satisfied.

Wyatt was pleased to see Doc again for they had got on well during their previous meeting in Texas. They now actively shared their gambling interests and were both now familiar faces at the faro, monte and poker tables. It was a double life for Doc; teeth by day, cards by night, and he pursued each activity with the same level of professionalism. The difference being that a sober Doc by day, dealing with his patients, would be far more likely to refrain from the alcohol fuelled reactions he was capable of in a smoky saloon.

With Earp keeping a lid on simmering problems, it was a lively yet mainly passive scene during that summer. The saloons and other dens of ribald entertainment never closed, the most wild period being between dusk and dawn, and it was in the early hours of the morning on July 26th. that Wyatt may have chalked up his only recorded kill in Dodge City.

The atmosphere was one of loud fun, with not too much aggression in the air. Just about everyone had been drinking for hours and were acting accordingly. In the Commy-Kew, the scheduled nightly performances had been put to bed but, at 3.00am., a square dance was now in full swing, accompanied by a banjo player and called by the season's star attraction, Eddie Foy. Foy had been engaged for the summer by the theatre. Being an enthusiastic, ambitious and hard working performer, he was glad to offer his talents for extra activities such as this. He would go on to become one of the biggest stars in American Vaudeville right through until his death in 1928. Right now he was touring the west and loving it.

As the music and dancing was being enjoyed by a surging crowd,

Doc Holliday and Bat Masterson sat engrossed in their monte game in a far corner. Wyatt, never one to totally relax, had a disagreement with one of the Texan cattlemen. Nothing odd about this, but this one was not letting things go. He either left the place seething of his own accord, or Wyatt ejected him.

The fun resumed in full but the miffed drover was not finished with his anger. He gathered together a group of armed friends and they galloped wildly down Front Street, opening up with their pistols as they passed the Commy-Kew riddling the place with bullets.

Inside the building, as the slugs zipped through the thin planking, the mood instantly changed as the revellers screamed, cursed and threw themselves flat on the floor. It was a miracle that no one was hit, although Eddie Foy's brand new stage coat became a casualty; hung up backstage yet perforated with several holes.

Wyatt and Jim Masterson reacted immediately, rushing to the door just as the last of the drovers cantered past, a few of them aiming blasts at the lawmen. Other armed men had joined Wyatt and Jim by now and they opened up their own fusillade at the horsemen as they disappeared into the darkness, heading for the rickety wooden bridge which would take them across the river.

An attempt was made at pursuit but the shooters had vanished onto the prairie. However, the posse did come across one young drover who had taken a bullet in the arm which had knocked him off his horse. Taken back to town, the wounded man was treated but infection set in and he was to pass away in about a month.

Whether or not it was one of Wyatt's shots which felled the man cannot be known for sure, but the incident was enough to fuel further flames for Earp's national fame. Dramatic retellings of the incident, naming and praising him, appeared in publications, notably the *Police Gazette*.

Wyatt actually became convinced that the attack was not mere chance but that it had been orchestrated as an attempt to kill him. He felt that it could have been a hit paid for by a leading merchant in town, a politician who had developed a grudge against Wyatt's no nonsense methods. This was logical but unprovable.

There were other close shaves for Wyatt, but his luck held. In August, yet again in the Commy-Kew, which appears to have developed as a magnet for trouble, another pair of Texans turned drunkenly belligerent. Wyatt was on the scene quickly, drawing his pistol for "buffaloing" purposes, but these two toughs were proving harder to put down than usual. Other Texans in the room took encouragement from this and signs grew of them offering support. Wyatt stood tall and bravely held his ground, concentrating on flooring one drover but showing his back to the other who drew his pistol.

Suddenly, a familiar southern drawled voice called out, *"Look out, Wyatt!"*

It was Doc Holliday who had been quietly observing events from his card table nearby. All eyes turned towards the voice as Doc drew his revolver and snapped off a shot. Whether he intended it as a warning or he just missed, Doc's action had the desired effect and the crisis was instantly diffused.

With the Texans sobered by the gunshot, Wyatt took control and would from that moment truly value Doc as a friend who had saved his life.

***

Wyatt, for all his quiet, disorientating seriousness, made quite a few friends during his Kansas period, not least of all connections with other famed lawmen such as Luke Short and Bill Tilghman. Dodge City was to one day form its own Peace Commission and there exists a famous and fascinating photograph which pictures the members, including Wyatt, Bat Masterson, Luke Short and Charlie Bassett.

He also found romance, of a sort, and began his quite long yet tempestuous relationship with Mattie Blaylock. They lived together but, although sometimes named as Mrs. Earp, there is no evidence that they married. No firm records either of Mattie's past, but she certainly worked as a prostitute in later times and probably already had when she took up with Wyatt.

Not quite so friendly was the arrival in town of the proven killer Clay Allison. He was a cattleman on legitimate business but it was also said that he had his eye on Wyatt because he had known George Hoy, the young drover who Wyatt may have shot during the Commy-Kew hurrahing incident.

Allison had a deadly reputation. Fond of shooting and lynching, his seemingly psychotic history of violence extended back to the Civil War. Some thought it possible that the homicidal Texan may have been provoked by the words and money of the same politician who wanted Wyatt dead.

It is alleged that Clay and Wyatt had a tense meeting in the street which was covered from a nearby building by a shotgun wielding Bat Masterson but it came to nothing. Some reports say that Allison decided that Wyatt deserved respect and he left town wishing him good luck.

Wyatt also received praise for tracking down and arresting a character named Spike Kenedy. Spike was the son of an influential Texan cattle baron and was, accordingly, of the opinion that he was above the law.

He was cocky and had already caused a few problems in Dodge for demeanours such as carrying firearms and disorderly conduct. Fined and riled by this treatment, he complained to Mayor "Dog" Kelly who responded by defending his peace keeping force, saying that they were only carrying out their duty.

This was not the reply Spike wanted and he left town severely miffed. He returned a while later to Dodge with out of proportion intentions of vengeance in mind.

Mayor Kelly was not in town having travelled to Fort Dodge for medical treatment. For whatever reason (and it is probably unfair to jump to conclusions!) he gave permission for his empty house to be used by a couple of actresses, Fannie Garretson and Dora Hand, who worked the town's theatres. Dora was actually asleep in Kelly's bedroom (Fannie was in the front room) at about 4.00am. when shots crashed through the wall of the shack killing Dora where she lay.

Rushing to the scene, Wyatt and others found Fannie sobbing with grief and pointing out the body of her friend dead in the mayor's bed.

This attractive actress had been a very popular figure in town, not just for her talent but as a philanthropic and warm person. Wyatt's investigation quickly pointed to Spike Kenedy, who had taken refuge in the Long Branch Saloon, as the culprit. By the time a friend of Kenedy's had been interrogated and blamed Spike for the act, Kenedy had made a run for it.

The townsfolk were incensed and baying for blood. Sheriff Bat Masterson raised an enthusiastic posse without delay, which included Wyatt, Charlie Bassett and Bill Tilghman, and they set off to pick up Spike's trail. Within a day or two they found him on the open prairie. Wyatt dropped the fugitive's horse with a rifle bullet and Bat put a round in his shoulder. The posse then dragged Spike cursing and struggling from under his horse.

Back in Dodge, Kenedy spent two weeks recovering before facing a preliminary hearing. Surprisingly, he was acquitted through lack of evidence.

Many thought his father's power and money may have had something to do with that.

By 1879, the writing was on the wall for Dodge City too. The

Kansas cowtowns were always subject to a limited life span and the old timers recognised the change which was beginning to encroach on their enterprise and fun. Sodbusters were inevitably taking over the surrounding grasslands, fences were going up and the anti-liqour temperance societies were making their mark of moral high ground upon the "sinners".

Wyatt saw all this coming and yet again he was looking ahead.

A letter from his brother Virgil would do the trick.

***

My extensive pursuit of the frontier has, so far, never taken me to the mid West, so, sadly, I cannot write firsthand of experiences in Wichita, Dodge City and the other cowtowns.

My understanding is that they have become teeming metropolises which would be unrecognisable to the folks I write of here. However, those of today do maintain respect for their history and, in the case of Dodge, for instance, they have built a partial replica of the old town Wyatt would have known. They even have a life-sized sculpture of him. There are museums and guides who proudly re-enact the past.

I left a disappointing stay in El Paso to drive the long route west across the border into Arizona. It was across harsh, desolate prairie, beneath a sky dark with ominous rain clouds. When those clouds broke, the deluge poured down with an almost frightening violence, bouncing high off the windscreen, the driving rains swirling like mini tornadoes in the heart of a savage storm.

The skies rapidly cleared, an arid dryness took the place of the rain and very soon I was manoeuvering my way through billowing dust storms. And all the while, for hour upon hour, the road stretched endlessly ahead like the path of a gigantic arrow.

For much of the relentless journey I was driving parallel to the huge locomotives of the Union Pacific Railroad, heaving their unbelievably long string of freight cars. At one point I could not resist pulling in to watch, at a distance, as cops dragged some poor bewildered and heavily bearded hobo out of one of those cars, spreading his meagre possessions across the dry sand, frisking him and defusing his free spirit.

Pausing briefly for a glance at the ghost town of Shakespeare, it was over the state line and through Willcox and Benson before entering the city limits of Tucson, Arizona.

The country changes dramatically here, the sun shining upon craggy rocks and palm trees. I found the approach roads quite confusing and earned myself a pullover by the siren of a police squad car. This led to an interesting little interlude when the officer approached my open window and, in very civil tones, explained that I had failed to "yield" when leaving the freeway.

In her crisp, black sleeveless uniform and shining silver badge on her breast,

I must admit I was more than a touch mesmerised by her image, even though she had a hand resting on the butt of the gun holstered at her shapely hip! Call me predictable but I did begin to wonder if I was undergoing a touch of fantasy because she did actually resemble Penelope Cruz!

"Sir," she drawled, "I must ask you to go on your way more carefully. I would spend more time on this but I've been called to a shooting...enjoy your vacation."

And that was that... off she went, leaving me to wonder if all female American police officers offer such a vision.

A pity, but they don't...

I had driven nearly 400 miles that day but still could not resist seeking out the Old Tucson movie set which, with the sun setting in spectacular fashion, was a further ten miles or so. It can be found by following a winding mountain road, the slopes alongside dotted with giant cacti and views across a vista of sweeping plains and distant peaks ... truly stunning.

Old Tucson itself was closed for the day but I was still able to get up close to the buildings for a solitary tour. I immediately recognised the backgrounds to so many Western movies from my youth and even stretching into more recent times, because the set was still being regularly used for film shoots. Livery stable, bank, saloons, hardware store, undertaker... all so familiar as a backdrop for the great Hollywood stars who rode in toting a Colt Peacemaker.

Back in the central modern city of Tucson itself, it was quite a contrast. We had found a decent enough motel on the outskirts, nicely cheap, but after I had checked in and was preparing to steer around to our room, my wife pointed out a couple of shady characters hanging around.

I never like to judge prematurely, but they did look like they might murder their grandmothers! Sergio Leone might well have signed them up on the spot... They were definitely sizing us up and when I pulled up outside the room, they followed us, as a third one appeared at a far corner. If he had begun picking his teeth with a Bowie knife, I would not have been surprised!

Well, neither of us fancied the idea of an assault in the middle of the night, so we checked out without delay. The desk clerk was very understanding when I explained, and acted as if it was a regular complication for clients. I overheard her on the telephone telling her boss that she was refunding an English couple because they were concerned about "traffic"!

With night falling, we found somewhere much nicer, safer and considerably more expensive but at least we slept easy.

Plus we were looking forward to the next day's destination...

CHAPTER 37
TOMBSTONE

The Earp brothers were scattered all over the west, pursuing their varied ambitions but keeping in touch, their paths crossing on occasion.

Virgil had more or less settled down in south west Arizona with his partner Allie. In Prescott, following various employments, the elder Earp had taken a position as a town constable during which time he gained respect for his role in a shootout with a pair of outlaws.

Always on the lookout for fresh opportunities, Virgil's attention was drawn to the establishment of a new settlement which was springing up in the remote and dusty hills close to the Mexican border. It was a largely neglected wilderness of desert, which had been previously occupied by Fort Huachuca as the only sign of so called civilized expansion. The soldiers there were responsible for keeping an eye on hostile Chiricahua Apache bands which roamed the territory, especially in the lower slopes of the distant Dragoon Mountains.

As such, the area was not viewed as a promising destination until the arrival of an eccentric adventurer named Ed Schieffelin. He was a big man, a loner and army scout whose appearance was almost bear-like, with an enormous black straggly beard and a thick mane of hair across his back. His clothes were ragged and patched, and he was thought crazy when he set off alone into the wilderness to find a rumoured strike of silver. The troopers he knew laughed and shook their heads, telling the would be prospector that all he would find would be the site of his tombstone. But Schieffelin was undeterred and his determination paid off when in late 1877 he struck lucky; a thick and very rich vein of the precious metal which he had valued at $15,000 per ton; an absolute fortune.

Safely staking his claim, Ed could concentrate on his good luck as word spread and hordes of other prospectors began flocking to this *mesa* which had previously been known only as Goose Flats, notable just for the birds which would settle there during migration. It was an area raised several thousand undulating feet above the scorching heat of the surrounding scrubby grasslands. First there spung up a sea of tents, then shacks, followed by a quite rapid order of settlement which began to resemble an actual town to house miners and all the many trades, legal and illegal, which would inevitably follow them. Even bigger strikes than Schieffelin's were soon discovered in surrounding areas, news of which drew even more hopeful souls to the latest boomtown which had now been christened Tombstone. It lay in Pima County.

Before long, Tombstone's inhabitants consisted of elements far more business-like and wily than the rough sorts who had originally turned up with nothing more complicated than a pick and shovel. It was not just the pimps, gamblers and usual dodgy characters who looked for ways to fleece the prospectors of their newly won riches. Potential had been quickly spotted by entrepreneurs of every description as they sought to create a well ordered little metropolis which they could mould to their own design. They came flocking in from the east and west coasts, establishing themselves by snapping up land and property, one group of them forming the questionable Tombstone Town Site Company. As adobe and brick buildings rose, businesses opened, proper streets began to be laid out and the town began to take on the characteristics of a recognised community, unscrupulous souls saw how much money was waiting to be made… far more than that which might be dug out of the hills.

The Town Site Company dealt in real estate, manipulating a situation which was not really understood by most in the frenzy of building and claim staking. Buying up lots under the pretence of advantage to the original owners, the Company was creating its own lucrative empire, blinding and baffling simple folks with science. The result was that property was being sold back to the original owners, the value being placed on work they had already completed themselves!

Arizona was still a territory and would not be granted statehood for years to come, so the legality of what transpired remained hazy. In the meantime, those who would not comply with any elements of corruption could find themselves in trouble, pressured by unsavoury sources. It was rumoured that threats from thugs were used to convince stubborn townsfolk to tow the line.

As time went by, and the town ostensibly grew more civilized, in theory anyway, many citizens started to realise what was happening and those with intelligence and backbone began to resist. The result was that Tombstone grew divided in its loyalties, a mish-mash of political bickering.

In the fall of '79, Tombstone's first newspaper, *The Nugget*, was published but it steered away from any contentious issues. This was rectified the following spring when a more fiery publication called *The Epitaph* was brought out to rival it. The editor was a spirited young man, an ex Indian agent named John Clum, and he was not afraid to challenge, in print, the activities of Tombstone's darker side.

But the town was growing in respectability, large parts of it anyway.

By mid 1880 and onwards the retail district blossomed with businesses of all kinds... clothing stores, butcher's shops, banks, stables, blacksmiths, churches, a school, offices, hotels, a photographic studio, even a bowling alley and ice cream parlour!

Alongside all this, of course, there were over 100 saloons (many of which were carpeted and well furnished), plenty of bordellos, gambling dens, dance halls and all the usual seedy places which accompanied a western boomtown. The town's founder, who was now a pillar of society, built his very own *Schieffelin Hall*, on the corner of Fourth and Fremont Streets, the biggest adobe structure in the county; 130 feet long and double storied. Masonic meetings were held there and it also staged opera performances by imported theatrical companies from San Francisco for the more refined citizens. Later on, *The Birdcage Theatre* would open on the corner of Allen and South Streets, catering for a more bawdy clientele.

The town was expanding with unseemly haste and this resulted in an almost never ending cacophony of noise and confusion as new structures rose on a daily basis. Building projects were in progress wherever one looked and the buzz of saws and thwack of hammers filled the air, alongside the mingling of swirling sawdust and clinging dust which filled every crevice, nook and cranny.

Indeed, Tombstone had become a desirable destination for many reasons and offered so much more than its eventual reputation (founded mainly by movies) would have most of us believe.

280 miles to the northwest in Prescott, Virgil Earp was receiving news of this exciting new town and the chances it offered to further oneself. Contacting his brother Wyatt in Dodge City, he described the potential of Tombstone in glowing terms, suggesting that they could all clinch their fortunes there.

Wyatt did not need a great deal of convincing. He was ready to move on, as was elder brother James. Packing up wagons, they commenced the journey south, Wyatt with Mattie, and James with Bessie and her two children from a previous marriage.

It was in September 1879 when the Earp party stopped off in Las Vegas, New Mexico, meeting up with Doc Holliday and Big Nose Kate who joined them on their trek. The next stop was in Prescott where they reunited with Virgil and Allie.

Doc and Kate decided to remain in Prescott for the time being, to check out the local action, but the three Earp brothers and their women pushed on, keen to experience the much talked about excitement of Tombstone.

***

They arrived in early December.

At this time the town still had an obvious rough edge with tents outnumbering proper structures, but this was changing rapidly, the constant building work adding to civilization by the day. The populace too was increasing in waves as stagecoaches and wagons arrived bursting with newcomers, all destined to do their part in creating the Tombstone of legend.

The Earps quickly absorbed the lay of the land and set about establishing themselves in the community. Virgil had already arranged a job for himself before travelling and was engaged as a deputy to territorial Marshal Crawley Dake. James soon found work as a bartender but Wyatt's initial intentions foundered.

He was hoping to convert the wagon he had arrived on into a stagecoach and start a line of transportation, but other companies had beaten him to it and were in heavy competition. Instead, Wyatt took to his other talent… gambling… setting himself up as a saloon dealer to secure an income. Before long, however, he was employed by Wells Fargo as a shotgun guard, sitting high up on their stagecoaches alongside the driver, responsible for protecting cargo and passengers in a dangerous land.

All of this was nothing more than a means to an end. The Earp brothers had not come to Tombstone to work for others. They sought opportunities to build their own fortunes and were always on the lookout for such. Industrious and wily as ever, the three of them were soon filing their own mining claims, making healthy profits by reselling them to hungry investors. In addition they acquired land holdings and water rights.

Wyatt kept his shotgun messenger role for a few months before passing it on to another notable town resident, the ambitious and gigantically built Bob Paul. By this time, the income of the collective Earps was handsome enough to allow them to relax a little. No need for Wyatt to spend so much time eating dust atop a stagecoach. They were all very well established in booming Tombstone, enjoying status on one side of the town's split elite. Wyatt joined Virgil as a deputy under town marshal Fred White, a popular figure who kept himself neutral within the simmering politics.

Of course, it was inevitable that brother Morgan would join them, and he did so in July 1880, immediately stepping into a deputy's role alongside his elder brothers as well as regular stints as a shotgun messenger.

Almost completing the set came youngest brother Warren, but he had a tendency to drift in and out of town rather than settle.

Morgan had been spending time in the patriarchal Earp family home in California, having sold his home in Montana. He brought his wife (probably common law) Louisa with him and left her with his parents because he felt that Tombstone might be too rough for her. She actually joined him later in the year once he realised that they might have a future there.

All four Earp couples actually set up homes in a trio of houses on the apex of First and Fremont Streets which were a few hundred yards down from the liveliest part of town. It was a stronghold of firm family ties, the women forging a tight bond as their menfolk indulged in their business around and beyond town. Allie and Bessie were the bedrock; delicate Louisa under their wing, but Wyatt's Mattie was beginning to draw concern. Addicted to opium based laudanum, she had become fragile and subject to emotional outbursts. Wyatt was losing patience with her, preferring to spend his time as a faro dealer at the Oriental Saloon.

Virgil and Wyatt were strikingly alike in appearance. People who knew them well were known to mistake one for the other. Morgan was similar but with a more carefree personality to his largely dour older brothers. All three seemed committed to their law enforcement duties and meant business, whilst James, shorter and darker haired, was a bartender through and through.

Wyatt's calmly quiet but effective skill as a lawman was much appreciated by the townsfolk in general, but not by everyone.

CHAPTER 38
THE COWBOYS

Tombstone had boomed on the back of mining silver but it was surrounded by cattle country. Unlike most of the other frontier towns known to the Earps, this place was dominated by the kind of crime they had not encountered before.

Drunken cattlemen were the least of the town's problems. Wyatt, in particular, could handle these incidents with ease but trouble in Tombstone mainly had much darker roots.

Offshoots from the Town Site Company spread tentacles amidst the business fraternity of the town, many of whose motives were not to everyone's benefit. Crooked merchants and selfish entrepreneurs sought every avenue they could to exploit others. Tombstone had become a magnet for that type of individual.

And political positions had split the town almost right down the middle.

Tombstone's newspapers were the symbols of the most simple understanding of the situation. *The Epitaph,* under editor John Clum, tended to give voice and support to those with Republican sympathies, and this was largely the Northern based business elite who represented apparent progress and modernity. The general populace of the working townsfolk were their backbone. On the other hand, *The Nugget* represented the much more wildly vocal and freewheeling Democrat stand which attracted the overwhelmingly Southern ranchers and cattlemen. Civil War resentments were still fresh for many… quite a few had actually fought in it. In a nutshell, townsmen were still the Union and the cattlemen still Rebs.

These two worlds clashed. The Republicans desired the creation of a peaceful modern city which would attract investment, but the Democrats tended to favour a more open community based on the Code of the West.

Of course, it could never be as straightforward as this.

In a largely lawless territory, the situation was ripe for the taking. Southeast Arizona became a magnet for men (and some women) on the run who could disappear from the radar of the day. Outlaws, runaways and reprobates of every description were drawn to this wild frontier society where few questions were asked and few even cared. Names were changed and characters drifted from place to place, minding their own business and expecting the same in return.

Many of those who fell into such a category made their living from outright banditry, skulking out in the wilderness or finding shelter in small towns like Charleston or Galeyville, or ranches which took advantage of their services. That involved the sale of cattle stolen from across the border in Mexico, or even from fellow American's herds. This rustling was largely overlooked because it kept the price of beef down. Consequently, the rustlers themselves usually had plenty of money to spend in Tombstone, so their rough ways were tolerated.

The term "cowboy", as we grew to know it, was not used in that way in 1870/80's Arizona. Men who worked with steers, on the trail or on ranches, were mainly called cattlemen or drovers. "Cowboy" was a derogatory term at that time, used to encompass the criminal element of that brood. It would take Buffalo Bill, dime store novels and Hollywood movies to make it glamorous.

The Cowboys honed a rough skill in their ability to alter brands on cattle to disguise their work. They found support in the business generated by some ranchers surrounding Tombstone who welcomed their illegal activity, notably ranches owned by the likes of the McClaury brothers, Frank and Tom, and the Clanton family. The latter establishment was run by Old Man Clanton and his sons, Phin, Ike and Billy.

Honest ranchers were soon sick of the Cowboy's activities, especially as they increasingly found themselves victims of the rustling. In particular, the biggest and most powerful spreads, overseen by the likes of cattle baron Henry Hooker, were losing patience as the bandits grew bolder. There was no way that legitimate cattlemen wished to be tarred with the same brush but it had become a confusing situation.

The Cowboys had no real organisation, as such. They were a loose confederation with no central leadership. Members would come and go out of the territory, their numbers would rise and fall, acting independently from each other but with a basic mutual goal… which was nothing more than to exploit the circumstances and raise hell on the illicit proceeds.

As a rule, these Cowboys were a tough bunch but their big spending in Tombstone made them plenty of friends. Boisterous behaviour led to regular fights and mayhem but enough dollars and pesos were flowing to cover the damage. Many townsfolk even welcomed their out of town presence because they were known to clash and keep a lid on renegade Apaches who were still feared as a threat to travellers.

But, as the months went on and the town grew, the Cowboys

began to take more chances, pushing the limit of their activities. What had begun as simple cross border rustling and occasional forays against American ranchers had extended into bolder and more violent crime. Things were getting out of hand as travellers on the dusty roads between towns reported robberies and assaults, alongside tales of gangs terrorizing innocent settlers. By the spring of 1880 the first of a string of stagecoach robberies took place, resulting in the death of a passenger and the driver wounded.

Clashes with Mexican ranchers were turning from plain opportunist theft into out and out shootouts as the victims began to fight back. The death toll rose.

The Earp brothers, were, of course, well aware of what was going on and actually knew many of these Cowboys who came to town and shared the card tables with them. On occasion it was necessary to bring a few of them to order with a spot of buffaloing but, as a rule, Wyatt and Co. kept their distance as much as they could, their main interest still being in their own futures and what they could glean from this wild boomtown. As a deputy sheriff, Wyatt and his fellow deputy, Newton Babcock, had their work out cut out dealing with various other crimes such as horse theft and drunks, but on occasion they would be drawn into wider and more complicated spats.

Although the Earps were far from actually being friends with the Cowboy fraternity, they largely tolerated them, but tensions were building. In July '80 the first major incident occurred to set the ball rolling.

The Cowboys were pushing their luck and they overstepped the mark by stealing some U.S. Army mules, probably feeling confident that they could get away with just about anything by now. Word came from an informer that the thieves were the McClaury brothers, young Billy Clanton and a renowned outlaw named Pony Diehl (or Deal). Interesting to note that Diehl had previously ridden with the Jesse Evans Gang and was part of the Murphy/Dolan faction fighting against Billy the Kid in the Lincoln County War.

Armed with this information, a posse was formed consisting of Wyatt, Virgil and Morgan Earp, a Wells Fargo agent, an army officer and four troopers, who rode out to the McClaury ranch. Here they redhandedly caught the outlaws in the process of rebranding the six stolen mules, turning the US into a D8.

A tense standoff followed. The posse had every right and enough evidence to seize the mules but they were outgunned and in dangerous surroundings. Diplomacy won through on this occasion, however, and a sharp exchange resulted in a deal wherein the army officer agreed that if the mules were returned by the following day, charges would be dropped.

It seems that the mules were never returned and the outlaws laughed openly about it in Charleston, telling the officer that they only made the promise to get the Earps off their backs.

Frank and Tom McClaury sought out Virgil Earp and threatened him with consequences if he were to persist in interfering in their business.

Virgil was unfazed and replied that he would certainly follow through with any warrant with their names on which came his way.

The elder Earp said that Frank's reaction was to state that he would never be taken alive.

The countdown to showdown was now ticking…

CHAPTER 39
TROUBLE BREWING

September of '80 brought some new arrivals into Tombstone who were of some significance to Wyatt.

First came his old friend from Dodge, Doc Holliday, with his volatile girlfriend Big Nose Kate on his arm. Doc had experienced his fill of Prescott and was now keen to seek out opportunities in this booming mining town he was hearing so much about. Kate was not so keen, instantly disliked the place and left. In later years she was to say that she disapproved and fought against the powerful hold the Earps seemed to have over her man, but Doc was under their spell. Kate left him to it but was to return eventually.

Around the same time, a charismatic figure named Johnny Behan turned up. He was a former sheriff who had held various government posts in the territory; now he had fixed his ambitious eye upon Tombstone. Behan was well connected and possessed a naturally appealing personality, making friends easily. These were qualities which he would cannily exploit over the coming months.

Not so popular was Doc Holliday who was soon in trouble. Within a month of his arrival, Doc got into a serious altercation at a gaming table in the Oriental. By this time, Wyatt had purchased a 25% share of this establishment but he was not present on the night in question when Doc faced off another gambler, John Tyler, in a row over a game. It got nasty and the pair had to be separated. True to form, Doc was not satisfied and continued to make a fuss after Tyler had left the building, so much so that the Oriental's owner, one Milt Joyce, ordered him to pipe down. When Doc got even louder, Joyce ejected him from the saloon by force.

Doc was soon back, this time with a pistol to take a potshot at Joyce. He missed but in the ensuing tussle, Joyce took a bullet through his hand before Marshal White and others managed to subdue the pair. Holliday was arrested and locked up to cool off.

Doc could have faced more serious consequences but ended up just paying court costs and a fine. He was lucky because prosecution witnesses failed to appear at the hearing and the case was dismissed.

Wyatt felt sympathy for his friend Holliday and made his feelings known. For all Doc's faults, Wyatt always seemed drawn to siding with him, and Joyce, and others, resented it. It was the beginning of a simmering rivalry between those with business interests in the Oriental.

The Earp brothers never specifically set out to seek trouble with the Cowboys and their shady supporters in and around town, but circumstances made it inevitable. In their lawmen's roles, Wyatt, Virgil and Morgan found themselves in unavoidable confrontations with the constant rustling activities and other sources of trouble brought about by these outlaws. The Earps became more than a nuisance to the Cowboys; they were now a dangerous liability and a feeling was growing that they needed to be dealt with.

One of the most prominent figures at the head of the Cowboys was Newman Clanton, with his bushy white beard, and known as "Old Man". Originally a Tennessee slave owner, he moved around, gaining a reputation for criminal activity and brutality before settling in Arizona in the mid 1870s. By the time the Earps were around Tombstone he was in his mid sixties and running a prosperous ranch a few miles outside of town on the San Pedro River. He and his sons provided beef for the local mining company, as well as many towns in the surrounding territory, particularly profitable because of their supply of stolen cattle from south of the border.

Acting as accomplices and middle men were the McClaury brothers who had established a ranch of their own on Babocomari Creek. The eldest, Frank, was around 31 years old in 1880, with his brother, Tom, about four years younger. They came from a large New York based family of Irish descent but moved west and entered the cattle business where they soon befriended the Clantons. Pretty soon they were sharing mutually ill gotten gains from rustling and robbery.

Old Man Clanton's most prominent sons in this story were Phin, Ike and Billy, who was considerably younger than his brothers, aged just eighteen in 1880.

This bunch and their numerous partners in crime enjoyed rich profits from their activities and seemed largely immune from prosecution. Most of the populace of Tombstone and its surroundings tended to turn a blind eye to what benefited them; i.e. beef at acceptable prices and, as previously stated, the business they generated in town. Some of the more honest folk tut-tutted a little and the Earps were developing a deep enmity from the criminal fraternity by refusing to play along.

In the meantime, any conflict was fought out in print in the pages of the *Nugget* and *Epitaph* as they spun headlines attacking their rival interests.

The Clantons and McClaurys also attracted the friendship of other colourful figures who took advantage of the easy pickings they offered by working for them.

Pony Diehl has been mentioned already. Having retreated south from the Lincoln County War, Diehl's experience as an outlaw and rustler earned him a prominent role in the Cowboys, alongside tough characters like Curly Bill Brocius.

Curly Bill was burly, freckle faced and handsome, they say, his dark, tightly ringleted hair furnishing him with his nickname. He was known for his wicked sense of humour and reckless behaviour when drunk... which was often. Plus he was renowned as a deadly shot with a pistol, rumoured to have already put men in their graves.

There was also Johnny Ringo whose reputation as a quick shooting killer surpassed any of those previously mentioned. He was feared for his hair trigger temper and unpredictability which bordered on some kind of psychosis. This could possibly be traced back to when he witnessed the traumatic accidental death of his father. Aged just fourteen, young Johnny watched in shocked horror as the elder Ringo stepped down from a wagon carrying a loaded shotgun which somehow discharged and blew half his head off.

Carrying this image, Ringo took his own path to Texas where he played a prominent and deadly part in the Mason County War of 1875. Having won his gunfighting spurs he carried on to Arizona, showing his true colours by shooting a man who turned down his offer of a drink. By 1880 he was closely associated with the Cowboys and was no doubt in the thick of their exploits.

***

It was a little after midnight on October 28th. 1880 and Tombstone was experiencing its usual lively bawdiness. The saloons and other hives of entertainment were bustling with the normal crowds of fun-seekers, mostly good natured, mindless japes, a row or two, but nothing too dramatic... that is until Curly Bill and a bunch of his cronies rolled into the street, truly inebriated and full of mischief.

One of them looked up at the moon and stars and came up with the notion that they made great targets. Within seconds, the whooping, drunken Cowboys were blasting their pistols skywards. Harmless, raucous fun, some might say, but the volume and pandemonium was a little too much at this time of night, even for Tombstone, so Marshal Fred White was soon on the scene to quell what was growing out of hand. As he approached, the shooters lowered their weapons and began to disperse. White had the respect of most of these toughs. He was a fair lawman... popular... no one wanted to give him grief, even in their cups...

The marshal's eye fell upon one of them in particular... Curly Bill, who was hurriedly leaving the scene. White called out to him, but he carried on, staggering behind a building and into a vacant lot.

Wyatt Earp was relaxing in a nearby barroom when he heard the shots and was swiftly on his feet to investigate. Out on the street, he ran into his brother Morgan who pointed in the direction of the fracas.

Marshal White had followed Curly Bill into the lot. The marshal approached him, his hand outstretched, eyeing the pistol in the Cowboy's holster and demanding that he surrender it.

Brocius was unsteady on his feet but he drew the weapon and raised it with the barrel pointing shakily at the lawman just as Wyatt and others arrived on the scene. Wyatt later said that he threw his arms around Curly Bill from behind just as the marshal reached out and grabbed the outlaw's pistol barrel, accompanied by another demand to give it up.

Whatever the intention, the pistol discharged, sending a ball directly into White's groin. The marshal yelled and fell, as Wyatt sent his own gun barrel crashing down on Curly Bill's skull, knocking him to the ground.

Others rushed forward to assist the stricken marshal as Wyatt dragged the dazed Brocius back onto his feet and placed him under arrest. Curly Bill protested his innocence, claiming the shot was accidental but Wyatt, Morgan and a friend named Fred Dodge dragged him off to jail before the shocked townsfolk could get hold of him. Fred White was a well liked man and some were already calling for a lynching.

All witnesses at the scene said that Wyatt dealt with it all in a calm and professional manner. Yet again he had proven his worth as a steady and dependable lawman, but he was determined to keep his prisoner safe from the wrath of the mob. Marshal White hung on for a couple of days during which time he, rather graciously, made the point that the shooting was indeed accidental. Wyatt agreed but Curly Bill would still have to face a trial. The marshal passed away and Wyatt made sure his killer was out of harm's way by taking him to another cell over seventy miles north west in Tucson. Brocius was to spend the next couple of months there, pondering over his fate.

Fred White's funeral was a grand affair, the biggest Tombstone had seen thus far and his death had repercussions. The town council immediately extended the existing firearms ordinance, now stating that, with the exception of law officers, no deadly weapons would be permitted to be carried in town.

And there was now a vacancy for town marshal, of course, a

position which was temporarily given to Virgil Earp, though not for long. A special election was called within two weeks and Virgil lost to Ben Sippy.

Pima County's sheriff was Charlie Shibell but he was facing a fierce challenge from Big Bob Paul. Shibell was a slightly built fellow who lacked the charisma and bulk of Paul, but the existing sheriff was a Democrat and therefore had the overwhelming support of the Cowboy faction and their numerous supporters. Although Wyatt was also Shibell's deputy, he favoured Republican Paul but Shibell won the election. There was an immediate outcry as word went around that the whole process had been rigged… hardly surprising when the likes of Ike Clanton and Johnny Ringo were serving as election officials!

Bob Paul wasted no time in contesting the result and demanded a recount. This was to become a messy affair with legal wrangling well into the following year as each side fought their corner.

Somewhat disgusted with the situation, Wyatt resigned from his deputy sheriff position on November 9th., feeling that he could not continue in Shibell's employ whilst supporting Paul. He was immediately replaced by Johnny Behan who at first tried to glean support from the Earps, but it was to no avail.

The courtcase in Tucson was a tangled affair, but by the end of January '81 the judge declared the whole vote for Shibell invalid with Bob Paul being the true winner, by a narrow margin. However, an appeal was lodged which delayed matters and Paul was not officially appointed until April. In the meantime, he carried on riding as a shotgun messenger for Wells Fargo.

Behan continued his attempts to befriend the Earps and tried to make a deal with Wyatt over their dual ambitions to be appointed sheriff of the new county which was due to be formed from the southern portion of Pima.

Losing his deputy sheriff's salary had not been an issue for Wyatt. He and his brothers were doing well having made quite a pile in land deals and mining interests. Wyatt was comfortable and could afford to bide his time but issues with the Cowboys would not go away.

For instance, some time before, a favourite horse of his had disappeared; obviously stolen. Rumours came his way that the animal could be found at the Clanton ranch and eventually, in late December '80, an informant told him that if he acted on it immediately, he would locate his horse corralled in Charleston.

This he did, and, lo and behold, there was his horse. Young Billy

Clanton was in charge of the herd which included Wyatt's mount and when he realised that Earp was on to him, he tried to remove the animal. Wyatt blocked his path and made it clear that the horse was his and could not be removed. He said he was waiting for the ownership papers to be delivered by his brother Warren but Billy sensibly made the decision not to protest. Never the less, before he surrendered it to its rightful owner, Billy cockily asked Wyatt if he had any more horses to lose.

When Ike got to hear of this he was livid... humiliated by the Earps again!

***

In mid January, another incident occurred to help foster Wyatt's growing reputation.

Virgil came galloping into town with a frightened young man on the back of his horse. (The horse was actually another belonging to Wyatt; a racer which Virgil had taken out to exercise.) Wyatt recognised the terrified youth, aged about eighteen, as Johnny Behind The Deuce, an inexperienced gambler who he knew from the faro tables. Virgil explained that he had encountered Johnny in a buggy on the road from Charleston, in the care of a panicky lawman from the town. Johnny had apparently killed a man in self defence and an angry mob from Charleston was now out for his blood. (The victim was the manager of a mining company's smelting equipment.)

Unfazed as ever, Wyatt led the young gambler across Allen St. into a saloon where his brother Jim was behind the bar. Wyatt quickly rallied support from Virgil, Morgan, Doc Holliday and a few others to stand guard around the manacled prisoner as a noisy crowd began to assemble outside. Taking up a shotgun, Wyatt stepped out to face them just as Johnny Behan and Marshal Ben Sippy turned up to observe things.

On the other side of the street stood a livery stable from where the posse would be leaving to take the prisoner away, but a mob was blocking their path... furious miners from Charleston and their followers who were determined to string up Johnny.

Cautiously, Wyatt's party left the saloon, his men forming a protective ring around their prisoner. Wyatt led them into the crowd, his shotgun levelled. The mob parted but the atmosphere remained tense as Wyatt pushed his way through them, his low, steady voice uttering stern warnings to stand aside.

Locking eyes with a mining foreman he knew, singling him out as a ringleader, Wyatt strongly inferred that the double barrels of his shotgun were ready to blast the first soul who made a move. Angry and heated though they were, the miners knew Earp wasn't bluffing.

"*Make way and let us through...*" he growled, "*I am taking this man to jail in Tucson.*"

And so he did.

As usual, Wyatt had courageously accomplished his mission, but Johnny Behind The Deuce never faced trial. He broke out of jail and vanished.

***

In February '81, the political situation in south eastern Arizona was complicated still more by the creation of that new region which broke away from Pima County. It was named Cochise County (after a Chiricahua Apache war chief) and the territorial governor delegated Johnny Behan as its first sheriff. Referring to their previous negotiations, Wyatt was expecting Behan to give him the role of under-sheriff, a lucrative position which would bring in not only a fine salary but a percentage of local taxes. As it turned out, the new sheriff overlooked him and appointed soon to be *Nugget* editor Harry Woods instead, a man who would be more politically beneficial to Behan's ambitions.

Wyatt apparently shrugged it off, but it was more power to the elbow of the Democrat faction as Behan took advantage of his new position.

Johnny Behan's persona not only gained him friends but attention from women. As was his nature, he took advantage of this, one of his more regular flames being a twenty year old actress who had arrived in Tombstone, around the same time as the Earps, as part of a theatrical troupe performing Gilbert and Sullivan's *H.M.S. Pinafore*. Her name was Josephine Marcus, known as "Sadie" to her friends.

She was said to be quite a beauty and caught the eye of the ever ready Johnny Behan. Sadie left Tombstone for the next part of the show's Arizona tour, and when it ended she wound up back home in San Francisco, but the lure of Tombstone, and probably Behan, brought her back. By the spring of '81 she was known around town as "Mrs." Behan.

The sheriff had apparently promised to marry her; they even lived together after a fashion, but Johnny's roving eye was forever straying. When Sadie caught him with another woman she terminated their engagement and took lodgings on her own. Deeply depressed, the young actress needed to pay her way and this is when she probably sold her charms in prostitution. That said, her looks and demeanour almost certainly kept her out of the lower end of the business and she would have found her clients amongst the more respectable, and discreet, gentlemen around town.

Wyatt would have known her, and by mid summer it became obvious that they had become an item. They made no secret of being seen together and Sadie would have been happy to be in a relationship again with a prominent member of Tombstone's elite. She had moved from involvement with one faction to the total opposite and it added considerable fuel to the fire of the growing conflict between Earp and Behan.

As for Wyatt's current common-law wife Mattie, she remained as part of the Earp clique, under the wing of the supportive womenfolk who must have been somewhat disapproving of Wyatt's blatant infidelity. Not that he seemed bothered. Mattie's decline in health from the ravages of her laudanum addiction had become a liability. Wyatt was tired of her behaviour and self pity, probably even repelled, but he had to accept that she was dependent upon him.

His antidote was to welcome the embrace of an attractive, loving woman who gave him what Mattie no longer could.

CHAPTER 40
LINES DRAWN

Curly Bill Brocius must have spent that last two months of 1880 in anguish. Locked up in his Tucson jail cell, he had plenty of time to reflect on the reckless actions which had put him there. He was no angel, for sure, but on this occasion he did seem to be feeling regret and sorrow about the man he had killed.

No doubt about Bill and his Cowboy friends being drunk and disorderly on that fateful night, but they were just having a little fun, eh? A few shots at the moon, some cussing and laughing... Marshal Fred White was just doing his job in facing them... Curly Bill liked Fred... who didn't?

But he shouldn't have grabbed my pistol barrel, argued Brocius. I was giving it up, he said... it went off half cocked when he pulled on it... I would never have shot Fred deliberately... they ain't gonna string me up for that, are they?

And so it went on, to anyone who would listen, until Bill could have his say in court. That finally happened on December 28th. and Curly Bill's mental torture came to an end when the whole case was laid out for the reasoning of Judge Joseph Neugass.

There were plenty of witnesses to confirm Brocius's version of events, even Wyatt and Morgan Earp who testified that they agreed that the shooting had been an unfortunate accident. For all the Earp's faults, which many delight in showcasing, it says a lot for their moral fibre and honesty when they actually helped an enemy (who would go on to give them much grief in the coming months) by simply telling the truth. Different words may well have sent the brash outlaw to the gallows.

But there was even a statement from the deceased Marshal White, who, decent man that he was, declared from his death bed that he believed the shooting was not deliberate.

The judge was satisfied and dismissed the case as accidental homicide.

Curly Bill was a free man again and he decided to remedy his miserable Christmas by celebrating the new year in style... *Cowboy* style!

He made for Charleston in the company of a *compadre*, both of them fuelled with liquor to make up for lost time. It was the second Saturday of 1881 and they found a dance hall packed with joyful Mexicans gyrating gleefully to a lively band. The two Cowboys burst in, drawing their pistols and positioning themselves at each door to block any exit. The band stopped playing and all eyes turned on Curly

Bill as, with a grin, he demanded that all the dancers strip naked!

Looking down the barrels of those volatile outlaw's guns was all the persuasion needed, and all clothing was quickly shed. Curly Bill and his friend were delighted by the compliance, laughing wickedly as they called for the band to strike up again and the dance to resume.

And so it did, like some kind of mad orgy of swinging genitals and breasts as the fandango carried on. A nightmarish humiliation for most, no doubt, but maybe Brocius wasn't the only one who enjoyed it!

It carried on for quite some time, as the swaying gun barrels of the outlaws ensured that the dance continued, but a passerby spotted through a window what was happening and alerted the law. A swiftly assembled posse were unsure how to handle this unique situation, but finally opted to lay in wait for the Cowboys when they emerged from their fun. This resulted in a few shots being exchanged but no one was hit; just a few corralled horses wounded.

The orchestrators of the naked fandango escaped and were probably highly pleased with themselves. It was typical of Curly Bill that when he had sobered up a little the next day, he sent money into town via a go-between, to pay for any damage done! Almost an act of appreciation...

It is intriguing to ponder on the effect the incident had on those dancers and how they would conduct their future celebrations, having seen so much of each other. Perhaps they made it a regular feature!

Curly Bill may have sobered up "a little", but his spree was far from over. The very next morning... Sunday... he and his drinking partner, who had not really stopped imbibing since the previous night's debauchery, rode just a few miles to the small town of Contention where they interrupted a preacher giving his sermon in church.

The terrified preacher, observed by his stunned and silent congregation, was forced to stand rigid as the Cowboys blasted holes in the wall all around him. He was then ordered to dance a jig but said he was not capable.

Curly Bill waved his pistol menacingly, saying "... *dance you must!*" to which the poor man found the ability to shuffle his feet enough to satisfy his tormentor. The Cowboys, highly amused by their pranks, congratulated the preacher for his pious talents and rode away laughing.

They followed this up by returning to Tombstone and spending the next few days running amok, shooting out lights and even indulging in a spot of armed robbery. Brocius had been making a nuisance of himself wherever he appeared but patience was being stretched. Chased out of town, there was a spatter of gunplay but without serious consequences.

Yet Curly Bill possessed a charm which won over many people, unless they found themselves on the sharp end of his unpredictable drunken temper. One irony was in the unlikely friendship he had with Deputy Sheriff Billy Breakenridge.

Breakenridge was an odd character, and he defended his decision to use Curly Bill as an assistant tax collector because of the talents he had for collecting money. Brocius thought it quite something to be riding around the back trails of the territory with a lawman. He even persuaded many of his fellow rustling friends that it would be a good idea to pay up because, if caught, they would be able to claim, truthfully, that they were tax payers!

Breakenridge actually had a high opinion of Curly Bill and said that he learned a lot from him. It was a friendship which almost brought about the rowdy outlaw's premature demise.

***

Such high jinks were all very well but there was a serious undercurrent to it all.

Curly Bill's recent antics caused quite a stir and influenced others to emulate him. The Cowboys in general began to up the scale of their troublemaking, progressing from simple rustling and robbery to feeling they had some kind of right to terrorise with impunity. Nameless groups of loud toughs rampaged around the territory's smaller towns and remote areas, picking on strangers, making them dance "Curly Bill" style to pistol shots, waylaying travellers and subjecting terrified townsfolk to demonstrations of their marksmanship, which could include shooting off their boot heels.

As if this nuisance wasn't enough, raids south of the border were growing even bolder. Mexican ranchers were heartily sick of the constant attacks on their herds and Mexico's army were getting involved, staging patrols along the borderline and tangling openly with the raiders. It was reaching the point of creating a grave international incident. Arizona's governor demanded action and even proposed the creation of a militia to take on the Cowboys. This notion was only shelved when politicians who controlled Arizona's purse strings decided that they did not wish to spend any of their budget on such a force.

Instead, members of the territorial Stock Association considered taking the law into their own hands. It was rumoured that various powerful figures had personally put up a $1,000 dollar reward for the apprehension of Curly Bill. Strange, in a way, that he should have been particularly singled out. As it was, Brocius himself was to disappear from the scene for quite a while, all because of that odd friendship with Deputy Breakenridge.

Mid May of '81, Curly Bill, with a string of nuisance shootings in his wake, apparently shot the horse of his friend Jim Wallace for a "joke" whilst on the trail, leaving Wallace to walk into town. Hilarious! Well, I guess it was to Bill, at least…

This was the kind of jape Curly Bill specialized in but it was understandably more than a little tiresome to the victims. He was drinking shortly afterwards in the small mining town of Galeyville with a group of rustling friends, including Jim Wallace, who was probably still smarting from the loss of his horse.

Billy Breakenridge turned up and when he entered the bar, something triggered Wallace to start loudly insulting the deputy who responded by just walking away. Curly Bill was offended by this slight to his friend and demanded that Wallace apologise. Surprisingly, Wallace gave way and extended the apology requested, but Brocius was on the brink of one of his foul, trouble making moods and threatened to kill him. Wallace, who was another Lincoln County War veteran, thought it best to leave but Curly Bill went for him. This was a big mistake because Wallace had taken enough and reacted by shooting Brocius in the face.

It was not a fatal wound but a very nasty one which laid Curly Bill up for the remainder of the summer. This was probably just as well for the wayward Cowboy because it kept him out of the trouble which would dominate that time period… out of it for now, that is.

***

Wyatt dealt a lot of faro throughout early '81, biding his time and taking note of the lay of the land. When John Clum was elected Mayor of Tombstone, this was to the considerable advantage of the Earps now that they had a firm ally in such a high post.

In mid March, Bob Paul was still waiting to take up his position as sheriff of Pima County, occupying his time on those Wells Fargo stagecoach runs between Tombstone and Benson. He had served before as a sheriff in California, earning an admirable reputation as a man to be trusted, but right now he made an imposing 6 foot 4 inch sight perched up on the box beside the driver, shotgun cradled across his broad chest.

On the evening of the 15th., Big Bob sat with his friend Bud Philpott, an experienced driver who handled the team smoothly and with ease. The coach rattled along the rough trail, bouncing from side to side, $26,000 of silver bullion intact, nine passengers aboard.

They were a couple of miles outside of Contention when a group of masked men spread out in the coach's path, forcing Philpott to pull on the reins. One of these would be bandits called out for them to stop but Bob Paul was having none of it.

"By God, I hold for nobody!" he yelled back defiantly, raising his shotgun and letting fly at the shadowy figures. The bandits scattered to avoid the speeding coach but eagerly returned fire. Philpott jerked in his seat, toppling forwards and down onto the rears of the nearest horses before rolling off onto the trail. Bob Paul grimaced but there was nothing he could do in that moment save reach down for the dropped reins and drive the team out of danger. Bullets still flew around him and he heard some strike the body of the coach.

About a mile or so further on, he managed to gain full control of the frantic horses and pulled them up to a halt. Checking his shaken passengers, he found that one of them had also taken a bullet and would soon die. Poor Bud Philpott's body was found lifeless in the dust where he had fallen.

Back in town, the news was received with shock and sorrow. Bud was a popular man and people were horrified and angered that he had been shot down so cold bloodedly. There was no shortage of volunteers to form a posse of pursuit but Sheriff Behan opted for a tight-knit, small group who would be able to travel swiftly. He also wanted experienced trackers and men with backbone, and so chose the Earps, Bob Paul, Bat Masterson and a Wells Fargo agent named Williams. Their first stop being the site of the robbery, they found discarded masks made of rope and from this point they picked up a trail.

Within a few days, this earnest posse came across a ranch owned by a man suspected of Cowboy sympathy. Here they discovered a character named Luther King whose attempt to flee was quickly foiled. King was nervous and acting suspiciously but some rough interrogation by Wyatt soon convinced him to open up about what he knew. He admitted to keeping check on the bandit's horses whilst three others committed the actual deed. King's sense of loyalty to his accomplices was soon broken down, probably owing to Wyatt's persuasive methods! He named the others as Harry Head, Bill Leonard and Jim Crane; known Cowboys, and King insisted that he, personally, had not joined in with the actual shooting.

Behan took charge of the prisoner and escorted him back to Tombstone whilst the rest of the posse took up the robber's trail again. They rode hard and determinedly, pushing their mounts to the limit. Virgil's telegraphed request to Behan for much needed fresh horses was not fulfilled and the posse began to suffer hardship, Wyatt and Masterson ending up on foot before making it back to town exhausted. The remainder of the posse pushed on as best they could.

In Tombstone, Wyatt was concerned to discover that the prisoner, King, did not seem to be held very securely. There were a lot of Cowboys in town who would very likely make a move to break him out of custody so Wyatt suggested that he be put in irons and the guard increased.

This suggestion was made to the newly appointed under-sheriff, Harry Woods, who now had the job Wyatt had been expecting to get. Woods agreed to do this but, almost immediately, King found a miraculous opportunity to escape, seemingly by just slipping out of the back door of the sheriff's office in an unguarded moment and grabbing a horse.

Wyatt was incensed at such apparent carelessness, dereliction of duty even. The law abiding townsfolk of Tombstone felt the same and there was a huge outcry that the only captured stage robber was allowed to get away so easily. It stank and word began to spread that elements within the law must be somehow compliant and sympathetic with the bandits.

Behan, not so enthusiastic as the Earps, took to the search again with others, intermittently joining up with the remainder of the original posse in their relentless tracking of the fugitives Head, Leonard and Crane. They covered many miles in what ultimately proved to be a wild goose chase. Behan was with them for a while, along with Breakenridge and Buckskin Frank Leslie (another colourful Tombstone character and saloon owner who was destined to make his own mark on the town). The members of the posse separated again into two groups, having reached the end of their tether. Hungry, drained and devoid of further ideas, their quarry always seemed one step ahead.

Reluctantly, following a harsh close to two weeks tracking, they returned to Tombstone. Bud Philpott had already received a grand funeral, with much grieving by the townsfolk, plus a show was staged which raised over $300 to present to Bud's widow. The Earps had failed, but their efforts were much appreciated.

Although before Wyatt and Behan's girlfriend Sadie took up

together, this whole incident was another major factor in the growing enmity between the Cochise County sheriff and the Earps. Behan's underhand, hesitant and even incompetent behaviour had driven quite a wedge between them. It was becoming more and more apparent that Behan's leanings were tilting with bias towards the Cowboys.

To make matters worse, there was also a dispute over money owed to the Earp brothers for their time spent chasing the stage robbers. Behan received a considerable sum, nearly $800, from the County, but none of it came the way of Virgil, Wyatt or Morgan, even though other members of the posse were paid.

This was read as a blatant snub to the Earps although the Wells Fargo company, when made aware of this, did make it up to them.

In the meantime, it seemed for a while that the elusive robbers had got clean away but there was a big reward on their heads so it was inevitable that someone would find them. Two ranch owning brothers named Haslett had their eyes on the money and it came to pass that they managed to ambush and kill Head and Leonard.

Jim Crane was still on the loose and he and his friends killed the Hasletts before they were able to claim the reward. Crane then went to ground for a while.

Before any of this took place, with the robbers still at large, Wyatt had come up with a scheme which he hoped might clear the air and be of mutual advantage to all.

It was well known that the Clantons and McClaurys were well acquainted with the stagecoach robbers but not so close as to turn down something which would be of benefit to them.

Wyatt maintained an ambition to eventually take the Cochise County sheriff's role from Behan, the next election being due in November '81. To curry favour with the territorial population and increase his chances of winning, Wyatt knew that he needed to achieve something of note which would bolster his image.

According to his version of events years later, he took a deep breath and approached Ike Clanton (and maybe Frank McClaury), neither of them having anything like fond thoughts of the Earps, but Wyatt was looking at the bigger picture. In secret talks, Wyatt suggested that it might be wise if they were to betray their "friends", Head, Leonard and Crane, who were apparently laying low somewhere up in New Mexico, by luring them to a spot where Wyatt and Co. would be able to kill them. In return, Wyatt would turn all the reward money over to Clanton (and McClaury). Wyatt's motive for this was to get the glory for terminating the killers of popular Bud Philpott, and the dead passenger, thereby increasing his vote winning chances.

Ike was intrigued and mulled over the offer. Apart from the money, he had a business problem with Leonard over some land and cattle, so it would be to his advantage to have these bandits removed from the scene. But, it was essential that the deal remain a deadly secret, literally. If any other Cowboys learned of it, Ike would be a dead man for sure.

Ike stressed the importance of the bandits being killed, so was the reward payable "dead or alive"? Wyatt showed him proof that such was the case... "dead or alive", and that he had every intention of dropping all three. It was a forgone conclusion that they, in any case, would not, by their own admission, be taken alive.

Ike did not fully trust Wyatt and was terrified that the details of their deal might leak out, but it was a tempting offer which would solve some problems for him. In fact, Ike would have his own version of his chat with Wyatt in which he claimed he never made any such deal, but then it was in his interest to state that, of course.

Anyway, as it turned out, with two of the robbers dead, the deal never came to fruition.

However, there were further complications.

***

The Earps were well established in Tombstone by now, as effective lawmen, successful entrepreneurs in business and, as a consequence, mainly respected, even feared, by the populace, and that included their enemies who remained wary of them.

In early June, Virgil officially replaced Ben Sippy as city marshal. Sippy had taken a fortnight's leave but stayed away under a cloud of unpaid debts. He failed to return so Virgil was given his job whilst retaining his own existing position as U.S. deputy marshal. This gave him extra power and wide ranging jurisdiction. Wyatt, of course, was on regular call as Virgil's deputy, often taking over his older brother's territorial duties whilst Virgil concentrated on matters in town.

Morgan was on hand too, and the Earps kept a close eye on the Cowboys expanding criminal activities which were growing more serious as the year wore on. It was a peculiar arrangement as all these frontier roughnecks lined up against the law on one hand whilst still sharing gaming tables with them in the saloons on the other. There was mutual suspicion all around, naturally, and both sides had a wealth of informers.

Bat Masterson, who had been a strong supporter of the lawmen, was suddenly called back to Dodge City to help his brother Jim in some matter, leaving the Earps bereft of a reliable ally. However, they remained in a strong position. The respectable clique of city fathers were content to have them in control of potential trouble, but with reservations. Storekeepers, bankers, merchants, mining surveyors and engineers, out of town investors... the Republican elite of Tombstone felt protected and represented lawfully by this trio of tall, tough gunmen who were not afraid to stand up for what was "right". But it was not as simple as that. The Earps were respected, yes, but were perhaps not quite as respectable as officialdom would have liked before fully accepting them into society.

Virgil, Wyatt and Morgan (and occasionally Jim when he emerged from behind his bar) were a common sight around town, dressed in their dark, frock coated suits, ties and broad brimmed black hats. They looked the part, striking and confident, self sufficient pillars of the community. Many were happy to shelter behind them and let them deal with any dirty business, *BUT*, accepting them into the higher class of town was still resisted.

And why was this? Well, there was a hurdle they just could not seem to cross. It was because of the saloon life which was the framework of their very being. Gamblers, dealers, frequenters of low dives (even though the Oriental was one of the finest establishments in town)... and their understanding and ability to deal with the rougher elements of humanity being what kept gentler people safe from harm... *PLUS*, heaven forbid, their women were known prostitutes.

Virgil's application to join the local Masonic Lodge was rejected but that was hardly surprising.

The Earps grew to accept and understand the town's reluctance to grant them full access to respectability but they were probably not overly concerned about it. They were doing fine.

Wyatt, who almost never indulged in alcohol, remained as cool as the ice cream scoops which he habitually enjoyed from the cosy little parlour on Fourth Street.

CHAPTER 41
THE SUMMER OF ILL INTENT

That summer of 1881 in Tombstone was typically dusty, and as hot as the simmering climate of trouble... like a pressure cooker straining to blow.

As the opposing sides in the coming conflict took stock and flexed their muscles, a major distraction eased the tension briefly when a fire broke out in the centre of town. It started somehow in a saloon on Fifth Street and spread rapidly eastwards, consuming several blocks in a raging inferno right on down to Seventh Street and across from Fremont to Toughnut Streets.

This area was an important hub and much was lost as the tinder dry wooden buildings crackled and burned... the Oriental Saloon was one of the first victims (although it was to be swiftly rebuilt). With no official fire fighting service, the townsfolk quickly rallied and did their best to combat the flames, hurling buckets of water and pulling down structures in a desperate attempt to stop the spread.

This disaster was brought under control within a day but left a fortune's worth of destruction in its wake. Many homes and businesses were lost but the people wasted no time in setting to work immediately to rebuild. This would prove to be a blessing in disguise, as the opportunity was taken to improve upon what had stood before... sturdy adobe structures to replace those of wood. Plans were soon in hand for water pipes to be laid and there was even talk of the introduction of that brand new miracle, the telephone.

The Earps did their bit helping out in the panic. Virgil gathered an emergency police force to take control of the situation and give aid to the victims. This was needed in various ways, notably to curb the activities of "lot jumpers" who quickly tried to take advantage the day after the fire when, in the smouldering ruins, they attempted to lay claim to land upon which previous owners had lost property. Virgil and his new force went around forcibly removing these lot jumpers and putting the original occupiers back in place.

Shortly after this, with the charred debris well on its way to clearance, the subject of the March stagecoach robbery attempt reared its head again. By now, serious though it was, the incident had begun to recede in collective memory but it was to be brought back to public attention in a most unlikely form.

Big Nose Kate, the highly strung on/off girlfriend of Doc Holliday was back in town and she and the consumptive dentist were soon at each other's throats again. Doc had remained almost fully occupied with professional gambling (when not supporting the Earps), largely in the Oriental which was, temporarily, a burned out ruin. He soon found places at the tables of other outlets but Kate was on his back. To say their relationship was stormy would be an understatement in the extreme, but it was like they could not actually be apart for long. When they were together, it was explosive.

Their latest clash, in the first week of July, was particularly loud and colourful and, for whatever reason, Kate reacted by getting spectacularly drunk. In a foul and vindictive mood, she sought out Sheriff Behan and demanded that a warrant be sworn out against Doc as she strongly suspected him of being involved in the robbery which had led to the death of Bud Philpott.

It was a mammoth allegation but Behan drew pleasure from this excuse to arrest Holliday. Rumours about Doc's possible involvement had been growing anyway. His friendship with the robber Bill Leonard was common knowledge… they often enjoyed gambling together… and some spoke of Doc being suspiciously out of town on the night of the robbery. His dubious reputation was such that a feeling grew in town that he could be guilty. When Wyatt stood some of his friend's bail money, word began to spread that maybe the Earps were involved too. Theories began to fly… perhaps those lawmen were not so straight after all… had they tipped off the bandits about the silver bullion on board the coach that night?

Kate herself was arrested within a day or two on a charge of "drunk and disorderly" as well as accusations of making threats, so she was not regarded as the most reliable of witnesses. Also, when she sobered up, she apparently regretted dropping Doc in it, but he was obviously none too pleased. Kate was fined and Holliday's case was dismissed through lack of evidence but the incident left a cloud over Doc and the Earps and a murmuring of distrust began to grow. Perhaps their efforts to track down the culprits were just a show…

It was a confusing time for all and Doc made himself scarce again for a while.

In the meantime, conflict on the border was really hotting up. The Mexican ranchers and authorities were hitting back. It was not only their cattle herds which were being decimated but traders were being robbed on a regular basis. Of course, many of these Mexican traders were acting illegally themselves; smugglers who were bringing gold and silver into American territory to purchase contraband goods such as tobacco and alcohol. Strict Mexican tax laws had provided a market for this illicit trade when the smugglers brought the goods back south to sell on cheaply. The richly laden crooks became a major target for the Cowboy outlaws, as well as stealing cattle.

But the Mexican army was officially involved now, with regular patrols scouring the border for the Yankee raiders. Bullets flew and men died on both sides. The situation was threatening out and out war.

In August, Old Man Clanton was part of a gang herding cattle; not an unusual past time for him and his kind. They camped on the American side of the border in Guadalupe Canyon when they were attacked as they slept in their bedrolls. The attackers were Mexican troops, it was claimed, pre-empting a strike by slipping across the line. Five Americans were killed in the volley of shots which tore into the camp site, one of them being the veteran old villain Clanton and another Jim Crane, the third of the stagecoach robbers.

The Mexican authorities had now more or less taken control of the border and the Cowboy raids dropped off dramatically. The killings caused uproar in Cochise County with many threats of retribution filling the air but the savage action had achieved the desired effect. It resulted in the Cowboys turning their attention more intensely to the rancher's herds on their own side of the border.

With all three of the hunted robbers now dead, the possibility of that deal between Wyatt and Ike Clanton (and Frank McClaury) was now off the table, but Ike became obsessed that word of it would get out to his fellow Cowboys. Wyatt swore that he would not say a thing, but Ike did not believe him. What if he told his loose lipped friend Holliday? It was a worrying thought…

Ike was now regarded as one of the leading lights of the Cowboy's antics, along with the McClaury brothers and various other outlaw types.

Many townsfolk regarded Frank and Tom McClaury as legitimate ranchers, oblivious to their nefarious activities as they acted as a front to the regular rustling and robberies. Ike was a volatile kind of character whose mouth ran away with him, especially when drunk, but he was prosperous and often dressed in genteel style. A verified photograph of him is evidence of his smart attire and well groomed appearance. He looks more like a Victorian poet than a grizzled cowboy. However, this can be balanced, for instance, by a female Tombstone resident who wrote of him being a despicable man who *"ate like a pig"*! I guess a true character assessment lies somewhere in the middle…

***

As fall began to creep into the fading embers of summer, Tombstone blossomed in an atmosphere of tense uncertainty. On the one hand, the city was thriving as refined and industrious folks arrived in larger numbers than ever. Brick buildings were springing up like well watered crops, new businesses were being established, art and culture spread to satisfy the tastes of the fine families who were beginning to inhabit the neighbourhoods. Opera and Shakespeare at the Schiefflin Hall, bookshops, tailors, a school, an oyster bar, Italian fruit markets, a Chinese eating house and the availability of gourmet food in an array of quality restaurants ... Tombstone had transformed enormously in less than a year from a rough and ready mining outpost into an oasis of pure civilization in the middle of nowhere. And yet all this refinement sat alongside the spirit of what the town had been built upon... the frontier and those who lived it. No matter what they may have preferred amidst their fine dining, fancy clothes and theatrics, the genteel folks were never far from the raucous saloons, bordellos, bawdy shows and gambling haunts which were still noisily inhabited by the rough, tough and coarse, not least of all those troublesome Cowboys.

At least they had the Earps to keep a lid on things in town, as well as some of the worrying incidents which were happening in the surrounding territory. Sheriff Behan, however, was proving to be a figure of disappointing authority. His cheery disposition kept his popularity on an even keel, but the simple fact remained that the Cowboys were still running amok under his watch. He may have made a few token efforts to contain them but it was obvious that his heart wasn't in it. On the contrary, the evidence pointed towards where his sympathies lay. Behan's personality and devious methods were suspiciously covering up a wealth of sins it seemed.

The sheriff's rivalry with the Earps was intensifying but they did unite briefly, putting their differences aside to ride together as part of Mayor John Clum's Tombstone Rangers militia. This had been hastily formed in an effort to combat the threat of a possible Apache attack on the town. A bunch of warriors had recently skipped the San Carlos reservation and tales were coming in of savage raids on remote settlements, even pitched battles with troops of Buffalo Soldiers. Could an assault on Tombstone be possible? The population did not want to take any chances so the militia was formed and rode out to negate the threat.

As it turned out, the Tombstone Rangers earnestly combed the land in a sincere effort to confront those eighty or so Chiricahua bucks but it came to nothing. The Apache threat faded away and was replaced by the next drama, another stagecoach robbery in early October.

Returning from their fruitless pursuit of Apaches, the Earps were swiftly on the case, finding evidence that the robbery culprits were a pair of known Cowboys named Frank Stilwell and Pete Spence. This pair had already been under suspicion for a previous and similar crime in September but now they were under arrest. Stilwell had been a deputy sheriff under Behan, so this made for another awkward situation between the opposing parties. He was also a prominent part of the rougher elite in Tombstone, fronting several business interests, such as 50% ownership of a saloon in Bisbee with fellow bandit Spence.

It was hardly a surprise that the two of them were released through lack of evidence again, much to the annoyance of the Earps.

The Clanton/McClaury faction were similarly annoyed that their friends had suffered the inconvenience of arrest and they voiced their objections by surrounding Morgan Earp outside the Alhambra saloon on Allen Street.

Morgan's dignity and courage were severely challenged when this mob of Cowboys publicly confronted him. It must have been intimidating as Ike Clanton and Frank McClaury yelled abuse at him with Johnny Ringo and others looking on menacingly.

Frank warned Morgan that he had better never come after him but the lawman just responded that if given the opportunity he would do so. This was like a repeat performance of the same confrontation which had taken place between the McClaurys and Virgil Earp the previous year.

Morgan was alone and outnumbered but stood his ground. This could have been the time, but the Cowboys let him go amidst violent threats, especially from Frank.

Wyatt and Virgil were furious when told of this by their younger brother. The three of them decided that the point had been reached where something drastic needed to be done to silence these big mouthed Cowboys.

So many threats and accusations, not least of all the word which had reached Wyatt that Ike was convinced that Doc Holliday had been told of their secret plotting. This would have been Ike's biggest fear. He could not believe that Wyatt would have kept this dangerous news from his friend. Wyatt strongly denied having done so but Ike was not convinced.

Doc was still out of town and had settled himself in Tucson to let the heat die down from his recent arrest. Wyatt asked Morgan to go and find him and ask him to return… for clarification and support.

There was a fair in progress in Tucson's Levin's Park and Morgan found Doc there playing faro. He and Big Nose Kate were together again so he must have been exceptionally forgiving or simply could not live without her. Morgan explained that he was needed in

Tombstone immediately. Doc would always respond without question to a request from Wyatt and he left without delay. He told Kate to stay behind but she insisted on going with them. Doc did not argue. There was enough of that without further ammunition...

CHAPTER 42
NEAR THE O.K. CORRAL...

Doc was back in Tombstone on the evening of Saturday October 22nd. where Wyatt immediately asked him if he had heard word of Ike's accusations and concerns. This was news to the deadly dentist and his reaction was one of anger. He wanted to confront Clanton about it without delay but Wyatt probably convinced him to sit on it for a while.

Doc (and probably Kate) had taken lodgings at Fly's boarding house, on Fremont Street near to the junction with Third Street. This was an addition, and separate business, to the gallery and photographic studio of Camillus Fly whose pictures were to provide some of the most famous images of the Old West.

Three days passed before Ike Clanton and Tom McClaury rode a wagon into town. Their brothers, Billy and Frank, were due to arrive the following morning so that they could conduct some business with Bauer's Union Market on Fremont Street. Ike decided to kill time by going on one of his regular mammoth drinking sprees. He started early, rolling from place to place, swigging whisky and getting more belligerent as the evening wore on. Everyone was aware of the tension in town and Ike was already drunkenly bad mouthing the Earps to anyone who might grant him the time to listen.

At around 1.00am., Ike felt hungry enough to seek out a late supper to sop up some of the alcohol. He swaggered into the Occidental Lunch Room, which was attached to the Alhambra Saloon, and sat at a table to order food. Wyatt was seated at the counter and Morgan was at the bar closeby, but Ike probably did not notice them at first. Likewise, the Earps probably did their best to not draw his attention.

Suddenly, Doc Holliday entered the room, spotted Ike and strode angrily up to his table. Doc had been drinking too and the combination of the pair of them face to face was a recipe for disaster. The gunfighting dentist steamed straight in, bawling at Clanton, calling him a liar and a *"son of a bitch of a cowboy"*. Ike shouted back, defying him, but Doc's hand slipped inside his shirt, a known place of concealment for a weapon.

Of course, under the rules, no one but lawmen were supposed to be carrying guns in town, but Doc was snarling threats and demanding that Ike defend himself. Ike growled back that he was unarmed, which was probably true, but Doc just demanded that he *"go heel"* himself.

At this point, Wyatt and Morgan looked meaningfully at each other and felt that it was time to intervene. Morgan swung himself over the counter and approached the highly strung opponents, grabbing Doc by the arm and pushing him towards the door. Ike was shaken but furious and followed them out onto the boardwalk of lamplit Allen Street where the row continued. Wyatt also left his seat and hurriedly joined the fray. Some said that Morgan aggravated the situation by openly siding with Doc, telling Ike if he wanted a fight then *"have it now"*. Ike was drunk but not so out of his mind as to take them all on unarmed.

Then Virgil turned up with a threat of arrests unless everything calmed down. This seemed to temporarily do the trick and those present drifted off in different directions, no doubt with a few parting verbal shots. Morgan had had enough and wandered off home as the others went in different directions to seek welcome distraction.

Wyatt had spent the earlier part of the night in the Golden Eagle Brewery, just a little further down on the corner of Fifth Street. He had a faro game running there and wanted to get back to it hoping the troubles were over for now. When he stepped back onto the street he bumped into Ike again who was still seething about what had happened.

Wyatt listened as Ike rattled on about Doc, saying that he would have fought him on the spot if he had been armed. As it was, Clanton said that it was about time to *"fetch this fighting talk to a close"*. Wyatt said that he responded, perhaps in a jocular fashion, that he did not intend to fight anyone because there was *"no money in it"*.

Ike was not amused. As he staggered away, he said, menacingly, *"I will be ready for all of you in the morning."*

Wyatt also felt it was time to call it a night. As he walked back he met Doc who was also, uncharacteristically, ready to turn in. It must have been quite a conversation.

Ike was still fired up and going to bed was probably far from his mind. Just a few paces from where he had left Wyatt, he saw that there was still some action going on in the Occidental Saloon. A poker game was just starting and he felt in the mood to join in.

The most amazing thing about this game was who the other players were. Virgil Earp was seated with Johnny Behan, Tom McClaury and a man who has never been identified. As the cards were dealt and with all their differences apparently, and miraculously, on hold for the night, it must be wondered if any of them had the slightest inclination of the momentous clash which would kick off in just a few hours time.

***

The game carried on through the small hours until, finally, at 7.00am., Virgil rose from his seat, pulled on his coat and hat, and announced that he was going to bed.

Ike would still not let his issue go, telling Virgil that he was to deliver a message to Holliday; that he *"had to fight"*. As he walked to the door, Virgil dismissed the request and told the Cowboy not to make such talk and that he did not wish to be woken up from his bed by more trouble.

As Virgil left, Ike shouted after him, *"You may have to fight before you know it!"*

Ike's mood and level of frustration must have added to his staying power because he carried on ranting and drinking. By 8.00am. he was seen on the streets brandishing a pistol and a Winchester rifle. This time, it seemed that he meant to carry out what had previously been empty threats. His tour of Tombstone's bars continued and he visited several throughout the morning, somehow staying on his feet as he made it known to one and all that he intended to make Holliday and the Earps pay for the way they had insulted him when he was unarmed.

Many of those he met tried to talk sense into him, with advice to get to bed and sleep it off, but Ike just grew more determined. Friends of the Earps went to their houses and tried to warn them but Virgil and Wyatt just turned over in their beds. Ike had never been a character to take seriously and they could not be bothered with him now.

Around about midday Ike hammered on the door of Doc's lodgings demanding to see him, but Mrs. Fly sent him away. Doc had been fast asleep but was woken by Kate who told him the news. He was out of bed quickly, still coughing, but eager to meet the threat.

Virgil, Wyatt and Morgan were also up and dressed by now, and informed of how Ike's aggressive behaviour was the talk of the town.

The streets were buzzing with apprehension. Ike was making quite a scene and Mayor Clum, who was on his way to his editor's desk at the *Epitaph's* office on Fremont Street, greeted him, unaware, at this point, of the huge scoop which was to occupy the rest of his working day.

Virgil and Morgan were hunting for Ike by now, the hunted hunting the hunter. It was an unseasonably chilly day… Wednesday October 26th. 1881… and a blustery wind was stirring up more dust than usual. The lawmen found the Cowboy Clanton, approaching him from behind as he lounged in an alleyway. Virgil grabbed Ike's rifle, totally surprising him. Although unsteady and bewildered, Ike reached for his pistol but Virgil was faster, drawing his own weapon and bringing it sharply down upon the Cowboy's head. Clanton fell heavily to his knees, still conscious but at the mercy of the Earps who promptly placed him under arrest for violating the town arms ordinance. Ike protested and cursed as Virgil dragged him to his feet with the defiant question, *"Hunting for me?"*

Ike was just as defiant, spitting back that he surely was and that a second sooner would have made the difference and Earp would have been the victim. Hours of threats had been terminated... it was now just words, and Ike was dragged off to the county courthouse and plonked down upon a bench to await the arrival of the Justice of the Peace. Clanton's head was bleeding profusely and he held a soiled kerchief against it to staunch the flow. He was a sorry sight but failed to raise much sympathy.

It was about 1.00pm. by now and Frank McClaury and young Billy Clanton had arrived in town on horseback. As they headed for a drink in the Grand Hotel on Allen Street, they quickly absorbed the excited news of what had been happening. Amongst those who greeted them was a grinning Doc Holliday who could not resist a sarcastic remark or two. At this stage Frank and Billy remained cautious and did not take the bait.

Over at the courthouse, things had moved swiftly. Ike was fined $25 plus costs, sent on his way with his weapons detained until he left town. Twenty one year old Billy Claiborne was on hand to help his Cowboy friend and he accompanied Ike to a nearby doctor's office for treatment to his battered head. Claiborne was also known as "Billy the Kid" but there was no connection to the more famous Kid who had been killed at Fort Sumner in July.

Tom McClaury had been on his way to the courthouse having heard of Ike's arrest but before he got there, he encountered Wyatt who had just left the proceedings. Wyatt was in a dark mood, infuriated by Ike's behaviour and the general tension which had been building. Seeing Tom McClaury taunted him further.

Witnesses described the scene... Wyatt challenged Tom, towering over him. *"Are you heeled?"* he growled, angrily.

McClaury, physically much shorter than Earp, resented the question, trying to retain his dignity as he replied that he was not seeking trouble but if Earp wanted it, he would fight him anywhere.

Wyatt had reached his limit and reacted by slapping Tom hard across the face with his left hand, then pulling a pistol with his right hand which he smashed against the side of McClaury's head. Tom rocked on his feet, dazed and bleeding, but Wyatt stalked away to buy a cigar at Hafford's Corner.

Most people, even Earp supporters, appeared to agree that even in view of prior provocation, Wyatt's behaviour on this occasion was somewhat over the top.

Billy Claiborne met up with Frank McClaury and Billy Clanton telling them all he knew and that Ike would be joining them shortly when the doctor had treated him. By many accounts it seems most likely that Frank actually wanted to avoid a fight that day. He spoke of wanting to get everyone out of town. Billy also showed concern about his brother Ike and just wished to get him home.

Even so, these Cowboys wanted to be prepared if trouble should come their way. Tom, his head still throbbing, had joined them and they made their way to Spangenberg's Gun Shop on Fourth Street where Frank and Billy bought ammunition to fill up their gunbelts. It is probably true that Tom was unarmed but the other two Cowboys were in violation of Tombstone's firearms restrictions.

Wyatt was stalking them and looked through the shop window at what they were doing. Frank's horse, presumably having got loose from its hitching rail outside, had stepped up onto the boardwalk and was starting to nose its way through the doorway into the shop. Wyatt, being busy and pedantic, stepped up and took the horse by its bridle to lead it back onto the street, prompting Frank to react by grabbing the bridle himself.

Wyatt demanded that the horse be taken off the sidewalk just as Ike, his head bandaged, joined them. Still spoiling for an excuse to escalate things, regardless of the present odds, Wyatt hung around, watching the Cowboys every move.

Ike's head wound was raw and painful. He felt nauseous, not just from Virgil's blow but, presumably, from the effects of the long, drunken night and morning he was still enduring. With his weapons confiscated and awaiting collection from the Grand Hotel, Ike tried to buy a handgun but the shop owner wisely refused the sale.

1.30pm. ... approximately. Sheriff Johnny Behan had settled himself into a barber's shop chair for a shave, having slept in late and in hope of a peaceful day. Unfortunately, people in the shop were talking anxiously of the danger brewing in town. Behan was not really a fighting man. His main deputies, like Breakenridge, were out of town, but he knew he needed to do something. Urging the barber to finish his work, the sheriff left the chair and headed for the door…

Virgil was receiving many warnings of what was building, including a tip off that Wyatt was facing the Cowboys all alone down at the gunshop. Having just picked up a shotgun he kept at the Wells Fargo office nearby, Virgil made his way towards the shop but before he got there he met Wyatt on the corner of Allen and Fourth Street, just outside Haffords. The Clantons, McClaurys and Billy Claiborne had just been seen making their way towards Fremont Street on their way to pick up their horses at the O.K. Corral.

There was a lot of commotion at Hafford's corner, with townsfolk surrounding Virgil and Wyatt, many of them probably relishing the drama of the moment. Cradling his shotgun, Virgil took in all the information and advice he was receiving but he was making his own plans. A representative of the local vigilance committee had already offered the support of as many as 25 armed men in support of the Earp faction, but Virgil turned them down, confident that they would not be needed. Morgan had joined him and Wyatt, and then Doc Holliday, striding up the street hunched in a heavy, long grey coat, head bent against the wind. Doc looked unwell and was leaning on a walking cane but he told his friends, the Earps, that they could count on him.

Behan came hurrying up to them and Virgil answered his concerns by stating that there were "sons of bitches" in town looking for a fight, but the sheriff said that he was sure it could be avoided by convincing them to disarm. The Earps seemed sure that the time for that had passed but Behan headed off hurriedly towards Fremont to try. Johnny, after all, had his own questionable relationship with these Cowboys, but maybe they would listen to him.

Nearing 3.00pm., Virgil, Wyatt and Morgan had made up their minds. The time had come. Word had now reached them that the Cowboy faction were no longer in the corral but had gathered in a vacant lot behind the two properties belonging to the photographer Fly, right on the corner of Fremont and Third Streets. Their guns were still on open display, it was said, so that was enough of an excuse for them to be confronted.

Had the Cowboys been planning to vacate the town to avoid trouble or had they decided to fight it out after all? The surviving evidence is contradictory. Some witnesses spoke of hearing them arguing heatedly in the corral, with more threats against Holliday and the Earps, but others said they were ready to leave. Feelings were mixed. Frank McClaury and Billy Clanton had both expressed their desire to go, Ike must have been drained to the limit, but, in the cold light of day, the further aggressive behaviour of the Earps must have riled them.

They were probably still all debating what best to do when Behan came hurrying up to ask them to surrender their weapons. Frank and Billy were armed and said they would only give up their guns when they had been assured that the Earp party had done the same. Behan later swore that he had searched Ike and Tom, both of whom were unarmed.

Back at Haffords Corner, Virgil handed his shotgun to Doc, reasoning that Holliday could conceal it beneath his long coat, which he did. Doc in turn passed his cane to Virgil.

The lawmen then set off with a firm and steady pace towards Fremont Street.

It was not a long walk around to their destination but it conjures up an image which has embedded itself as one of the most iconic pictures of the Old West.

The Earp brothers, clad almost identically in black… thick frock coats and ties on this cold afternoon, hats pulled low, marching purposefully towards the fulfilment of their legend… strung out in an almost military line with the ever faithful Doc Holliday at their side. The wind blew, flapping back their coat tails, sweeping their drooping mustaches and occasionally revealing Doc's concealed scatter gun.

They all carried pistols, of course. Virgil, it is said, had his tucked in his waistband and Wyatt's was deep in the specially waxed pocket of his coat. Morgan and Doc may have been sporting holsters and the handguns were probably all Colt .45's, Doc's being fancily nickel plated. (That said, Wyatt was known to also carry an 1869 model Smith & Wesson, but it was probably a Colt that day.)

The people of Tombstone were mesmerised as they watched them walk, knowing they were surely about to witness something desperate and memorable. They watched from the shelter of doorways, windows and sidewalks as the four men turned left at the corner of Fourth Street and into Fremont without slowing their pace. Soon they were walking between the facing offices of the *Nugget* and *Epitaph*. Clum was hard at work at the desk of the latter, maybe Woods at the former…

The Cowboys were out of sight, backed into that empty lot, but Behan looked up the street and saw the lawmen coming. The sheriff was still hopeful that he would be able to diffuse the situation and told those in the lot that he would go and speak to the approaching group. As he walked away, another witness later said that he heard one of the Cowboys call out for him not to be afraid for there would be no trouble.

Behan confronted the Earps and Holliday just as they reached the awning above the porch of Bauer's. The sheriff raised his hands as if to try and stop them but they carried on without hesitation, ignoring his words which declared that, as the county sheriff, he would not allow any trouble. It had no effect. Behan had to step aside as they walked right on but he followed them, calling out, *"For God's sake, don't go down there or you will be murdered!"* (As recalled by Wyatt.)

Without turning, Virgil just sternly replied, *"I am going to disarm them."*

Behan then said something to the effect that he had already disarmed them all, which was a contradiction to the warning within his previous statement.

A friend of the Cowboys, one Wes Fuller, had run ahead to give a warning, but by the time he got there, the Earps and Holliday were positioning themselves at the entrance of the lot, almost blocking it. The space was constricted, less than twenty feet wide.

The Clantons and McClaurys, with Billy Claiborne, stood at an angle with their backs to the home of William Harwood, (who had been the original mayor of Tombstone) facing Fly's Boarding House. Fuller gave up his intention and slipped out of sight behind the buildings, as did Billy Claiborne who had second thoughts about facing down those sinister looking Earps. Behan had also removed himself from the line of fire, drawing back to the shelter of Fly's. Two horses were also in the lot; Frank and Billy's.

Ike, Billy, Frank and Tom almost froze but made a slow move deeper into the lot. It was claimed by some that Frank and Billy had their hands ready on the butts of their pistols. Tense seconds passed as the two sides glared at each other with just a few feet between them. The McClaurys sported almost identical mustaches and neat chin beards, nineteen year old Billy Clanton's boyish face totally clean shaven. These men would all have been wearing coats against the chill of the day.

"Boys, throw up your hands... I want your guns..." demanded Virgil, Doc's cane clutched in his raised right hand.

It was later said that this was the moment that Frank and Billy reacted by drawing and cocking their pistols, with Virgil throwing his other hand in the air as he yelled, *"Hold... I don't want that!"*

Wyatt's pistol was drawn in that same moment and it is probable that he and Billy fired simultaneously. Knowing that Frank McClaury was the most dangerous of their opponents, Wyatt had already earmarked him as his first target and that initial bullet tore into

Frank's stomach. The elder McClaury was knocked back by the shot but still game, stumbling but raising his gun.

Billy's first shot missed as Virgil changed hands with the cane, drawing his pistol at the same time Morgan did. Tom McClaury, who was said to have opened his coat to show he was unarmed, had now realised that he needed to fight and was desperately trying to pull a rifle from the saddle scabbard of one of the frightened, rearing horses.

Doc produced the shotgun from under his coat and walked quickly around the horse to get a clear shot. Tom's right arm was raised as he struggled to control the animal and Doc seized that opportunity to quickly aim and fire a charge at close range into Tom's armpit. The younger McClaury moaned, spun sideways and staggered into Fremont Street.

There had been the briefest of pauses before all the participants played their part and the shooting started in earnest. Ike threw his hands in the air, his face a picture of sheer terror as he sprung at Wyatt, grabbing his arm. It was not an assault; just an act of desperation as he confirmed that he was not sporting a weapon.

Wyatt pushed him away with a contemptuous shout, *"This fight has commenced. Get to fighting or get away!"*

Ike did not need to be told twice, taking to his heels and bursting into Fly's house, tearing through it and running on across a couple of blocks to put as much distance as he could from the gunfire. So much for his bold talk which had led to this mayhem.

Though severely wounded, Frank was shooting back, as was Billy Clanton, but a flurry of fire, mostly from Morgan, hit Billy several times… in the wrist, stomach and chest. Virgil fell to one knee, a bullet having torn a nasty flesh wound in his lower right leg, as Billy was thrown back against the wooden boards of Harwood's House. Showing quite amazing fortitude, the young Cowboy slid down the wall into a cross legged sitting position, performing an action known as the "border shift" as he transferred his pistol from his immobilised right hand to his left. Incredibly, he was still in the fight and it was probably a shot from him which hit Morgan. As the younger Earp was most likely standing side on in a duelling stance, this is probably why the bullet took an odd course, hitting him in the shoulder and tracing a groove, chipping his backbone before ripping out of the opposite shoulder.

Frank, though badly hit, had grabbed the bridle of the nearest horse, pushing the animal towards the street, using its bulk as cover as he returned fire, but it broke loose, galloping away and leaving him totally exposed. The elder McClaury was nearly finished, but not quite. Dropping into a squat, he was still firing. Then he levelled his pistol at Doc Holliday, fierce determination in his eyes as he gasped, *"I've got you now…"*

Doc, forever out to make a game of everything, reportedly snapped back, *"You're a daisy if you have!"* He had tossed aside the empty shotgun and had drawn his nickel plated revolver.

Morgan had stumbled to the ground, maybe just tripping over a mound of earth, but was on his feet again. He may have already been hit, or maybe it was just before, but he and Doc were concentrating on Frank, both of them opening up on him, Morgan's shot striking the Cowboy in the head and Doc's in the chest. McClaury's last bullet grazed Doc's hip, making him yelp and think he was wounded more seriously than he actually was.

Standing at the entrance to Fly's house, a stray bullet whistled close to Billy Claiborne and that was what made him and Behan duck quickly inside. Some witnesses said they heard shots actually come from this area, drawing suspicion that outside participants may have joined the fray, but this was never proved. Maybe those sounds were just ricochets from the main fight… the Earps were never convinced.

Billy Clanton had emptied his pistol and was feebly calling out for more cartridges as he leaned back against the wall, his face twisted in pain. Camillus Fly emerged from his house and cautiously knelt down beside him, gently coaxing the spent weapon from his grasp. Tom McClaury had staggered as far as the telegraph pole on the corner of Third and Fremont where he fell dying. His brother Frank was sprawled just outside of the alley in Fremont.

As the intense barrage of shots subsided, an eerie silence prevailed, the swirling white gunsmoke already blowing away in the stiff breeze.

Three fatalities, three wounded, with Wyatt Earp the only one present still fully on his feet untouched by lead. Shielded momentarily by the fleeing Ike Clanton, this ironic moment no doubt contributed to his luck. Ike was nowhere to be seen.

Wyatt pocketed his gun and looked around at the chaos. Sprawled bodies, his brothers knocked off their feet, his friend Doc stooped and clutching at his side.

The fight which had taken so long in coming had lasted less than half a minute.

CHAPTER 43
THE SMOKE CLEARS...

That frozen moment and silence following the gunfire was abruptly broken by the shrill scream of a steam whistle from one of the mine workings outside town. This was a signal, unknown to most, to alert the Tombstone Vigilance Committee, the members of which began to appear on the streets as soon as they heard a second blast. Model citizens, armed, had been told to prepare for such a moment, to respond to an event such as this, be it outlaw domination or Apache attack, but an outright gun battle between the town's main rival factions had not been expected in such a dramatic form.

There had been quite a few direct witnesses to the fight, even though most of them understandably ducked for shelter as the bullets began to fly. It was difficult to agree on how many shots had been fired but it must have been in the region of thirty.

Wyatt's first concern was for his brothers. Virgil's leg wound was painful but not too serious. Morgan's was more of a worry. The bullet had creased the width of his upper back; a nasty injury but it could have been much worse. Another inch inwards would most likely have killed him. Doc had been even luckier in receiving that graze to his hip.

Crowds of people were now beginning to congregate at the scene, already mumbling their diverse views of what had just happened. The *Nugget's* editor Harry Woods was one of the first on the scene, tending to the suffering Billy Clanton as he writhed in agony against the wall of Harwood's home. Woods was probably already composing in his head the biased report which would appear in his newspaper the following day.

Others rushed to the McClaury brothers. It was too late for Frank who had just breathed his last, but Tom was clinging to life... just. He and Billy were carefully lifted up and carried into a nearby house to be made as comfortable as possible. A doctor attended them and quickly confirmed that there was nothing that could be done to save them. Tom did not even speak and soon passed away. Nearly $3,000 in cash, cheques and receipts was found in his pockets, demonstrating the level of business which had been conducted recently.

As for Billy, he twisted, turned, kicked and moaned as the doctor examined his wounds, injecting him with morphine in the hope of dulling the pain. The young Cowboy choked on his words, exclaiming through gritted teeth that he had been murdered. His last words before drifting into a final sleep were an agonised request to clear the crowd away from the door and give him air.

Onlookers sympathetic to the Earps were, at Wyatt's urging, tending to Virgil and Morgan and they were conveyed to their homes for medical attention. Doc, as "walking wounded", drifted away from the chaotic scene. Big Nose Kate was to claim that he returned to his room in Fly's, sat on the edge of his bed and wept. Well, perhaps, but it does not sound like Doc's behaviour.

Fred Dodge offered as much help as he could, remarking later that Wyatt was dealing with the situation in his usual "cool and collected" manner. Together he and Dodge left the scene but were soon approached by Johnny Behan who sombrely told Wyatt that he was going to have to arrest him.

Wyatt paused and fixed the sheriff with a long, hard stare before forcefully responding that he would not be arrested. *"You deceived us, Johnny,"* he continued, *"you told us they were not armed."* Before walking on, Wyatt indicated that he was willing to answer for what he had done and would not leave town.

Already the Earps, and Holliday, were receiving praise for their action from a large percentage of the townsfolk who were gathering on the streets to discuss the excitement. It was not unanimous, of course, for the Clantons and McClaurys had their supporters too, but the initial general buzz did seem to be that the Cowboys had got what they had been asking for. Many were already saying that the Earps had *"done just right"* in killing them and that the *"people will stand by them"*.

"You bet we did right..." uttered Wyatt softly but firmly.

Ike Clanton was found later that afternoon, skulking in a dancehall on Toughnut Street and he *was* promptly arrested. Locked up in the jailhouse, he was visited that evening by his brother Phin who had just been to view Billy's corpse. Several extra deputies were drafted in to guard Ike from any possible vigilante action. Likewise, down at the Earp's homes, their friends, heavily armed, had created a ring of protection.

Behan visited the Earps that night where Virgil and Morgan were being tenderly comforted by their womenfolk, Allie and Louisa. It was not a warm reception for the sheriff where, despite his pain, Virgil, supported by his brothers, accused him of coercion with their enemies and of trying to drum up aggression from the vigilance committee. Behan was shown the door and left in no doubt that sides had been drawn with severe repercussions to follow.

By the next day, word of the gun battle had spread far and wide, reported in newspapers right across to San Francisco and beyond. Naturally, the two Tombstone publications printed very different interpretations of what had taken place, the *Nugget* inferring accusations of unnecessary murderous violence whilst the *Epitaph* praised the lawmen, stating that they had rid society of bad elements.

Over the next couple of days widespread sympathy for the Earps and Holliday reached an overwhelming level of virtual hero worship from many commentators, but this attitude was short lived.

Balance changed quite abruptly on October 28th., the day of the slain Cowboy's funerals. The bodies of Billy Clanton and the McClaurys had been prepared for display, dressed in fine suits and placed in expensive, silver trimmed open coffins. These coffins were tilted almost upright in the front window of the undertaker's shop with a large sign above them… "MURDERED IN THE STREETS OF TOMBSTONE". A photograph of this grim sight was taken; a picture which has become one of the most famous to emerge from the Old West.

The funeral itself was an even bigger affair than Marshal Fred White's or Bud Philpott's. Ornate hearses conveyed the dead men to the cemetery, Billy in one glass sided carriage and the McClaurys in the other. Ike and Phin rode mournfully in a carriage behind, accompanied by many a long faced Cowboy. Hundreds followed the procession, led by a marching brass band which blared out a string of tragic melodies. This was the first major step in growing sympathy for the victims of the shootout. People were beginning to wonder, were the Earps and Holliday really justified in gunning down these men?

The coroner's inquest began the same day as the funeral and it immediately raised questions about the previously assumed legality of the killings. Conflicting testimonies grew and when the coroner released his report on October 29th., just three days after the gunfight, there appeared to be enough evidence to stage what would prove to be a long and complicated hearing.

It was enough to make the city council act immediately by suspending Virgil from his trusted position as Chief of Police, although he did retain his role as Deputy U.S. Marshal.

Virtually overnight, the Earps and Doc Holliday were being viewed in a totally different light. Suspicion and outright accusation began to shadow them; such is the fickle nature of public opinion.

Worried about retribution before any hearing, the Earps decided to relocate, centralizing themselves, with their women, in rooms at the Cosmopolitan Hotel where they felt they could more easily defend themselves. The Cowboys had a similar idea, some of them establishing a shuttered headquarters almost directly across the street in the Grand Hotel to keep their enemies under observation.

Witnesses were claiming that the lawmen opened fire whilst the Cowboys were in the act of surrendering. Some swore that Tom McClaury had opened his coat as he said, *"I ain't got no arms…"* and Billy Clanton had called out that he did not wish to fight. One of the Earps was said to have growled, *"You sons of bitches have been looking for a fight…"*

Ike and his supporters felt strongly that they had a case and murder charges were filed against the three relevant Earp brothers and Holliday. Because Virgil and Morgan were laid up with their wounds, only Wyatt and Doc had to face Justice of the Peace Wells Spicer who set their bail at a whopping $10,000 dollars each. Fortunately, these were sums which were easily covered, not just by the comfortably off Earps themselves but also by their many well heeled supporters.

***

There was to be a hearing to decide whether or not the case would actually go to trial. Both sides invested in serious legal representation. Within a day or so another high profile figure arrived from Fort Worth, Texas, to bolster the power of the prosecution team which was already headed by District Attorney Lyttleton Price. This was another McClaury brother, William, a lawyer by profession, fiery by nature and a passionate asset for the case. He was determined to get justice for Tom and Frank.

On the other side, the Earps put their faith in one Tom Fitch, a colourful and well connected figure who came with an impressive reputation as a convincing and successful speaker in important litigation cases. Doc Holliday was represented by the firm of Howard & Street.

The hearing began on November 1st. and got off to a flying start for the prosecution with witnesses Bill Allen and Johnny Behan solemnly relating all they knew, with bias against the defendants. In contrast to what had previously been believed, they were both adamant that the first shots had come from the Earp/Holliday side and that the defendants on the day of the gunfight were determined to settle things with violence. What of the bullying provocation dished out by Virgil and Wyatt when they pistol whipped Ike and Tom? And Holliday's verbal assault on Ike at the Occidental on the night before the shootout?

Behan stressed that his attempts to defuse the situation were brushed aside.

Further testimony from on the spot witness Wes Fuller led to the prosecution requesting that the able bodied defendants be placed in custody, such was the damning evidence to date, regardless of their bail. The defence team argued against this but a decision was made and Sheriff Behan must have felt rather smug as he led Wyatt and Doc off to his jailhouse. Will McClaury was delighted but not fully satisfied. He felt pretty sure that he could put a noose around the necks of his brother's "murderers".

Billy Claiborne next took the stand and he reiterated the words of those who had preceded him. Regardless of fine efforts by the defence to discredit him, Claiborne left the stand with public opinion well and truly turned against their clients.

So far it was not looking good for the Earp faction. The hearing had been lumbering on for over a week before Ike Clanton was finally called to give his evidence and a general feeling had already settled that the case was won and Ike's words may just be icing on the cake.

To everyone's surprise, and Tom Fitch's joy, Ike's woeful performance turned the tide back again. For the prosecution, he portrayed himself as the wronged, grieving brother who had never made any threats against the Earps or Holliday, and of how they had bullied, beat and threatened *him*. He even made up an elaborate tale of how he had heroically taken on Wyatt during the shooting, unarmed as he wrestled him around a corner, the lawman's gun blazing.

However, under pressure from the defence team, he tied himself in knots of contradiction and absurdity. He was so obviously lying and confused that it became embarrassing. All the strong, convincing work achieved thus far by the prosecution team began to unravel.

His accusations and tall tales fell apart under clever cross examination to the point where his testimony was simply not credible. When he was faced with questions about the deal he was supposed to have made with Wyatt, he seemed to panic. He denied everything and lost himself in a tirade of direct attacks on the Earps and Holliday which just resulted in humiliating and potentially incriminating him.

At one point, he asked to be excused for the day because he was suffering from pains in the head. When he returned, his over the top, deluded ranting brought his legal team to the point of despair. His behaviour had become almost irrational.

This was good news for the defence team. Up to this point, the prosecution had built a strong convincing case which had resulted in an abrupt decrease in sympathy for the Earp faction. Ike's performance was now making people think yet again.

Tom Fitch's side would need to up their game but they had some strong cards to play. Wyatt took the stand, despite objections from the prosecution which were overruled. The only Earp not hit by a bullet in the gunfight had prepared a long, detailed, written statement which outlined the whole complicated background which had led to such violence on the streets of Tombstone.

He spoke with a clear, strong voice and was far more convincing than Ike had been. His explanations of the history of conflict with the Cowboys made sense, along with his personal description of the shootout itself. To sum up, Wyatt's dignified conclusion, without apology, was that he had acted morally and legally in defence of his own life, as well as that of his brothers and his friend Holliday, and to uphold the law.

He even presented written declarations from the authorities at Dodge City and Wichita which gave multi signed glowing references of his competence, character, morality and law enforcement skills.

Doubt had now been cast upon the previously accepted testimonies of Behan and other witnesses. Wyatt's solid performance proved to be an excellent opening gambit for the defence.

The hearing continued for another fortnight during which time Fitch's team had a field day gradually wearing down the prosecution. Further witnesses were called whose testimony largely supported Wyatt's words. Sheriff Behan's version of events was shown to be full of holes and Will McClaury's former swaggering confidence began to buckle.

Unable to appear in the courtroom owing to his raw leg wound, Virgil was visited in his room at the Cosmopolitan. It must have been a crowded scene as the court convened around him, but the elder Earp firmly reiterated his brother's statement. Virgil emphasised that he had not been motivated by dark thoughts on the fateful day and his only intention had been to uphold the law.

On November 30th., Justice Spicer read from his long and explanatory verdict. Considering all the complex facts, he had arrived at the decision that *"the defendants were fully justified in committing these homicides… a necessary act done in the discharge of official duty".*

There would be no need for the case to be heard in a murder trial and the Earps and Holliday could go free.

***

It is approximately a seventy mile drive from Tucson to Tombstone, back east along Interstate 10 and turning south at Benson.

I loved it from the moment I motored down the first of the wide, gorgeously recreated streets. Of course, almost all of the town known to the Earps was gone, destroyed in those fires or demolished, but, ever since the popular resurgence of Wyatt's name and all those movies and T.V. shows, it has been reborn.

Not long after the Earp era, the mines were played out and Tombstone fell into a swift decline. People left in droves and the town went through a lengthy period of bleak emptiness. Once the potential of a booming tourist trade was recognised, investment in the recreation of what had once thrived was embraced with enthusiasm. Having almost become a ghost town, Tombstone's revival began in the late 1930s with a sign erected outside town in the hope of luring travellers to experience the flavour of the Old West.

It really took off after World War Two.

I was delighted to see rebuilt versions of the Oriental, the Crystal Palace (including large Victorian ceiling lamps and a 45 foot long mahogany bar), and take a beer in the Longhorn and Big Nose Kate's saloons. The Schieffelin Hall (still presenting performances) and Cochise County Courthouse still stand (as a museum). The Birdcage Theatre remains intact and allows tours inside, which was a dream for me. Now this theatre, contrary to popular belief, was not in operation at the time of the O.K. Corral gunfight. It actually opened officially in December of that year of '81, originally intended for family shows and refined performances but did not do well with that policy. It quickly became the scene of more ribald entertainment for the miners and cowboys where prostitutes plied their trade in the cosy balcony booths which give the place its name. It is gloriously dusty and rundown and I was able to walk around it alone, drinking in the wonderful atmosphere. I stepped onto the stage and made my way down into the basement room where the ambience of old time gambling is recreated.

All rather creepy, but a thrill indeed. It is said to be haunted and I can well believe it.

Walking Fremont and Allen Streets were pure inspiration, avoiding the tourist toting stagecoaches which trot the whole lengths throughout the day. Cowboys on horseback seemed to be everywhere. Old Western mementoes appear in virtually every establishment, a highlight of which was one of the actual hearses which took the O.K. Corral victims to Boot Hill graveyard.

The site of the gunfight itself is well preserved, although the rickety, cartoon like mannequins which represent the participants could be much improved upon. There are also daily reenactments of the famous confrontation, played out by actors, which is fine but left me feeling a little uncomfortable. Yes, all for the tourists, I know, but the cheesy quality of it does not sit well if one respects the history. Good that it is kept alive though...

That said, one must appreciate that Tombstone only thrives today because of tourism so I would not be too critical. And, to be fair, although there is an emphasis on the fun aspect of it all, it is generally tasteful and authentic and just a great place to spend time. So many period relics wherever you look. Good ol' boys drinking at the bars, and gargantuan, wholesome portions of vittals, cowboy style. Live country music in the bars was very entertaining, the locals were friendly and the sun shone... what more could you want?

We stayed on Fremont Street itself in a comfy place whose rooms were all named after the famous figures of Tombstone's history, and we were put in the Ed Schieffelin Room.

Around town, located at the actual spots (they claim) were signs indicating various other gunfights. Where Curly Bill shot Marshal White... where Luke Short terminated Charlie Storms... and where Buckskin Frank Leslie put a bullet through Billy Claiborne (more on that later...)

The Old West Bookshop on Allen Street absorbed me for a while, as I perused some terrific titles which were unobtainable back on my side of the Atlantic. I tried to interest the owner in my recently released tome From Crockett to Custer and she did seem to take note. It reminded me of another time on this trip when I had approached another small bookshop in a town on the road with the same proposition.

A lady ran that place too and, as she thumbed through the pages of my efforts, she called over an old grizzled character from the back room.

"Hey, Ira," she said to him, "We've got a British writer here who's writ a real fine book about the Alamo n' Custer's Last Stand."

Ira shuffled over and glanced at my book with no attempt to pick it up.

"Has it got pictures?" he sniffed, in a Texas drawl, "We liiiiiiike pictures..."

On our way out of town, located high on its impressive plateau, we visited the renowned Boot Hill cemetery. The sun was setting, giving the most fantastic panoramic backdrop to our wander around the gravestones.

Most famously, the McClaurys and Billy Clanton are buried here, but also Billy Claiborne and many other names from back in the day, victims of gunshots and lynchings. Like "George Johnson 1882: Hanged by mistake... He was right, we was wrong...but we strung him up and now he's gone" and "Here lies Lester Moore... four slugs from a .44... NO LES NO MORE".

CHAPTER 44

RESENTMENT AND REVENGE

In several ways, it was a hollow victory.

Legally, for now, Virgil, Wyatt, Morgan and Doc were in the clear with no murder trial to endure. Although their support in town was still strong, with jubilance and relief at the verdict, there remained an overriding sense of injustice from many others. Resentment and anger became the main topic on the streets of Tombstone as rival supporters argued and seethed.

Many felt that the freed men had got away with murder. The overreaction of gunplay had been unnecessary, they grumbled. Why would the Clantons and McClaurys have sought that kind of conflict? Most of them were not even the main players in any potential showdown. Where were the more prominent suspects? Johnny Ringo, Pony Diehl and Curly Bill Brocius, for instance?

It was a tense time as further battle lines were drawn. Without any concrete evidence, the rumours and Chinese whispers had created poisonous suspicion about the Earp's and Holliday's involvement in stagecoach robberies and general criminality. There was talk of a hit list having been drawn up to assassinate those who were held to blame, a list which it was said had been written in actual blood at a secret ceremony in the darkness of a canyon at night. Top of the list were the Earp brothers and Doc, of course, but also the likes of Judge Spicer, Attorney Tom Fitch and Mayor John Clum.

Everyone was on alert. When Clum left town on the evening of December 14th. to head east for a business trip, the stagecoach he was travelling on had barely covered a few miles before it was accosted by armed men who ordered them to halt. The driver whipped up the horses to escape and received a fusillade of shots in response. A little further down the trail, the coach reined in to assess the damage... a wounded horse and driver... but Clum decided he did not want to take the chance of staying on board with the possibility of further attack. He disembarked and let the stage carry on without him, convinced that the incident was an assassination attempt rather than a robbery. Carrying a pair of pistols, and feeling that he would be safer to trudge through the night on foot, he set off on a 20 mile trek to Benson.

The *Nugget* took great delight in ridiculing Clum's desperate experience, and this was swiftly responded to in the *Epitaph* with a piece shaming such insensitivity.

When the news reached Tombstone, it almost caused another

shootout. In the Oriental Saloon, which was now thriving again, Milt Joyce (longtime Earp rival) confronted Virgil (still limping), taunting him by suggesting that such a stagecoach attack was only to be expected since Wyatt and Doc had been released from jail. It was too much for Virgil who silenced Joyce by slapping him across his grinning face. Several Earp supporters were present and they moved forward protectively, forcing Joyce to back off. It did not end there because, according to the recollection of Billy Breakenridge, Joyce faced them the following day, armed with a brace of pistols and asking if they were still keen to fight. Bloodshed was only avoided, it was said, by Sheriff Behan, whose loyalties were always open to question, grabbing him from behind and placing him under arrest for disturbing the peace.

This kind of confrontation was always a hair's breadth away from erupting and it created a most uncomfortable atmosphere wherever people gathered and took sides.

In their shuttered room at the Grand, watching the street through a single absent slat, were a string of Cowboys, their attention rooted to the frontage of the Cosmopolitan where the Earps maintained their headquarters of sanctuary. One of the main occupants was Johnny Ringo, biding his time inbetween his continuing criminal activities. Pony Diehl too, and Curly Bill who was on the scene again following his long recovery from being shot in the face. They, with Ike and their cohorts, were waiting for a chance to strike...

It is worth speculating at this point about a connection between Ringo and Big Nose Kate. Left alone during the recent hearing whilst her man Doc Holliday spent weeks in jail, she was visited at Fly's Boarding House by the Cowboy outlaw. This was an odd relationship and one can only wonder at the extent of it. According to Kate, Ringo was a gentleman and *"... a fine man, anyway you took him..."* (???) She appreciated his intelligence and good looks and called him *"wistful"*. It seems pretty obvious that she was attracted to him, regardless of his enmity with her lover. Ringo even openly told her that the Clantons were watching for Doc to return to his room where they intended to deal with him.

Kate was short of money and she said that Ringo gave her $50 so that she could return to Globe, Arizona, where she had connections. This, it seems, is what she did, effectively yet again terminating her relationship with Doc around the time he was released, although she did continue to visit him in Tombstone from time to time.

Doc must have been aware of the strange friendship between his woman and the outlaw and it must have stoked the already existing enmity between him and Ringo which was to flare over the coming months.

As Christmas approached, accusations and threats infected every major aspect of life in Tombstone, dominating the daily newspaper coverage in the *Nugget* and *Epitaph*, each one outdoing the other in their bias towards their chosen faction.

Morgan was slowly recovering from his gunshot wound and Virgil was hobbling around, having been replaced as city marshal by one of his deputies, Jim Flynn. Virgil still technically, though not very practically, held his position as U.S. deputy marshal in the county, with Wyatt as his occasional deputy, so the Earps did maintain some authority as lawmen. As it was, however, Wyatt drifted back to his regular occupation dealing faro, brassing out any threats which came his way. Doc was in a similar position.

And what of Sadie Marcus and Wyatt's probable romance? Very little detail has survived regarding their relationship during this volatile period and years later, neither of them were forthcoming about it. Wyatt was undoubtedly preoccupied with the drama and danger surrounding him and his brothers, but it can be assumed that he and Sadie were seeing each other. Mattie was still very much part of the Earp clan but the existence of Sadie, and Wyatt's interest in her, must have added to the pressure within the family.

Helping to protect them all was Wyatt's priority.

It was only a matter of time before something broke the deadlock.

***

On the night of December 28th., around about 11.30pm., Virgil and Wyatt said goodnight to each other following an average evening in the Oriental. Wyatt remained as Virgil pulled on his coat, adjusted his hat, and stepped out onto Allen Street to make his way back to his room at the Cosmopolitan.

He had only walked a few paces when his attention was drawn towards a vacant burned out building, about 20 yards away across the street. A figure was hurrying into it and Virgil recognised the man as Frank Stilwell, the Cowboy and ex Behan deputy who had been arrested, then released, under suspicion of stagecoach robbery back in the fall.

The blasts of three double barrelled shotguns ripped through the cold night air, the heavy buckshot charges striking Virgil and hurling him into the dirt. He took the brunt of it, but part of one blast smashed through the window of the adjacent Golden Eagle Brewery narrowly missing those inside.

Virgil was a tough customer and pulled himself to his feet just as people rushed into the street from the surrounding buildings. A trio of figures were spotted immediately, running out from the charred timbers then down Fifth Street towards Toughnut Street. There were shouts of *"There they go"* and *"Head 'em off"* as Virgil, bleeding profusely from his shattered left arm and peppered back, staggered back the way he had come and into the Oriental. Shocked but ever professional Wyatt was there for him.

Earp supporters rallied around, some of them spreading out in pursuit of the would be assassins while others formed a protective ring around those who helped the dazed and bleeding Virgil back to his hotel room. Doctors were summoned and an examination revealed the wounds to be serious. Virgil had taken the full force of those scattergun blasts in his left arm between the shoulder and elbow, severely mangling the whole length of that limb. More buckshot had raked a broad area of his back but, luckily, without penetrating anything vital.

A long section of shattered bone was removed from the elder Earp's arm, alongside a struggle to stem the copious loss of blood. Virgil was growing pale, sweating with the pain of the ordeal, as his woman Allie sobbed by his side. Stoically, the wounded lawman put on a brave face as he tried to comfort her with the words *"Never mind... I've got one arm left to hug you with."*

The doctors grimly debated their next course of action. That destroyed arm would need to be amputated surely, but then again they were also 80% certain that the wounded man could not survive his injuries. But Virgil was made of strong mettle and, to most everyone's relief, he was to pull through, even though he lost the use of that arm.

The hunt for the shooters had been fruitless, but had at least revealed some clues. Although the hunted had disappeared into the night, Virgil had identified one of the main suspects as Frank Stilwell who he had seen just moments before the shooting. And, almost comically, at the site where the shots had come from, a hat was found with Ike Clanton's name stitched inside! He was later to claim that he had indeed lost his hat but had no idea how it had ended up there! This fact really does sum up so much about Ike's character...

The latest drama caused uproar in town. Rival factions were at each other's throats again with a renewed sense of purpose. Wyatt moved quickly. By the following afternoon he had sent a concise telegraph wire to U.S. Marshal Crawley Dake in Phoenix outlining the latest news. He actually stated that Virgil's wounds were fatal, adding that local authorities were doing nothing and asking for the appointment of power to choose his own deputies.

Dake agreed and wired back the permission. Wyatt now had the official authority to conduct his own legal retribution but, for now, his priority lay with his ailing brother. Virgil was dangerously weak and there followed a worrying ten days of touch and go before he began to show promising signs of recovery. They did manage to save his arm but it hung useless for the rest of his life.

Wyatt and the rest of the family remained at his bedside for virtually the whole ten days, but now attention could begin to be devoted to justice.

However, as the new year of 1882 opened, Tombstone was bubbling with the further drama of municipal elections, to choose the placement of various political offices. The voting was hugely influenced by whatever side one may be choosing in the Earp/Clanton feud. It was a most complicated situation, the details of which I will not attempt to outline here. Suffice to say that the results were not favourable to the Earps and, regardless of considerable sympathy for the stricken Virgil, they and their supporters found themselves in a weakened position. Many people had lost faith in the brother's brand of law enforcement and clung to the perception of them being nothing more than hard vigilantes.

In contrast, Behan and his cronies were enjoying a new lease of popularity.

January saw a flurry of action in various ways. More stagecoach robberies which were yet again, by some, muttered about as being the work of the Earps.

Anti Earp Milt Joyce was back in control of the Oriental which made Wyatt sell off his interest in the business. This was not such a loss to him as his focus was now very much upon getting justice for his brother. Gathering a posse of his chosen men he commenced a campaign of riding out in pursuit of those he felt to be guilty.

In the middle of January, there was almost another shootout which would have become legendary… had it actually come to the expected violent conclusion. Most of the detail is sadly lost, but Doc Holliday and Johnny Ringo almost drew on each other when they met in the street. It was a close thing with such enmity between them… their hands were on the butts of their pistols before they were separated by the fortunate close proximity of the law. Each of them was fined $32.

With Virgil still weak but on the mend, laid up at the Cosmopolitan, Wyatt felt ready to act. He and Morgan chose some deputies and managed to obtain warrants for the apprehension of the surviving Clanton brothers, Ike and Phin, and also Pony Diehl. They rode out with determination, making for the Cowboy haunt of Charleston where, with a captured Cowboy held at gunpoint as a human shield, they ran roughshod through the town searching for their prey. Miraculously, Charleston proved empty of any names on their list, so they moved on to scour the surrounding country beyond, which also proved fruitless.

Johnny Ringo was also being hunted by a separate posse on an unrelated charge of robbery. Avoiding the Earps, the Clantons gave themselves up to this posse feeling, sensibly, that it was by far the safer option. Ringo returned to Tombstone and surrendered to Behan, no doubt having reached the same conclusion, but... surprise, surprise... it came to nothing.

Wyatt's frustrated posse made it back to town to find the Clantons and Diehl facing a charge of the attempted murder of Virgil Earp, but it was a very temporary slice of satisfaction. All three of them were released owing to lack of evidence.

The Earps must have been wholly sickened by this. It was looking like a conspiracy with some kind of underhanded determination from corrupt officialdom to keep the Cowboys off the hook. They, the Earps, also felt that they were receiving too much criticism.

Demoralised, Wyatt and Virgil sent in written resignations from their roles as lawmen but U.S. Marshal Dake refused to accept them. A judge took Wyatt to one side and strongly inferred that these Cowboys would never face justice by legitimate means. He suggested that the only effective remedy would be to *"take them out in the brush where alibis don't count."*

This was food for thought indeed...

***

Surprisingly, and much out of character, Wyatt must have taken a very deep breath to reevaluate his entire view of the crisis.

He had choices to make.

Continue this feud via lawful means and expend energy pursuing men who would inevitably wriggle their way free from any legality?

Or bypass the law and seek personal retribution...

This was tempting, and justified in Wyatt's mind, but it went against the grain of the Earp's code. For all the suspicion and darker aspects of what the brothers may have been into, it does appear that when it came to law enforcement, they always went by the book.

True, Virgil had been gunned down, but at least he had survived, unlike the McClaurys and young Clanton. Looking at the bigger picture, the surviving Clantons, Will McClaury and their friends were only looking for the retribution that the Earps were now seeking.

And where would it end? Endless killing, a lifetime of having to look over one's shoulder...

There was one more choice... try to reason with his enemies, talk things through, reconcile differences and arrive at some kind of understanding so that everyone could move on. Incredibly, Wyatt actually suggested all this in a message to Ike Clanton and was promptly rebuked.

Ike made it clear that he had no intention of any interaction with the Earps and obviously had other solutions in mind. In fact he immediately tried to revive murder charges against them and Doc Holliday but this was quickly rejected on the grounds that the case had already been heard. This decision just further deepened Ike and Co.'s determination to make them pay, one way or another.

In the meantime, life went on. Snow fell and the battle of the newspapers resumed as those rival publications hammered away at each other with fresh daily accusations and insults. Wyatt rode out with another posse, possibly in search of Pony Diehl, plus anyone else he could pin down.

The Earp faction still maintained its solid fortress in their rooms at the Cosmopolitan. Virgil recuperating slowly with Allie attending to him, his brothers and their "wives" close at hand. Morgan was very concerned about his Louisa who was not dealing well with such threats hanging over the family. In February he persuaded her to travel by train to California so as to be under the protection of stern patriarch Nicholas Earp at the family homestead in Colton.

Wyatt and Mattie endured what must have been a highly strained relationship during this time but the pressure was lessened slightly when, by early in the new year, Sadie Marcus left town, returning to her own family in San Francisco.

As stated before, Wyatt was deeply preoccupied by the troubles which were assailing him from every side, but the presence and mutual interest of voluptuous Sadie must have been something of a relief. That said, her absence removed a complication but they were destined to meet again.

Johnny Behan followed her to San Francisco in March, presumably in the hope of rekindling their connection but he returned alone, rejected we can assume.

The youngest Earp brother, Warren, had been making more frequent and longer visits to Tombstone in support of his siblings and had been accompanying them on their posse rides. Unlike previous times, Warren was now seriously involving himself in the dangerous business of South Arizona.

Throughout that month of March, the oppressive and threatening atmosphere in town, and even outside, began to ease off. It seemed that major crime was taking a rest, posses were on patrol and outlaws appeared to have backed off, at least for the time being.

With spring approaching, the populace were beginning to relax. Perhaps the worst was over. Was true civilization really gaining the upper hand in Cowboy country?

Alas, it was to prove to be the calm before the storm.

***

Morgan Earp was the outwardly fun loving brother. He was as tough as any of them but apparently laughed and took it easy more than the others. Despite all the anxious pressure and dangers of the last few months, he still welcomed any excuse to cut loose and relax whenever possible.

The most seriously wounded of them in October, that nasty injury of his had taken a long time to heal and he probably still felt the effects of it. But he was out and about again now and seeking a little partying. Louisa was many miles away and he was missing her.

Saturday night, March 18th. '82. Wyatt was still the most vigilant amongst them and always had his eye on the shadows and around corners. It was true that things seemed calmer these days but Wyatt stressed that none of the family should let their guard drop. Johnny Ringo and Frank Stilwell were around town and had both made it known that there might be trouble brewing and that they would have nothing to do with it. Strange things to say… almost as if they were seeking to establish alibis.

Generally speaking, the main Cowboy suspects had been keeping a low profile of late but Wyatt was on the alert, as usual.

A new theatre company was making a one night visit to town to stage a performance of the comedy play *Stolen Kisses*. Morgan said he would like to see it but Wyatt had an uneasy feeling as he watched his brother make his way towards the theatre near the Schieffelin Hall. That stormy evening, scouting around Tombstone's streets, Wyatt had identified a few unwelcome faces who had not been seen for a while.

When Morgan left the theatre that night, in good spirits having enjoyed the show, a cautious Wyatt met him on the street, urging that they both make their way back to the hotel. Morgan was still lively however and suggested a game of pool before calling it a night. Wyatt gave in and agreed. Together they made their way across to Campbell & Hatch's cosy little pool room, sandwiched between the Alhambra Saloon and the Wells Fargo Office on Allen Street.

They met friends there... fellow posse members Dan Tipton and Sherman McMaster. Tipton was a fairly new arrival in town but McMaster had been around for quite a while. He had history as a Texas Ranger and known outlaw and had ridden on escapades with the Cowboys, but he was friendly with the Earps. It seems probable that he operated as an informer for them.

It was an amiable, small gathering. Late night chat and shooting some pool. Morgan pitted himself against owner Bob Hatch, each of them dab hands at the game. Wyatt took a seat to watch his brother play.

The room was well illuminated by bright lamps, especially above the baize of the pool table. A glass door at the rear of the room backed onto a darkened alley. The top half of the glass was clear, the lower section fogged by either ground glass or painted over... accounts differ.

It was shortly before 11.00pm. when Morgan, clutching his cue, strolled around to the end of the table, his eyes on the balls as he calculated his next shot. His back was to that glass door as he took the cue in both hands and moved to line it up.

The tranquil moment was abruptly shattered by a gun blast from the alley which smashed the glass, throwing Morgan face down onto the table. A spectator named George Berry cried out as the bullet took him in the leg, having ripped through Morgan's left lower back, exiting a few inches below the rib cage.

Within a second or two another shot flew through the door, the slug penetrating the wall just above Wyatt's head.

Everyone's first instinctive reaction was to dive for cover, but most were soon back on their feet, reeling from the horror of what had just happened. Wyatt rushed over to the table as his brother slowly toppled from it, hitting the floor awash with blood.

McMaster, Hatch and others made for the smashed rear door, throwing caution to the wind as they became aware of shadowy figures fleeing into the darkness. It would be pointless trying to pursue them so full attention turned to the wounded Earp.

Wyatt and others tried to lift Morgan up but the pain was too much for him and he begged them to stop. Even in his agony, a hint of his humour shone through as he weakly quipped that he had played his last game of pool.

They managed to move him to another room and lay him down where a trio of doctors attended him, but there was nothing they could do. Unlike the mistaken prediction when Virgil was shot, this time there was no mistake. The single bullet had inflicted immense damage, narrowly missing Morgan's spine but mangling his internal organs beyond repair. He was losing an enormous amount of blood and was in terrible pain but stayed conscious.

Wyatt remained close to him, exchanging as many words as possible. The rest of the family gathered there too… James, Bessie, Allie, probably Mattie, even Virgil apparently, but Warren was not in town that night. Louisa, of course, was many miles away in California and would hear the tragic news via a telegraph message.

What actually passed between them was never recorded in entirety but Wyatt himself left a few clues. One memory speaks of Morgan referring to his interest in spiritualism, reminding Wyatt of their promise to contact one another as to what could be seen at the point of death. It was said that Morgan gasped that he could not see a thing.

Aware that he was dying, Morgan also asked that Wyatt get those who had killed him. His hands soaked with his brother's blood, Wyatt promised that he would.

As he slipped away, Morgan, according to Wyatt, seemed comforted by this, whispering, *"That's all I ask… but Wyatt, be careful…"*

By midnight it was all over. Morgan breathed his last, aged thirty.

Another poignant fact, which almost seems to have been lifted straight from the pages of some melodrama, concerns the presence of a dog which was moping at the door of the room. It was an Earp family pet which they had collectively raised, and it began to whine and howl mournfully.

When Morgan's body was carried along to the Cosmopolitan, the dog followed, downcast and whining.

As they laid out the still warm corpse in the hotel in the early hours of Sunday March 19th., all the Earps must have realised that the date was significant.

No reason to celebrate now… but it was Wyatt's 34th. birthday.

CHAPTER 45
RIDING FOR VENDETTA

Morgan's murder was the most dramatic turning point in Wyatt's colourful life.

It changed his attitude to law enforcement overnight, immediately realising that there would be little point in trying to pursue retribution through legitimate means. He had been there too often. In his heart he knew who was responsible and there was enough suspicion and evidence to bring certain characters before a judge, but what would be the point?

Sheriff Behan had his own questionable agenda, more interested in lining his pockets than true justice. It was also obvious who his friends were and how he would do his utmost to protect them. The Cowboy fraternity would always come up with an alibi, backed by a strong element in town who watched their backs. Numerous hearings had come to nothing, so why should anything be any different now?

No, Wyatt had simply had enough and was not prepared to waste any further time on playing a losing game. The death of his brother made it all a deeply personal issue and he reacted with grim determination, especially because of the cowardly manner of the assassination. War had now undoubtedly been declared and he was prepared to meet fire with fire… literally.

On the very next morning, Wyatt must have given barely a thought to his birthday. Morgan's body had already been placed in a casket and, just after noon, a solemn procession transported it by carriage to the rail station at Contention. From here, James Earp was to accompany his brother's remains all the way to the family home in Colton, California, for burial.

Returning to Tombstone, Wyatt spoke to his brother Virgil later that day. They were both grief stricken but dealt with it by resolving to avenge Morgan without delay. Virgil was in agreement but his injury was life changing. There was no practical way he would be able to be of use on a vendetta ride anymore.

With a degree of reluctance, he saw sense in Wyatt's suggestion that he take Allie and follow Morgan's coffin to California. It would be safer and leave Wyatt free to concentrate on his hunt for the killers.

They were taking no chances. By night they made the journey, via Contention, to Tucson where they could join the train connection out to the west coast and safety. Wyatt would be going with them as far as Tucson, making sure they were well guarded by armed friends.

Warren was back with them now, also Doc Holliday, Sherm McMaster and John Johnson (later known as Turkey Creek Jack). Like McMaster, Johnson had also ridden with the Cowboys, acting as an informant for the Earps. Although their loyalties may have previously been a little shaky, Morgan's killing seems to have made the pair of them throw in their lot totally with Wyatt's cause.

In the darkness at Tucson's rail hub, the tracks and platforms lit by the yellowy glow of the town's newly installed gas lamps, the weapon heavy Earp party were tipped off that familiar Cowboys had been seen at the station, watching every connecting train that pulled in. With extra vigilance, Wyatt and the bodyguards escorted Virgil and Allie to a nearby hotel for supper.

When the California bound train was ready to leave, Wyatt's group made sure that Virgil and Allie were securely ensconced in their carriage but were concerned by the way they were so well lit through the window as targets for any skulking assassins. Allie carried Virgil's gunbelt, his pistol loose in the holster. Virgil's one good hand was closeby. The train was about to leave as Wyatt, Warren, Doc and the others fanned out, their eyes scouring faces and shadows.

The engine hissed, steam billowed, as Wyatt's keen gaze spotted a couple of figures lying prone on a nearby flat car. He saw their gun barrels pointed towards his brother illuminated inside the train carriage. One of the men was definitely Frank Stilwell and the other, Wyatt thought, probably Ike Clanton... both men at the top of Wyatt's list.

Seeing Wyatt rushing towards them, his shotgun raised, the would be shooters jumped up and fled. Wyatt stayed with them but one was faster than the other. Stilwell lagged behind and turned to face Wyatt as he caught up with him. It must have been a moment of satisfying triumph for that vengeful deputy marshal. This time there would be no arrest to wriggle away from.

Wyatt's account of what happened next is rich with his vengeful pleasure, speaking of how Stilwell stood trembling in terror, making no attempt to defend himself. *"What a coward he was..."* Wyatt recalled grimly, *"... he who killed my brother..."* The Cowboy who had taunted the Earps for so long could do nothing more than reach out and grasp the barrels of Wyatt's levelled shotgun, knowing that his fate was sealed. As the rest of his avenging party caught up and gathered around, Wyatt pulled the double triggers, a short range blast which must have virtually cut the victim in two. Judging by the state of the corpse when it was studied later, it seems that the others joined in for their own amusement. A witness remarked that Stilwell was *"the worst shot-up man I ever saw"*.

With his blood lust up, Wyatt turned his attention to Ike Clanton, as he was sure that he was the other fleeing Cowboy, but he had managed to get away. Other Cowboys were also believed to be present but had all managed to melt into the night.

Virgil and Allie, still seated in the carriage, heard the shots just as the train began to move out of the station. They could see no clues in the surrounding darkness until, it was said, Wyatt appeared, sprinting alongside the moving carriage, mouthing the words to his brother, *"One for Morgan!"*

Wyatt had crossed the line and there could be no doubt that Stilwell's killing had been in cold blood. The vengeful brother made no attempt to deny it, nor to make it known that he intended to do it again… and again… as soon as he got the chances. The stern, tough lawman who had so often avoided gunplay and stood between vigilantes and their intended victims was now out for blood.

Pima and Cochise counties were in uproar. The newspapers called out for justice but the Earp supporters maintained that the killing had been justified. Virgil was swift to state that without such drastic action, he would have been the victim himself that night. The swiftly convened inquest, which included Ike's usual unsound and absurd claims of innocence and victimization, resulted in a warrant for the arrest of Wyatt, Warren, Doc, McMaster and Johnson for murder.

The coroner's inquest on the killing of Morgan took place at around the same time in Tombstone and it was to reveal some startling new information. The Mexican wife of another Cowboy suspect, Pete Spence, had turned against him, largely it seems because he beat her and generally treated her badly. She testified that she felt sure her husband and Stilwell were involved in Morgan's murder, judging by their behaviour on the night of the shooting. She named others too, including Florentino "Indian Charlie" Cruz. Her mother verified the claim.

Terrified, and for his own safety, Spence gave himself up and was locked in Sheriff Behan's jail. It says a lot about Behan when he allowed Spence to keep a pistol in his jail cell out of fear of a possible assault from the Earps.

A wire was received from the Justice of the Peace in Tucson stating that Wyatt and his friends were wanted in his town for the murder of Frank Stilwell. Behan was told that he had to arrest them. Always a little nervy about this sort of thing, Johnny B., dithered but informed his deputies, Breakenridge and Dave Neagle, that they had best get on with it.

Wyatt and the other wanted men had returned to the Cosmopolitan and were already virtually ready to saddle up and continue their Vendetta Ride, as it became known. That evening, just as Wyatt, Warren, Doc, McMaster and Johnson came out of the hotel on their way to collect their horses, Behan and the deputies confronted them on the sidewalk. It was another tense meeting. Wyatt was not prepared to endure any complications or further hold ups which might get in his way and Behan recognised that. The Sheriff avoided mentioning any intention of arrest but merely told Wyatt he wished to see him. Wyatt responded that he had seen him once too often and just walked on.

Behan was to claim that the Earp party resisted arrest by drawing their guns but bystanders seem to corroborate the first version. Wyatt's men were soon on horseback and cantering out of town, *en route* to carve the next chapter in the Arizona war. This time they had been joined by Texas Jack Vermillion, an ex deputy of Virgil's who had probably known Wyatt and Doc since Dodge City days. He was a wild hombre who wore his hair flowing across his shoulders Wild Bill style and was said to be a deadly pistoleer.

Jim's Bessie and Wyatt's Mattie left town soon after, taking the train to California. The Earp's physical Tombstone connection was now history.

***

Late morning, Wednesday March 22nd. The Vendetta riders rode purposefully towards their first port of call; the logging camp which Pete Spence managed in a pass on the south side of the Dragoon Mountains. Presumably they were unaware of Spence's incarceration in Behan's jail because Wyatt confronted the workers there to ask his whereabouts. Told that he was not around, further questions were asked… how about Hank Swilling, another suspect? Wyatt knew that this camp was a popular rendezvous for Cowboys when up to no good.

At least one of Earp's targets was in the vicinity… Indian Charlie, watching nervously from the top of a hill. Realising the fierce looking bunch were after him, he began to run. Wyatt's group turned their horses, spreading out as they rode up the slope in pursuit. Some witnesses said they opened fire as Indian Charlie ran, leaping from side to side as he desperately tried to dodge the bullets.

Wyatt was convinced that Charlie had acted as lookout on the night of Morgan's murder and that was enough to justify a death sentence. The riders easily caught up with him and he was at their mercy. Conflicting versions of how Florentino "Indian Charlie" Cruz died are all we are left with, but the outcome was pure fact. Wyatt may have questioned the terrified Cowboy, obtaining a confession and gleaning further information. One story claimed that Wyatt gave him a chance to live by challenging him to a duel, but that is highly unlikely. Most probably Indian Charlie met his end in a barrage of shots fired *en masse*, an undeniable execution.

Workers at the camp described how the Earp party calmly rode away, obviously satisfied with their grim work. Whether or not their victim had spoken before his death, Wyatt was sure of his next targets, the men who had been in that alley when that bullet had killed Morgan. Not just Indian Charlie, Hank Swilling, Spence and Stilwell, but the obvious ones like Johnny Ringo and Curly Bill Brocius. And surely Ike Clanton must have had quite a role to play...

Back in Tombstone, Behan was receiving criticism for failing to arrest the Vendetta Riders before they set out on their deadly mission. Many former Earp supporters were now doubting his methods, feeling that he had gone too far, no matter what the justification. Most newspapers railed against the Vendetta Ride, except the *Epitaph* which still boldly made excuses. In San Francisco, officials of the Wells Fargo Company openly defended their former highly respected employee Wyatt, praising his dignity and courage, backing him for doing what the law seemed unwilling to do. They also dismissed all those allegations of Wyatt's involvement in robbery of their stagecoaches. Others like Sheriff Bob Paul were sympathetic too, but not quite so vocally.

Behan had to be seen to take action so he formed a posse to supposedly hunt down the Earps. Some of those he deputised raised a few eyebrows... men such as Phin Clanton and Johnny Ringo. They took to the trail at the same time as another posse from Charleston, this one made up totally of about a score of Cowboys led by Curly Bill. Brocius claimed his men had been officially deputised by Behan, although the slippery sheriff later denied it. Ike must have been floating somewhere in the midst of all this.

Behan had also made an effort to make a point by arresting two of Wyatt's supporters, Dan Tipton and Charlie Smith, on dubious charges that didn't stick.

***

Galloping around the hills and back country, sleeping under the stars beside open fires, Wyatt and his men needed practical finance to keep going. He sent word to friends to arrange a loan of $1,000 from a sympathetic businessman, a sum which was to be brought to Wyatt for collection at a remote watering hole. This was Iron Springs on the lower slopes of the Whetstone Mountains, a few miles to the south west of Contention.

Leaving Warren Earp behind to scout for any sign of an approaching messenger with the cash, the remainder of Wyatt's riders cantered on towards Iron Springs, approaching from another direction to avoid any possible clash with a posse.

A description of what happened next can be found in the opening of this section of this book, but here I will add a little further detail...

When Wyatt and Texas Jack, with the others lagging a short way behind, approached the watering hole, they were faced by several of Curly Bill's posse, surprising them as they relaxed on the bank beneath the trees. Apart from Brocius himself, accounts agree that other Cowboys present were Pony Diehl, Johnny Barnes, brothers Milt and Bill Hicks, Frank Patterson, "Rattlesnake" Johnson and the Lyle brothers, Ed and John.

As described earlier, the opposing sides commenced blasting away at each other from pretty short range. As Wyatt dismounted and grabbed his shotgun, Texas Jack's horse went down, trapping its rider beneath its bulk.

Wyatt's recollections spoke of how he was sure his time had come but that he was determined to take at least Curly Bill with him. This he managed to do in part, responding to the outlaw's shooting (which shredded Wyatt's coat tails) with a double blast which knocked the Cowboy down by the water's edge. Wyatt recalled that he *"yelled like a demon"* as he fell.

Wyatt tossed aside his spent shotgun but was unable to free his rifle from his rearing horse. Instead he managed, with difficulty, to draw a pistol from his drooping gunbelt and exchange fire with the remaining Cowboys. Yet again, Wyatt's uncanny luck held. Curly Bill's gang were blasting away, the air thick with gunsmoke, and maybe this helped to divert their aim. As for Wyatt, his cool and collected persona paid off as he took his time to send a pair of shots which found their mark, hitting Milt Hicks in the arm and fatally wounding Johnny Barnes.

Finally managing to remount his terrified horse, Wyatt made his escape with Texas Jack clinging on behind him, Cowboy bullets blasting harmlessly into their raised dust.

Wyatt and Texas Jack, double mounted, rejoined their fellow riders further back along the trail. Relief was expressed all around but Wyatt was none too pleased that his friends had high tailed it just when they were needed.

Doc Holliday was pleased to find his friend unharmed save for a ripped coat and numb leg, caused by a bullet striking his boot heel. The deadly dentist felt sure that Wyatt must have been *"shot all to pieces"*. Anxious to make amends for not staying by his side, Doc suggested that they all ride back and make a charge against the remaining Cowboys but Wyatt declined. He had done his part for the day.

Back at the waterhole, the surviving Cowboys were taking stock. Curly Bill dead, Johnny Barnes nursing a wound which would eventually see him off, Milt Hicks clutching his punctured arm… it had been quite a price to pay for tangling with Earp. The posse remained where they were for a while, trying to decide on their next move when another pair of riders approached them. The Cowboys levelled their guns again, recognising these newcomers as familiar faces… "Austrian" Kraker and "Whistling Dick" Wright. The atmosphere relaxed and the two men sat down to eat with the Cowboys who were still reeling from the shock of the unexpected gunfight. Kraker and Wright managed to hide the real reason for their presence there, convincing Diehl and Co. with a false story about searching for lost mules. In actual fact, the two men were carrying the $1,000 which had been promised to Wyatt. Naturally, they kept quiet about that as they listened to the Cowboy's account of the recent shootout before returning to Tombstone with the money intact.

Many inaccurate and fanciful versions of the gun battle rapidly began to circulate in the pages of publications far and wide… not least of all the *Nugget* and *Epitaph*. The former even claimed that Wyatt himself had been gunned down.

All the papers went into overdrive either praising or condemning Earp's effective methods.

Although the certain details of the Iron Springs battle were shrouded in controversy, the most viable evidence does appear to verify the version outlined in these pages, but some sources sought to find advantage in stating differences. The Cowboys present at the shootout obviously discussed the best course of action. They almost certainly buried Curly Bill at some remote spot and decided that admitting he was dead would not further their cause. Instead, it seems they decided to deny it, starting a campaign to claim that he was still alive and kicking. One motive for this would have been a refusal to allow Wyatt any credit for killing their leader, and to stop him from collecting the $1,000 reward which had been put up by the Cattle Grower's Association.

The *Nugget*, in particular, backed this claim, underlining alibis which denied he was even in the county at the time. They even printed the offer of a $1,000 grant to anyone who could supply definitive proof of Curly Bill's death, a ploy which was outmatched by the *Epitaph*'s response... $2,000 for charity if Brocius himself were to turn up in person at their office to prove that rumours of his passing were somewhat exaggerated!

No claimants, alive or dead, were to appear.

So, did Wyatt really kill Curly Bill? Most reliable sources would agree he did, endorsed by several of those who were there... even the mortally wounded Johnny Barnes. The other Cowboys tried to stay silent, spreading rumours of how their leader had lit out for Texas, or maybe Colorado, using the false news of his death to cover up his disappearance so that he could start anew with a clean slate.

This would have been a most unlikely course for a brash, over the top character like Curly Bill to take. Not like him at all. He loved the limelight, and, remember, there was not even a warrant out for his arrest. It simply does not ring true that such a personality, who made preachers dance to gunfire, shot up towns and forced Mexican party goers to cavort naked, would just disappear into a life of low profile.

I think we can be pretty sure that Curly Bill's remains are buried somewhere out near the Whetstone Mountains.

CHAPTER 46
ARIZONA FAREWELL

Wyatt's riders rode back towards Tombstone, reuniting with Warren and being joined by Charlie Smith. Naturally, they could not risk going back into town, so they headed again for the Dragoon Mountains where they searched a train at Summit Station in the hope that someone might be on board with the promised loan. There wasn't, so their next stop was a small ranch run by some sympathetic brothers. Unfortunately, these brothers, though affable, were afraid of repercussions should Cowboys hear that they had helped the Earps. Although pretty desperate by now for fresh mounts and a decent night's rest, Wyatt and Co. understood and rode on.

They pushed north, urging their exhausted horses to the extreme until they reached a more welcoming greeting at Henry Hooker's vast Sierra Bonita Ranch.

54 year old, grizzled veteran Hooker was very much on Wyatt's side. He was heartily sick of the Cowboy's antics and the trouble they had caused him over the last few years, decimating his herds so blatantly. The Earp faction were fed and watered and were able to rest properly for the first time in several days, as well as trading their spent horses for fresh ones.

Wyatt was not able to enjoy the well earned rest for long. Word came of approaching riders who proved to be Sheriff Behan's dogged posse. Viewing the distant dust cloud, Hooker made it clear that he had no fear of any threat from Behan and that the Earps should not feel the need to hide. A gun battle seemed likely but Wyatt had no wish to involve his host unnecessarily. Instead he took his party out to a bluff a few miles away where he would await an attack from the posse in a prepared and neutral defensive position.

Behan, Harry Woods and their men arrived at Hooker's ranch house with an attitude but the veteran rancher was not in the least bit intimidated.

The sheriff asked for information about the Earp's whereabouts but Hooker said he didn't know and would not tell even if he did. Behan tried accusing him of covering for *"murderers and outlaws"* but Hooker stubbornly replied that he had no problem with the Earps. With a disdainful look at Behan's companions, Hooker made a point of *"damning"* this posse and referring to them as *"cut-throats and horse thieves"*.

Taking offence, one of Behan's men cursed the rancher and

suggested forcing information out of him. Big mistake. Hooker was surrounded by his own men and his ranch foreman stepped forward with a levelled Winchester, calling out the loudmouth for daring to insult a gentleman on his own property. He added, forcefully, that they could get themselves a fight *"right here"* before they found the Earps.

At this, Behan back-pedalled a little to defuse the growing tension, even making a remark that he was only associating with such types out of necessity!

Hooker agreed that if this was the case, he would feed Behan and Woods at one table whilst the others, the Cowboy faction, sat separately!

Unable to get useful support from Hooker, Behan's posse carried on up to Fort Grant where they requested the loan of Apache army scouts, but the Colonel there, when hearing of Hooker's stand, refused to cooperate.

Somewhat demoralised, the sheriff and his men made their way back to Sierra Bonita where Behan told Hooker that he was heading back to Tombstone, having already run up a huge expenses bill for Cochise County during his ten day pointless pursuit. Hooker would later comment that he felt that the posse was *"willing to ride in any direction... except where the Earps were waiting for them!"*

Guns at the ready, Wyatt and his group watched and waited patiently from their nearby position on that bluff, but were surprised to see Behan's large dust cloud disappearing in the opposite direction. When certain that the posse had gone, the Earps returned to the ranch house where Hooker told them the whole story.

Wyatt and his friends could relax properly now and they spent the next few days doing just that. Hooker said that he actually offered Wyatt the Cattle Grower Association's $1,000 reward for killing Curly Bill but that Wyatt had graciously turned it down. Apparently, he was grateful enough for Hooker's support and hospitality. He was also said to have declared, *"I don't want any reward for carrying out my promise to Morgan."*

However, Dan Tipton soon turned up at the ranch carrying the $1,000 which Wyatt was supposed to have received at Iron Springs. Then another courier arrived with yet another $1,000, this time a grant from the Wells Fargo company.

Financially sound and well rested, the Vendetta Riders took the time to compose a mischievous letter to send to the *Epitaph*, in response to Harry Wood's biased account in the *Nugget*. The educated and tongue in cheek style of the missive does suggest that it was penned by Doc Holliday, maybe. It was full of artistic licence, designed to downplay any wrongdoing and protect those who had helped them. It was signed, impishly, by *"One of Them"*.

Whatever plans were made at Hooker's ranch relating to a continuance of the Vendetta Ride have never really come to light. Had they achieved enough of their goal? Were they content with the victims they had already claimed? Had they made their point?

Of course, most of those deemed responsible for Morgan's murder were still at large... especially the remaining Clantons and Johnny Ringo... but Wyatt had certainly struck some blows. Could he be satisfied with things as they stood? Could he continue to play this dangerous and difficult game with more than half the county out for his blood?

Years later, Wyatt stated that there were further "skirmishes", but no details have survived. If there were any more confrontations between posses or individuals then they cannot have been very significant. It is worth noting though that Frank Stilwell's brother, "Comanche Jack", had arrived in Tombstone, anxious to avenge the killing of his sibling. Jack was a tough customer, renowned as an Indian fighter, and when he joined the Cowboy posse on the trail of Frank's killers, it kind of balanced out the level of who was most justified in carrying out a vendetta. Maybe Wyatt's passion for vengeance was tempered a little by the arrival of a man who could match him... maybe...

What we do know is that Earp's riders called in at Fort Grant where the Colonel made a less than half hearted effort to arrest them, acting on the warrant which he was obliged to fulfil. Wyatt dealt with some official business, compiling documents to transfer the deed of his Tombstone property to his surviving sister Adelia.

With no attempt to stop them, the Earp party carried right on up to Silver City, New Mexico, so they were obviously intent on putting distance between themselves and Arizona. With some of them giving false names, they sold their horses and travelled on, by stagecoach and train, to Albuquerque.

They hung around town for about a week during which time Wyatt agreed to interviews with a couple of local newspapers on the condition that his location not be identified until he and his friends had managed to secure a safe refuge from their enemies. The press were complimentary of their behaviour, praising the courteous, low profile they kept whilst in town. One exception was when a drunken and out of order Doc Holliday fell out with his friend Wyatt. The source of the argument is not clear but Doc's remarks about some issue, were enough to drive a wedge between them and Doc left town with Dan Tipton, heading for Denver, Colorado.

The posse continued to drift apart. Smith left at some point, with Sherm McMaster and Turkey Creek Johnson following suit. This was just after they all travelled by train into Colorado where they set up camp on the outskirts of Trinidad, leaving Wyatt, Warren and Texas Jack to decide on their next move. There would be no pressure on them there as the City Marshal was their stalwart friend Bat Masterson.

Gunnison was their next stop, in early May, where they continued to bumble along under the radar on the perimeter of the town. Wyatt could not resist involving himself in a saloon where he was soon running a faro game.

At this time, Wyatt, having cooled down from his initial vengeful fury, was beginning to consider his future again. He had no desire to burn *all* those bridges he had built in Tombstone; the mining interests, the land deals, the numerous useful and largely still supportive connections he and his brothers had worked so hard to create over the last couple of years.

That spring of '82, the situation remained too hot for him to risk a return to town, with a warrant out for his arrest and teams of armed men on his trail. But, time could be a great healer and he held out hope that, by the fall, he would have secured an official pardon which would allow him to get back to his old stamping ground. He even had plans to officially run for sheriff and finally take the role from the troublesome Johnny Behan. True, there would still be those around who would never forgive him, but, once back in an accepted official capacity, he felt that would be something he could easily handle.

In the meantime, Doc Holliday had found himself up to his neck in trouble again, having made his way to Denver where he was arrested at gunpoint by a man named Mallen, who turned out to be a bogus lawman. This situation makes an interesting tale in itself, but I will not go into it here as it would be too much of a digression. Suffice to say that, following a complicated legal wrangle which Bat Masterson instigated, Doc wriggled off the hook yet again and made his way to Gunnison where he reunited with Wyatt in June.

Their friendship was still intact, the breathing space between them having helped. As previously stated, the reason for their falling out is vague, but it may have been over remarks which Doc had made about Wyatt's relationship with Sadie. Holliday was a typical southern "gentleman" at heart, with some deeply ingrained racial issues. Sadie was Jewish and, when drunk, Doc let his real feelings slip, accusing his friend of having turned into a *"damned Jew Boy!"* Wyatt was understandably pretty offended by this, thus the rift, but Doc was back now, all forgiven. As it turned out, he did not stick around for long and was moving on again within a couple of weeks.

The months went on and it eventually became apparent that the Earp influence in Tombstone was all but spent. From a distance, the brothers got the message that their absence had resulted in the almost total erosion of all that they had achieved there. Tax demands melted their mining concessions and all their other interests were soon swallowed up in the chaos of rival political ambition. Not being on the spot, they were helpless to do anything about it.

By the end of the year, it was obvious to Wyatt and Warren that there was no way they could return. Instead they travelled to San Francisco on the Pacific Coast to visit Virgil who had been seeking expert medical advice about his useless left arm. The three brothers shared lodgings in the city where they no doubt indulged in the pleasures to be found in such a lively metropolis, Virgil having already been in trouble for running an illegal faro game. This was very much Wyatt's area of expertise and he would have become involved, obviously. Another obvious route for him would be to seek out the charms of his Tombstone dalliance, Miss Josephine "Sadie" Marcus, who was still in town. Having shown Behan the door. Sadie welcomed her tall, stern, blonde haired flame keenly. She possessed that rare talent of being someone who could coax a smile, even an occasional rye laugh, out of him.

About 400 miles away, at the Earp family residence in Colton, Wyatt's Mattie waited… and waited… he was in no hurry to rekindle his responsibility to her.

CHAPTER 47
A NEW LIFE

Tombstone was undergoing many changes which within a few years transformed everything which had created the heart and soul of this unique town.

Apart from the arguments between the rival political factions, a catalyst was reached when, in May '82, yet another fire devastated the central district destroying many of the key establishments. Major hotels were swept away, including the former Earp headquarters at the Cosmopolitan, also the Eagle Brewery and the offices of the *Nugget*. This was symbolic as that paper's owners had recently purchased the *Epitaph*. With republican editor Clum replaced by the democrat Sam Purdy, there was no need for the *Nugget* anymore but attacks on the Earps, and all they had stood for, trundled on for months to come.

Cowboy activities continued but lost impetus, kicking off a long decline which would reduce their influence to virtually zero.

Most of their main players were gone anyway, leaving the territory, driven out by encroaching "civilization" or falling victim to their own code of violence.

Johnny Ringo suffered an abrupt exit from the scene. He had ridden out of Tombstone's July 4th. fiesta celebrations, still drunk and festooned with liquor bottles. Deputy Billy Breakenridge spoke of having seen him a few days later, reeling in the saddle out in the hills, and tried to convince him to end his lone ride. Ringo was known to suffer from bouts of depression and morose ramblings but he stubbornly rode on.

At a ranch close to West Turkey Creek Canyon in the Chiracahua Mountains, about sixty miles east of Tombstone, workers heard a single shot in the middle of the afternoon. It had come from just a few hundred feet away, and the next day Ringo's body was found in most peculiar circumstances.

Five oak trees clustered together, their roots partially entangled above ground and with a large, flat rock in the centre, created a kind of natural throne upon which sat the sun blackened body of Johnny Ringo.

The gunman's Colt .45 was clutched in his limp hand, the hammer resting on an empty chamber. There was a neat bullet hole in his right temple, the shot having exited through the back of his head. Strips of cloth had been torn from his undershirt and wrapped around his bootless feet, as if he had walked a short distance like that. And, for some unexplained reason, his cartridge belt was buckled upside down around his waist.

Stranger still, cut marks to his head suggested that there might have been an attempt to scalp him.

Finally, his horse was found over a week later, just a few miles away, with his boots slung across the saddle.

Ringo was buried at the base of the trees where he was found.

Lack of powder burns seemed to negate the solution that he had shot himself, although he had darkly spoken of suicide on several occasions. Such was the official verdict, but the mystery became a huge topic of theoretical debate. Had Ringo actually fallen before the pistol of one of his enemies? The return of Doc Holliday perhaps? It was even suggested that Wyatt had slipped back into Cochise County to carry out another part of his vow and take revenge on a key player in Morgan's murder. Over the years, it was reported that Wyatt himself confessed to Ringo's shooting but that notion is laced with doubt.

In more modern times, a lot of researchers seem to believe that the culprit was probably Buckskin Frank Leslie, who may have done it in an attempt to curry favour with the Earps.

Who knows?

Johnny Behan's fortunes took a nosedive when he did badly in the nominations to be re-elected as sheriff of Cochise County. By November he had been ousted in favour of Larkin Carr.

Also that month saw the end of another prominent figure from the Earp days.

Billy "the Kid" Claiborne had left Tombstone for a while after his sensible decision to dodge out of the firing line in the shootout which had seen off his friends Billy Clanton and the McClaurys. Returning to town, it seems that he became obsessed with the popular idea that Buckskin Frank had killed Johnny Ringo, another friend.

At around seven one morning, probably filled with drunken courage, Claiborne confronted Leslie in the Oriental, lambasting him with accusations and insults. Frank led the belligerent young Cowboy out onto the street in an attempt to cool things down, but it led to Claiborne raising his Winchester and opening fire.

He missed but Buckskin Frank's pistol response did not. "Kid" Claiborne died a few hours later.

***

Wyatt and Sadie rekindled their prior romance in the bright lights and good times of San Francisco. By now it was certain that they had made the decision to contemplate a solid future together. With Mattie well and truly sidelined, Wyatt made his way back to Gunnison with Sadie at his side to continue his role as a faro dealer.

It was becoming more and more apparent that Wyatt was happily leaving his old way of life behind. He no longer wished to carry the badge of a lawman, putting his survival on the line in the sights of newly acquired (as well as previous) enemies. But, before long, another appeal from an old friend, which twisted his conscience, forced him back.

Memories of Dodge City recalled him to Kansas where a complicated series of events, involving close comrades Luke Short and Bat Masterson, required his assistance. Yet again, the extent of this situation is beyond the scope of this book, but it involved Short's confrontation with the mayor owing to an attempt to run Luke out of town and shut down various businesses. Tempers grew heated, threats were made, and it culminated in a potentially nasty conflict which became known as the *Dodge City War*. Some of the good time girls at Short's Long Branch Saloon were arrested.

Short was having none of it. Enraged at the trumped up charges, which he felt were unfairly victimising him, he took his revolver to the jailhouse where a terrified town clerk panicked and took a potshot at him. The bullet missed, but as the clerk turned, ran and tripped, Luke returned fire, thinking that he had hit him. Short then barricaded himself in the Long Branch until he was convinced that no one had been hurt.

As the situation grew close to boiling point, Short, forced out of town, called for the help of old friends who he knew could help him handle things. Wyatt arrived in Dodge backed up by several hard cases like Texas Jack, Charlie Bassett and others. Sworn in as deputies by a sympathetic local constable, they made a formidable force for Luke Short's cause, especially when Bat Masterson joined them.

When interviewed about their purpose, Wyatt played it down in his customary cool way but the presence of all these renowned toughs was intimidating. Eventually, under the cloud of this threat, the mayor and his council backed down, the businesses were allowed to re-open and the crisis was over before another shot had been fired.

It was June 1883, and to celebrate, Wyatt and several members of their "Peace Commission" visited a photographic gallery to have that famous picture taken.

Back in Gunnison, Wyatt and Sadie were soon travelling again; the start of a long period when they seemed unable to settle. It was if they were in constant search of somewhere to plant roots, but that was a long time coming. They drifted through settlements all over the far west, gambling, staking mining claims which seldom paid off and keeping their eyes open for opportunities.

By 1884, Wyatt's brother Jim joined them in Idaho to pursue the possibilities of striking it rich in the Couer d'Alene gold rush. Alongside a creek in the small town of Eagle City they set up a circus style tent which they ran as the White Elephant Saloon and Dance Hall, a popular house of fun for the hordes of miners who were swamping the area. This was Wyatt's particular forte for making money, although he did make forays into mining which often led to accusations of lot jumping and various other legal complications.

As if this wasn't enough, the restless character of Wyatt Earp was tempted, yet again, to wear a lawman's badge, taking on the part time role of deputy marshal for the county of Kootenai. The town, like any of its kind, had its share of trouble, but nothing like Wyatt had experienced in his previous jobs. There was a touch or two of gunplay which Wyatt resolved without having to resort to drawing his own pistol. In fact he acquired a fresh reputation as a man of reason whose skills in diplomacy and bare faced courage drew admiration from far and wide. When the bullets flew, he could be in the middle of it and yet emerge the victor without getting violently involved.

In fact, this latest gold rush was not to last for long and the Earps uprooted themselves again to search for new adventures. Via El Paso, Texas, Aspen, Colorado and across to San Diego, California, Wyatt and Sadie chased their dream of making that elusive fortune. Wyatt's reputation and talents were such that he was never short of offers which came his way thick and fast... it was just that his many opportunities never seemed to blossom for long, his fortunes rising and falling like the ebbing tide. At one point he was approached by an Arizona lawman who wanted his help in assisting to arrest a stagecoach robber, a task which Wyatt carried out effortlessly.

***

Sometime in late '85 or early '86, the wandering couple were in Denver staying at the Windsor Hotel. Sitting in the foyer they were approached by an emaciated looking man, unsteady on his legs. As he joined them, a wide smile spread across his skull-like features. It was Doc Holliday.

Wyatt greeted his old friend warmly, the first time they had met since the troubles of '82. Doc's sandy hair was almost gone now in a sea of premature grey. His appearance was skeletal, his demeanour drained and weary, but he was obviously overjoyed by this meeting. He and Wyatt sat together and indulged in a lengthy bout of affectionate nostalgia which was only punctuated by Doc's continuous wracking cough. Obviously, his consumption had advanced to an extreme level, but he said that when he heard Wyatt was in town, he knew that he must make the effort to see him. It would almost certainly be the last chance.

Earp and Holliday had a special relationship, fuelled by Wyatt's gratitude for Doc having saved his life from those threatening drovers in Dodge all those years ago. Doc felt affinity for Wyatt, appreciating the fact that he was virtually the only soul who had stood by him over the years. In return, their mutual loyalty was solid.

Since their last meeting, Doc had continued to roam the west, getting himself in and out of trouble, including a gunfight or two. As his health rapidly deteriorated, he began to lose that edge with his gambling skills, gradually finding increased dependence upon whisky and laudanum to ease the outward effects of his painful symptoms. He was alone now and knew he was facing the end.

Wyatt was visibly moved and observed the irony of how, if it was not for Doc, he would not be alive today, and yet it was his loyal friend who *"must go first"*.

As Doc rose to leave, he placed a thin arm on Wyatt's shoulder.

Sadie wrote that his last words were. *"Goodbye, old friend… it will be a long time before we meet again."*

She also recalled how there were tears in Wyatt's eyes.

Following this poignant farewell, Doc spent some time in Leadville, but the high altitude gave him further problems. Somehow clinging to life, he sought relief by booking into the sanitorium at Glenwood Springs where the waters were said to have medicinal qualities. However, the sulfurous nature of the springs may have actually had an adverse effect on his ravaged lungs.

It was near to 10.00am. on November 8th. 1887 and his time had come. As he lay dying in bed, he asked an attentive nurse if he could drink a last shot of whisky and she, rather insensitively, told him he couldn't. This seemed to amuse him and he looked down at his bare feet. Weren't gunfighters supposed to pass over with their boots on?

"This is funny…" he grinned, weakly, just before taking his last breath.

He was 36 years old and had once been asked in an interview if he had a conscience about the wild side of his notorious life. His reply was, *"I coughed that up with my lungs long ago."*

Big Nose Kate later claimed that she was with him at the end but there is little evidence of that.

Wyatt would get the news a couple of months later.

***

Ike Clanton was to eventually get his comeuppance but not at Wyatt's hands.

By 1885, he and his brother Phin had gradually put distance between themselves and Tombstone, acquiring ranches close to the border of New Mexico. No doubt they would continuously be looking over their shoulders for the long shadow of Earp vengeance, but it did not halt their rustling activities.

In April '87, the Pinkerton Detective Agency was hired by the Apache County Stock Association to hunt them down. The team included an agent named Jake Brighton and they soon caught up with Phin who was jailed for his crimes.

Hot on Ike's heels, Brighton received information which led him to a ranch just south of Springerville where he and his men waited.

Ike came riding up to the ranch on the morning of June 1st. and was surprised to be greeted by the lawmen. Brighton called out to him to halt but he foolishly responded by turning his horse's bridle in an attempt to gallop away. As his mount gathered speed, Ike reached down to pull his Winchester from its scabbard. Raising the weapon, he was shot from the saddle before he could pull the trigger. By the time Brighton reached his body, sprawled in the dust, Ike Clanton had expired.

Phin Clanton was sentenced to ten years imprisonment but was released early on a technicality. He then raised goats with his friend Pete Spence (another unfulfilled name on the Earp list) near Globe. Apart from one or two further minor scrapes with the law, Phin contracted pneumonia and died in the early 1900s. Spence survived for a few more years and the outlaw friends lie buried side by side.

Wyatt's Tombstone connections were ebbing away, but there were none who must have played on his mind more than Mattie Blaylock; she who had unofficially taken on the mantle of "Mrs. Earp".

They had been together for several years, but Wyatt's loyalty to her was severely stretched as her laudanum reliance grew. Then, along had come Sadie and it did not take him long to decide who he would prefer to share his life with.

Mattie was a part of the close Earp family bond by now, however, and she received much sympathy from the womenfolk who felt protective of her. She could see that she was losing Wyatt and became increasingly pitiful; her neediness merely succeeding in driving him further away. This was complicated by the intensity of his troubles with the Cowboys during this time. That said, it does seem that his treatment of her left much to be desired. He lost patience and began to openly shun her, his methods, according to what evidence we have, being unnecessarily cruel. Wyatt's notorious cold streak was showing itself and any guilt he might have felt was well concealed.

When Mattie sought shelter in Colton with the bulk of the Earp brood, she would have received a level of solace, but Wyatt was blood so there was probably a limit to it. She waited to hear from him but his silence spoke volumes as he lived it up in San Francisco and other towns with Sadie on his arm.

Finally accepting that her relationship was over, Mattie left Colton in a state of drug fuelled depression and made her way to Globe, a popular destination for those with Earp connections. She returned to low level prostitution as a means to survive, but it was ultimately a sad and tragic existence.

She told her few remaining friends that she was *"tired of life"* and in mid summer '88 she overdosed on laudanum.

CHAPTER 48
BOXING AND PROSPECTING

When the news of Mattie's suicide reached Wyatt, it is probably fair to say that he did not mourn much. A tragic figure who had ended up as a thorn in his side, but they went back a long way. Of course, we cannot know the exact details of what went on between them, but it does appear that he could have dealt with the problem more sympathetically, being more straight with her, perhaps, instead of allowing her hopeless desire to drag on.

Whatever, although a sad kind of relief to Wyatt and Sadie, it was a dark cloud over their new happiness which was to dog them for the remainder of their lives, no matter how much they tried to forget it.

In the meantime, they enjoyed a four year stay in San Diego on the Californian coast which lasted until the dawn of the '90s.

This was a prosperous period for the Earp couple as they exploited the opportunities of a boom in land sales. Purchasing several properties, they were then able to rake in considerable profit from leasing out. Although it was a comfortably pleasant time for them, they did not acquire a huge fortune and Wyatt still felt the need to indulge in a spot of part time lawman-ship, helping out old friends like Bat Masterson when called upon. He also spread his time in various other pursuits which included running another saloon, managing stables and judging horse races. Racing became another passion for the aging lawman along with a newly acquired skill as a referee of boxing matches. He actually oversaw about thirty bouts during this time, as far out as Tijuana, but they were rough and tough contests and certainly not subject to the Marquis of Queensbury rules.

Wyatt was still a striking looking man, although a touch portlier now, with streaks of grey beginning to appear in his blonde hair and moustache. Sadie grew homesick and expressed a desire to spend time with her family again in San Francisco. They had made many trips there throughout their wandering years but now they settled, after a fashion, in a string of different accommodations.

Life in such a big city suited them and Wyatt became an accepted "man about town". He dressed the part in fine quality attire, tailored suits and even a derby hat. His fame as a Wild West legend remained quite strong and the newspapers still showed interest in the far away events of more than a decade previously. This was helped by the fact that Wyatt made a point of mixing in high brow circles which included the family of publishing giant William Randolph Hearst.

The Examiner (a Hearst publication) printed a three part series chronicling Wyatt's Wild West adventures, written in the sweeping, vainglorious style of the day but all helping to bolster his image.

The Earps ate in the finest restaurants and were often spotted at the race tracks of Oakland and Ingleside, rubbing shoulders with the fashionable sporting clique. They could hold their own in this company; never fabulously wealthy but well heeled enough to keep up appearances and fit in. Previously dry Wyatt also began to drink alcohol regularly, never to excess but enough to not stand out as a teetotaller in the crowd which he now blended with.

As their fortunes rose and fell, with the gambling that was the mainstay of their life, the Earps were always able to keep their heads high. And woe betide anyone who might get the mistaken impression that Wyatt Earp was growing soft. On more than one occasion it was reported that he physically took down anyone who dared to confront or belittle him. The old frontier spirit still burned strong.

And he was not above still taking on the odd freelance job which called upon his most basic skills; like as a guard for a payroll which had to make it through dangerous country.

Sadie was not happy with this and begged him not to do it, but he brushed her concerns aside. Deep down, he probably still needed this kind of thing in his life and he always won through unscathed.

When on a winning streak, Wyatt was generous and made a point of buying jewellery for Sadie. But Sadie had grown fond of the track herself and began to indulge in her own betting binges which were usually a disaster. She resorted to borrowing money from friends, even handing over her sparkly gifts as collateral. When Wyatt found out, he was not pleased, and, having bailed her out a few times, he gave her a strong lecture about mending her ways and to stop squandering their hard-earned cash. When it came to gambling, he knew what he was doing; she did not.

As a leading light in the sporting community, Wyatt was about to receive an offer which would result in probably the biggest regret of his life.

***

By the mid 1890's, boxing was a popular sport nationwide but officially illegal in most states. It had been around since the late 1700s, brought over from England, and gaining popularity throughout the following century. However, it was usually an underground activity in a brutal world of machismo, the opponents slugging it out bare knuckled in unofficial, backstreet venues and on board barges. There were no rules as such and it was a game for the hardest of men.

But it was a sport which grew and became so popular that the police and other authorities turned a blind eye to it, many of them becoming some of the most prolific bet placers.

"Gentleman Jim" Corbett battled his way to emerge as one of the leading lights as a fighter, winning the title of World Heavyweight Champion when, in '92, he knocked out John L. Sullivan in the 21st. round of their clash in New Orleans. These were the days before regulations had been founded under the boxing commission, so it was a free for all business when it came to contenders. Corbett actually became more interested in theatrical style demonstrations of his methods, reluctant and evasive when issued challenges. When he made it clear that he intended to retire from professional bouts (although he did eventually return), it left the way clear for separate arrangements to be made by those who wished to seize the title.

That was when Bob "The Freckled Wonder" Fitzsimmons became prominent on the scene. Fitzsimmons was an Englishman, raised in Cornwall, whose tough work at the family blacksmith's forge hardened him for his future career. Via moves through Australia, he found himself in the U.S.A. as an ambitious and formidable fighter. In 1896 he was 34 years old, just under six feet in height and in his prime, with an impressive record behind him. He already held the world middleweight title and now had his eyes on raising the bar.

Irishman Tom Sharkey, a sailor, was a few years younger than Fitzsimmons and about three inches shorter, but he was renowned for his incredibly broad shoulders and iron punch. Like Bob, he had many wins behind him and was reaching for the ultimate prize.

It was inevitable that they should meet in the ring, a much anticipated clash, and this was arranged and sponsored by the San Francisco Sporting Club towards the end of 1896. With Corbett off the scene, it was declared that this would be fought for the coveted title of World Heavyweight Champion at the city's Mechanic's Pavilion.

New rules were in place now. The recent acceptance of those refined by the Marquis of Queensbury had turned the art of boxing into a much more civilized sport, although it was still not for the faint hearted. Gloves, and no hitting below the belt were now officiated, for instance, but the matches could still go on for many rounds.

As the press grew excited around the activities of the two fighter's training regimes, disagreement arose over who should be chosen to referee this much anticipated clash of the titans. Fitzsimmons and Sharkey's people simply could not find someone who suited everyone. All suggestions were rejected for one reason or another until the sponsors themselves stepped in with a controversial solution.

How about a local, highly respected sporting gentleman; the "heroic, upright and honest" ex-lawman Wyatt Earp?

When approached, Wyatt was not initially keen. It had been years since he had refereed any boxing, and those he had were under very different circumstances to what was now being proposed. His experience had been in overseeing free for all brawls in mining camps, prairie settlements, railroad shacks and a host of other dodgy outlets, but this was something else altogether. A high profile, crowded event which was drawing the attention of the entire nation. And under these new Queensbury rules too. What did he know of those?

But the choice of Earp was seen as a compromise, an outsider who, it was thought, should not attract any kind of bias. Even so, the Fitzsimmons camp objected right to the end, beyond the eve of the match when it was too late for the consideration of anyone else suitable.

Wyatt reluctantly agreed but as soon as the announcement was made, word began to circulate that his appointment was suspicious... some kind of fix. It made for a most uncomfortable atmosphere as the huge event swung into being.

On the evening of Wednesday December 2nd., the stands of the Pavilion were packed to bursting point with an estimated crowd of ten thousand or more. The elite of San Francisco, the high fliers, politicians, police chiefs, judges and anyone with money had snapped up the expensive tickets, with everyone else packed in tiers behind, much of which had needed to be especially constructed to cope with the demand.

The atmosphere must have been buzzing, vendors made a killing, police officers with their tall, coned helmets and blue uniforms patrolling the crowds, watching for trouble in an event which, strictly speaking, had no legal status.

A few preliminary bouts stirred up the crowd, then shortly after 10.00pm. the opponents in the main event approached the ring. Right up until virtually the last minute their respective managers could be seen arguing about the choice of referee but the decision had been made.

Wyatt was also at ringside by now, well aware of the doubts his appointment had raised. Some said that he offered to step down but representatives of the Sporting Club insisted that he go ahead with his agreed duty.

With possible reluctance, Wyatt gave in and made to climb through the ropes. Seated in the front row, the city's police captain, Charles Wittman, spotted something which made him step forward to challenge the referee. Pointing to the bulge in Wyatt's pocket, Wittman asked if he was packing a gun.

Wyatt unhesitatingly admitted that he was and, at Wittman's stern request, surrendered a Colt revolver. Earp later said that he had simply forgotten he was carrying it, in contravention of the law, and this is possible considering that it was lifelong second nature for him to be so armed.

In the heat of the moment, with anticipation of the coming fight at fever pitch, the incident, though surprising, barely seemed to attract much attention. It would become an issue later, however.

From the opening bell, it seemed that Fitzsimmons had quite an edge over Sharkey, with Wyatt prowling around them, intently watching every move. For round after round, Fitzsimmons countered the sailor's assaults, gamely not getting riled by a string of fouls, but Sharkey put up a good fight. By the eighth round, it seemed pretty obvious that it was Fitzsimmons' bout, especially when he suddenly launched into a flurry of sharp and savage blows to the sailor's head and body. Sharkey was driven back against the ropes, shaken by a particularly vicious swing which Fitzsimmons followed up with a low jab.

Sharkey fell heavily to the canvas, curling up and crying out in agony. His team rushed into the ring as Fitzsimmons triumphantly played to the crowd who were cheering madly.

Intense moments followed as Wyatt briefly conferred with Sharkey's manager. Sharkey himself was being attended, lifted into a sitting position, obviously in terrible pain and unable to carry on fighting.

Wyatt made one of his instant, characteristic decisions and declared that Sharkey was the victor, Fitzsimmons being guilty of hitting below the belt, an indisputable foul.

A towel was waved over Sharkey's head to announce this result to the crowd and the response was instant confusion and disbelief. Uproar spread like wildfire through the benches and the crowd began to surge towards the ring, screaming their disapproval and outright fury at such an unexpected decision. How could Earp have possibly arrived at such a swift conclusion, flying in the face of popular opinion and shattering the expectations of thousands? How could a man who was being carried out of the ring be awarded the championship and $10,000 prize money when his opponent was fresh as a daisy and obviously the better man?

Fitzsimmons' manager and team immediately voiced their objections. Within seconds word was openly spreading of Wyatt having been part of a blatant fraud, a plot to fix the fight. No wonder he had carried a pistol into the ring, looking ahead to what could well happen following such a controversial outcome.

As pandemonium erupted, Wyatt nonchalantly ducked under the ropes and made his way unceremoniously through the mob before it was even noticed that he had gone. Leaving behind a scene of total disruption, he went home where Sadie said he seemed drawn and depressed. He had no regrets about the decisions he had made that night but certainly expressed a wish that he had never allowed himself to get involved in the first place.

The repercussions dragged on painfully. Within a couple of days, Wyatt was summoned to court and fined $50 for carrying a concealed weapon. Hearings and court appearances, instigated by the understandably miffed Fitzsimmons faction, took considerably longer.

Complications resulting from the technically illegal status of the whole event meant that the judge could not really make an official ruling, regardless of the many contradictory arguments. The outcome was that no one was actually disciplined on any account, and Sharkey was permitted to keep his prize money. As for Wyatt, he was mercilessly lampooned in the newspapers, including the indignity of seeing grotesque cartoon caricatures of himself as a figure of derision and fun.

So what was the truth behind all this?

Once again, it is something which is lost in the myriad of conflicting tales within history. The situation was a complex one and there seems little doubt that there was something untoward going on in the shady world of behind the doors dealings. It was a shadowy scene which ultimately bore little relation to sportsmanship and fairplay. Like in so much else where money rules, corruption was often the name of the game, the details of which lie hidden.

Did Wyatt allow himself to be corrupted, then? He was no angel and had a lifelong record of accusations which had more than a basis in truth, so, it is possible. Then again, perhaps he was out of his depth and duped, and was actually just a scapegoat in a conspiracy much larger than he realised.

Alternatively, maybe it was simply that Wyatt genuinely made the decision to declare Sharkey the winner because he thought it was the right one to make.

Whatever, as he got older it seems likely that he grew tired of these never ending clouds which darkened every enterprise he originally saw as his path to a brighter, more peaceful future.

It was time to move on again… to seek out a completely fresh and distant scenario.

***

In 1897/8, way up north on the shores of the freezing Bering Sea in Alaska, gold was discovered. As always with such strikes, this instigated an immediate mass influx of hopeful miners who, almost overnight, threw up a ramshackle, tented settlement which quickly morphed into the boomtown of Nome. At this time, the settlement was a long, skinny affair along the beach, just a couple of blocks wide and five miles long. It had an open sewer and diseases were rife.

Wyatt and Sadie had spent the previous year doing their best to ignore the controversy surrounding the Fitzsimmons/Sharkey fight but it just would not go away, nor ever really would. Earp's attempts to lose himself in other aspects of the sporting world, racing and gambling, were not really working and he needed to find an escape.

The Nome Gold Rush was just the opportunity he had been looking for and he and Sadie booked passage on a steamship to take them there with no further ado.

The primitive town was full of promise for a man with Wyatt's experience and he wasted no time in establishing saloons and gambling concessions. This was Wyatt back in a world he fully understood, taking a leading role amongst the frontier types he knew how to control, although it did take a year or two to become fully established. As a headquarters he went into partnership to build and run the Dexter Saloon in Nome itself, which proved to be a popular haunt for miner's recreation. It was the first double storied wooden building in town and the upper rooms were said to operate as a busy whorehouse, although Sadie always denied it. There was plenty of competition, however, with about sixty other drinking dens in operation. But the Dexter prospered and Wyatt even went back to some boxing refereeing on the premises.

Winters were savage in Alaska, making mining difficult, even impossible, so the Earps would sail back to San Francisco during these months to enjoy the money they had made. At the dawn of the 20th. century, Nome had expanded considerably and was drawing visits from celebrities. Consequently, Wyatt accumulated friendships with the likes of celebrated *Call of the Wild* author Jack London, as well as visits from old Tombstone friends such as John Clum and George Parsons whose detailed diaries furnish us with much detail about the Arizona years.

Of one affable meeting, Parsons wrote of spending a *"memorable time"* in the company of Earp and Clum, reminiscing the night away which *"… would have been worth $1,000 or more to the newspapers…"*

The years spent in Alaska, on and off, were generally fraught with difficulty for the Earps, regardless of their elusive successes. As was the usual case wherever they settled, they were local celebrities again with stories of Wyatt's colourful past never out of reach. Wyatt fed on this, as much as he could to his advantage, and they were well connected. Sadie, pushing forty, fell pregnant a couple of times but sadly suffered miscarriages, so the couple never had children.

Wyatt was in his early fifties by now but there appeared to be little sign of any dimming of his tough, steady frontier spirit. However, apparently he ended up in a barroom brawl on a visit to San Francisco during the spring of 1900. This came about following an argument he had with a well known figure from the racing world, a stubborn fellow named Tom Mulqueen. They disagreed over the merits of a jockey and it got nasty, resulting in Mulqueen knocking Wyatt out with a single punch.

This was an unusual result for a Wyatt Earp confrontation. Maybe it was the drink which he now partook of, maybe his age, maybe he was growing a tad soft… but it happened, they say. When he came to, Mulqueen had been ushered away and Wyatt was sent back to his lodgings in a street car.

Back in Alaska there were more scrapes and problems. An arrest for *"interfering with an officer while in the discharge of his duty"* but he was released without charge. Quarrels with saloon customers; even a report on the front page of a New York newspaper that Wyatt had been shot, but there is no substance as to where that came from. It was also reported that Wyatt was involved in dishing out a beating to a soldier in the Dexter, an incident which also ended up in court.

Wyatt also complained about Sadie's ongoing gambling which was haemorrhaging cash. She, in turn, accused him of carrying on with other women. It was a stormy time for the couple but they remained together.

Later in the year 1900, Wyatt received tragic news which, owing to the distance involved, had taken a long time to reach him.

In early July, his brother Warren had been shot dead in a saloon in Willcox, Arizona.

At 45, Warren was the youngest of the Earp brothers and, following the troubles of '81/'82, his life had become fairly aimless. Forced out of the Tombstone area, like all the vendetta riders, he returned to the town about a decade later, when the heat had died down. He worked as a stagecoach driver and, perhaps, a range detective for sympathetic rancher Henry Hooker, but Warren had issues. Off the backs of his more famous brothers, and maybe with echoes of resentment, the younger Earp developed something of an attitude towards others. He acquired a bullying manner, especially when drinking, and gained a reputation as one to avoid. His elder brother Virgil often spoke of his concerns that Warren's wild temper would get him killed one day.

Such was the case when he honed in on Johnny Boyett, Hooker's range foreman in Brown's saloon. Warren had been pushing Boyett all evening, it was said, the culmination of a long standing feud between them.

Boyett endured lengthy abuse but, eventually, it became too much. He opened up on Warren with a brace of pistols, missing several times. Warren kept coming at him, armed only with a knife, but a ball finally took him in the chest and he fell dead.

Boyett made himself scarce, fearing retribution, but it was only Virgil who made any attempt to follow things up. With one useless arm, he made the trip to Willcox to find out what he could but the trail was cold. For Wyatt, it was too far and too late. He let it go.

Yet another Earp had fallen to the gun.

CHAPTER 49

A TALE WORTH TELLING

The years were pushing in on Wyatt Earp but there was plenty of life left in the veteran adventurer yet.

By 1902 he and Sadie had left Alaska, but, by accounts, they came out of it with a reputed $80,000 or so, which was a considerable fortune back then. They probably felt that this nest-egg was enough to keep them stable for the foreseeable future, and so it should have been, but, as was the pattern with their escapades, the money soon dwindled as they dabbled in a string of further ventures.

An earlier plan to open a saloon in Seattle had failed and they carried on to Los Angeles to take stock, settling themselves for a few months in the Hollenbeck Hotel before trying their luck in the Nevada silver strikes. Wyatt opened another saloon and, as a sideline, served briefly as a deputy marshal in Tonopah but prospects were not as promising as hoped. They tried prospecting in the deserts of Esmeralda County but returned to L.A. in the winter when mining got too difficult, constantly on the move through various rented addresses. Wyatt staked many claims over a wide area, even nearly as far out as Death Valley, with varying degrees of modest success and, in this way, he and Sadie got by comfortably enough.

In 1905, when they were in Esmerelda County, they visited brother Virgil who had been hired as a deputy marshal for the area. Virgil was not the man he had been. Apart from his crippled arm, his general health had deteriorated and he was suffering from the effects of a mining accident which had crushed him in a tunnel. He contracted pneumonia and died that October. Wyatt was deeply affected having lost yet another close brother.

Sadie had a sister living in Oakland and she spent quite a bit of time staying with her as Wyatt took off chasing dreams all over the place. Although they always seemed to get back together, it appears there was a lot of friction between them. In appearance they were man and wife... Mr. & Mrs. Earp... with Sadie proudly stating that they had married many years ago on board a rich friend's yacht off the Californian coast. No official record of this has been found, however, so, as with most of the Earp siblings, it was probably a common law relationship.

"Mrs. Earp" did not care for her commonly held name of Sadie, preferring to be addressed by her actual name, Josephine. Wyatt had always called her Sadie, an annoyance she reluctantly got used to, but he probably continued to use it out of a little rebellious devilment. His "wife", after all, was beginning to become something of a pain as they grew older together. Plus her gambling habit had not lessened, putting a continual strain on their finances.

Wyatt was still game and went his own way, happy to gamble within his own limits and pursue his interests. He was never able to stay far away from his passion for upholding the law, regardless of his disappointments in the system over two decades before around Tombstone. Consequently, he remained open to offers which came his way from lawmen when they approached him for assistance based upon his long-held reputation.

At the age of 62, in 1910, Wyatt was hired by the LAPD as a kind of special duties officer, which meant carrying out tasks which were, technically, "outside the law", but it was in a very different world to the one he had once thrived in. Rickety motor vehicles were now beginning to replace horses and the "badmen" were a different breed to the Cowboys.

Part of Wyatt's job, along with another agent named King, involved tracking elusive criminals into Mexico and bringing them back, illegally, to face American justice without the lengthy process of extradition. Wyatt and King often operated in disguise for these missions and their success rate was high. This, after all, was very much Wyatt's bag… not quite like the old days, but as close as he could get in a modern world. They dealt with strike breakers too.

King's recollections of working with the aging Earp were not wholly complimentary, but he did say that he was *"… a fine man, one of the coolest… afraid of nothing."*

That October proved to be Wyatt's last known armed confrontation when he led a posse for the protection of a company who were trying to take control of potash mining claims. Another company had a more acceptably legal claim to these rights and they sent armed men to make their point. Wyatt's posse spread out in the brush during a long night awaiting their arrival in the wilderness of San Bernardino County.

In the cold light of day, Wyatt walked out to face them. Guns were drawn on both sides but the old lawman's persona dominated the proceedings, his opponent's side agreeing to his demand to back off. It was said that he may have fired a shot into the ground and had sternly grumbled that he had no desire for gunplay before breakfast!

Wyatt and some of his men were arrested for contempt of court but it went no further.

***

The following year, Wyatt was in trouble again, this time accused of attempting to work a confidence trick to fleece money from a real estate agent. It was a complicated business involving Wyatt's long toothed skill with faro games, but he ended up paying $500 bail before his case was discharged. It was yet another example of the old lawman's dubious relationship with his interpretation of the law.

Los Angeles became the main base for Wyatt and Sadie although they would venture out, especially in the winter, to stake further mining claims and invest in oil wells. They rented cheap accommodation or took advantage of the hospitality of friends, but they continued to get by.

Wyatt's father, Nicholas, had passed on in an old soldier's home in 1907 at the ripe old age of 93, another symbolic severance from the past. Earp's connections to the life he had shone in were disappearing fast.

Regular word reached him over the years of the vanishing nature of those he had known in the wild old days... Clay Allison, the deranged Texas killer, had met his end unceremoniously in 1887 by falling from the seat of a wagon he was driving, the wheel of which ran over his neck.

Gun toting Luke Short had died with his boots off... struck down by Bright's Disease in 1893... Big Bob Paul from cancer in 1901... Pony Diehl, released from prison following a five year sentence for robbery and rustling, just vanished in the late 1880s, although there were rumours that he had died in a gunfight.

Those who had ridden with Wyatt in his vendetta of '82 were all gone... Doc and Warren, of course... Sherm McMaster possibly died in the Spanish American War in '98 but his family claimed it was natural causes in '92. Jack Johnson died of consumption in '87 in Salt Lake City and Texas Jack Vermillion had settled in Virginia to become, surprisingly, a methodist preacher. He may have drowned in 1900, or, according to more reliable reports, in his sleep in 1911.

And what of Wyatt's arch enemy Johnny Behan? Following all the Earp based troubles, Behan tried again for the sheriff's nomination in November '82 but failed. He hung around Tombstone for a few more years until taking charge of Yuma Prison as superintendent between '87-'90 where he personally killed an escaping prisoner. More than one old timer said that he spent this period on the "wrong side of the bars"! There followed accusations of false accounting but he moved east, all the way to Philadelphia, where he commenced a lifelong role working for the government nationwide in various capacities... customs officer, Chinese exclusion inspector (arresting illegal immigrants) and then, in

1900, even serving overseas in the Chinese Boxer Rebellion. The new century saw him back roaming over the U.S.A. serving in Washington, Tucson and El Paso, and by 1910 he was engaged as a railroad policeman in Arizona. It was like he had come full circle but he succumbed to arterial problems and passed on in Tucson in 1912.

Wyatt still had a couple of brothers sharing the aging process... James, running bars, and their half brother, Newton, farming and working as a carpenter, both in different parts of California.

Wyatt's close friend from the old days, who had shared so much of it with him... Bat Masterson... was still going strong, although he had undergone a total change of occupation. Bat had lived a pretty amazing life, experiencing virtually every aspect of the Old West. He had been one of a party of 28 buffalo hunters who had held out for five days in the shacks of Adobe Walls in the Texas Panhandle in 1874 against a huge force of determined Comanche, Cheyenne and Kiowa braves... a legendary fight. He went from there to a gun battle in Denver where he killed an army corporal, receiving a wound which caused him to use a walking cane for the rest of his life. (This cane became a trademark for him.) There followed numerous roles as a lawman, with associated tales, true and false, but he gradually gained additional notoriety as an expert on sporting matters, especially boxing. In 1902, he relocated to the big eastern seaboard city of New York where he was respected for his fame as an authentic frontier legend. He swiftly became very well connected, including a close friendship with Teddy Roosevelt, and he penned a series of articles for *Human Life Magazine* on gunfighters he had known... including Wyatt, Doc, Luke Short, Ben Thompson and Bill Tilghman. *The New York Morning Telegraph* engaged him to write a regular column on sports and all manner of topics which proved highly popular.

Wyatt had a whole new circle of friends and acquaintances now, but very few who truly understood him. His very essence was rooted in a vanishing world which was all but gone in the fast paced advance of modern progress.

However, he could still hold his own and refused to surrender into a shell of compliance. He was living in the heart of America's latest phenomenon... the movies! The world of black and white silent films had been growing rapidly since the end of the last century and was blooming into a gigantic industry centred around what would become Hollywood. From short, novelty one reelers, the scope of films was expanding into an exciting, soon to be global, explosion. So many stories to be told, so much dramatic potential...

From simple, highly popular comedies featuring experienced vaudeville performers right through to gigantic epics which boasted magnificent sets and thousands of extras... films such as D.W. Griffith's stunning *Birth of a Nation* and *Intolerance*... this was an industry which would take the world by storm.

It seemed that everyone wanted to be a part of it. Film sets were much more open situations in those days, access to which was, in the early days, pretty easily achieved. Like everybody else, Wyatt's curiosity was aroused and he took an interest in whatever filming was going on, especially the early silent westerns which were gaining popularity, largely as an extension of Buffalo Bill's touring extravaganzas.

Wyatt even found himself merging into the background as a faceless supporting artiste on some of these films. A fascinating thought. It would be great if we were able to identify him in these old moving images...

Because of his own fame, Wyatt got to know quite a number of the pioneering names from film history, including the director Raoul Walsh, who was fascinated by him. John Ford too, who later said that he based his film *My Darling Clementine* on what Wyatt had told him. On at least one occasion he was introduced to an impressed Charlie Chaplin.

In 1915 or '16, Wyatt made a particular friend of the biggest western movie star of the day; William S. Hart. This actor was obsessed with the Old West and was deeply intrigued to hear about it first hand from a man who had lived it, and largely created it. Hart actually hero worshipped Wyatt and did much to publicly praise him.

With the terrible slaughter of World War One trundling on over in Europe and the U.S.A.'s eventual involvement, Wyatt tried to keep a fairly low profile. He enjoyed some level of his celebrity and the doors that it opened for him, but, as a rule he did not speak out about his past, especially the more shady parts of it. A gambler, prospector and entrepreneur is how he liked to think of himself, but the general public, and media, thought differently.

Publications were still raking up the old Tombstone sagas and most of them were not complimentary to the Earps. Stagecoach robbery, villainy and corruption were being more than implied, with at least one farcical article in the *Los Angeles Times* even making Johnny Behan the hero of the day and stating that Wyatt had passed on.

This was all too much for the old lawman and he began to protest regularly to those who would listen. The notion of setting the record straight with his own first hand version of events became deeply important to him. One of his more powerful allies was, naturally, his great friend and admirer Hart, whose influence in the movies could be enormously effective.

Wyatt contacted him, outlining his concerns in a passionate, yet diplomatic, letter. Not wishing to exploit their friendship, he wrote, he appealed to the famous actor for help in making things right, to tell the true story before it was too late. A big screen version could be the answer.

Hart was sympathetic and they met to discuss it, leading to a suggestion that Wyatt would first need to find a writer who could put his story into book form from which a film script could be created.

By now, Wyatt was over seventy and knew he needed to act fast.

He was smart and fairly well educated for a man of his time and his letters show that he could string words together well. But, he was no serious writer, as such, so the hunt was on for someone who could tell the tale.

***

An obvious contender would have been Bat Masterson; he who had become a highly respected, professional wordsmith and had lived the West at the same time as Wyatt. He would have done a splendid job, though perhaps a little biased in his old friend's favour. However, Bat had died of a massive heart attack at his desk in 1921.

By 1923, Wyatt and Sadie were still between addresses, juggling their business interests as they sought some more permanent accommodation. An old pal from Dodge City/Alaska days, an ex-railroad man named Charlie Welsh, had moved to the Los Angeles area with his family and the Earps were often invited around for meals and general socialising. Charlie extended the invitation by handing over an apartment on the top floor of his house for them to live in until they found a place of their own.

This generous gesture was gratefully received around about the time that Wyatt took a more or less ceremonial position as a deputy sheriff in San Bernardino County. This must have done his ego some good and, aged 75, he could still show spirit when he had to. He proved that he retained his ability by disarming a fugitive with sheer force of personality.

The hunt for a biographer was finally solved when the job was taken by John Flood, a mining engineer who had been friends of Wyatt and Sadie for quite a few years. He was very fond of the couple and had spent much of his time acting as Wyatt's unofficial secretary, dealing with his correspondence and generally helping out. He knew how to handle a typewriter and that seems to have been his qualification to offer to take on the mammoth task of attempting to transfer Wyatt's story to the written page.

It proved to be a long process. Day after day, night after night, Flood and Wyatt sat in a cigar smoke wreathed room as the old lawman plumbed the depths of his memory. Flood was enthralled, taking copious notes and doing his best to tolerate Sadie who was often present, interfering and making demands about what he could, or could not, write. She wanted what she called a "clean story".

Unfortunately, Flood's enthusiasm was not matched by his talent as a writer which was sadly lacking. After nearly two years, the manuscript he presented failed to impress a long list of publishers who rejected it quite brutally. Even with the backing of famous William S. Hart, who did his best to promote it, there was no way this nearly 350 page book would make it into proper published print.

The problem was not the story but the way it was written. Overblown, jumbled, cornily exaggerated and filled with unnecessary onomatopoeia in the action scenes... *"Crack, crack, crack... Zing, zing, zing..."* for gunshots and so on. It was actually appalling and rather embarrassing but all Wyatt had to give, at this stage.

The dilemma might have been solved had Wyatt accepted an offer which came to him in the summer of 1926 when he was approached by the successful writer and literary critic Walter Noble Burns. Having just published his well received tome *The Saga of Billy the Kid*, Burns was on a roll to continue his mission to glorify the West's legendary figures and Wyatt was the next on his list.

Regardless of all the rejections, Wyatt remained loyal to Flood, thanked Burns but told him that the book was already in hand. However, he was happy to furnish the writer with a ream of pages detailing his knowledge of Doc Holliday who Burns considered covering instead. As it turned out, Burns used Wyatt as his central character after all, seeking out other old timers and newspaper records for his research.

By the end of 1927, with Wyatt, Hart and Flood still dithering over their manuscript, and finally realising that it simply was below par, Burns published his *Tombstone; An Iliad of the South West*. It was quite a hit and succeeded in bringing the character of Wyatt Earp back into the public arena, but there would be no money for the great man himself. He had declined to cooperate and it was his loss.

Wyatt was at the age where his earning ability had faded dramatically. He and Sadie had managed to obtain a modest cottage in the small hamlet of Vidal, south eastern California, and close to the Arizona state line. It was a home of their own, but it was about 250 miles from L.A. and travel was difficult for Wyatt now. They retained their copper mine, which they called *Happy Days*, but the old pattern of mining seasonally and spending leisure time in the big city was no longer easy.

Making a living was a real concern now. Sadie did receive regular financial help from her sister, whose deceased husband had left her financially secure, but she tended to use that up with her gambling addiction.

Wyatt's friends had been concerned about his welfare for a long time. Even when the Earps were living under the hospitality of the Welsh family, it was noticed that Sadie was neglecting Wyatt. He would be left alone for long periods while she was off at the illegally run card tables. Often he went without food and she did not seem to care, so the Welsh's would feed him, regardless of her lack of concern and *"Oh, he's alright…"* attitude.

Wyatt himself, never a man to overuse words, grew quieter with the passing years. His thick hair had thinned, his sweeping blonde mustache, now trimmed, turning from grey to snow white, yet his stature remained upright, maintaining every ounce of the dignity he had always had. When Sadie nagged him, which was often, he sometimes told her to *"shut up"* but, more often than not, he would set off on long walks on his own.

All the Welsh family liked Wyatt. They spoke of him as a gentleman, no trouble at all. As for Sadie, her behaviour reached the point where they just tolerated her for Wyatt's sake. It was quite a relief when they moved out.

The Earps had found a tiny, dark and dreary one room apartment on 17th. Street in L.A.; not the most salubrious part of town. Wyatt would sit there alone all day, seemingly at peace, and no doubt enveloped in memories of better times.

His big time friends continued to visit on occasion and this brightened him up, but, all in all, everyone acknowledged the sadness of what had become of him. The only bitterness lay in Wyatt's frustration that his story had not been told with his approval. After all, his past was all he had now. Such irony that the Burns book had made him a celebrity again but without any supportive benefit.

When all seemed lost, a beam of hope shone out in the closing weeks of 1927.

CHAPTER 50

"THE GOOD LORD OWES ME AN EXPLANATION FOR THE THINGS THAT HAVE HAPPENED IN MY LIFE..."

So said Wyatt Earp in the autumn of his years. What kind of explanation could he expect? Like all of us, the culmination of all things in his life was the result of the choices he had made, good and bad.

Brother James had passed away in 1926 leaving Wyatt as the only Earp who had experienced the Tombstone period. His options were all but spent when he began receiving correspondence from Stuart Lake, a magazine writer with an impressive track record who had also been a wrestling promoter and press aide for Teddy Roosevelt.

Lake's interest in Wyatt had developed from his meetings with Bat Masterson in New York years before. Bat's stories about the Old West, and Wyatt in particular, had intrigued him, so when the Earp name became significant again, as the decade progressed, the ambitious writer decided to seek him out.

With the dreadful Flood manuscript long since put aside, Wyatt had grown despondent, resigned to the acceptance that any hope of boosting his sullied reputation had passed. The best he could hope for was a legacy as a flawed frontier gunman and a charlatan who had cheated Fitzsimmons out of his world title.

Lake's letters were like a breath of fresh air... a proper writer who actually seemed genuinely interested in creating Wyatt's version of events.

Wyatt and Sadie (of course) gladly met Lake and this led to further meetings. They clicked immediately (Wyatt and Lake, that is) and the writer spoke of their "beautiful" connection. Earp was very cooperative, naturally, patiently answering all the questions which were put to him as Lake studiously noted it all down in chronological order. Apart from the meetings there was also a mountain of correspondence passing between them as Lake collected all the details of Wyatt's colourful and complicated life. The writer was pleased that Wyatt spoke to him so freely... he obviously knew what he wanted written... but, at the same time, there was an element of frustration regarding Wyatt's laid back nature. He had always been cautious with words. Lake described this as being *"delightfully laconic or exasperatingly so"*.

The writer did separate research too, also speaking to the surviving old timers and raking through those crumbling newspapers to verify what he was being told. A promising book was beginning to take shape.

Wyatt perked up as he began to regain faith in a future which might look upon him favourably. His old friend George Parsons, the diarist, met him one afternoon and was pleasantly surprised to see that the old lawman still possessed his younger charm. For a man pushing eighty he appeared impressively healthy and full of spirit. There exists a photograph from that period showing Wyatt sitting with Sadie and their dog beneath the awning of their property. Another poignant image has Wyatt standing in shirtsleeves and braces, alone in profile, hands in pockets as he stares wistfully across a river. One of him sitting thoughtfully in a rocking chair too. What appears to be going on in his mind is almost tangible.

In recent years Wyatt had also renewed his acquaintance with an enemy from the old days… Billy Breakenridge, Behan's deputy who had ended up dismissed and moving on to working for the railroad. During the Flood manuscript years, it is said that Wyatt had a couple of meetings with Breakenridge, in Tucson and L.A.. Why this happened is unclear but Wyatt reported that his old enemy appeared friendly towards him. Maybe it was considered that enough time had elapsed to let bygones be bygones. Two old men enjoying chewing the fat about a past long gone…

As it happened, Breakenridge seems to have had an ulterior motive as he coaxed information out of Wyatt. To the surprise of most, in 1928, just as Lake's biography was gaining momentum, Breakenridge brought out a ghost written version of his own memoirs. It was called *Helldorado* and, although entertainingly readable and deceivingly authentic, it was yet another character assassination of Wyatt and his brothers.

The survivors from the old Tombstone days were incensed at this blatantly biased version of their history, which laughingly portrayed Breakenridge as some kind of hero who had cleaned up the territory. None were more furious than Wyatt himself who objected strongly to the book's many untruths. He even personally complained to the ghost writer, but the book was out there, distributed widely and selling well.

It must have made Wyatt more determined than ever to get his own version into print. Lake was beavering away at the manuscript but Earp was up against time. By the end of 1928, Wyatt's health had deteriorated. He had liver and prostate problems, had developed chronic cystitis and was more or less confined to the one room of that shabby rented bungalow.

In late December he took a turn for the worse. The tough old lawman was nearing the end of the trail.

As he lay in bed, or shuffled around the room, fading slowly,

Wyatt's half brother Newton passed away, aged 91, up in Sacramento, so now he really was the last of the Earp boys.

Sadie tended him at his bedside. He made it through Christmas and into the new year of '29, occasionally still weakly speaking of making it out to the mines again when he got better... but it was not to be.

On January 12th. he remained in bed, with Sadie, a doctor and a nurse tending to him. There was nothing else to be done. He slept and spoke only to ask for a glass of water before dawn on Sunday the 13th. ... then, sometime before 8.00am he spoke for the last time. In a clear tone, he uttered, *"Suppose... suppose..."* By the time Sadie had asked him to repeat it he was gone.

What did he suppose? A glowing portrayal of his truth to balance history? The longing for a more peaceful and satisfying life?

He had outlived just about everyone from his golden days... certainly all those who mattered, and he died with his boots off.

***

Wyatt made it to the age of eighty, passing on almost fifty years after the violent events which shaped his legacy. So much else had happened in his long life.

He lived to see the age of the motor car, aeroplanes, radio, the telephone, amazing advances in technology and exploration, and... of course, moving pictures. And, on that note, he never got to see that long hoped for portrayal of himself on screen, but it was to happen... a lot.

I find something awesome in the fact that my parents were running around as children whilst Wyatt was still living. To me, that is a tangible connection with history.

His funeral took place within a few days of his passing, at the Pierce Brothers Chapel in Los Angeles. The event stirred quite a bit of interest in the press, even reaching the pages of the New York Times, so his legend was intact, albeit flawed. His pall bearers included faithful Tombstone characters John Clum and George Parsons, as well as the high profile celebrity presence of William S. Hart and the latest cowboy movie star Tom Mix. Mix was seen to unashamedly weep beside the casket.

It was not a burial, however. Wyatt was cremated and Sophie received his ashes in an urn which she kept at home for many months. It was eventually interred in her family's plot near San Francisco.

Sadie had not even attended the funeral service or cremation. She claimed she had become too ill and grief stricken to do so. They had been together for 46 years.

Her almost immediate main concern following her husband's demise was for Lake to complete the book which was still very much a work in progress. Money was tight and she needed this biographer to secure her future.

With Wyatt out of the way, Sadie took it upon herself to badger Lake relentlessly, pressuring him to complete. Worse than that, she insisted that the contents must meet with her approval for that "clean" story, so that her late husband would emerge in a highly positive light. All questionable material must be omitted, she said, including any mention of herself and especially no word of Mattie and the way she had been treated. Brothels, gambling, arrests, accusations… none of it must appear on the printed page.

This was quite a stranglehold on Lake over the coming months as he brokered a deal with publishers Houghton Mifflin. Sadie had become an immense irritation and their relationship took a nose dive. When the book finally made the stores in late 1931, they were barely speaking.

But, after a slowish start, *Wyatt Earp; Frontier Marshal*, took off and became a top best seller. Sadie was still far from happy but the clump of money she made from it helped to ease the blow.

Lake had indeed produced a biography which sold Wyatt as some kind of Wild West super hero. The nucleus of facts were present but it was all laid out in a fabricated style as if Wyatt was boldly relating it all in the first person, and that was not the way it had been created at all. Those who had known Wyatt personally quickly picked up on the fact that he simply did not speak like that. He was known for his quiet and dignified manner but Lake excused it on the basis of artistic licence, to give life and "authenticity" to the tale. Wyatt himself would have surely disapproved of being presented in such a manner.

The events themselves were greatly embellished, much of it total fabrication, but it undoubtedly made a stirring saga which the public lapped up enthusiastically.

It was not so much a pack of blatant lies as a cover up. Wyatt himself had not told untruths, as such, but he had deliberately failed to mention anything which might reflect badly upon him. Add to this Lake's intention of creating a whiter than white saviour of the West and the result was almost fiction. It seems that he may have totally made up the existence of Wyatt's famous pistol, the Buntline Special. This was an impressive weapon, a long barrelled Colt uniquely commissioned by Ned Buntline for presentation to a select group of lawmen, Wyatt being one. According to Lake, it was wielded at the O.K. Corral, but, sadly, no concrete evidence has emerged that it was ever made.

The extremely complex politics of Tombstone's troubles were sanitized and simplified in the extreme, but only those who knew the truth cared, and they were in the minority. As the years went on, and more serious researchers unpicked the errors, the credibility of Lake's book was severely damaged but, for now, it was put on a pedestal as an historic and fascinating work of art.

By 1932 Lake had sold the film rights and the first of many movies based on his work rolled into production, but Sadie kicked up with threats, so the film *Frontier Marshal* had to change the lead character's name to Michael Wyatt!

She was an extremely hard woman to please and people began to question her sanity. Filled with self pity and taking advantage of everyone around her, Sadie continued to be a thorn in many sides. She also fell out with Virgil's widow, Allie, a feisty woman herself who had never had much time for Wyatt, feeling that he unjustly stole the thunder from her late husband.

Deeply depressed by the death of her supportive sister, Sadie struggled on, complaining and threatening law suits, even though money was coming in from Lake's efforts. A couple of female Earp descendants with writing credits tried to assist her in penning yet another version of Wyatt's life but the project was abandoned when she became too difficult to work with.

Even so, in 1939, she was engaged as a technical advisor on another filmed version of *Frontier Marshal*, with Randolph Scott playing Wyatt with his actual name. Yet again she was full of criticism and demands for script changes, but the film itself was a great success, even though it bore almost no relation to the known facts. They even changed Doc Holliday's name to Halliday out of fear that his relatives might object to something.

Poor Sadie, well into her seventies and suffering with signs of senility, finally joined Wyatt in December 1944, her ashes being buried alongside his.

Big Nose Kate, by the way, had died in 1940, at the grand old age of ninety.

***

The legend of Wyatt Earp had become something nobody ever expected.

His name was now the symbol of all good things in the Old West and Hollywood began to model all their heroes upon his image.

Director John Ford made his version (mentioned earlier) *My Darling Clementine* in 1946 with a superb portrayal of Wyatt by Henry Fonda and Victor Mature as a muscle bound Doc. With the wonderful

Walter Brennan as Old Man Clanton dying at the O.K. Corral, it was a delightful picture, a Western classic, but, despite Ford's claims, about as accurate as a Mickey Mouse feature.

The advent of television in the 1950s brought a massive project starring Hugh O'Brian in the titular role and *The Life and Legend of Wyatt Earp* ran for years. I still find myself humming the theme tune, along with the one from Fess Parker's *Davy Crockett*. That other very long running television series *Gunsmoke*, starring James Arness, was obviously based upon Wyatt, although they called him Matt Dillon.

With the interest in Westerns at a peak, Hollywood sought to pull audiences back into the cinema from their T.V. sets with director John Sturges' *Gunfight at the O.K. Corral* in 1957 and it worked. Burt Lancaster as a stoic Wyatt and Kirk Douglas as a consumptive but stalwart Doc, it kept a slim hold on accuracy but was very entertaining. Sturges revisited the story a decade later with his remake *The Hour of the Gun* which, with James Garner and Jason Robards as Wyatt and Doc, was a much harsher, but more accurate, take on the tale.

Before Westerns went out of fashion for quite a few years, there was another attempt to expose the so called gritty "truth" of it all in 1971's *Doc*, but it was a typical debunking stab which was popular at the time. It even inferred some kind of gay attraction between Earp and Holliday. Yeh... right... excuse me while I yawn...

Years passed, but in 1993 it all came back at a gallop with the rather stunning *Tombstone*, a glorious looking epic which did much to revive interest in cowboy films. Kurt Russell's tough but charismatic Wyatt ticked the boxes and critics still praise Val Kilmer's brilliantly subtle portrayal of Doc. The film was stylish and largely very accurate in much of its depiction of true events, taking a few liberties but staying close enough to please the pedantic types such as myself. I just thought it such a shame that they felt the need to open the film with a ridiculously over the top scene where Curly Bill, Ringo, Ike and the Cowboys slaughter a wedding party, laughing and joking as the bride is dragged away to be raped. Never did such a thing happen there. How do I know? I just do! And then another gratuitous blood bath at the end when Wyatt's vendetta appears to wipe out just about every bad man in Arizona.

Within a few months that serious Western enthusiast Kevin Costner brought out his own version of the saga; *Wyatt Earp*. It was a very long retelling of not just the Tombstone years but an edited view of Wyatt's long life... a lot of it anyway. It was a darker, more dour experience than *Tombstone*, but, in many ways, a more realistic one. Costner did capture the essence of Earp's sombre, uncommunicative nature, but, following the fast moving, colourful tone of the previous film, it failed at the box office.

There have been many other filmed attempts to tell this well worn story, especially in the modern world of works which go straight to streaming. Documentaries, new theories explored, more debunking... A Netflix series called Wyatt Earp and the Cowboy War claims authenticity but those responsible for the casting and costume design need severe history lessons! But I guess we Western enthusiasts should just be pleased that it is all being kept alive.

As previously mentioned in the first two sections of this book, social media plays an enormous part in making information available to those who are interested.

Like with Wild Bill and the Kid, there are groups devoted to Tombstone and Wyatt and they are, with caution, worth visiting and, in some cases, joining.

So Wyatt did achieve lasting fame, after all. But, as with the other subjects of this book, I am sure he could never have perceived the route it would take and the conclusions reached.

Wyatt Earp was neither a hero or a villain, but he was certainly a product of his times who came through with admirable qualities.

His courage was indisputable... there is no end of clarification of that. He was loyal too, to those who mattered to him, family particularly. As for honesty, well, he had his own code of morals. I feel sure there was nothing inherently sinister about him or his brothers. He was not averse to a little back handed coercion to fleece a greenhorn or two, but it does seem that, following an uncertain youth, he did mature into a lawman who sincerely believed in keeping order. That is until the law, in his eyes, let him down, and he became convinced that he would need to take it into his own hands to get results.

Breakenridge outlived him, but only just. How must Wyatt have felt reaching his eightieth year, never having taken a bullet and looking back on all those who had fallen?

He took so much of his full story to the grave.

Ultimately, he endured a pretty sad and lonely end to his life but I would like to think that he could look back on much of it with some sense of satisfaction.

Wyatt Earp walked tall and shot straight. That is no bad legacy for a Wild West legend.

Writing this book has been a labour of love for me and its completion has resulted in a pure sense of relieved satisfaction.

The original idea was conceived over two decades before I actually sat down to begin the actual physical act of writing it. I was travelling a lot then, especially across the U.S.A. from coast to coast, my motive being my fascination in North America's history. As I experienced the many different faces of this amazing country's past and present, witnessing first hand those things which had fascinated me ever since I could walk and talk, a vision gradually formed in the depths of my being.

I became determined to set out my personal impressions of characters who, for some unknown but deep reason, had made a mark on me, so that such a record could play a part in my own legacy. As I have previously stated, I simply cannot explain just why this became so important, but it did… and remains so. These iconic legends from the Old West touch a resounding chord, having created an affinity which I feel has furnished me with an understanding of their characters, an understanding which goes beyond the 167,000 words which I have used to tell their stories.

I apologise if that statement comes across with a shade of arrogance. Many have told their stories in numerous forms and I have the greatest respect for the best of them. I do not reserve the sole right to feel passionate about it all… far from it… I tip my hat to those historians and writers who have produced such great works, many of which have been my basic sources for what I have achieved here. They have passion and dedication too, and obviously their own deep motives for preserving their conclusions on paper.

All I know, regarding my own path, is that I have shared my entire life with a subject which, on the face of it, logically, should not resound so deeply with my typically English background and all the other things which have shaped me as a person. It has always bemused and amused my friends and family but has forever been present.

I do not profess to "know" any more factually than all my fellow historians. My sources are the same as theirs, but it has been important, in fact essential, to take on board everything which is available for scrutiny, analyse it in depth, sift through the wheat and chaff before arriving at what one sees as the "truth". Not even all serious historians agree on their conclusions, of course. The "truth" is always subject to interpretation, but writers owe it to their readers to present it as closely as possible so that they can decide for themselves.

In addition to the known facts, I can only add something which is unique to us all… not just my own interpretation, but also my own "feelings". I really am convinced that my affinity with the Old West was in me anyway, long before I began to absorb the recorded history.

So, if you have got this far, (and not skipped the pages!) I sincerely hope that you have enjoyed the ride.

I have done my best and hope that I may have inspired at least a few more souls to gallop on into the sunset and beyond…

www.ingramcontent.com/pod-product-compliance
Lightning Source LLC
Chambersburg PA
CBHW060350190426
43201CB00044B/1926